D1415930

D1417742

♣

....

A GIFT TO

....

FROM

....

ON THIS DATE

LESSONS *from*

GOD IS IN
THE SMALL STUFF

(and it all matters)

bruce & stan

A DAYMAKER BOOK

APPRECIATE
GOD'S CREATION

*The heavens tell
of the glory of God.
The skies display
his marvelous
craftsmanship.*

PSALM 19:1 NLT

(i n   t h e   s m a l l   s t u f f)

⊱   When it comes to origins, there are only
two alternatives: Either God created
the heavens and the earth, or He didn't.

⊱   Don't get hung up on how long ago
God made the heavens and the earth.

⊱   When you experience beauty in nature,
praise the Creator.

⊱   Science is not the enemy of God,
and religion is not the enemy of science.
After all, when God made the world,
He made science possible.

⊱   You can learn a great deal about God
by studying His creation.

PRAYER

(THE GREAT CONNECTER)

The eyes of the Lord

watch over those

who do right,

and his ears are open

to their prayers.

1 PETER 3:12 NLT

(*in the small stuff*)

- Prayer changes things.

- Pray for people you dislike.

- When you pray, be careful to distinguish your needs from your desires.

- Live humbly and pray likewise.

- Don't pray for a lighter load. Pray for a stronger back.

- Prayer is listening to God as well as speaking to Him.

- Pray with perseverance and expectancy.

- At its core, prayer is giving yourself to God.

- Pray as if the task depends on God; and work as if it depends on you.

GOD WANTS YOU

(TO GROW)

Brothers and sisters...
we are thankful that
your faith is flourishing
and you are all growing
in love for each other

2 Thessalonians 1:3 nlt

(in the small stuff)

🙢 Recognize that you can't get holy in a hurry.

🙢 Little is much if God is in it.

🙢 Rejoice in the Lord's discipline
as well as His blessings.

🙢 Be cautious in telling others what you can do,
but be bold in asserting what God can do.

🙢 Realize your inadequacy without God
and your sufficiency with God.

🙢 Faith does not demand miracles,
but often accomplishes them.

🙢 It's a good thing to delight in the Lord,
but how much better when the Lord
delights in you.

CONTENTMENT

(IT'S GOOD FOR THE SOUL)

True religion

with contentment

is great wealth.

1 TIMOTHY 6:6 NLT

(*in the small stuff*)

- Don't acquire everything you want.

- Contentment with your situation
  breeds satis faction.

- If you believe for a moment that you own even a
  single possession, your contentment will be tied to it.

- Enjoy happiness; treasure joy.

- The best time to relax is when you're too busy.

- Beware the barrenness of a busy life.

- Cherish tranquillity.

- Since exhaustion begins and ends on the inside,
  that's where genuine rest must originate.

- Learn to relax without feeling guilty.

- Live somewhere between complacency and crisis.

REALIZE THAT
GOD LOVES YOU

This is real love.

It is not that

we loved God,

but that he loved us....

1 JOHN 4:10 NLT

❧ Whenever you feel insignificant, remember how important you are to God.

❧ We love God because we know who He is. God loves us despite who we are.

❧ Unconditional love comes only from our heavenly Father.

❧ Find your self-worth in God's unconditional love for you, not your accomplishments.

❧ The love of God has no limits.

❧ The reason we can love God is because He loved us first.

❧ God's unconditional love for us should motivate us to love others unconditionally.

❧ Never confuse love with lust.

❧ Love isn't an option. We are commanded by God to love others.

❧ Loving God is the greatest thing you can do.

CHARACTER

(WHAT YOU ARE WHEN NO ONE'S LOOKING)

May integrity and
honesty protect me,
for I put my
hope in you.

PSALM 25:21 NLT

(*in the small stuff*)

 Let your word be your bond:
Keep your promises, meet your deadlines,
honor your commitments, pay your bills.

 It's one thing to know what's right,
and another thing entirely to do it.

 Others determine your reputation.
You determine your character.

 If you want to know what's in your heart,
listen to your mouth.

 If you find yourself in a questionable situation,
get out immediately.

 Before you can ask integrity of others,
you must attempt to be blameless yourself.

 Be honest with yourself.
Be honest with other people.
Be honest with God.

 Character is one of those qualities
that takes time to develop.

Understand God's Nature

> *Do you not know?*
>
> *Have you not heard?*
>
> *The LORD is the ever-*
>
> *lasting God, the Creator*
>
> *of the ends of the earth.*
>
> *He will not grow tired*
>
> *or weary, and his under-*
>
> *standing no one can fathom.*

ISAIAH 40:28 NIV

(*in the small stuff*)

-    God knows what's in our hearts.
  We might as well get right to the point.

-    Remember that God values you for who
  you are, not what you do.

-    God is more likely to speak to you with a gentle
  whisper than with a loud voice.

-    God won't take away a sin until
  you give it over to Him.

-    Faith is not an emotion. It is objective trust
  placed in a very real God.

-    One quality of God's nature that should
  make us tremble is His justice.

-    One quality of God's nature that should
  give us comfort is His love.

-    Thank God that your salvation does
  not depend on you.

SELF-DISCIPLINE

(ONLY YOU CAN DO IT)

To learn,

you must love

discipline....

PROVERBS 12:1 NLT

(*in the small stuff*)

    ✑   Discipline begins with small things done daily.

    ✑   The secret behind most success stories?
Discipline.

    ✑   Every morning you choose your attitude for the day.

    ✑   The first step on the path to commitment
is making up your mind.

    ✑   You can plan to succeed or you can plan to fail.
The choice is yours.

    ✑   Develop a cause for your life.
Whatever it is, dedicate yourself to it daily.

    ✑   Use your free time productively.

    ✑   Worthwhile activities may be tough in the
short-term but rewarding in the long-term.

    ✑   Motivation can fade. Habits prevail.

IMPROVE YOURSELF

(NO ONE ELSE CAN)

No, dear brothers and sisters, I am still not all I should be, but I am focusing all my energies on this one thing: Forgetting the past and looking forward to what lies ahead....

PHILIPPIANS 3:13 NLT

(*in the small stuff*)

⚘   Self-improvement is a lifelong process.

⚘   Learn from the mistakes of others.
You'll never live long enough to make
them all yourself.

⚘   Don't take pride in exceeding your
expectations if your goals were only mediocre.

⚘   Study and evaluate your own behavior.

⚘   Learn to tell a good story.

⚘   Now and then, set a goal that absolutely
terrifies you.

⚘   Learn to thrive on challenge and change.

⚘   It's hard to learn from a mistake
you won't acknowledge making.

⚘   Never mistake activity for achievement.

⚘   Develop a unique style.

Simplify

(AND ENJOY LIFE MORE)

This should be your ambition: to live a quiet life, minding your own business.

1 Thessalonians 4:11 NLT

(*in the small stuff*)

- ✍ Learn to have a good time
  without spending a lot of money.

- ✍ Satisfaction begins when comparison stops.

- ✍ While the poor dream of having riches,
  the wealthy long for simplicity.

- ✍ Anything can last more than one year.

- ✍ Don't throw money at problems.

- ✍ If you can't afford it, you don't need it.

- ✍ Be as satisfied with what you don't have
  as with what you have.

- ✍ Never buy something for the purpose
  of impressing others.

- ✍ If you can't live without it, go home and sleep on it.

- ✍ Make it a lifelong goal to remove clutter.

- ✍ What you are bears little resemblance
  to what you have.

ARRANGE YOUR PRIORITIES

Your heavenly Father already knows all your needs, and he will give you all you need...if you live for him and make the Kingdom of God your primary concern.

MATTHEW 6:32–33 NLT

(*in the small stuff*)

   ✑   You can start your day without God,
but you'll never really get started.

   ✑   Don't be so involved with the *when*
that you miss the *now*.

   ✑   Strive to be a person of faith rather than fame.

   ✑   If what you are doing won't make a difference
in five years, it probably doesn't matter now.

   ✑   You can't plan for the future by looking
in the rearview mirror.

   ✑   Whenever you look to the future, be bold.

   ✑   What you think about when you have nothing
to do reveals what is important to you.

   ✑   Embrace the power of love. Reject the love of power.

   ✑   A good life is of more value than a good living.

STOP WORRYING

(AND START LIVING)

*"So I tell you,
don't worry about
everyday life—
whether you have
enough food, drink,
and clothes.
Doesn't life consist
of more than food
and clothing?"*

MATTHEW 6:25 NLT

(in the small stuff)

& Live longer by worrying less.

& When you're feeling overwhelmed, remember
   to take things one at a time, one day at a time.

& Anxiety is short-lived if we give it to God.

& If you prepare for the future,
   you won't have to worry about it.

& Rather than worrying about change,
   learn to thrive on it.

& Worry is a choice.

& When you choose to worry,
   you are choosing not to trust God.

& The best way to stop worrying is to start praying.

& Prayer changes things; worry changes nothing.

EMBRACE ADVERSITY

Dear brothers and sisters,

whenever trouble comes

your way, let it be an

opportunity for joy.

For when your faith

is tested, your endurance

has a chance to grow.

JAMES 1:2–3 NLT

(i n   t h e   s m a l l   s t u f f)

❧ Convert your failures into successes
by learning from them.

❧ You will learn more from adversity
than from prosperity.

❧ Let your difficulties be opportunities
for God's control.

❧ God will either protect you from hardships
or give you the strength to go through them.
You win either way.

❧ You don't know you're fortunate
until you're unfortunate.

❧ Deal creatively with adversity.
When you can't pay the electric bill,
have a romantic dinner by candlelight.

❧ Difficulties are opportunities for growth.
If you try to avoid all trials, you are simply
arresting your development.

COMMUNICATION

(IT'S MORE THAN TALKING)

*Dear brothers
and sisters,
be quick to listen,
slow to speak,
and slow to get angry.*

JAMES 1:19 NLT

(*in the small stuff*)

- People are attracted to enthusiasm.

- Be the first one to ask a question.

- A card sent with a personal note inside is more meaningful than a card sent but only signed.

- Develop exceptional listening habits.

- Listen with your eyes as well as your ears.

- No one will ever accuse you of being a boring conversationalist if you let people talk about themselves.

- A truly eloquent speech includes all that is necessary—and no more.

- Thoughtful compliments wear better than impulsive flattery.

- You learn more by listening (you already know what you would say).

ENCOURAGEMENT
IS A GIFT

So encourage

each other

and build each

other up....

1 THESSALONIANS 5:11 NLT

(in the small stuff)

- Enthusiasm encourages positive behavior.

- Ask for advice often. Offer advice sparingly.

- Be kind to unkind people. It gets to them.

- Encouragement, praise, and recognition are often more effective than a raise or bonus, and they're always cheaper.

- Love first if you long to be loved.

- You will encourage more people by listening than by talking.

- Be happy for others in their good fortune.

- Never expect gratitude, but always express appreciation.

- You can't always control the kind of service you receive, but you can always control the kind of gratitude you deliver.

- Compliment people as soon as it occurs to you.

- Make it a habit to encourage youngsters.

LEADERSHIP IS AN ART

If God has given you leadership ability, take the responsibility seriously.

ROMANS 12:8 NLT

(*in the small stuff*)

⅋ Empowering is more effective than delegating.

⅋ Have the courage to hold people accountable.

⅋ Find a mentor.

⅋ Being a good example is better than giving good advice.

⅋ If you want to lead, read.

⅋ When you find a leader, follow.

⅋ Use your influence sparingly. It will last longer.

⅋ Be available to take someone's place in an emergency.

⅋ Managing people begins with caring for them.

⅋ One of the sobering characteristics of leadership is that leaders are judged to a greater degree than followers.

A GENEROUS
SPIRIT

*The generous prosper
and are satisfied;
those who refresh
others will themselves
be refreshed.*

PROVERBS 11:25 NLT

(*in the small stuff*)

   Money is like fertilizer:
It's not much good unless it's spread around.

   If you want to be rich—give.

   Initiative is seeing what needs to be done and
doing it before you are asked.

   Filling an existing need can be as valuable as
anticipating a new one.

   Give the gift of time. It's a gift more valuable
than money can buy.

   Support a missionary financially.

   When you give a gift, expect nothing in return.

   Generosity does not include giving away
something you'll never miss.

   Share your blessings with others.

COMPASSION

(IS MORE THAN SELF-PITY)

If you think you are
too important to
help someone in need,
you are only fooling
yourself. You are
really a nobody.

GALATIANS 6:3 NLT

(in the small stuff)

    Let your primary motivation be the still, small voice of the Holy Spirit.

    Don't wait to do one great thing for God in your lifetime. Rather, do many good little things for the sake of His kingdom, which in itself is a great thing.

    Get to know your intuitions; God may be speaking to you.

    What happens to you may be an accident. How you respond is not.

    Make sure your caring includes doing.

    No one does the right thing naturally. It takes effort and practice.

    Feeling good about yourself begins with serving others.

    Your care for others is a measure of your greatness.

♣

LAUGH

(AND THE WORLD LAUGHS WITH YOU)

We were filled
with laughter,
and we sang for joy.

PSALM 126:2 NLT

(*in the small stuff*)

- Our five senses are incomplete without the sixth—a sense of humor.

- The best jokes are painless and profaneless.

- Laugh at yourself. Laugh with others.

- You know you have a good sense of humor if you can laugh when someone tells your joke better than you.

- Leave funny and enthusiastic messages on answering machines and voice mail.

- If you can laugh at yourself, you are guaranteed a lifetime of chuckling.

- If someone tells you a joke you've already heard, let them finish and laugh anyway.

- Develop the art of telling stories that are short, clean, and funny.

- If you doubt that God has a sense of humor, look in the mirror.

- Humor works best when it brings joy to others.

CRITICIZE

(AND YOU WALK ALONE)

Stop judging others,

and you will not

be judged. For others

will treat you

as you treat them.

MATTHEW 7:1–2 NLT

(*in the small stuff*)

✂ Motivate, don't denigrate.

✂ If you agree to bury the hatchet,
   don't leave the handle sticking out.

✂ Criticism and success are both difficult
   to handle, but one is ultimately more enjoyable.

✂ Never criticize your hair cutter—
   at least not while yours is the hair being cut.

✂ A word spoken in anger cannot be erased.
   It plays over and over again.

✂ Be generous with praise and stingy with criticism.

✂ Appreciate differences instead of criticizing them.

✂ The urge to criticize someone
   usually comes from feelings of resentment.

✂ Rather than taking criticism personally,
   look at it objectively.

RELATIONSHIPS
TAKE TIME

Don't just pretend

that you love others.

Really love them....

Love each other with

genuine affection,

and take delight in

honoring each other.

ROMANS 12:9–10 NLT

(in the small stuff)

- When someone does something good for you, never forget it.

- When you do something good for someone else, let it go immediately.

- Be a peacemaker.

- You can tell a little about a person by what he says about himself.

- You can tell a lot about a person by what others say about him.

- You can tell even more by what he says about others.

- Ask questions.

- A smile is your most important accessory.

- Examine your life for the faults you find most irritating in others.

FAMILIES ARE FOREVER

"There are secret things that belong to the LORD our God, but the revealed things belong to us and our descendants forever, so that we may obey these words of the law."

DEUTERONOMY 29:29 NLT

(*in the small stuff*)

❦ Establish family traditions and faithfully keep them.

❦ Be as considerate with your family as you are with your friends.

❦ Friendships can fade. Families are forever.

❦ There are a few nuts (and squirrels) in every family tree.

❦ Stay in touch with family members. It's easy to ignore those closest to you.

❦ Call your mother—you know how she worries.

❦ Eat at least one meal a day together as a family.

❦ Develop a recreational activity your family can do together, and then enjoy it regularly.

You Need
Your Friends

*A friend is always
loyal, and a brother
is born to help in
time of need.*

PROVERBS 17:17 NLT

(*in the small stuff*)

    A friend is one whose strengths
complement your weaknesses.

    Your best friends will criticize you privately
and encourage you publicly.

    Friendships are built gradually but can be
destroyed quickly.

    Have lots of acquaintances and a few close friends.

    Make friends with persons of advanced years and
let them know how much their friendship means.

    Make a list of six people you could count on to
carry your casket at your funeral. If you can't
come up with six, develop some new friendships,
or plan to be cremated.

    Remember to ask friends to pray for your needs.

    Select friends based on their character,
not their compliments.

Carpe Diem

(SEIZE THE DAY)

*Don't brag about
tomorrow, since
you don't know what
the day will bring.*

PROVERBS 27:1 NLT

(in the small stuff)

- Live life on purpose, not by accident.

- Place fresh flowers in the places where you live and work.

- Visit the Holy Land once in your life.

- Smile at babies.

- Always go the extra mile. . .whether for a friend or mint chocolate chip ice cream.

- Change is a process, not an event.

- Plan to be spontaneous.

- Have someone over on the spur of the moment.

- Enjoy each day as if it were your last.

- When you spend time with God, His Word, and other people, you are investing in eternity.

- People who ask "Why?" keep others from getting things done. Ask "Why not?" and get things done.

(*in the small stuff*)

❧   Daily thank the Lord for His gifts.

❧   Display what you believe by how you behave.

❧   As you go through the day,
look for opportunities too good to miss.

❧   Be teachable every day.

❧   Have a sharp mind, a keen wit,
and a discriminating tongue.

❧   Enjoy life's detours.

❧   Refuse to be lazy. Take control of your time.

❧   Be a person of principle, passion, and purity.

❧   When you see God in the small stuff,
your life becomes more meaningful.

About the Authors

BRUCE BICKEL is a lawyer and STAN JANTZ is a marketing consultant. But don't let those mundane occupations fool you. Bruce and Stan have collaborated on fifteen books, with combined sales of more than a million copies. Their passion is to present biblical truth in a clear, correct, and casual manner that encourages people to connect in a meaningful way with the living God.

Bruce and his wife, Cheryl, live in Fresno, California; they are active at Westmont College where Bruce is on the Board of Trustees and their two children attend. Stan and his wife, Karin, also live in Fresno; they are involved at Biola University where Stan is on the Board of Trustees and their two children attend.

Contact Bruce & Stan at:
www.bruceandstan.com

If you enjoyed this book, look for the best-selling
God Is in the Small Stuff and it all matters
wherever books are sold.

© 2003 by Bruce Bickel and Stan Jantz

ISBN 1-58660-704-6

Cover photo © Calvin Polley/Photonica
Book design by Kevin Keller/designconcept

All rights reserved. No part of this publication
may be reproduced or transmitted in any form
or by any means without written permission of the publisher.

Scripture quotations marked NLT are taken from the HOLY BIBLE:
NEW LIVING TRANSLATION, © 1996. Used by permission of
Tyndale House Publishers, Inc., Wheaton, Illinois 60189, USA.
All rights reserved.

Scripture marked NIV is from the HOLY BIBLE: NEW INTERNATIONAL VERSION®. NIV®
Copyright © 1973, 1978, 1984 by International Bible Society. Used by permission
of Zondervan Publishing House.

Published by Barbour Books, an imprint of Barbour Publishing, Inc.
P.O. Box 719, Uhrichsville, Ohio 44683, www.barbourbooks.com

ecpa Member of the
Evangelical Christian
Publishers Association

Printed in China.
5 4 3 2

PROGRAM OBJECTIVE

The goal of the *Pediatric Clinics of North America* is to keep practicing physicians and residents up to date with current clinical practice in pediatrics by providing timely articles reviewing the state-of-the-art in patient care.

TARGET AUDIENCE

All practicing pediatricians, physicians and healthcare professionals who provide patient care to pediatric patients.

LEARNING OBJECTIVES

Upon completion of this activity, participants will be able to:

1. Review the treatments and genetic components of disorders such as pediatric epilepsy and Duchenne and Becker Muscular Dystrophy.
2. Discuss the ethical issues associated with newborn screening for neurological and developmental disorders.
3. Recognize how advances in genomics have affected the diagnosis and management of pediatric neurologic and developmental disorders.

ACCREDITATION

The Elsevier Office of Continuing Medical Education (EOCME) is accredited by the Accreditation Council for Continuing Medical Education (ACCME) to provide continuing medical education for physicians.

The EOCME designates this enduring material for a maximum of 15 *AMA PRA Category 1 Credit*(s)™. Physicians should claim only the credit commensurate with the extent of their participation in the activity.

All other health care professionals requesting continuing education credit for this enduring material will be issued a certificate of participation.

DISCLOSURE OF CONFLICTS OF INTEREST

The EOCME assesses conflict of interest with its instructors, faculty, planners, and other individuals who are in a position to control the content of CME activities. All relevant conflicts of interest that are identified are thoroughly vetted by EOCME for fair balance, scientific objectivity, and patient care recommendations. EOCME is committed to providing its learners with CME activities that promote improvements or quality in healthcare and not a specific proprietary business or a commercial interest.

The planning committee, staff, authors and editors listed below have identified no financial relationships or relationships to products or devices they or their spouse/life partner have with commercial interest related to the content of this CME activity:

Guyla Acsadi, MD, PhD; Lindsay Alfano, PT, DPT, PCS; Elizabeth Baker, BA; Stormy J. Chamberlain, PhD; Liam Crapper, BSc; Basil T. Darras, MD; Francis J. DiMario Jr, MD; Darius Ebrahimi-Fakhari, MD; Carl Ernst, PhD; Anjali Fortna; Yael Hacohen, MRCPCH; Abeer Hani, MD; Guy Helman, BS; Kerry Holland; Ahm M. Huq, MD, PhD; Saumya S. Jamuar, MD; Agnes Jani-Acsadi, MD; Louisa Kalsner, MD; Indu Kumari; Ming Lim, MRCP PhD; Husam Mikati; Mohamad Mikati, MD; Sylvia Ounpuu, MSc; Kristan Pierz, MD; Fatema J. Serajee, MD; Bonita Stanton, MD; Megan Suermann; Keith Van Haren, MD; Christopher A. Walsh, MD, PhD; Nicolas Wein, PhD.

The planning committee, staff, authors and editors listed below have identified financial relationships or relationships to products or devices they or their spouse/life partner have with commercial interest related to the content of this CME activity:

Maria L. Escolar, MD is a consultant/advisor for Shire Plc; Synageva BioPharma Corp; and GlaxoSmithKlein plc., and has research support from Shire Plc and Synageva BioPharma Corp.
Kevin M. Flanigan, MD is a consultant/advisor for PTC Therapeutics, Inc.; Prosensa Inc; Sarepta Therapeutics; Audentes Therapeutics; and Italfarmaco SpA, and has research support from Akashi Therapeutics.
Lainie Friedman Ross, MD, PhD has stock ownership in General Electric; Bristol-Myers Squibb Company; and Mead Johnson & Company, LLC.
Jeste SS, MD is a consultant/advisor for F. Hoffman-La Roche Ltd.
Mustafa Sahin, MD has research support from Novartis Pharmaceuticals and Shire.
Adelin Vanderver, MD's spouse/partner has an employment affiliation with Aetna Inc.
Angela Vincent, FMedSci FRS receives royalties/patents from Athena Diagnostics, Inc.

UNAPPROVED/OFF-LABEL USE DISCLOSURE

The EOCME requires CME faculty to disclose to the participants:

1. When products or procedures being discussed are off-label, unlabelled, experimental, and/or investigational (not US Food and Drug Administration [FDA] approved); and

2. Any limitations on the information presented, such as data that are preliminary or that represent ongoing research, interim analyses, and/or unsupported opinions. Faculty may discuss information about pharmaceutical agents that is outside of FDA-approved labelling. This information is intended solely for CME and is not intended to promote off-label use of these medications. If you have any questions, contact the medical affairs department of the manufacturer for the most recent prescribing information.

TO ENROLL

To enroll in the *Pediatric Clinics of North America* Continuing Medical Education program, call customer service at 1-800-654-2452 or sign up online at http://www.theclinics.com/home/cme. The CME program is available to subscribers for an additional annual fee of USD 290.

METHOD OF PARTICIPATION

In order to claim credit, participants must complete the following:

1. Complete enrolment as indicated above.

2. Read the activity.

3. Complete the CME Test and Evaluation. Participants must achieve a score of 70% on the test. All CME Tests and Evaluations must be completed online.

CME INQUIRIES/SPECIAL NEEDS

For all CME inquiries or special needs, please contact elsevierCME@elsevier.com.

Contributors

CONSULTING EDITOR

BONITA F. STANTON, MD
Vice Dean for Research and Professor of Pediatrics, School of Medicine, Wayne State University, Detroit, Michigan

EDITOR

GYULA ACSADI, MD, PhD
Associate Professor; Chief of Pediatric Neurology, Connecticut Children's Medical Center, Departments of Pediatrics and Neurology, University of Connecticut, School of Medicine, Farmington, Connecticut

AUTHORS

GYULA ACSADI, MD, PhD
Associate Professor; Chief of Pediatric Neurology, Connecticut Children's Medical Center, Departments of Pediatrics and Neurology, University of Connecticut, School of Medicine, Farmington, Connecticut

LINDSAY ALFANO, DPT
The Center for Gene Therapy, The Research Institute, Nationwide Children's Hospital; Department of Physical Therapy, Nationwide Children's Hospital, Columbus, Ohio

ELIZABETH BAKER, BA
Department of Psychiatry and Biobehavioral Sciences, Semel Institute for Neuroscience and Human Behavior, David Geffen School of Medicine, UCLA, Los Angeles, California

STORMY J. CHAMBERLAIN, PhD
Raymond and Beverly Assistant Professor, Departments of Genetics and Genome Sciences and Pediatrics, Connecticut Children's Medical Center, University of Connecticut Health Center, Farmington, Connecticut

LIAM CRAPPER, BSc
Integrated Program in Neuroscience, McGill University; McGill Group for Suicide Studies, Douglas Mental Health University Institute, Montreal, Quebec, Canada

BASIL T. DARRAS, MD
Associate Neurologist-in-Chief; Chief, Division of Clinical Neurology; Joseph J. Volpe Chair, Department of Neurology, Boston Children's Hospital, Harvard Medical School, Boston, Massachusetts

FRANCIS J. DIMARIO Jr, MD
Professor Pediatrics and Neurology; Associate Chair, Department of Pediatrics; Director, Neurogenetics–Tuberous Sclerosis Clinic, Connecticut Children's Medical Center, Hartford, Connecticut

DARIUS EBRAHIMI-FAKHARI, MD
Fellow Child Neurology, Boston Children's Hospital, Boston, Massachusetts

CARL ERNST, PhD
Integrated Program in Neuroscience, McGill University; Department of Psychiatry, McGill University; McGill Group for Suicide Studies, Douglas Mental Health University Institute; Department of Human Genetics, McGill University, Montreal, Quebec, Canada

MARIA L. ESCOLAR, MD
Associate Professor, Department of Pediatrics, University of Pittsburgh, Pittsburgh, Pennsylvania

KEVIN M. FLANIGAN, MD
The Center for Gene Therapy, The Research Institute, Nationwide Children's Hospital; Departments of Pediatrics and Neurology, Ohio State University, Columbus, Ohio

YAEL HACOHEN, MRCPCH
Clinical Academic Fellowship, Nuffield Department of Clinical Neurosciences, John Radcliffe Hospital, University of Oxford, Oxford, United Kingdom

ABEER J. HANI, MD
Division of Pediatric Neurology, Department of Pediatrics, Duke Children's Hospital and Health Center, Durham, North Carolina

GUY HELMAN, BS
Department of Neurology, Children's National Health System; Center for Genetic Medicine Research, Children's National Health System, Washington, DC

SAUMYA S. JAMUAR, MD
Adjunct Assistant Professor, Department of Paediatrics, KK Women's and Children's Hospital, Singapore; Division of Genetics and Genomics, Manton Center for Orphan Disease Research, Howard Hughes Medical Institute, Boston Children's Hospital; Departments of Pediatrics and Neurology, Harvard Medical School, Boston, Massachusetts; Paediatrics Academic Programme, Duke-NUS Graduate Medical School, Singapore

AGNES JANI-ACSADI, MD
Associate Professor; Interim Chair, Department of Neurology, University of Connnecticut School of Medicine, Farmington, Connecticut

SHAFALI SPURLING JESTE, MD
Department of Psychiatry and Biobehavioral Sciences, Semel Institute for Neuroscience and Human Behavior, David Geffen School of Medicine, UCLA, Los Angeles, California

LOUISA KALSNER, MD
Assistant Professor, Departments of Pediatrics and Neurology, Connecticut Children's Medical Center, University of Connecticut School of Medicine, Farmington, Connecticut

MING LIM, MRCP, PhD
Consultant Pediatric Neurologist, Nuffield Department of Clinical Neurosciences, John Radcliffe Hospital, University of Oxford, Oxford; Children's Neurosciences, Evelina London Children's Hospital at Guy's and St Thomas' NHS Foundation Trust, King's Health Partners Academic Health Science Centre, London, United Kingdom

A.H.M. MAHBUBUL HUQ, MD, PhD
Professor, Departments of Pediatrics and Neurology, Children's Hospital of Michigan, Wayne State University, Detroit, Michigan

HUSAM M. MIKATI, RA
Center of Human Genome Variation, Duke University, Durham, North Carolina

MOHAMAD A. MIKATI, MD
Division of Pediatric Neurology, Department of Pediatrics, Duke Children's Hospital and Health Center, Durham, North Carolina

SYLVIA OUNPUU, MSc
Director of Research and Education, Center for Motion Analysis; Associate Professor, School of Medicine, University of Connecticut, Farmington, Connecticut

KRISTAN PIERZ, MD
Medical Director, Center for Motion Analysis, Connecticut Children's Medical Center; Associate Professor, School of Medicine, University of Connecticut, Farmington, Connecticut

LAINIE FRIEDMAN ROSS, MD, PhD
Carolyn and Matthew Bucksbaum Professor of Clinical Ethics, Professor, Departments of Pediatrics, Medicine and Surgery, University of Chicago, Chicago, Illinois

MUSTAFA SAHIN, MD
Director, Multidisciplinary Tuberous Sclerosis Program; Associate Professor, Department of Neurology, Boston Children's Hospital, Boston, Massachusetts

FATEMA J. SERAJEE, MD
Assistant Professor, Departments of Pediatrics and Neurology, Wayne State University, Detroit, Michigan

KEITH VAN HAREN, MD
Assistant Professor, Department of Neurology, Lucile Packard Children's Hospital, Stanford University School of Medicine, Stanford, California

ADELINE VANDERVER, MD
Associate Professor, Department of Neurology, Children's National Health System; Center for Genetic Medicine Research, Children's National Health System; Department of Integrated Systems Biology, George Washington University School of Medicine, Washington, DC

ANGELA VINCENT, FMedSci, FRS
Professor of Neuroimmunology, Nuffield Department of Clinical Neurosciences, John Radcliffe Hospital, University of Oxford, Oxford, United Kingdom

CHRISTOPHER A. WALSH, MD, PhD
Professor of Pediatrics and Neurology, Division of Genetics and Genomics, Manton Center for Orphan Disease Research, Howard Hughes Medical Institute, Boston Children's Hospital; Departments of Pediatrics and Neurology, Harvard Medical School, Boston, Massachusetts; Program in Medical and Population Genetics, Broad Institute of MIT and Harvard, Cambridge, Massachusetts

NICOLAS WEIN, PhD
The Center for Gene Therapy, The Research Institute, Nationwide Children's Hospital, Columbus, Ohio

Contents

Malformations of cortical development (MCDs) are a common cause of neurodevelopmental delay and epilepsy and are caused by disruptions in the normal development of the cerebral cortex. Several causative genes have been identified in patients with MCD. There is increasing evidence of role of de novo mutations, including those occurring post fertilization, in MCD. These somatic mutations may not be detectable by traditional methods of genetic testing performed on blood DNA. Identification of the genetic cause can help in guiding families in future pregnancies. Research has highlighted how elucidation of key molecular pathways can also allow for targeted therapeutic interventions.

Three distinct neurodevelopmental disorders arise primarily from deletions or duplications that occur at the 15q11-q13 locus: Prader-Willi syndrome, Angelman syndrome, and 15q11-q13 duplication syndrome. Each of these disorders results from the loss of function or overexpression of at least 1 imprinted gene. This article discusses the clinical background, genetic cause, diagnostic strategy, and management of each of these 3 disorders.

Although the diagnosis of autism spectrum disorder (ASD) is based on behavioral signs and symptoms, the evaluation of a child with ASD has become increasingly focused on the identification of the genetic etiology of the disorder. In this review, we begin with a clinical overview of ASD, highlighting the heterogeneity of the disorder. We then discuss the genetics of ASD and present updated guidelines on genetic testing. We then consider the insights gained from the identification of both single gene disorders and rare variants, with regard to clinical phenomenology and potential treatment targets.

Self-injury is a complex and poorly understood behavior observed in people with psychopathology or neurodevelopmental disorders (NDD). Despite the differences in etiology and progression of these distinct disease domains, it is possible that overlapping molecular pathways underlie the expression of self-injurious behaviors (SIBs). This review outlines the similarities and differences at the behavioural and molecular level, where SIBs in both conditions may involve opioid, nucleoside, and dopamine signalling. These points of convergence have important implications for treatment and research of SIB in both populations.

Tuberous sclerosis complex is an autosomal-dominant, neurocutaneous, multisystem disorder characterized by cellular hyperplasia and tissue dysplasia. The genetic cause is mutations in the *TSC1 gene*, found on chromosome 9q34, and *TSC2 gene*, found on chromosome 16p13. The clinical phenotypes resulting from mutations in either of the 2 genes are variable in each individual. Herein, advances in the understanding of molecular mechanisms in tuberous sclerosis complex are reviewed, and current guidelines for diagnosis, treatment, follow-up, and management are summarized.

The leukodystrophies are a heterogeneous group of inherited disorders with broad clinical manifestations and variable pathologic mechanisms. Improved diagnostic methods have allowed identification of the underlying cause of these diseases, facilitating identification of their pathologic mechanisms. Clinicians are now able to prioritize treatment strategies and advance research in therapies for specific disorders. Although only a few of these disorders have well-established treatments or therapies, a number are on the verge of clinical trials. As investigators are able to shift care from symptomatic management of disorders to targeted therapeutics, the unmet therapeutic needs could be reduced for these patients.

Antibody-mediated diseases of the central nervous system are a relatively new and challenging field in autoimmune neurologic disease and of major clinical importance in children and adults. The antibodies bind to cell-surface epitopes on neuronal or glial proteins, and the patients demonstrate either focal or more generalized clinical signs depending on the extent of brain regions targeted by the antibodies. The presence of seizures, movement disorders, autonomic dysfunction and sleep disorders, alongside neuroimaging and electrophysiological features may indicate a specific antibody-mediated disorder. However, phenotypic variation may be observed in children with the same antibody. Regardless, many patients benefit from immunotherapy with substantial improvement.

Fatema J. Serajee and A.H.M. Mahbubul Huq

Tourette syndrome (TS) is a childhood-onset neurodevelopmental disorder characterized by multiple motor tics and at least one vocal or phonic tic, and often one or more comorbid psychiatric disorders. Premonitory sensory urges before tic execution and desire for "just-right" perception are central features. The pathophysiology involves cortico-striato-thalamo-cortical circuits and possibly dopaminergic system. TS is considered a genetic disorder but the genetics is complex and likely involves rare mutations, common variants, and environmental and epigenetic factors. Treatment is multimodal and includes education and reassurance, behavioral interventions, pharmacologic, and rarely, surgical interventions.

Abeer J. Hani, Husam M. Mikati, and Mohamad A. Mikati

As the genetic etiologies of an expanding number of epilepsy syndromes are revealed, the complexity of the phenotype genotype correlation increases. As our review will show, multiple gene mutations cause different epilepsy syndromes, making identification of the specific mutation increasingly more important for prognostication and often more directed treatment. Examples of that include the need to avoid specific drugs in Dravet syndrome and the ongoing investigations of the potential use of new directed therapies such as retigabine in KCNQ2-related epilepsies, quinidine in KCNT1-related epilepsies, and memantine in GRIN2A-related epilepsies.

Nicolas Wein, Lindsay Alfano, and Kevin M. Flanigan

 Videos showing a boy with DMD climbing stairs and a boy with DMD arising from the floor, accompany this article

Mutations in the DMD gene result in Duchenne or Becker muscular dystrophy due to absent or altered expression of the dystrophin protein. The more severe Duchenne muscular dystrophy typically presents around ages 2 to 5 with gait disturbance, and historically has led to the loss of ambulation by age 12. It is important for the practicing pediatrician, however, to be aware of other presenting signs, such as delayed motor or cognitive milestones, or elevated serum transaminases. Becker muscular dystrophy is milder, often presenting after age 5, with ambulation frequently preserved past 20 years and sometimes into late decades.

Basil T. Darras

Spinal muscular atrophies (SMAs) are hereditary degenerative disorders of lower motor neurons associated with progressive muscle weakness and atrophy. Proximal 5q SMA is caused by decreased levels of the survival of motor neuron (SMN) protein and is the most common genetic cause of infant mortality. Its inheritance pattern is autosomal recessive, resulting from mutations involving the *SMN1* gene on chromosome 5q13. Unlike other autosomal recessive diseases, the *SMN* gene has a unique structure (an inverted duplication) that presents potential therapeutic targets. Although there is currently no effective treatment of SMA, the field of translational research in this disorder is active and clinical trials are ongoing. Advances in the multidisciplinary supportive care of children with SMA also offer hope for improved life expectancy and quality of life.

Heritable diseases of the peripheral nerves (Charcot-Marie-Tooth disease [CMT]) affect the motor units and sensory nerves, and they are among the most prevalent genetic conditions in the pediatric patient population. The typical clinical presentation includes distal muscle weakness and atrophy, but the severity and progression are largely variable. Improvements in supportive treatment have led to better preservation of patients' motor functions. More than 80 genes have been associated with CMT. These genetic discoveries, along with the developments of cellular and transgenic disease models, have allowed clinicians to better understand the disease mechanisms, which should lead to more specific treatments.

Genetic testing for neurologic and developmental disorders spans the spectrum from universal newborn screening for conditions like phenylketonuria to diagnostic testing for suspected genetic conditions, to predictive genetic testing for childhood-onset conditions. Given that virtually all children in the United States undergo genetic screening in the newborn period, this article focuses on 3 actual case studies of neurologic and developmental disorders that have been included or proposed for inclusion in newborn screening programs: Duchenne muscular dystrophy (a neuromuscular disorder), Krabbe disease (a neurodegenerative disorder), and fragile X syndrome (a neurodevelopmental disorder).

PEDIATRIC CLINICS OF NORTH AMERICA

THE CLINICS ARE AVAILABLE ONLINE!
Access your subscription at:
www.theclinics.com

Foreword

Transformative Technologies and Understanding

Bonita F. Stanton, MD
Consulting Editor

This exciting volume of *Pediatric Clinics of North America* eloquently tells the story of the advances in our understanding and treatment of many previously misunderstood psychological, neurologic, and developmental disorders over the last few decades. With the increased knowledge of clinical conditions and genetic patterns arising from the rapidly expanding field of genome research coupled with expanded neurologic imaging and neuropsychological testing, previously unrecognized and misidentified disorders can now be diagnosed. Diagnosis in many cases can be followed by therapeutic regimens that result in far better outcomes, and in some cases, cures. This is an area of pediatrics in which great advances are continually being made, allowing much brighter futures for impacted children and families.

These disorders are not obscure, hopeless, or rare, and thus, it is important that practicing pediatricians be aware of the new diagnoses and diagnostic criterion and the substantial therapeutic options available for most affected children. This issue will enable pediatricians to bring clarity and hope to distressed families and map a path forward for affected children. Dr Gyula Acsadi and the outstanding group of geneticists, pediatric neurologists, and developmental pediatricians he has assembled have written an exciting and enlightened set of treatises that will be very helpful in every day practice.

Bonita F. Stanton, MD
School of Medicine
Wayne State University
1261 Scott Hall
540 East Canfield, Suite 1261
Detroit, MI 48201, USA

E-mail address:
bstanton@med.wayne.edu

Pediatr Clin N Am 62 (2015) xv
http://dx.doi.org/10.1016/j.pcl.2015.03.015
0031-3955/15/$ – see front matter © 2015 Published by Elsevier Inc.

Preface

Pediatric Neurology in the Era of Genomics

Gyula Acsadi, MD, PhD
Editor

"Our knowledge of the pathological substratum of the various forms of mental derangement is still very imperfect. In the majority of cases, there may be no marked changes in the structure of the brain; or, if there be any changes at all, they are entirely beyond our ken, and cannot be made out by our present methods of investigation." Bernard Sachs started his paper with these words in 1887, describing a disease that was later named Tay-Sachs disease.[1] This quote by Sachs may apply to the term "idiopathic," with regard to the etiology of neurologic diseases.

For a long time, many childhood developmental and neurologic diseases were characterized as "idiopathic," but now it is used less often thanks to rapidly increasing genetic discoveries. Since the introduction of cytogenetics in the middle of the twentieth century, the evolution of genetic technologies, from positional cloning to the next-generation sequencing, has allowed us to discover the causes of hundreds of pediatric neurologic diseases.[2–4] The recognition of genetic and phenotypic variability constantly redefines nomenclature and disease classification. However, a better understanding of molecular mechanism of diseases has been made possible by genetically engineered cell cultures and animals as disease models. This, in turn, provided platforms for screening therapeutic molecules. The rapidly evolving research has led to development of rational therapies for many diseases that were thought to be incurable in the past.

In this special issue of *Pediatric Clinics of North America*, it is our pleasure to provide updates on various common childhood developmental and neurologic conditions that have directly or indirectly benefited from genome research. For many of these, therapeutic interventions are available or being considered. There is no doubt that our efforts in supportive treatments have improved the quality of life and extended the life expectancy of children suffering from neurologic diseases. Our renewed hope is that new therapies, based on molecular mechanisms, will significantly improve the outcome.

Pediatr Clin N Am 62 (2015) xvii–xviii
http://dx.doi.org/10.1016/j.pcl.2015.03.014
0031-3955/15/$ – see front matter © 2015 Published by Elsevier Inc.

pediatric.theclinics.com

The increasing availability of new genetic tests, such as whole-exome sequencing, is bound to change traditional diagnostic approaches.[5,6] We will likely order less biochemical, histological, and other neurodiagnostic tests. We will have to tailor the treatments based on individual genotypes. For example, the antisense oligonucleotide-based "exon skipping" treatment for Duchenne muscular dystrophy is designed to treat patients with specific mutations.

In the meantime, considerable limitations exist for the new genetic technologies. Whole-exome sequencing covers only 1.5% of the human genome, and it may miss some large deletions, triplet repeat expansions (eg, CTG repeat expansion in myotonic dystrophy), mutations in introns (eg, regulatory sites), and gene promoters. Epigenetic regulation is important in the phenotypic expression of some neurologic diseases, such as chromosome 15–related conditions. Testing for these requires additional laboratory processes.[7] Whole-genome sequencing will further improve the genetic testing of neurologic diseases; however, the differentiation of disease-causing genetic mutations from benign or irrelevant DNA alterations requires the aid of genetic specialists. This is a very time-consuming task that is not reimbursed by most insurance carriers in the United States. Another significant problem regarding test results is dealing with unexpected disease-causing gene abnormalities, which may have a significant impact for the future health of the individual.

I am delighted to present thirteen excellent review articles written by well-recognized experts in the field of Pediatric Neurology and Developmental Pediatrics. We trust that these articles are going to be helpful resources for the practicing pediatric specialists.

Gyula Acsadi, MD, PhD
Connecticut Children's Medical Center and
Departments of Pediatrics and Neurology
University of Connecticut School of Medicine
505 Farmington Avenue
Farmington, CT 06032, USA

E-mail address:
gacsadi@connecticutchildrens.org

REFERENCES

1. Sachs B. On arrested cerebral development with special reference to cortical pathology. J Nerv Ment Dis 1887;14(9-10):541–4.
2. Jiang T, Tan MS, Tan L, et al. Application of next-generation sequencing technologies in Neurology. Ann Transl Med 2014;2(12):125.
3. Guerreiro R, Brás J, Hardy J, et al. Next generation sequencing techniques in neurological diseases: redefining clinical and molecular associations. Hum Mol Genet 2014;23(R1):R47–53.
4. Poduri A, Evrony GD, Cai X, et al. Somatic mutation, genomic variation, and neurological disease. Science 2013;341(6141):1237758.
5. Coe BP, Girirajan S, Eichler EE. A genetic model for neurodevelopmental disease. Curr Opin Neurobiol 2012;22(5):829–36.
6. Pittman A, Hardy J. Genetic analysis in neurology the next 10 years. JAMA Neurol 2013;70(6):696–702.
7. Gropman AL, Batshaw ML. Epigenetics, copy number variation, and other molecular mechanisms underlying neurodevelopmental disabilities: new insights and diagnostic approaches. J Dev Behav Pediatr 2010;31(7):582–91.

Genomic Variants and Variations in Malformations of Cortical Development

Saumya S. Jamuar, MD[a,b,c,d,e],
Christopher A. Walsh, MD, PhD[b,c,d,f],*

KEYWORDS

- Malformations of cortical development • Genomic variants • Somatic mutation
- Microcephaly • Megalencephaly • Cortical dysplasia • Lissencephaly
- Polymicrogyria

KEY POINTS

- Development of the cerebral cortex is a tightly regulated process, and disruption in any part of this process can lead to malformations of cortical development (MCDs).
- MCD can primarily be classified into abnormalities of neurogenesis, abnormalities of neuronal migration, and abnormalities of postmigrational development.
- Recent advances in genomic technology have allowed for an unprecedented expansion in the knowledge of these disorders and have elucidated molecular pathways that can serve as targets for therapeutic interventions.

Disclosure: No conflicts of interest to declare.
C.A. Walsh is supported by grants from the National Institute of Mental Health (R01MH083565 and 1RC2MH089952), the National Institute of Neurological Disorders and Stroke (R01NS032457, R01NS079277 and R01NS035129), the Simons Foundation, the Paul G. Allen Family Foundation, and the Manton Center for Orphan Disease Research. C.A. Walsh is an Investigator of the Howard Hughes Medical Institute.
[a] Department of Paediatrics, KK Women's and Children's Hospital, 100 Bukit Timah Road, Singapore 229899, Singapore; [b] Division of Genetics and Genomics, Manton Center for Orphan Disease Research, Howard Hughes Medical Institute, Boston Children's Hospital, Boston, MA 02115, USA; [c] Department of Pediatrics, Harvard Medical School, Boston, MA 02115, USA; [d] Department of Neurology, Harvard Medical School, Boston, MA 02115, USA; [e] Paediatrics Academic Programme, Duke-NUS Graduate Medical School, 8 College Road, Singapore 169857, Singapore; [f] Program in Medical and Population Genetics, Broad Institute of MIT and Harvard, Cambridge, MA 02138, USA
* Corresponding author. Division of Genetics and Genomics, Boston Children's Hospital, Center for Life Sciences 15062.2, 3 Blackfan Circle, Boston, MA 02115.
E-mail address: christopher.walsh@childrens.harvard.edu

Pediatr Clin N Am 62 (2015) 571–585
http://dx.doi.org/10.1016/j.pcl.2015.03.002   **pediatric.theclinics.com**
0031-3955/15/$ – see front matter © 2015 Elsevier Inc. All rights reserved.

CLINICAL BACKGROUND

The development of the human cortex is a complex and tightly regulated process. During development, distinct cell types must proliferate, differentiate, migrate, and integrate to form a highly complex structure, capable of complex cognition, language, and emotion.[1] Disruptions in any of these processes lead to malformations of cortical development (MCD), which are common causes of neurodevelopmental delay and/or epilepsy.[2] Individuals presenting early can show feeding difficulties soon after birth (in some instances, in utero swallowing difficulty may present as polyhydramnios), abnormal head size (microcephaly or macrocephaly), epileptic encephalopathies, or global developmental delay. Some patients with MCD may present early with severe neurologic impairment, whereas others present with epilepsy and mild functional impairment at a later age. Individuals who present later may exhibit focal epilepsy, learning difficulty, and behavioral issues, such as attention deficit hyperactivity disorder.[3] Occasionally, a few individuals may be diagnosed only on screening, as their deficit may not be clinically apparent.

Classification systems for MCDs, first introduced in 1996 and subsequently revised in 2001, 2005, and 2012 to incorporate the improved understanding of cortical development, divide MCDs into 3 major groups, namely, malformations secondary to abnormal neuronal and glial proliferation or apoptosis, malformations due to abnormal neuronal migration, and malformations secondary to abnormal postmigrational development. This system is based on the developmental steps at which the process is first disrupted, the underlying genes and biological pathways affected, and imaging features,[2] although there is surprising overlap in the phenotypes of many genes, reflecting involvement of some genes in more than one stage of development.

Genomic variants are changes in one allele of a gene of an individual compared with a reference genome. Variants may be small (<1 kilobasepair) and include substitutions and small insertions and deletions (indels) or may be large (>1 kilobasepair) and include copy number variants (CNVs) (larger insertions or deletions) and rearrangements, such as translocation and inversion. Lastly, genomic variants also include whole chromosome numerical alterations such as aneuploidy. Although many variants are not associated with disease (and instead are referred to as benign variants), certain deleterious variants that alter the function of a gene may cause disease, representing disease-causing mutations. Human genetic diseases have traditionally been thought to reflect either inherited or de novo (spontaneous) variants. These mutations are present in all the cells of the affected individual and can be detected in any cell of the body, including readily available peripheral blood, and are referred to as germline mutations. Somatic mutation, on the other hand, is a postzygotic mutational event that leads to an individual having 2 or more populations of cells with distinct genotypes, despite developing from a single fertilized egg[4,5]; somatic mutations thus represent a subset of the larger category of de novo mutations.

This review focuses on the recent advances in understanding the genetics of MCDs, including recent updates on the role of somatic mutations in MCDs. Large-scale sequencing projects have led to an exponential increase in the knowledge of the genes associated with MCDs, and the authors address some of these recent discoveries. Although most MCDs are caused by genomic variants, a proportion of MCDs (such as schizencephaly) are associated with nongenomic mechanisms and may be secondary to environmental causes.

EMBRYOLOGY OF CEREBRAL CORTICAL DEVELOPMENT

The normal human cortex is composed of 6 distinct histologic layers. Its development begins from neuroepithelial progenitors lining the lateral ventricles, which divide to expand the progenitor pool and then give rise to intermediate progenitors that subsequently divide and give rise to neurons. The neurons migrate from the proliferative ventricular zones toward the pial surface of the brain to form the layered cortex, where the connections between neurons form and mature.[1,6]

The principal excitatory neurons of the cerebral cortex and hippocampus are derived from an embryonic neuroepithelium, with progenitor cells lining the ventricular surface deep in the brain. In animal models, inhibitory neurons that populate the cerebral cortex are formed outside the cortex in a second proliferative zone in the basal forebrain called the ganglionic eminence, which generates the basal ganglia. These neurons migrate large distances in nonradial direction before turning radially to enter the cortex.[7] There is recent evidence that human interneurons are formed by a similar mechanism.[8] Astrocytic glial cells arise from several sources, including progenitors that also generate principal neurons,[9] whereas oligodendrocytes arise in the basal forebrain that generates cells for the entire forebrain.[10]

RECENT ADVANCES IN GENETICS AND PATHOMECHANISM OF MALFORMATIONS OF CORTICAL DEVELOPMENT
Overview

Historically, geneticists have relied on principles of mendelian inheritance to identify genes, which when perturbed, lead to development of specific symptoms. Linkage analysis, homozygosity mapping, positional cloning, and/or candidate gene sequencing have helped identify the genetic causes of many forms of MCDs.[11–14] Studying individuals/families with MCDs allows one to understand the critical components of normal brain development and function.

High-throughput next-generation sequencing (NGS) allows one to interrogate multiple regions of the genome at once to identify tens of thousands of genetic variants in an individual's genome.[15] These variants can then be filtered bioinformatically using certain criteria, such as absence in control population, allele frequency, predicted pathogenicity, and inheritance model, to narrow down the candidate gene list to a few genes. With NGS, causal variants can be identified in a few weeks, and this has led to a surge in the identification of novel genes as well as new alleles in known disease genes. With these recent advances in genetics, certain MCD-related genes, such as *WDR62* and *DYNC1H1*, have been associated with a broad range of malformations, suggesting that some of these genes are implicated in many developmental stages that are functionally and genetically interdependent.[3]

Improved genomic tools have shed light on the role of de novo mutations in intellectual disability.[16] Although traditionally, de novo mutations were considered to have developed in the egg or the sperm of the unaffected parents, there is increasing evidence of the role of postzygotic (or somatic) de novo mutations in neurologic disorders as well. As these mutations may be present in only a small proportion of the cells in the body, traditional methods of testing using leukocyte-derived DNA have been shown to miss most of these somatic mutations.[17] Some of these mutations may be present only in the affected tissue, and testing of nonaffected tissue, such as blood DNA, may not be informative.[17–19]

Microcephaly

Primary microcephaly

Primary microcephaly (or microcephaly vera) is defined as the clinical finding of a head circumference less than 3 standard deviations (SD) less than the age- and sex-related mean, which is present at birth and is commonly associated with intellectual disability.[20] Genes known to cause primary microcephaly affect pathways involving neurogenesis, resulting in decreased number of neurons and smaller brain size.[2] These pathways include cell cycle progression and checkpoint regulation (*MCPH1, CENPJ, CDK5RAP2*[21]), centrosome duplication (*NDE1*[22]), centrosome maturation (*CDK5RAP2, CENPJ*[21]), cell proliferation (*STIL, ASPM*[23,24]), mitotic spindle formation (*WDR62, NDE1*[25,26]), and DNA repair (*PKNP, PCNT*[27,28]). Aberrations in these pathways highlight the important role of centrosome in neuronal proliferation. The centrosome is a key microtubule-organizing center that helps maintain the cellular cytoskeleton and coordinate the segregation of duplicated chromosomes during cell division. Mutations in genes encoding centrosomal proteins, or proteins required for proper chromosomal segregation, account for the largest number of genetic causes of microcephaly and may form a common pathway to regulate neuronal progenitor proliferation.[20]

With the exception of *WDR62* (polymicrogyria [PMG], subcortical heterotopia)[25] and *ARFGEF2* (periventricular nodular heterotopia [PVNH]),[29] primary microcephaly genes do not produce obvious brain anomalies except for simplified gyral pattern and hypoplasia of the corpus callosum.[27,30,31] No definable clinicoradiologic characteristics that separate the different types of microcephaly caused by mutations in different stages of the cell cycle have been identified,[2] suggesting that sequencing panels of genes is an efficient diagnostic approach.

Postmigrational microcephaly

In contrast to primary microcephaly, individuals whose head circumference are normal or slightly small (2 SD below mean) at birth, but develop severe microcephaly in the first 1-2 years are referred to as postmigrational microcephaly.[2] In these individuals, brain growth slows during late gestation or early postnatal period after normal early development. Examples of genes involved in this condition include *CASK* (associated with microcephaly with disproportionate cerebellar and brainstem hypoplasia),[32] *MECP2* (Rett syndrome),[33] and *UBE3A* (Angelman syndrome)[34] and genes of proteins related to protein synthesis, including transfer RNA (tRNA) splicing endonuclease subunit genes such as *TSEN54, TSEN2,* and *TSEN34*; aminoacyl-tRNA synthetases such as *RARS2*; and *SEPSECS* associated with pontocerebellar hypoplasias.[2,35] Mutations in *QARS*, a cytoplasmic aminoacyl-tRNA synthetase, has been reported in individuals with progressive microcephaly, intractable seizures, diffuse atrophy of the cerebral cortex, and cerebellar vermis and considerably mild atrophy of the cerebellar hemispheres.[36] As the disruption occurs late in cerebral development, these disorders may someday be good candidates for intervention once the molecular causes have been elucidated.

Overgrowth-Related Disorders

Megalencephaly and hemimegalencephaly

Megalencephaly with PMG is a sporadic overgrowth disorder associated with markedly enlarged brain size (head circumference more than 3 SD), sometimes seen with developmental vascular anomalies, distal limb malformations (polydactyly and syndactyly), and mild connective tissue dysplasia, when it is referred to as megalencephaly-capillary malformation-polymicrogyria (MCAP) syndrome.[37] Hemimegalencephaly, on the other hand, refers to asymmetric brain enlargement that is typically isolated, although it has been reported in association with tuberous sclerosis, hypomelanosis of Ito, and Proteus syndrome.[18] Hemimegalencephaly is associated with dysmorphic immature neurons, neuronal heterotopia, and cortical dyslamination.[18,19]

Exome sequencing and targeted deep sequencing have identified de novo germline and postzygotic (or somatic) point mutations in *AKT3*, *PIK3CA*, and *PIK3R2* in individuals with MCAP syndrome and hemimegalencephaly.[18,19,38] Somatic CNV increases of chromosome 1q involving *AKT3* have also been identified in individuals with hemimegalencephaly.[19,39] Mutations in *PTEN* also lead to megalencephaly, autism, and tumor predisposition.[40] The phosphoinositide 3-kinases (PI3Ks) are a family of signaling enzymes that regulate a wide range of cellular processes, including growth, proliferation, survival, migration, and brain development. *PTEN* is a tumor suppressor gene that antagonizes the PI3K signaling pathway, whereas AKT kinases are downstream effectors of PI3K signaling and have a critical role in growth regulation. Gain of function mutations or increased copy number of *AKT3* hyperactivates the mammalian target of rapamycin (mTOR) pathway, causing increased cell growth, ribosome biogenesis, and messenger RNA translation. The tuberous sclerosis complex (TSC) genes encode negative regulators of mTOR, so that loss of these genes (in tuberous sclerosis) also leads to hyperactivation of mTOR, leading to overgrowth of normal cells and production of abnormal cells in many organs.[38]

Focal cortical dysplasia

Focal cortical dysplasias (FCDs) are a heterogeneous group of disorders that are characterized by abnormal cortical lamination and defects of neuronal migration, growth, and differentiation involving 1 discrete cortical region, several lobes, or even the entire hemisphere.[41] FCDs are the most common cause of medically refractory epilepsy in the pediatric population. The cause is heterogeneous and can be genetic or environmental. FCDs are classified into 3 groups[42]:

- FCD I: This condition presents with mild symptoms and is often seen in adults, and changes are typically seen in the temporal lobe. Evidence suggests that prenatal and perinatal insults, including extreme prematurity, asphyxia, bleeding, stroke, hydrocephalus, and shaking injury, are commonly observed in patients with FCD I.
- FCD II: Clinical symptoms are more severe with onset typically in childhood. Radiologic changes are seen outside the temporal lobe with predilection for the frontal lobes. Histologic characteristics of FCD II are more homogenous across patients, and evidence points toward genetic mutations that lead to perturbation of the mTOR pathway in the pathogenesis of FCD type IIb.[43] Patients with mutations in *DEPDC5*, which typically cause epilepsy without any imaging abnormality, have been reported with FCD, suggesting a second hit phenomenon, analogous to TSC, with a somatic mutation in the other allele of *DEPDC5* or another gene in the mTOR pathway, causing the malformations in these patients.[44]
- FCD III: This condition is associated with acquired pathology during early development, such as hippocampal sclerosis, vascular malformations, epileptogenic tumor or injury secondary to head trauma, encephalitis, or hypoxic ischemic injury. As seen in FCD IIb, dysregulation of mTOR pathway has been described in certain forms of FCD III.[43]

Abnormal Neuronal Migration

Heterotopia

Heterotopia can range from PVNH (**Fig. 1**A) to periventricular linear heterotopia to columnar heterotopia and is secondary to abnormalities of the neuroependyma and failure to initiate migration. Although the exact pathophysiology remains to be elucidated, evidence suggests that injury to the neuroependyma is an important factor in the formation of PVNH. Classic PVNH is associated with mutations in *FLNA*.[13] The phenotype of patients with *FLNA*-related PVNH has been expanded to include a wide spectrum of connective tissue and vascular anomalies, including aortic root dilatation.[45,46] Autosomal recessive forms of PVNH have been described in patients with

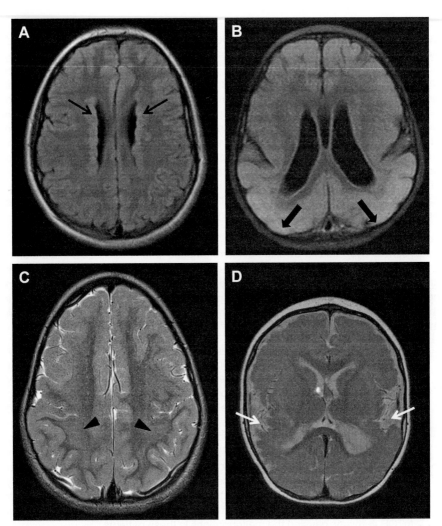

Fig. 1. Axial magnetic resonance images of the brain showing (*A*) periventricular nodular heterotopia (*black arrows*), (*B*) pachygyria (*black arrows*), (*C*) subcortical band heterotopia (*arrowheads*), and (*D*) polymicrogyria (*white arrows*).

mutations in *ARFGEF2*[29] and *C12orf57*.[47,48] Other potential genetic loci for genes associated with PVNH include 7q11.23, 5p15.1, 5p15.33, 5q14.3-q15, and 4p15.[49]

Lissencephaly and subcortical band heterotopia

Abnormal transmantle migration can lead to agyria (complete absence of gyri), pachy-gyria (reduced but thickened gyri) (see **Fig. 1**B), and subcortical band heterotopia or double cortex syndrome (see **Fig. 1**C). Most cases of lissencephaly are attributable to mutations in *LIS1* (also known as *PAFAH1B1*) and *DCX* and are commonly loss of function alleles. *LIS1* alleles include genic deletions, missense mutations, and nonsense mutations; *DCX* alleles include nonsense mutations, frameshift mutations, genic deletions, and splicing mutations that are distributed across the entire length of the protein, whereas missense mutations cluster predominantly around the 2 functional microtubule-binding domains and disrupt tubulin binding.[50–53] Germline null mutations in *LIS1* cause classic lissencephaly, whereas germline mutations in *DCX*, which is on the X-chromosome, result in lissencephaly in males and subcortical band heterotopia in females. Somatic mutations in *DCX* and *LIS1*, affecting as few as 10% of leukocytes, have been associated with variable degree of subcortical band heterotopia.[17]

With use of NGS, mutations in additional genes have been identified. These include *TUBA1A* (encoding a neuronal α-tubulin),[54] *DYNC1H1* (encoding a dynein heavy chain isoform), *KIF2A* (encoding a kinesin heavy chain), *KIF5C* (encoding a member of the kinesin superfamily of proteins), and *TUBG1* (encoding γ-tubulin) and have been reported in patients with milder disease on the lissencephaly spectrum.[17,55] These discoveries highlight the role of cytoskeletal proteins in neuronal migration. In addition, the complex of cytoplasmic dynein with Lis1, Nde1, and Ndel1 has been known to be essential for neuronal migration, and patients with mutations in *NDE1* have been reported in association with microlissencephaly, highlighting the link between microcephaly and lissencephaly.[22]

Cobblestone malformations

Cobblestone malformations are associated with abnormal migration of neurons into the leptomeninges and are a result of deficiencies in the cerebral basement membrane due to defects in O-mannosylation of α-dystroglycan.[56] This condition leads to abnormal cortical lamination and overmigration of neurons through the incomplete basement membrane into the pial layer.[2] Mutations in multiple genes in the glycosylation pathway have been identified, and mutations in the same gene can cause widely different phenotypes.[57] For example, mutations in *FKRP*, encoding a fukutin-related protein, were initially identified in patients with only severe congenital skeletal muscle defects[58] but since have been identified in patients with milder skeletal system defects[59] and in patients with central nervous system (CNS) malformations and eye involvement.[60] Genes associated with glycosylation within the endoplasmic reticulum (*SRD5A3*)[61] or Golgi apparatus (*ATP6V0A2*)[62] have also been reported in patients with cobblestone malformations.

Dystroglycanopathies can cause a wide range of disorders ranging from isolated brain malformation to intellectual disability with microcephaly and skeletal muscle and eye involvement. These syndromes are commonly referred to as Walker-Warburg syndrome, muscle-eye-brain disease, Fukuyama congenital muscular dystrophy, and congenital muscular dystrophy type 1C and 1D, depending on the extent of tissue involvement.[60] However, elucidation of the genetic underpinnings has prompted a reclassification of the dystroglycanopathies.[57]

Patients with mutations in *GPR56* may also present with cobblestone malformations but do not show a known glycosylation defect. GPR56 is a G protein–coupled receptor that is preferentially expressed in the neuronal progenitor cells of the cerebral cortical ventricular and subventricular zones during periods of neurogenesis but not in the cortical plate or intermediate zone. GPR56 is postulated to regulate cortical patterning, and patients with mutations in *GPR56* have a thin cortex, suggesting a role in cell fate control during neurogenesis.[63]

Polymicrogyria

PMG (see **Fig. 1**D) refers to a cerebral cortex with many excessively small gyri.[3] The cause of PMG is highly heterogeneous and can be subdivided into two: with schizencephalic clefts likely due to infection or vascular causes and without clefts but with and without associated CNS and non-CNS malformations and with certain types of inborn errors of metabolism (IEM).[2]

Polymicrogyria without clefts

PMG without clefts can be secondary to a genetic or disruptive process. Isolated PMG is classified by location; however, the genetic cause remains unknown for most of the PMG syndromes.[2] The most common form is bilateral perisylvian PMG, which presents with oromotor dysfunction, intellectual disability, and epilepsy. The clinical presentation of patients with other forms of PMG varies widely and depends on the extent of PMG and presence of other brain malformations, such as cerebellar hypoplasia or microcephaly. PMG can affect cortical areas representing language or primary motor functions, yet these functions can be retained with minimal or no disability.[3]

CNVs, especially deletion of chromosome 1p36.3 and chromosome 22q11.2, have been reported in association with PMG, although the causal genes remain to be identified. Common syndromic associations with PMG include Adams-Oliver syndrome,[64] Joubert syndrome and related disorders,[65] Goldberg-Shprintzen syndrome,[66] Warburg Micro syndrome,[67,68] and Aicardi syndrome.[69] Mutations in genes encoding α-tubulins, such as TUBA8,[70] and β-tubulins, such as TUBB2B[71] and TUBB3,[72] have been reported in patients with PMG in isolation or in the presence of other brain malformations, including corpus callosum anomalies and optic nerve hypoplasia.

PMG-like cortical malformations have also been reported in patients with IEM, including peroxisomal disorders (such as Zellweger syndrome, neonatal adrenoleukodystrophy), fumaric aciduria, glutaric aciduria type 2, maple syrup urine disease, and mitochondrial diseases.[2,3] However, the pathomechanism of these associations is not well established. Some forms of PMG are also associated with the megalencephalic conditions and cobblestone disorders described earlier, and so those genes should be considered in the differential genetic diagnosis.

Schizencephaly

In schizencephaly, the cortex edges can be fused (closed lip) or remain at a distance (open lip) and may be unilateral or bilateral. Patients with closed-lip unilateral schizencephaly may present with hemiparesis or motor delay, whereas patients with open-lip schizencephaly present with hydrocephalus or seizures.[3] Histologically, the cortex surrounding the cleft shows loss of laminar architecture, forming irregular heterotopic aggregates of gray matter. Although there was initial evidence of role of mutations in EMX2 as a cause of schizencephaly,[73] subsequent analysis has not further confirmed this,[74,75] and current understanding supports a nongenetic cause for most cases, likely infection (commonly cytomegalovirus)[76] or vascular event.[77] In addition, young maternal age and monozygotic twin pregnancies have been associated with higher incidence of schizencephaly.[77]

DIAGNOSTIC STRATEGY

Brain Imaging

In patients presenting with clinical features suggestive of MCD, diagnostic imaging with MRI is recommended to delineate the type of MCD.[3] The key features to look for include distribution and severity of MCD, the cortical surface and border between white and gray matter, cortical thickness, and any other associated brain malformations (such as anomalies of the corpus callosum, brainstem, and cerebellum). Identification of the type of MCD allows the clinician to focus on the malformation-relevant genes.

Tissue Consideration

Leukocyte-derived DNA from peripheral blood is the most readily accessible tissue for genetic analysis in the clinic and can be used to detect any inherited or de novo germline genomic variants. However, in patients who present with a specific radiologic phenotype but show negative results on testing for the known malformation-related genes, it is important to consider the role of somatic mutations. In this scenario, DNA derived from buccal swabs has been shown to be more effective in detecting these mutations.[38,78] However, some mutations require direct examination of the affected tissue (in this case, brain), which can be obtained from patients undergoing resection of the affected tissue, for example, for epilepsy surgery.[18,19]

GENETIC TESTING
Single Nucleotide Variants

In cases in which 1 or 2 genes are known to be the predominant cause of the MCD phenotype, for example, *LIS1* and *DCX* for lissencephaly and *FLNA* for PVNH, targeted Sanger sequencing of these genes may still be the best approach, although targeted panels are increasingly the first-line test. Given the known genetic heterogeneity of the MCD, such as in pachygyria or PMG, targeted gene panels are useful and cost-effective, by efficiently analyzing multiple genes at once. An alternative strategy is to perform whole exome sequencing (WES), which is the process of sequencing the coding regions of the entire genome in 1 reaction and has been shown to improve diagnostic yield to 25% in undiagnosed cases with mendelian disorder.[79] However, one advantage of targeted gene panel sequencing is that the coverage of the genes of interest is more uniform than in WES. Another advantage is that targeted gene panel obviates the issue related to incidental findings detected on WES (such as mutations in a *BRCA1*, which may place the patient at risk for breast cancer in the future but are not related to the primary phenotype).[80] Lastly, targeted gene panel sequencing also allows for deeper coverage, which in turn is more likely to detect low-frequency somatic mutations.[17]

Copy Number Variants

CNVs have been associated with certain forms of MCDs, including PMG. Traditionally, these CNVs were detected by cytogenetic analysis with karyotype and fluorescence in situ hybridization (FISH) analysis for specific regions of the genome. However, karyotype analysis has a resolution of approximately 5 megabasepairs, and CNVs smaller than this are not detectable by this method. FISH is specific only for certain regions (eg, 22q11.2) but may be costly and laborious when probing multiple regions across the genome. The advantage of karyotype analysis and FISH is that it provides structural information and can detect translocation. Translocations that disrupt genes of interest have been paramount in mapping of disease-related genes during the past 2 decades.

Chromosome microarray analysis (CMA) allows a clinician to detect submicroscopic CNVs across the genome. The diagnostic yield of CMA in patients with neurologic disorders is about 10% to 15%, and CMA has replaced karyotype analysis as the first-tier test in the evaluation of a child with multiple congenital anomalies, developmental delay, or autism spectrum disorders.[81] Certain forms of CMA using single nucleotide polymorphisms allow for detection of homozygosity in individuals with shared ancestry or consanguinity and can aid in narrowing the list of candidate genes.[82]

CURRENT MANAGEMENT OF THE DISEASE
Investigations

Brain imaging with MRI is the first step in managing any patient who presents with signs and symptoms of MCD. If the patient presents with seizures, electroencephalography is prudent to detect any epileptogenic focus, which may be amenable to surgical resection. Other imaging modalities include diffusor tensor imaging, which can be used to better characterize the perturbation in brain development by evaluating the neuronal tracts,[83] and functional MRI, including magnetoencephalography, which can be used to map brain activity and localize regions affected by pathology.[84]

Management

The treatment of these individuals is predominantly symptomatic. Developmental delay is managed with neurorehabilitation, including physical and occupational therapy and speech and feeding therapy. Learning disability should be managed based on the severity of learning disability and neurocognitive delay; this could range from additional help in regular school to special education classrooms. Patients with seizures need to be managed with appropriate antiepileptic medications, under the guidance of a neurologist. Occasionally, patients with focal epileptogenic focus may benefit from surgical resection.[85]

Genetic counseling should be provided to individuals in whom a genetic cause is identified and their families and even in those who do not have an identifiable cause but the lesion is known to be genetic, through a referral to a clinical geneticist or genetic counselor. In X-linked disorders, such as *DCX*, *FLNA*, and *ARX*, the carrier mother may be completely asymptomatic and has a 50% risk of having another affected child. Similarly, for disorders inherited in an autosomal recessive manner, the couple has a 25% risk of having another affected child and 50% risk of having an unaffected but carrier child. For disorders with dominant inheritance, both parents should be assessed carefully with detailed physical examination and pertinent investigations, as some of these diseases can have variable expression even within a family. If the parents are affected, albeit mildly, they have a 50% risk of having another affected child. However, if the parents are unaffected, the risk of them being mosaic carriers for the apparent de novo mutations is approximately 4%.[86] In families with known molecular cause, prenatal testing in the form of chorionic villus sampling or amniocentesis can be offered to guide subsequent pregnancies. Preimplantation genetic diagnosis may also be an option for families in which the pathogenic variant has been identified.

FUTURE TREATMENT APPROACHES

The understanding of the genes and pathways associated with MCDs is expanding rapidly. For example, identification of somatic mutations in the *PI3K-AKT-mTOR* pathway in patients with overgrowth-related disorders offers potential opportunity for pharmacologic intervention for these disorders, although this remains untested.[41] *mTOR* encodes the mammalian target for rapamycin and is used commonly as an immunosuppressant. The antiepileptic effects of rapamycin have been evaluated in animal models of cortical dysplasia. For example, in mice with inactivated *TSC1*, rapamycin prevents epilepsy when given early and ameliorates seizure activity when given at a later stage.[87] In patients, administration of rapamycin has been demonstrated to show reduction in the duration and frequency of seizures in a child with TSC[88] and has been associated with reduction in the size of the subependymal giant-cell astrocytomas in patients with TSC.[89]

Similarly, patch clamp recordings from dysplastic neurons from patients with FCD type IIb show excitatory responses of γ-aminobutyric acid type A receptors that are significantly attenuated by the SLC12A2 inhibitor bumetanide,[90] which may justify trials with bumetanide in patients with FCD administered anticonvulsants that increase GABAergic function.[3]

With advances in genomic technology, the understanding of the molecular basis of these MCDs, including the diversity within each MCD and the associated secondary phenotypes, will continue to improve, which will allow for more rational and targeted treatment options. Identification of pathogenic variant can also allow for prenatal testing to guide future pregnancies in these families.

REFERENCES

1. Hu WF, Chahrour MH, Walsh CA. The diverse genetic landscape of neurodevelopmental disorders. Annu Rev Genomics Hum Genet 2014;15:195–213.
2. Barkovich AJ, Guerrini R, Kuzniecky RI, et al. A developmental and genetic classification for malformations of cortical development: update 2012. Brain 2012; 135:1348–69.
3. Guerrini R, Dobyns WB. Malformations of cortical development: clinical features and genetic causes. Lancet Neurol 2014;13:710–26.
4. Poduri A, Evrony GD, Cai X, et al. Somatic mutation, genomic variation, and neurological disease. Science 2013;341:1237758.
5. Biesecker LG, Spinner NB. A genomic view of mosaicism and human disease. Nat Rev Genet 2013;14:307–20.
6. Greig LC, Woodworth MB, Galazo MJ, et al. Molecular logic of neocortical projection neuron specification, development and diversity. Nat Rev Neurosci 2013;14: 755–69.
7. Pleasure SJ, Anderson S, Hevner R, et al. Cell migration from the ganglionic eminences is required for the development of hippocampal GABAergic interneurons. Neuron 2000;28:727–40.
8. Hansen DV, Lui JH, Flandin P, et al. Non-epithelial stem cells and cortical interneuron production in the human ganglionic eminences. Nat Neurosci 2013;16: 1576–87.
9. Reid CB, Tavazoie SF, Walsh CA. Clonal dispersion and evidence for asymmetric cell division in ferret cortex. Development 1997;124:2441–50.
10. Kessaris N, Fogarty M, Iannarelli P, et al. Competing waves of oligodendrocytes in the forebrain and postnatal elimination of an embryonic lineage. Nat Neurosci 2006;9:173–9.
11. Ross ME, Allen KM, Srivastava AK, et al. Linkage and physical mapping of X-linked lissencephaly/SBH (XLIS): a gene causing neuronal migration defects in human brain. Hum Mol Genet 1997;6:555–62.
12. Gleeson JG, Allen KM, Fox JW, et al. Doublecortin, a brain-specific gene mutated in human X-linked lissencephaly and double cortex syndrome, encodes a putative signaling protein. Cell 1998;92:63–72.
13. Fox JW, Lamperti ED, Eksioglu YZ, et al. Mutations in filamin 1 prevent migration of cerebral cortical neurons in human periventricular heterotopia. Neuron 1998; 21:1315–25.
14. Collins FS. Positional cloning moves from perditional to traditional. Nat Genet 1995;9:347–50.
15. Ng SB, Buckingham KJ, Lee C, et al. Exome sequencing identifies the cause of a mendelian disorder. Nat Genet 2010;42:30–5.
16. Rauch A, Wieczorek D, Graf E, et al. Range of genetic mutations associated with severe non-syndromic sporadic intellectual disability: an exome sequencing study. Lancet 2012;380:1674–82.
17. Jamuar SS, Lam AT, Kircher M, et al. Somatic mutations in cerebral cortical malformations. N Engl J Med 2014;371:733–43.
18. Lee JH, Huynh M, Silhavy JL, et al. De novo somatic mutations in components of the PI3K-AKT3-mTOR pathway cause hemimegalencephaly. Nat Genet 2012;44:941–5.

19. Poduri A, Evrony GD, Cai X, et al. Somatic activation of AKT3 causes hemispheric developmental brain malformations. Neuron 2012;74:41–8.

20. Gilmore EC, Walsh CA. Genetic causes of microcephaly and lessons for neuronal development. Wiley Interdiscip Rev Dev Biol 2013;2:461–78.

21. Thornton GK, Woods CG. Primary microcephaly: do all roads lead to Rome? Trends Genet 2009;25:501–10.

22. Alkuraya FS, Cai X, Emery C, et al. Human mutations in NDE1 cause extreme microcephaly with lissencephaly [corrected]. Am J Hum Genet 2011;88: 536–47.

23. Desir J, Cassart M, David P, et al. Primary microcephaly with ASPM mutation shows simplified cortical gyration with antero-posterior gradient pre- and post-natally. Am J Med Genet A 2008;146A:1439–43.

24. Kumar A, Girimaji SC, Duvvari MR, et al. Mutations in STIL, encoding a pericen-triolar and centrosomal protein, cause primary microcephaly. Am J Hum Genet 2009;84:286–90.

25. Yu TW, Mochida GH, Tischfield DJ, et al. Mutations in WDR62, encoding a centrosome-associated protein, cause microcephaly with simplified gyri and abnormal cortical architecture. Nat Genet 2010;42:1015–20.

26. Feng Y, Walsh CA. Mitotic spindle regulation by Nde1 controls cerebral cortical size. Neuron 2004;44:279–93.

27. Shen J, Gilmore EC, Marshall CA, et al. Mutations in PNKP cause microcephaly, seizures and defects in DNA repair. Nat Genet 2010;42:245–9.

28. Griffith E, Walker S, Martin CA, et al. Mutations in pericentrin cause Seckel syndrome with defective ATR-dependent DNA damage signaling. Nat Genet 2008; 40:232–6.

29. Sheen VL, Ganesh VS, Topcu M, et al. Mutations in ARFGEF2 implicate vesicle trafficking in neural progenitor proliferation and migration in the human cerebral cortex. Nat Genet 2004;36:69–76.

30. Passemard S, Titomanlio L, Elmaleh M, et al. Expanding the clinical and neurora-diologic phenotype of primary microcephaly due to ASPM mutations. Neurology 2009;73:962–9.

31. Rimol LM, Agartz I, Djurovic S, et al. Sex-dependent association of common variants of microcephaly genes with brain structure. Proc Natl Acad Sci U S A 2010; 107:384–8.

32. Najm J, Horn D, Wimplinger I, et al. Mutations of CASK cause an X-linked brain malformation phenotype with microcephaly and hypoplasia of the brainstem and cerebellum. Nat Genet 2008;40:1065–7.

33. Amir RE, Van den Veyver IB, Wan M, et al. Rett syndrome is caused by mutations in X-linked MECP2, encoding methyl-CpG-binding protein 2. Nat Genet 1999;23: 185–8.

34. Kishino T, Lalande M, Wagstaff J. UBE3A/E6-AP mutations cause Angelman syndrome. Nat Genet 1997;15:70–3.

35. Namavar Y, Barth PG, Kasher PR, et al. Clinical, neuroradiological and genetic findings in pontocerebellar hypoplasia. Brain 2011;134:143–56.

36. Zhang X, Ling J, Barcia G, et al. Mutations in QARS, encoding glutaminyl-tRNA synthetase, cause progressive microcephaly, cerebral-cerebellar atrophy, and intractable seizures. Am J Hum Genet 2014;94:547–58.

37. Mirzaa G, Dodge NN, Glass I, et al. Megalencephaly and perisylvian polymicro-gyria with postaxial polydactyly and hydrocephalus: a rare brain malformation syndrome associated with mental retardation and seizures. Neuropediatrics 2004;35:353–9.

38. Riviere JB, Mirzaa GM, O'Roak BJ, et al. De novo germline and postzygotic mutations in AKT3, PIK3R2 and PIK3CA cause a spectrum of related megalencephaly syndromes. Nat Genet 2012;44:934–40.

39. Cai X, Evrony GD, Lehmann HS, et al. Single-cell, genome-wide sequencing identifies clonal somatic copy-number variation in the human brain. Cell Rep 2014;8:1280–9.

40. Marsh DJ, Dahia PL, Zheng Z, et al. Germline mutations in PTEN are present in Bannayan-Zonana syndrome. Nat Genet 1997;16:333–4.

41. Marin-Valencia I, Guerrini R, Gleeson JG. Pathogenetic mechanisms of focal cortical dysplasia. Epilepsia 2014;55:970–8.

42. Blumcke I, Thom M, Aronica E, et al. The clinicopathologic spectrum of focal cortical dysplasias: a consensus classification proposed by an ad hoc Task Force of the ILAE Diagnostic Methods Commission. Epilepsia 2011;52: 158–74.

43. Liu J, Reeves C, Michalak Z, et al. Evidence for mTOR pathway activation in a spectrum of epilepsy-associated pathologies. Acta Neuropathol Commun 2014;2:71.

44. Scheffer IE, Heron SE, Regan BM, et al. Mutations in mammalian target of rapamycin regulator DEPDC5 cause focal epilepsy with brain malformations. Ann Neurol 2014;75:782–7.

45. Sheen VL, Jansen A, Chen MH, et al. Filamin A mutations cause periventricular heterotopia with Ehlers-Danlos syndrome. Neurology 2005;64:254–62.

46. Reinstein E, Frentz S, Morgan T, et al. Vascular and connective tissue anomalies associated with X-linked periventricular heterotopia due to mutations in Filamin A. Eur J Hum Genet 2013;21:494–502.

47. Zahrani F, Aldahmesh MA, Alshammari MJ, et al. Mutations in c12orf57 cause a syndromic form of colobomatous microphthalmia. Am J Hum Genet 2013;92:387–91.

48. Akizu N, Shembesh NM, Ben-Omran T, et al. Whole-exome sequencing identifies mutated c12orf57 in recessive corpus callosum hypoplasia. Am J Hum Genet 2013;92:392–400.

49. Guerrini R, Parrini E. Neuronal migration disorders. Neurobiol Dis 2010;38: 154–66.

50. Haverfield EV, Whited AJ, Petras KS, et al. Intragenic deletions and duplications of the LIS1 and DCX genes: a major disease-causing mechanism in lissencephaly and subcortical band heterotopia. Eur J Hum Genet 2009;17:911–8.

51. Bahi-Buisson N, Souville I, Fourniol FJ, et al. New insights into genotype-phenotype correlations for the doublecortin-related lissencephaly spectrum. Brain 2013;136:223–44.

52. Saillour Y, Carion N, Quelin C, et al. LIS1-related isolated lissencephaly: spectrum of mutations and relationships with malformation severity. Arch Neurol 2009;66: 1007–15.

53. Taylor KR, Holzer AK, Bazan JF, et al. Patient mutations in doublecortin define a repeated tubulin-binding domain. J Biol Chem 2000;275:34442–50.

54. Keays DA, Tian G, Poirier K, et al. Mutations in alpha-tubulin cause abnormal neuronal migration in mice and lissencephaly in humans. Cell 2007;128:45–57.

55. Poirier K, Lebrun N, Broix L, et al. Mutations in TUBG1, DYNC1H1, KIF5C and KIF2A cause malformations of cortical development and microcephaly. Nat Genet 2013;45:639–47.

56. Clement E, Mercuri E, Godfrey C, et al. Brain involvement in muscular dystrophies with defective dystroglycan glycosylation. Ann Neurol 2008;64:573–82.

57. Godfrey C, Foley AR, Clement E, et al. Dystroglycanopathies: coming into focus. Curr Opin Genet Dev 2011;21:278–85.

58. Brockington M, Blake DJ, Prandini P, et al. Mutations in the fukutin-related protein gene (FKRP) cause a form of congenital muscular dystrophy with secondary laminin alpha2 deficiency and abnormal glycosylation of alpha-dystroglycan. Am J Hum Genet 2001;69:1198–209.

59. Brockington M, Yuva Y, Prandini P, et al. Mutations in the fukutin-related protein gene (FKRP) identify limb girdle muscular dystrophy 2I as a milder allelic variant of congenital muscular dystrophy MDC1C. Hum Mol Genet 2001;10:2851–9.

60. Mercuri E, Topaloglu H, Brockington M, et al. Spectrum of brain changes in patients with congenital muscular dystrophy and FKRP gene mutations. Arch Neurol 2006;63:251–7.

61. Al-Gazali L, Hertecant J, Algawi K, et al. A new autosomal recessive syndrome of ocular colobomas, ichthyosis, brain malformations and endocrine abnormalities in an inbred Emirati family. Am J Med Genet A 2008;146A:813–9.

62. Kornak U, Reynders E, Dimopoulou A, et al. Impaired glycosylation and cutis laxa caused by mutations in the vesicular H+-ATPase subunit ATP6V0A2. Nat Genet 2008;40:32–4.

63. Piao X, Hill RS, Bodell A, et al. G protein-coupled receptor-dependent development of human frontal cortex. Science 2004;303:2033–6.

64. Snape KM, Ruddy D, Zenker M, et al. The spectra of clinical phenotypes in aplasia cutis congenita and terminal transverse limb defects. Am J Med Genet A 2009;149A:1860–81.

65. Gleeson JG, Keeler LC, Parisi MA, et al. Molar tooth sign of the midbrain-hindbrain junction: occurrence in multiple distinct syndromes. Am J Med Genet A 2004;125A:125–34 [discussion: 17].

66. Brooks AS, Bertoli-Avella AM, Burzynski GM, et al. Homozygous nonsense mutations in KIAA1279 are associated with malformations of the central and enteric nervous systems. Am J Hum Genet 2005;77:120–6.

67. Morris-Rosendahl DJ, Segel R, Born AP, et al. New RAB3GAP1 mutations in patients with Warburg Micro syndrome from different ethnic backgrounds and a possible founder effect in the Danish. Eur J Hum Genet 2010;18:1100–6.

68. Borck G, Wunram H, Steiert A, et al. A homozygous RAB3GAP2 mutation causes Warburg Micro syndrome. Hum Genet 2011;129:45–50.

69. Aicardi J. Aicardi syndrome. Brain Dev 2005;27:164–71.

70. Abdollahi MR, Morrison E, Sirey T, et al. Mutation of the variant alpha-tubulin TUBA8 results in polymicrogyria with optic nerve hypoplasia. Am J Hum Genet 2009;85:737–44.

71. Jaglin XH, Poirier K, Saillour Y, et al. Mutations in the beta-tubulin gene TUBB2B result in asymmetrical polymicrogyria. Nat Genet 2009;41:746–52.

72. Poirier K, Saillour Y, Bahi-Buisson N, et al. Mutations in the neuronal ss-tubulin subunit TUBB3 result in malformation of cortical development and neuronal migration defects. Hum Mol Genet 2010;19:4462–73.

73. Granata T, Farina L, Faiella A, et al. Familial schizencephaly associated with EMX2 mutation. Neurology 1997;48:1403–6.

74. Tietjen I, Bodell A, Apse K, et al. Comprehensive EMX2 genotyping of a large schizencephaly case series. Am J Med Genet A 2007;143A:1313–6.

75. Merello E, Swanson E, De Marco P, et al. No major role for the EMX2 gene in schizencephaly. Am J Med Genet A 2008;146A:1142–50.

76. Barkovich AJ, Lindan CE. Congenital cytomegalovirus infection of the brain: imaging analysis and embryologic considerations. AJNR Am J Neuroradiol 1994;15:703–15.

77. Curry CJ, Lammer EJ, Nelson V, et al. Schizencephaly: heterogeneous etiologies in a population of 4 million California births. Am J Med Genet A 2005;137:181–9.

78. Huisman SA, Redeker EJ, Maas SM, et al. High rate of mosaicism in individuals with Cornelia de Lange syndrome. J Med Genet 2013;50:339–44.

79. Yang Y, Muzny DM, Reid JG, et al. Clinical whole-exome sequencing for the diagnosis of mendelian disorders. N Engl J Med 2013;369:1502–11.

80. Green RC, Berg JS, Grody WW, et al. ACMG recommendations for reporting of incidental findings in clinical exome and genome sequencing. Genet Med 2013;15:565–74.

81. Miller DT, Adam MP, Aradhya S, et al. Consensus statement: chromosomal microarray is a first-tier clinical diagnostic test for individuals with developmental disabilities or congenital anomalies. Am J Hum Genet 2010;86:749–64.

82. Wierenga KJ, Jiang Z, Yang AC, et al. A clinical evaluation tool for SNP arrays, especially for autosomal recessive conditions in offspring of consanguineous parents. Genet Med 2013;15:354–60.

83. Poretti A, Meoded A, Rossi A, et al. Diffusion tensor imaging and fiber tractography in brain malformations. Pediatr Radiol 2013;43:28–54.

84. Bast T, Oezkan O, Rona S, et al. EEG and MEG source analysis of single and averaged interictal spikes reveals intrinsic epileptogenicity in focal cortical dysplasia. Epilepsia 2004;45:621–31.

85. Hader WJ, Mackay M, Otsubo H, et al. Cortical dysplastic lesions in children with intractable epilepsy: role of complete resection. J Neurosurg 2004;100:110–7.

86. Campbell IM, Yuan B, Robberecht C, et al. Parental somatic mosaicism is underrecognized and influences recurrence risk of genomic disorders. Am J Hum Genet 2014;95:173–82.

87. Zeng LH, Xu L, Gutmann DH, et al. Rapamycin prevents epilepsy in a mouse model of tuberous sclerosis complex. Ann Neurol 2008;63:444–53.

88. Muncy J, Butler IJ, Koenig MK. Rapamycin reduces seizure frequency in tuberous sclerosis complex. J Child Neurol 2009;24:477.

89. Krueger DA, Care MM, Holland K, et al. Everolimus for subependymal giant-cell astrocytomas in tuberous sclerosis. N Engl J Med 2010;363:1801–11.

90. Talos DM, Sun H, Kosaras B, et al. Altered inhibition in tuberous sclerosis and type IIb cortical dysplasia. Ann Neurol 2012;71:539–51.

Prader-Willi, Angelman, and 15q11-q13 Duplication Syndromes

Louisa Kalsner, MD[a,b,*], Stormy J. Chamberlain, PhD[a,c,*]

KEYWORDS

- Prader-Willi syndrome • Angelman syndrome • Chromosome 15q11-q13 duplication
- Genomic imprinting • Copy number variation • DNA methylation • *UBE3A* • *SNRPN*

KEY POINTS

- Three distinct neurodevelopmental disorders are caused by copy number variation at human chromosome 15q11-q13: Prader-Willi syndrome (PWS), Angelman syndrome (AS), and 15q11-q13 duplication syndrome (Dup 15q syndrome).
- PWS and AS can also be caused by uniparental disomy, microdeletions and/or single gene mutations, and imprinting defects. An organized diagnostic strategy is required to confirm or fully exclude the diagnosis.
- PWS is characterized by infantile hypotonia and failure to thrive followed by obesity, hyperphagia, small stature, and behavioral issues. Early growth hormone (GH) treatment improves body habitus and stature.
- AS is characterized by severe intellectual disability, absent speech, epilepsy, and characteristic happy affect. This syndrome is caused by the loss of function of the maternal *UBE3A* gene.
- The Dup 15q syndrome is characterized by developmental delay, epilepsy, and autism. Duplications that lead to this syndrome are almost always of maternal origin.

INTRODUCTION

The 15q11-q13 region harbors several genes regulated by genomic imprinting, a phenomenon in which genes are expressed preferentially from 1 parental allele. As a result, genes subject to regulation by genomic imprinting are functionally haploid,

The authors have nothing to disclose.
[a] Department of Pediatrics, Connecticut Children's Medical Center, University of Connecticut School of Medicine, 505 Farmington Avenue, Farmington, CT 06032, USA; [b] Department of Neurology, Connecticut Children's Medical Center, University of Connecticut School of Medicine, 505 Farmington Avenue, Farmington, CT 06032, USA; [c] Departments of Genetics and Genome Sciences and Pediatrics, Connecticut Children's Medical Center, University of Connecticut Health Center, 400 Farmington Avenue, Farmington, CT 06030-6403, USA
* Corresponding authors. Department of Pediatrics, Connecticut Children's Medical Center, University of Connecticut School of Medicine, 505 Farmington Avenue, Farmington, CT 06032.
E-mail addresses: Lkalsner@connecticutchildrens.org; chamberlain@uchc.edu

http://dx.doi.org/10.1016/j.pcl.2015.03.004
0031-3955/15/$ – see front matter © 2015 Elsevier Inc. All rights reserved.
pediatric.theclinics.com

having only a single functional copy. Three distinct neurodevelopmental disorders arise primarily from deletions or duplications at the 15q11-q13 locus: PWS, AS, and Dup15q syndrome. Each of these disorders results from the loss of function or overexpression of at least 1 imprinted gene. Each of them occur with a frequency of approximately 1/15,000 to 1/30,000 live births.

The deletions and duplications of chromosome 15q11-q13 that cause PWS, AS, or Dup15q syndrome are mediated by local DNA repeats that occur at the common breakpoints. There are 5 such elements, which are composed of breakpoints 1 through 5 (BP1–BP5). Deletions involving either BP1 or BP2 and BP3 are most common, while the duplications are more complicated, but can frequently involve BPs 4 and 5 and are discussed below. A map of the 15q11-q13 genetic region is shown in **Fig. 1**. This article discusses the clinical background, genetic cause, diagnostic strategy, and management of each of these 3 disorders.

PRADER-WILLI SYNDROME
Clinical Background of the Disease

PWS is characterized by hypotonia, failure to thrive with poor suck, hypogonadism, short stature with small hands and feet, hyperphagia leading to morbid obesity beginning during early childhood, developmental delay/intellectual disability, and behavioral issues, including obsessive-compulsive disorder (**Table 1**). Characteristic facial features are also evident.

Hypotonia
Hypotonia becomes evident during pregnancy as decreased fetal movement and atypical presentation at delivery. Assisted delivery and caesarean delivery are increased with PWS births.[1] Hypotonia is nearly universal in infants with PWS, thus, a molecular test for PWS should be performed whenever neonatal hypotonia is observed. Infants with PWS are lethargic with reduced movement, often having a weak cry, poor suck, and failure to thrive.[2] The infantile hypotonia improves, but mild to moderate hypotonia persists throughout life in children and adults with PWS.

Hypogonadism
Hypogonadism is often evident at birth as gonadal hypoplasia in both males and females. Males typically have a small scrotum and may have a small penis. Unilateral or bilateral cryptorchidism is frequent. Females often have a small labia minora and clitoris. Puberty can be delayed or disorganized in adolescents with PWS, and most adults are infertile. Hypogonadism is thought to result from both hypothalamic dysfunction resulting in low levels of gonadotropins (and therefore gonadal hormones) and primary gonadal deficiency.[3]

Growth deficits
Growth deficits associated with PWS likely begin in utero. Infants with PWS are typically 15% to 20% smaller than their siblings.[1,4] Short stature is often apparent in childhood and persists through adulthood. The lack of a pubertal growth spurt may exacerbate the growth deficit.[5] Hands and feet are often particularly small, usually averaging below the fifth percentile. Growth deficits are caused, at least in part, by GH deficiency,[6] which seems to result from hypothalamic-pituitary dysfunction. Indeed, GH replacement therapy improves body mass index (BMI) and muscle mass in children with PWS and may even improve body habitus in adults with PWS.[7–9]

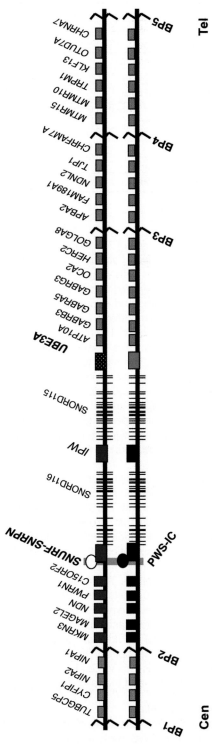

Fig. 1. Map of 15q11-q13 region. Individual genes are depicted as boxes with their respective names above them. Genes shown in blue and red are imprinted and expressed from the paternal and maternal alleles, respectively. Black boxes mark the silenced allele. Gray boxes indicate genes expressed from both parental alleles. BP1–5 indicate the common breakpoints 1–5. PWS-IC indicates the Prader-Willi imprinting center. Cen and Tel mark the centromere and telomere, respectively, to indicate orientation relative to the rest of the chromosome.

Table 1		
Features of PWS		
Consistent (100%)	**Frequent (80%)**	**Associated (20%–80%)**
Hypotonia	Hypopigmentation	Speech articulation defects
Failure to thrive	Behavioral problems	Autism
Feeding difficulty	Developmental delay	—
Hypogonadism	Short stature, if untreated with growth hormone	—
Obesity, in absence of intervention	Distinctive facial features	—
Hyperphagia	Sleep disturbances	—
	Small hands/feet	—

Hyperphagia and obesity

Individuals with PWS pass through a series of 7 nutritional phases relating to appetite and weight gain.[10] The first phase, phase 0, occurs from the prenatal period to birth with reduced fetal movement and lower birth weight than their siblings. The second phase, phase 1a, occurs from birth to approximately 9 months and is characterized by failure to thrive with difficulty feeding and decreased appetite. The third phase, phase 1b, occurs from approximately 9 months to 2 years and is marked by improved feeding and appetite and appropriate growth. The fourth phase, phase 2a, occurs between approximately 2 and 4.5 years. This phase involves weight gain without increased appetite or excess calories. The fifth phase, phase 2b, occurs between approximately 4.5 and 8 years. This phase involves continued weight gain with increased appetite and calories; however, individuals in this phase can still feel full. The sixth phase, phase 3, lasts from approximately the age of 8 years to adulthood. This phase is characterized by extreme hyperphagia, and individuals rarely feel full. If food consumption is not limited, obesity is inevitable. The seventh and final phase, phase 4, occurs throughout adulthood. During this phase, appetite is no longer insatiable.

The cause of hyperphagia in PWS is poorly understood, although it is likely to result from hypothalamic dysfunction.[5] It has been suggested that increased ghrelin levels may underlie hyperphagia in individuals with PWS[11]; however, there are no consistently identified hormonal abnormalities that explain the hyperphagic behavior in PWS. Nonetheless, it is not unusual for individuals in phase 3 to exhibit extreme food-seeking behaviors, including consumption of nonfood items, hoarding of food, or stealing money to buy food.[5]

The cause of obesity in PWS is manifold. The onset of weight gain in phase 2a, before there is an increased appetite, suggests that individuals with PWS have lower caloric requirement.[10] This low caloric requirement is partly because of the decreased resting energy expenditure caused by decreased activity and decreased lean muscle mass when compared with neurotypical individuals.[12] Increased appetite and hyperphagia also contribute to obesity. The obesity in PWS primarily occurs in the abdomen, buttocks, and thighs; there is less visceral fat than would be expected.[13] Obesity is the major cause of morbidity and mortality in PWS.

Developmental delay/intellectual disability

Motor development and language skills are delayed in most individuals with PWS, although nearly all individuals with PWS walk and can effectively communicate verbally. Individuals with PWS have mild to moderate intellectual disability,[14,15] and poor academic achievement is typical and may be exacerbated by behavioral difficulties in addition to developmental and intellectual disability.[14]

Behavioral difficulties

Up to 90% of individuals with PWS have characteristic behaviors including stubbornness, temper tantrums, manipulative behaviors, compulsivity, and difficulty with change in routine.[16] Features similar to obsessive-compulsive disorder and skin picking are common. Some of the behaviors are consistent with autism, and indeed some individuals with PWS meet diagnostic criteria for autism. This situation may be more common in individuals with maternal uniparental disomy (matUPD).[14] Psychosis is also prevalent in approximately 10% to 20% of adults with PWS.[17,18]

Other features

Facial features associated with PWS include almond-shaped eyes; narrow, but prominent nasal bridge; high, narrow forehead; thin upper lip; and downturned mouth. Other features associated with PWS include sleep disorders such as sleep apnea,[19] strabismus (60%–70%),[5] scoliosis (40%–80%),[5] light-colored hair and skin, striae, and tapering of fingers.

Recent Advances in Genetics and Pathomechanism of the Disease

PWS is caused by the loss of paternally inherited chromosome 15q11.2-q13. The loss of expression from this chromosomal region typically occurs by one of the following 3 mechanisms: (1) approximately 70% of individuals with PWS have a large deletion of the entire 15q11-q13 imprinted region, (2) approximately 25% of individuals with PWS have matUPD in which both copies of chromosome 15 have been inherited from the mother; and (3) less than 5% of individuals with PWS have an imprinting defect that causes paternal 15q11-q13 to behave as though it were inherited from the mother.[5] However, there are no instances of a point mutation in any gene causing PWS, suggesting that PWS is a true contiguous gene syndrome, resulting from the loss of more than 1 gene.

In the vast majority of individuals with PWS, approximately 20 paternally expressed genes are missing, including *Necdin* (*NDN*), *Makorin ring 3* (*MKRN3*), *Mage-like 2* (*MAGEL2*), *PWRN2*, *PWRN1*, *Nuclear pore-associated protein 2* (*NPAP2*), *SNURF*, *SNRPN*, *SNORD109A*, *SNORD116*, *SNORD115*, *SNORD109B*, and *SNHG14* (formerly known as *UBE3A-ATS*). Typical individuals with deletions of paternal *NDN*, *MKRN3*, and *MAGEL2* and with deletions of paternal *SNORD115* and distal portions of *SNHG14* have been identified, suggesting that these genes are not causative for PWS. Conversely, individuals with PWS have been identified with smaller, atypical deletions that have narrowed down the PWS critical region to a 91-kb region that includes *SNORD109A*, *SNORD116*, and *IPW*.[20–23] Mouse models further suggest that deletions of *Snord116* are sufficient to cause PWS; however, no human patient with PWS caused by deletion of *SNORD116* alone has been reported to date.

The *SNORD* genes that are located in 15q11.2-q13 are orphan CD box small nucleolar RNA (snoRNA) genes that have been reported to modify messenger RNAs (mRNAs)[24–26] and ribosomal RNAs (rRNAs),[27] as well as act as small interfering RNAs.[28] *SNORD116* is actually a cluster of 29 similar but not identical snoRNA genes that although evolutionarily related may affect different mRNAs and rRNAs. It is not known how loss of *SNORD116* results in the phenotypic manifestations of PWS.

Diagnostic Strategy

Methylation analysis

DNA methylation analysis using Southern blot or methylation-specific polymerase chain reaction (PCR) diagnoses PWS in 99% of cases, including all 3 classes, paternal deletion, matUPD, and imprinting defect (**Fig. 2**).[5] The most widely used assays target the 5′ CpG island of the *SNURF-SNRPN* (*SNRPN*) locus, a region known as the imprinting center (IC). The promoter, exon 1, and intron 1 of *SNRPN* are unmethylated on the paternal allele and thus expressed, whereas they are methylated on the maternal, nonexpressed allele. A normal individual has both a methylated and an unmethylated *SNRPN* allele, whereas individuals with PWS have only the maternal methylated allele.[5]

Methylation analysis allows for identification of patients with PWS, but it provides no information about the molecular class of the disease. As discussed, 65% to 75% of cases result from deletion at 15q11.2-q13, 20% to 30% result from uniparental disomy in which both copies of chromosome 15 are maternally inherited, and less than 5% are caused by some form of imprinting defect.[5] Differentiation of the molecular class of PWS allows the physician to provide more accurate prognostic information and is crucial for accurate recurrence risk counseling. Testing should proceed in the order outlined below, from the most to the least common cause.

Search for a deletion Fluorescence in situ hybridization (FISH) with an *SNRPN* probe is the most cost-efficient means of identifying a deletion. If done with simultaneous chromosomal analysis, rare cases caused by translocation or inversion are identified. Increasingly, chromosomal microarray analysis (CMA) is performed instead of FISH, and this method allows for accurate measurement of deletion size in addition to providing information about other genomic changes, if present. The extent of the deletion is expected to become increasingly important as the understanding of genotype-phenotype correlations in PWS grows. CMA is more expensive than FISH, but it is increasingly available and typically the first test done when a patient with a suspected genetic condition is evaluated, particularly if PWS was not initially considered. In this

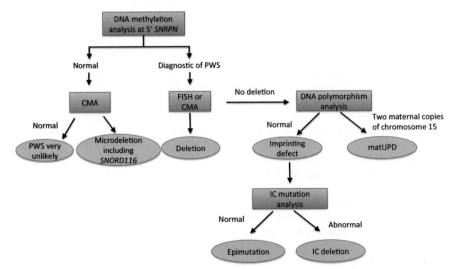

Fig. 2. Diagnostic strategy for PWS. Blue boxes indicate the diagnostic test, and pink boxes indicate the diagnostic decision. IC, imprinting center.

case, methylation testing is important as a confirmatory test, because identification of a deletion does not distinguish between PWS and AS, which may have considerable clinical overlap in the young child. In addition, CMA may identify rare patients who have deletions that do not include the IC.

Uniparental disomy testing DNA polymorphism analysis of chromosome 15 loci on the proband and parents' DNA identifies cases of matUPD in which both copies of chromosome 15 are maternally inherited.[29]

Imprinting defect Sequencing of the IC can be done in specialized laboratories. Mutations are found in 15% of those with imprinting defects, with the remainder caused by epimutations. Epimutations carry a low recurrence risk, whereas an IC mutation on the paternal allele may be associated with a 50% recurrence risk. Thus searching for a mutation provides important information to families about future risk.

Additional options
Multiplex ligation-dependent probe amplification (MLPA) testing is another increasingly popular option as a first-line test for diagnosis of PWS, particularly in Europe. MLPA testing has the ability to assess methylation at 5 sites in the PWS region, as opposed to 1 site in the standard methylation assay. This method also detects a deletion, if present, but cannot distinguish between UPD and imprinting defects.

Current Management

Diet and nutrition
Failure to thrive in infancy results from poor suck in the setting of hypotonia. Special nipples or gavage feeding are often required. Close monitoring of growth parameters is required in the first year of life.[2] If failure to thrive is noted, despite adequate caloric intake, testing for hypothyroidism is indicated, because this is not uncommon in infancy.[30]

As weight gain begins to increase from the age of 2 years, careful supervision of caloric intake is necessary. Weight gain often begins after the age of 2 years, although appetite increase is not typical until after the age of 4 years. It is important to monitor food intake, before the onset of obesity. Nutritional supervision to assess appropriate intake and supplementation of vitamin D, calcium, and other nutrients is recommended. Locking of cupboards and refrigerator is often necessary as appetite increases. Evidence suggests that early dietary intervention with a controlled prescribed diet as early as 14 months of age may result in a normal BMI.[31] Continued monitoring of diet and weight is central to long-term health including avoidance of diabetes mellitus and other obesity-related complications.

Hormonal/endocrine
Treatment with GH is now recommended as the standard of care for children with PWS. Early treatment seems beneficial with normalization of height, increase in muscle mass, and decrease in fat mass. Treatment should begin between 4 months and 2 years of age because benefits in head circumference, gross motor and language development, and cognition have been demonstrated with early treatment.[32,33] Owing to concern about the possibility of an increase in the rate of sudden death from upper airway obstruction in the first months of treatment, a sleep study is recommended before initiating treatment, 6 to 12 weeks after initiation of treatment, and on an annual basis thereafter.[34] Children with PWS are at increased risk of obstructive and central apnea, and this risk may rise with GH treatment, possibly because of lymphoid hyperplasia. While receiving GH treatment, close monitoring for scoliosis, hypothyroidism, diabetes, and elevation of levels of insulinlike growth factor 1 is suggested.[32]

Treatment with GH may need to continue into adulthood, because recent studies suggest that BMI may increase significantly after cessation of GH therapy.[35]

Cryptorchidism should be addressed with referral to urology and treatment if noted in infancy. Treatment of hypogonadism should be considered, with human chorionic gonadotropin (hCG) or testosterone, to assist with testicular descent, as well as scrotal and phallic development and growth.[2] In early adolescence, replacement of sex hormones may be appropriate; low-dose estrogen or combined estrogen/progestin should be administered in girls beginning at the age of 11 to 12 years, particularly if there is amenorrhea/oligomenorrhea or low bone mineral density in the setting of low estradiol levels. Testosterone or hCG (increases endogenous testosterone production) should be administered in the setting of hypogonadism in boys beginning at the age of 12 to 13 years.[36]

Monitoring of levels of free thyroxine in addition to that of thyrotropin should be done annually in childhood.[36] Awareness of elevated risk for adrenal insufficiency is important because it may be present in up to 60% of children. Central adrenal insufficiency has been observed in PWS, although the frequency is unclear. Considering measuring adrenocorticotropic hormone (ACTH) and cortisol levels with illness is appropriate, and some have advocated stress dose steroids with illness or before surgery.[36] Monitoring for type 2 diabetes mellitus is essential in adults.

Behavioral and educational
Physical therapy beginning in infancy assists with motor skills development with speech therapy often warranted by 2 years of age. Requirement for educational support should be anticipated including personal classroom aides and behavior management given the frequency of challenging behaviors such as tantrums as well as compulsive and stubborn behaviors. Serotonin reuptake inhibitors can be helpful for severe behavioral issues, including psychosis, which may emerge in adolescence.[37] Adolescents and adults are often successful residing in a group home where attention to daily exercise and diet can be emphasized.

Other
Annual assessment for scoliosis should begin in the early childhood. Ophthalmologic evaluation for strabismus and impaired acuity should be done in the first year of life and continue thereafter. Given the increased risk for osteoporosis, bone density studies (dual energy X-ray absorptiometry studies) are recommended beginning in adolescence and continuing to adulthood.[38]

Future potential therapies
Several medication trials are ongoing, aimed at addressing the hyperphagia and associated symptoms of PWS. Oxytocin nasal spray is being studied, because there is a reduction in oxytocin-producing neurons in the hypothalamic periventricular nucleus in individuals with PWS. A recent publication, however, did not demonstrate benefit in 30 individuals in an 18-week double-blind, placebo-controlled crossover trial.[39] Other trials are ongoing. A trial of a candidate obesity drug called Beloranib is also underway. Belonarib is an inhibitor of methionine aminopeptidase-2 and works to reduce fatty acid synthesis, insulin levels, and food consumption. This drug also increases mobilization of fats and energy expenditure.[40]

Recommendation for family counseling
Family counseling is recommended. Most deletions, UPD, and epimutations are associated with a low recurrence risk. However, IC mutations and some translocations may be associated with a 50% recurrence risk.

ANGELMAN SYNDROME
Clinical Background of the Disease

AS is characterized by developmental delay, intellectual disability, absent speech, seizures, ataxic gait, easily excitable happy demeanor, and characteristic facies (**Table 2**). This disorder has been referred to as happy puppet syndrome because of the ataxic gait and disposition of children with AS.

Developmental delay/intellectual disability

Most infants with AS do not show any signs of the disorder at birth. However, delayed attainment of gross and fine motor skills, language, and social skills is usually evident within the first year of life.[41] Motor skill delays can be severe, and many individuals with AS are not able to walk. Tremors can further complicate fine motor skill development. Toilet training is typically severely delayed but is achieved in many adults with AS. Functionally, individuals with AS only reach a developmental level of approximately 24 to 30 months.[42] Cognitive ability is severely impaired; however, cognition is difficult to ascertain because of the profound lack of speech, hyperactivity, and inability to pay attention in individuals with AS. Adults with AS are not capable of independent living, although many can perform tasks with supervision, can dress themselves, and can use feeding utensils.[43,44]

Speech

Language development in individuals with AS is severely impaired. Most individuals with AS are entirely nonverbal, some speak a few words, and a rare few have some phrase speech. Augmentative communication devices and sign language can be successfully used to communicate with individuals with AS. Their receptive communication exceeds expressive communication.[45]

Epilepsy

Epilepsy occurs in 80% to 95% of those with AS, typically with onset before 3 years of age.[44,46] AS is typically associated with generalized epilepsy, although focal seizures occur in up to one-third, often in combination with other seizure types.[44,46,47] Myoclonic, atypical absence, generalized tonic-clonic, and atonic seizures are most common, and status epilepticus, frequently myoclonic or nonconvulsive, has been reported to occur in up to 90%.[48] Epilepsy tends to be more severe in early childhood, often easing as children reach puberty, although its risk seems to persist into

Table 2
Features of AS

Consistent (100%)	Frequent (80%)	Associated (20%–80%)
Developmental delay	Seizures	Hypotonia
Ataxia and/or tremors	Microcephaly	Strabismus
Absent speech	—	Frequent drooling, mouthing behaviors
Happy demeanor, including hand flapping, frequent laughter/smiling	—	Protruding tongue, tongue thrusting
—	—	Wide mouth, wide spaced teeth sleep disturbances
—	—	Sleep disturbances
—	—	Fascination with water
—	—	Anxiety

adulthood.[44] Epilepsy tends to be more severe in those with a maternal deletion, as does disease severity in general.[47,49] Electroencephalogram (EEG) often shows a characteristic pattern, most classically with posterior predominant spike and sharp waves mixed with high-amplitude, sharply contoured 3- to 4-Hz activity.

Movement disorder

Ataxic gait and/or tremulous movement of the limbs is a consistent finding in AS.[50] Individuals with AS have a slow, stiff-legged gait. Typical posture includes raised arms, flexed at the elbows and wrists. Hand flapping is common when walking or excited. Movements are generally jerky and abrupt. The specific brain region responsible for the movement disorder is not known.

Happy demeanor

Individuals with AS have a characteristic happy demeanor and are easily excitable. These individuals have frequent, sometimes inappropriate laughter. Hyperactivity and hypermotoric activity often accompany the happy disposition. Individuals with AS are typically highly social, with social interest beginning in infancy. Most children with AS are eager to communicate, despite difficulty in doing so.[41] Social disinhibition is common, and there is little fear of strangers.

Other features

Other behavioral features associated with AS include stereotypic movements (such as hand flapping), difficulty sleeping, and anxiety. Individuals with AS are frequently fascinated with water. Facial features associated with AS include lightly pigmented skin, hair, and eyes; strabismus; tongue protrusion; prognathia; and widely spaced teeth.

Recent Advances in Genetics and Pathomechanism of the Disease

AS is caused by the lack of function of maternal *UBE3A*.[51,52] This lack of function arises because of 1 of the following 4 mechanisms: (1) deletion of maternal 15q11.2-q13 is found in approximately 74% of individuals with AS, (2) loss of function mutation of maternal *UBE3A* is found in approximately 11% of individuals with AS, (3) paternal uniparental disomy (UPD) is found in approximately 8% of individuals with AS, and (4) imprinting defect is found in approximately 7% of individuals with AS.[53] In contrast to PWS, AS caused by point mutations in the maternal copy of the *UBE3A* gene demonstrates that AS is a single-gene disorder, although other genes in the deletion region can contribute to the severity of AS.

The mechanism by which loss of *UBE3A* causes AS is still not completely understood. The UBE3A protein, also known as E6AP, is an E3 ubiquitin ligase, which transfers an activated ubiquitin from an E2 ubiquitin ligase to its target protein.[54] UBE3A/E6AP typically adds lysine 48 (K48)-linked polyubiquitin chains to its substrates, thus targeting them for degradation by the proteasome.[55] Some substrates of UBE3A/E6AP, such as HHR23A,[56] RPN10,[57] and EPHEXIN5,[58] have been identified. HHR23A (also known as RAD23A) stimulates nucleotide excision repair, RPN10 is a subunit of the proteasome, and EPHEXIN5 is a rho guanine nucleotide exchange factor (rhoGEF) involved in regulating dendritic spine density.

Mouse models of AS have suggested some underlying neuronal pathologic conditions associated with the disorder. Deficits in long-term potentiation,[59,60] inhibitory calcium/calmodulin dependent protein kinase (CaMKII) phosphorylation,[60] presynaptic release probability in inhibitory neurons,[61] and Golgi acidification and protein surface sialylation[62] have been reported. Full connections between UBE3A/E6AP substrates and the neuronal pathologic conditions have not yet been made.

Diagnosis

Methyation analysis

Methylation analysis using Southern blot or methylation-specific PCR of the promoter region of the *SNRPN* gene/IC is able to identify roughly 75% to 80 % of cases of AS (**Fig. 3**). Absence of a maternal methylation pattern indicates AS, but typically does not distinguish between deletion, UPD, and imprinting defect as the cause. If methylation testing is consistent with AS, testing should proceed as follows.

Deletion testing Most cases of AS (65%) are caused by de novo microdeletion of the 15q11.2-q13.1 region, which can be identified by FISH or microarray, and are associated with very low recurrence risk.

UPD testing If a deletion is not found, UPD testing can identify the presence of 2 paternal copies of chromosome 15 in 8% of cases, although parental samples are required. UPD is also generally associated with a low recurrence risk.

Imprinting center sequencing If the result of methylation testing is positive, but those of microdeletion and UPD testing are negative, an IC defect is suspected. Imprinting defects account for roughly 3% of cases of AS. Molecular testing to look for deletion in the IC is successful in roughly 10% to 20 % of these cases and carries up to 50% recurrence risk. If an IC deletion is not found, an epimutation is presumed, and the recurrence risk again seems low.

UBE3A sequencing

For patients with clinically suspected AS, but a negative result of methylation test, *UBE3A* sequencing should be sought. Mutations in *UBE3A* are the second most common molecular cause of AS, found in 12% of cases, and can carry a 50% recurrence risk.

If methylation testing and *UBE3A* sequencing yield negative results, AS is unlikely to be the diagnosis, and diagnosis of Angelman-like syndromes should be considered including Pitt-Hopkins syndrome, *CDKL5* mutation, and Kleefstra syndrome.

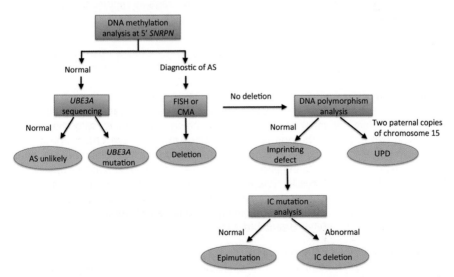

Fig. 3. Diagnostic strategy for AS. Blue boxes indicate the diagnostic test, pink boxes indicate the diagnostic decision.

Management of Angelman Syndrome

Epilepsy

Seizures are often difficult to control. Patients may require polypharmacy, and status epilepticus is not uncommon.[47,63] Seizures typically respond best to medications traditionally effective for generalized epilepsy including valproic acid, levetiracetam, lamotrigine, clonazepam, and clobazam. Seizures may also respond well to the ketogenic diet. Medications most likely to exacerbate seizures include vigabatrin, tiagabine, oxcarbazepine, and carbamazepine.[64]

Sleep disturbance

Children with AS frequently have disrupted sleep with difficulty both in falling asleep and maintaining sleep and possibly a reduced requirement for sleep.[65,66] Sleep disturbance can be a tremendous strain on caregivers and families. Treatment with melatonin 1 hour before bedtime has been shown to decrease sleep latency and nighttime awakening.[67] Doses as low as 0.3 mg can be effective, with typical doses ranging from 0.3 to 5 mg nightly.[68] Additional medical management may be needed as well as providing a safe and restricted environment for children when they do wake at night.

Diet and nutrition

In infancy and early childhood, feeding issues may require special nipples and gastroesophageal reflux can lead to poor weight gain and vomiting, typically managed with positioning and/or medication.

Muscle tone and gait

Hypotonia is frequent in young children, although spasticity of limbs often develops over time. Gait is typically ataxic.[50] Children should receive physical and occupational therapy services. Orthotics and other adaptive devices are often helpful, and orthopedic consultation may be warranted for issues including scoliosis.

Speech

Early intervention with speech therapy is important to maximize communication, with emphasis on nonverbal methods of communication such as picture boards and devices recommended.

Other

Children with AS should have regular ophthalmologic assessment for management of strabismus, and hyperopia.[69]

Future potential therapies

Strategies to augment DNA methylation through administration of supplements such as betaine, folate, or other supplements are being investigated with the goal of increasing expression of the dormant allele, although the results of trials have been disappointing. Recent studies are focusing on methods of unsilencing the paternal UBE3A allele. Studies by Huang and colleagues[70] and others using topoisomerase inhibitors or other approaches to "unsilence" the paternal UBE3A allele are ongoing in animal models. A recent report of restoration of paternal Ube3a expression in the AS mouse model by genetically terminating transcription of the antisense RNA also provides hope for improving disease treatment in the future.[71]

Recommendation for family counseling

Family counseling is recommended. Most deletions, UPD, and epimutations are associated with a low recurrence risk. However, IC mutations, UBE3A mutations, and some translocations may be associated with a 50% recurrence risk.

DUP15Q SYNDROME
Clinical Background of the Disease

Individuals with Dup15q syndrome have features of both PWS and AS, as well as some features unique to the disorder. Dup15q syndrome is characterized by central hypotonia, developmental delay, intellectual disability, seizures, and autism (**Table 3**). There is remarkable diversity in the severity of these symptoms, even in individuals with exactly the same genotype. Duplications involving 15q11.2 or 15q13.3 alone are distinct from 15q11.2-q13 duplications and are not discussed in this article.

Hypotonia

Muscle hypotonia is observed in almost all individuals with Dup15q syndrome and can be severe, prompting testing for PWS.[72] Feeding difficulties are common. Joint hyperextensibility and drooling accompanies the hypotonia in most individuals. Major motor milestones such as rolling over, sitting, and walking are delayed. Weak cry is often reported. Although hypotonia can persist in some adults, it also can subside or progress to hypertonia in the limbs.[72]

Developmental delay/intellectual disability

Gross and fine motor skill delays are common in individuals with Dup15q syndrome. Hypotonia contributes to these delays. Sitting is reportedly achieved between 10 and 20 months, with walking typical between 2 and 3 years. Although some children with Dup15q syndrome do not walk, the vast majority do walk independently. Fine motor delays include nonfunctional use of objects and immature exploration of objects. Cognitive and social/emotional delays are apparent in all children with Dup15q. Comprehension is very limited. Cognitive impairment/intellectual disability is frequently in the severe to profound range.

Epilepsy

Seizures affect up to 60% of children with Dup15q syndrome, with the typical onset occurring before the age of 5 years.[73] Seizures are more common in children with isodicentric chromosome 15 [idic(15)] than in those with interstitial duplications. In children with idic(15), seizures often first present as infantile spasms and later progress to a Lennox-Gastaut-type syndrome. Affected children may have multiple seizure types, including infantile spasms, tonic, atonic, tonic-clonic, myoclonic, complex partial, and atypical absence.[73] Seizures can be intractable. There is an increased risk of sudden unexpected death in epilepsy (SUDEP) in individuals with Dup15q syndrome. Many individuals without overt seizures have abnormal EEG activity.[74]

Table 3
Features of Dup15q syndrome

Consistent (100%)	Frequent (80%)	Associated (20%–80%)
—	Hypotonia	Characteristic facial features
—	Speech/language disorder	Reduced growth
—	Developmental delay	Autism
—	Behavior challenges	Sensory processing disorders
—	Abnormal EEG	Seizures
—	—	Hyperpigmentation
—	—	Autism

Autism

Most individuals with Dup15q syndrome meet the diagnostic criteria for autism.[74] Speech and language delays occur in most individuals. Some individuals are completely nonverbal, whereas a few are highly verbal. Expressive language is typically severely affected and may even be absent. Language is often echolalic with pronoun reversal.[72] Intent to communicate is also absent or very poor in many individuals. Inappropriate social interactions are typical in individuals with Dup15q. Gaze and bodily contact avoidance is common. Symbolic play is almost never acquired, and individuals with Dup15q syndrome usually do not show interest in their peers. Difficult behaviors such as tantrums, shouting, and aggressiveness often occur, as do stereotypies. Hand flapping, clapping, or wringing are frequently seen, as well as finger biting, head turning, and repeated spinning. Despite a frequent diagnosis of autism, many individuals with Dup15q syndrome score well on the Autism Diagnostic Observation Schedule-general (ADOS-G) test.

Other

Subtle facial features that are characteristic for Dup15q syndrome can be seen in most affected individuals. These features include a small button nose, downslanting palpebral fissures, and low-set and/or posteriorly rotated ears. Increased pigmentation can be observed. Growth retardation occurs in approximately 20% to 30% of individuals.[72] Hypogonadism occurs in approximately 20% of affected individuals, although precocious puberty sometimes occurs.[72]

Recent Advances in Genetics and Pathomechanism of the Disease

Dup15q syndrome usually occurs in one of 2 forms-idic(15) and maternal interstitial duplication[74]; idic(15) is the most common presentation. In addition to the 2 normal chromosomes 15, individuals with idic(15) have a small supernumerary chromosome harboring 2 extra copies of the maternal 15q11.2-q13 region in a tail-to-tail orientation. As the name implies, the idic(15) chromosome also contains 2 centromeres but is apparently stable despite this, possibly owing to the inactivation of one of the centromeres. Individuals with idic(15) are tetrasomic for the 15q11.2-q13 region, having 3 maternal copies and 1 paternal copy of the locus. Maternal interstitial duplications consist of 1 extra copy of the maternal 15q11.2-q13 region inserted inverted and in tandem with another copy of the region. Thus, these individuals are triploid for the 15q11.2-q13 region; 2 maternal copies and 1 paternal copy of the locus are present. Individuals with paternal interstitial duplications do exist in the population but seem to have a distinct, milder phenotype when compared with individuals with maternal interstitial duplications.

Owing to the dependence of the phenotypes of individuals on the parent of origin of the duplicated allele or alleles, it is assumed that *UBE3A*, the gene whose loss of function causes AS, contributes significantly to the Dup15q syndrome. A mouse model carrying 2 extra copies of murine *Ube3a* has autistic features and supports this hypothesis,[75] although mice with only a single extra copy of maternal *Ube3a* do not have an autistic phenotype.[75,76] Other, biallelically expressed genes could also play important roles. A cluster of γ-aminobutyric acid receptor subunit genes (*GABRB3*, *GABRA5*, and *GABRG3*), and a gene encoding another ubiquitin ligase, *HERC2*, are duplicated in individuals with both maternal interstitial duplication and idic(15). These genes may also contribute to the disorder.

Diagnosis

Duplications in the 15q11-q13 region, which is prone to genomic rearrangement because of the presence of repeated DNA elements, are most often detected through array comparative genomic hybridization (CGH),[77] which has become a standard screening tool when evaluating children with hypotonia, autism, or developmental delay. Before the widespread use of this technology, standard high-resolution karyotype along with FISH analysis identified cases of inverted duplication 15 (idic 15) syndrome, visible as a marker chromosome.[72] Cases of idic (15) may still be identified in this manner, although interstitial duplications would typically not be detectable by chromosomal analysis. Array CGH also allows for the precise delineation of breakpoints and size of the duplicated material.

Identification of an interstitial duplication or idic(15) should be followed by a test to clarify the parent of origin, which affects phenotype.[74] This clarification could be done either by methylation analysis of the proband sample or targeted array of parental samples.

Treatment/Management

Several studies have confirmed that phenotype is more severe for those children with idic(15) than for those with interstitial duplications.[78,79] In addition, maternally inherited interstitial duplications seem to be more consistently expressed than paternally inherited ones and are associated with significantly higher risk of autism spectrum disorder.[74] The impact of paternally inherited duplications remains unclear, although some pathogenicity is clear.

Muscle tone/growth and nutrition

Hypotonia, particularly affecting orofacial musculature, can lead to feeding difficulties in infancy, more often in children with idic(15), and may require special attention to feeding and growth. Delay in acquisition of motor milestones is also more pronounced in those with idic(15) than in those with interstitial duplications, and early intervention with physical therapy may be beneficial.

Autism

Given the high risk of autism with idic(15) and maternally inherited duplication, evaluation by a developmental pediatrician is recommended. This evaluation should be considered for paternally inherited duplications as well, particularly if concerns about behavior and social relatedness exist. Children with Dup15q syndrome also benefit from early intervention with speech and educational therapies.

Epilepsy

Seizures are significantly more common and severe in children with idic(15), affecting roughly two-thirds, as opposed to 25% of those with interstitial duplications.[73] Risk for infantile spasms is high in idic(15), and parents should be advised to watch for early signs of this seizure type, because early treatment is beneficial. Screening EEG may be warranted. Treatment with ACTH/steroids for infantile spasms seems to be more effective in this group than vigabatrin (75% vs 29%),[73] and thus should be considered as initial therapy. Seizures often evolve into Lennox-Gastaut syndrome and seem to respond to medications typically beneficial for those with generalized epilepsy including valproic acid, rufinamide, lamotrigine, and zonisamide, although formal studies remain limited. Carbamazepine was also reported to be effective in many, suggesting that epilepsy may be multifocal as opposed to primary generalized. Children with idic(15) do not respond well to benzodiazepines, and seizure exacerbation was also reported in almost half of those treated with leviteracetam.[73] There is little information regarding the efficacy of the ketogenic diet or vagal nerve stimulator in this population. Unfortunately, epilepsy risk seems persistent in idic(15) with seizures continuing into adulthood in two-thirds.[73] Refractory epilepsy does seem to be associated with the risk of early death secondary to status epilepticus or SUDEP, reported in 8% of patients with idic(15) with seizures.[73]

Behavior and sleep
Behavioral difficulties with defiant and aggressive behaviors, particularly in patients with idic(15), can be challenging and may require medical management.[80] In addition, sleep difficulties may be noted, possibly secondary to epileptic discharges, thus overnight EEG and sleep study may be helpful in directing management.

Future potential therapies
Current work toward future therapies may focus on reducing UBE3A expression levels or activity in patients with Dup15q,[81] although no specific therapies have been reported.

Recommendation for family counseling
Family counseling is recommended. The recurrence rate of idic(15) is low. However, interstitial duplication may be associated with a 50% recurrence risk.

SUMMARY

The 15q11-q13 region contains several genes that are regulated by genomic imprinting and impact neurodevelopment. Despite being caused by variation of the same genetic region, PWS, AS, and Dup15q syndrome are distinct disorders with different phenotypic manifestations and diagnostic strategies. As imprinted genes are involved in these disorders, potential therapies may involve modulating expression of the implicated genes and provide optimism for improved outcomes in the future.

REFERENCES

1. Butler MG, Sturich J, Myers SE, et al. Is gestation in Prader-Willi syndrome affected by the genetic subtype? J Assist Reprod Genet 2009;26:461–6.
2. McCandless SE, Committee on Genetics. Clinical report-health supervision for children with Prader-Willi syndrome. Pediatrics 2011;127:195–204.
3. Eldar-Geva T, Hirsch HJ, Benarroch F, et al. Hypogonadism in females with Prader-Willi syndrome from infancy to adulthood: variable combinations of a primary gonadal defect and hypothalamic dysfunction. Eur J Endocrinol 2010;162: 377–84.
4. Butler MG, Sturich J, Lee J, et al. Growth standards of infants with Prader-Willi syndrome. Pediatrics 2011;127:687–95.
5. Cassidy SB, Schwartz S, Miller JL, et al. Prader-Willi syndrome. Genet Med 2012; 14:10–26.
6. Burman P, Ritzen EM, Lindgren AC. Endocrine dysfunction in Prader-Willi syndrome: a review with special reference to GH. Endocr Rev 2001;22:787–99.
7. Carrel AL, Moerchen V, Myers SE, et al. Growth hormone improves mobility and body composition in infants and toddlers with Prader-Willi syndrome. J Pediatr 2004;145:744–9.
8. Carrel AL, Myers SE, Whitman BY, et al. Long-term growth hormone therapy changes the natural history of body composition and motor function in children with Prader-Willi syndrome. J Clin Endocrinol Metab 2010;95:1131–6.
9. Whitman B, Carrel A, Bekx T, et al. Growth hormone improves body composition and motor development in infants with Prader-Willi syndrome after six months. J Pediatr Endocrinol Metab 2004;17:591–600.
10. Miller JL, Lynn CH, Driscoll DC, et al. Nutritional phases in Prader-Willi syndrome. Am J Med Genet A 2011;155A:1040–9.

11. Cummings DE, Clement K, Purnell JQ, et al. Elevated plasma ghrelin levels in Prader Willi syndrome. Nat Med 2002;8:643–4.
12. Butler MG, Theodoro MF, Bittel DC, et al. Energy expenditure and physical activity in Prader-Willi syndrome: comparison with obese subjects. Am J Med Genet A 2007;143A:449–59.
13. Goldstone AP, Thomas EL, Brynes AE, et al. Visceral adipose tissue and metabolic complications of obesity are reduced in Prader-Willi syndrome female adults: evidence for novel influences on body fat distribution. J Clin Endocrinol Metab 2001;86:4330–8.
14. Whittington J, Holland A. Neurobehavioral phenotype in Prader-Willi syndrome. Am J Med Genet C Semin Med Genet 2010;154C:438–47.
15. Whittington J, Holland A, Webb T, et al. Cognitive abilities and genotype in a population-based sample of people with Prader-Willi syndrome. J Intellect Disabil Res 2004;48:172–87.
16. Dykens EM, Cassidy SB, King BH. Maladaptive behavior differences in Prader-Willi syndrome due to paternal deletion versus maternal uniparental disomy. Am J Ment Retard 1999;104:67–77.
17. Butler JV, Whittington JE, Holland AJ, et al. Prevalence of, and risk factors for, physical ill-health in people with Prader-Willi syndrome: a population-based study. Dev Med Child Neurol 2002;44:248–55.
18. Boer H, Holland A, Whittington J, et al. Psychotic illness in people with Prader Willi syndrome due to chromosome 15 maternal uniparental disomy. Lancet 2002;359: 135–6.
19. Festen DA, de Weerd AW, van den Bossche RA, et al. Sleep-related breathing disorders in prepubertal children with Prader-Willi syndrome and effects of growth hormone treatment. J Clin Endocrinol Metab 2006;91:4911–5.
20. Sahoo T, del Gaudio D, German JR, et al. Prader-Willi phenotype caused by paternal deficiency for the HBII-85 C/D box small nucleolar RNA cluster. Nat Genet 2008;40:719–21.
21. Duker AL, Ballif BC, Bawle EV, et al. Paternally inherited microdeletion at 15q11.2 confirms a significant role for the SNORD116 C/D box snoRNA cluster in Prader-Willi syndrome. Eur J Hum Genet 2010;18:1196–201.
22. de Smith AJ, Purmann C, Walters RG, et al. A deletion of the HBII-85 class of small nucleolar RNAs (snoRNAs) is associated with hyperphagia, obesity and hypogonadism. Hum Mol Genet 2009;18:3257–65.
23. Bieth E, Eddiry S, Gaston V, et al. Highly restricted deletion of the SNORD116 region is implicated in Prader-Willi syndrome. Eur J Hum Genet 2014;23(2):252–5.
24. Cavaille J, Buiting K, Kiefmann M, et al. Identification of brain-specific and imprinted small nucleolar RNA genes exhibiting an unusual genomic organization. Proc Natl Acad Sci U S A 2000;97:14311–6.
25. Bazeley PS, Shepelev V, Talebizadeh Z, et al. snoTARGET shows that human orphan snoRNA targets locate close to alternative splice junctions. Gene 2008; 408:172–9.
26. Kishore S, Khanna A, Zhang Z, et al. The snoRNA MBII-52 (SNORD 115) is processed into smaller RNAs and regulates alternative splicing. Hum Mol Genet 2010;19:1153–64.
27. Bortolin-Cavaille ML, Cavaille J. The SNORD115 (H/MBII-52) and SNORD116 (H/MBII-85) gene clusters at the imprinted Prader-Willi locus generate canonical box C/D snoRNAs. Nucleic Acids Res 2012;40(14):6800–7.
28. Shen M, Eyras E, Wu J, et al. Direct cloning of double-stranded RNAs from RNase protection analysis reveals processing patterns of C/D box snoRNAs and

provides evidence for widespread antisense transcript expression. Nucleic Acids Res 2011;39:9720–30.

29. Shaffer LG, Agan N, Goldberg JD, et al. American College of Medical Genetics statement of diagnostic testing for uniparental disomy. Genet Med 2001;3: 206–11.

30. Miller JL, Goldstone AP, Couch JA, et al. Pituitary abnormalities in Prader-Willi syndrome and early onset morbid obesity. Am J Med Genet A 2008;146A: 570–7.

31. Schmidt H, Pozza SB, Bonfig W, et al. Successful early dietary intervention avoids obesity in patients with Prader-Willi syndrome: a ten-year follow-up. J Pediatr Endocrinol Metab 2008;21:651–5.

32. Deal CL, Tony M, Höybye C, et al. Growth Hormone Research Society workshop summary: consensus guidelines for recombinant human growth hormone therapy in Prader-Willi syndrome. J Clin Endocrinol Metab 2013;98:E1072–87.

33. Festen DA, Wevers M, Lindgren AC, et al. Mental and motor development before and during growth hormone treatment in infants and toddlers with Prader-Willi syndrome. Clin Endocrinol (Oxf) 2008;68:919–25.

34. Berini J, Spica Russotto V, Castelnuovo P, et al. Growth hormone therapy and respiratory disorders: long-term follow-up in PWS children. J Clin Endocrinol Metab 2013;98:E1516–23.

35. Oto Y, Tanaka Y, Abe Y, et al. Exacerbation of BMI after cessation of growth hormone therapy in patients with Prader-Willi syndrome. Am J Med Genet A 2014; 164A:671–5.

36. Emerick JE, Vogt KS. Endocrine manifestations and management of Prader-Willi syndrome. Int J Pediatr Endocrinol 2013;2013:14.

37. Soni S, Whittington J, Holland AJ, et al. The course and outcome of psychiatric illness in people with Prader-Willi syndrome: implications for management and treatment. J Intellect Disabil Res 2007;51:32–42.

38. Goldstone AP, Holland AJ, Hauffa BP, et al. Recommendations for the diagnosis and management of Prader-Willi syndrome. J Clin Endocrinol Metab 2008;93: 4183–97.

39. Einfeld SL, Smith E, McGregor IS, et al. A double-blind randomized controlled trial of oxytocin nasal spray in Prader Willi syndrome. Am J Med Genet A 2014; 164A:2232–9.

40. Heymsfield SB, Avena NM, Baier L, et al. Hyperphagia: current concepts and future directions proceedings of the 2nd international conference on hyperphagia. Obesity (Silver Spring) 2014;22(Suppl 1):S1–17.

41. Bird LM. Angelman syndrome: review of clinical and molecular aspects. Appl Clin Genet 2014;7:93–104.

42. Peters SU, Beaudet AL, Madduri N, et al. Autism in Angelman syndrome: implications for autism research. Clin Genet 2004;66:530–6.

43. Clayton-Smith J, Pembrey ME. Angelman syndrome. J Med Genet 1992;29: 412–5.

44. Laan LA, den Boer AT, Hennekam RC, et al. Angelman syndrome in adulthood. Am J Med Genet 1996;66:356–60.

45. Gentile JK, Tan WH, Horowitz LT, et al. A neurodevelopmental survey of Angelman syndrome with genotype-phenotype correlations. J Dev Behav Pediatr 2010;31: 592–601.

46. Galvan-Manso M, Campistol J, Conill J, et al. Analysis of the characteristics of epilepsy in 37 patients with the molecular diagnosis of Angelman syndrome. Epileptic Disord 2005;7:19–25.

47. Thibert RL, Conant KD, Braun EK, et al. Epilepsy in Angelman syndrome: a questionnaire-based assessment of the natural history and current treatment options. Epilepsia 2009;50:2369–76.
48. Valente KD, Koiffmann CP, Fridman C, et al. Epilepsy in patients with Angelman syndrome caused by deletion of the chromosome 15q11-13. Arch Neurol 2006; 63:122–8.
49. Varela MC, Kok F, Otto PA, et al. Phenotypic variability in Angelman syndrome: comparison among different deletion classes and between deletion and UPD subjects. Eur J Hum Genet 2004;12:987–92.
50. Williams CA. Neurological aspects of the Angelman syndrome. Brain Dev 2005; 27:88–94.
51. Kishino T, Lalande M, Wagstaff J. UBE3A/E6-AP mutations cause Angelman syndrome. Nat Genet 1997;15:70–3.
52. Matsuura T, Sutcliffe JS, Fang P, et al. De novo truncating mutations in E6-AP ubiquitin-protein ligase gene (UBE3A) in Angelman syndrome. Nat Genet 1997; 15:74–7.
53. Dagli A, Buiting K, Williams CA. Molecular and clinical aspects of Angelman syndrome. Mol Syndromol 2012;2:100–12.
54. Scheffner M, Huibregtse JM, Vierstra RD, et al. The HPV-16 E6 and E6-AP complex functions as a ubiquitin-protein ligase in the ubiquitination of p53. Cell 1993; 75:495–505.
55. Wang M, Pickart CM. Different HECT domain ubiquitin ligases employ distinct mechanisms of polyubiquitin chain synthesis. EMBO J 2005;24:4324–33.
56. Kumar S, Talis AL, Howley PM. Identification of HHR23A as a substrate for E6-associated protein-mediated ubiquitination. J Biol Chem 1999;274:18785–92.
57. Lee SY, Ramirez J, Franco M, et al. Ube3a, the E3 ubiquitin ligase causing Angelman syndrome and linked to autism, regulates protein homeostasis through the proteasomal shuttle Rpn10. Cell Mol Life Sci 2014;71:2747–58.
58. Margolis SS, Salogiannis J, Lipton DM, et al. EphB-mediated degradation of the RhoA GEF Ephexin5 relieves a developmental brake on excitatory synapse formation. Cell 2010;143:442–55.
59. Jiang YH, Armstrong D, Albrecht U, et al. Mutation of the Angelman ubiquitin ligase in mice causes increased cytoplasmic p53 and deficits of contextual learning and long-term potentiation. Neuron 1998;21:799–811.
60. Weeber EJ, Jiang YH, Elgersma Y, et al. Derangements of hippocampal calcium/calmodulin-dependent protein kinase II in a mouse model for Angelman mental retardation syndrome. J Neurosci 2003;23:2634–44.
61. Wallace ML, Burette AC, Weinberg RJ, et al. Maternal loss of Ube3a produces an excitatory/inhibitory imbalance through neuron type-specific synaptic defects. Neuron 2012;74:793–800.
62. Condon KH, Ho J, Robinson CG, et al. The Angelman syndrome protein Ube3a/E6AP is required for Golgi acidification and surface protein sialylation. J Neurosci 2013;33:3799–814.
63. Pelc K, Boyd SG, Cheron G, et al. Epilepsy in Angelman syndrome. Seizure 2008; 17:211–7.
64. Thibert RL, Larson AM, Hsieh DT, et al. Neurologic manifestations of Angelman syndrome. Pediatr Neurol 2013;48:271–9.
65. Bruni O, Ferri R, D'Agostino G, et al. Sleep disturbances in Angelman syndrome: a questionnaire study. Brain Dev 2004;26:233–40.
66. Didden R, Korzilius H, Smits MG, et al. Sleep problems in individuals with Angelman syndrome. Am J Ment Retard 2004;109:275–84.

67. Braam W, Didden R, Smits MG, et al. Melatonin for chronic insomnia in Angelman syndrome: a randomized placebo-controlled trial. J Child Neurol 2008;23:649–54.
68. Braam W, Smits MG, Didden R, et al. Exogenous melatonin for sleep problems in individuals with intellectual disability: a meta-analysis. Dev Med Child Neurol 2009;51:340–9.
69. Michieletto P, Bonanni P, Pensiero S. Ophthalmic findings in Angelman syndrome. J AAPOS 2011;15:158–61.
70. Huang HS, Allen JA, Mabb AM, et al. Topoisomerase inhibitors unsilence the dormant allele of Ube3a in neurons. Nature 2012;481:185–9.
71. Meng L, Person RE, Huang W, et al. Truncation of Ube3a-ATS unsilences paternal Ube3a and ameliorates behavioral defects in the Angelman syndrome mouse model. PLoS Genet 2013;9:e1004039.
72. Battaglia A. The inv dup (15) or idic (15) syndrome (tetrasomy 15q). Orphanet J Rare Dis 2008;3:30.
73. Conant KD, Finucane B, Cleary N, et al. A survey of seizures and current treatments in 15q duplication syndrome. Epilepsia 2014;55:396–402.
74. Urraca N, Cleary J, Brewer V, et al. The interstitial duplication 15q11.2-q13 syndrome includes autism, mild facial anomalies and a characteristic EEG signature. Autism Res 2013;6:268–79.
75. Smith SE, Zhou YD, Zhang G, et al. Increased gene dosage of Ube3a results in autism traits and decreased glutamate synaptic transmission in mice. Sci Transl Med 2011;3:103ra97.
76. Nakatani J, Tamada K, Hatanaka F, et al. Abnormal behavior in a chromosome-engineered mouse model for human 15q11-13 duplication seen in autism. Cell 2009;137:1235–46.
77. Wang NJ, Liu D, Parokonny AS, et al. High-resolution molecular characterization of 15q11-q13 rearrangements by array comparative genomic hybridization (array CGH) with detection of gene dosage. Am J Hum Genet 2004;75:267–81.
78. Bolton PF, Dennis NR, Browne CE, et al. The phenotypic manifestations of interstitial duplications of proximal 15q with special reference to the autistic spectrum disorders. Am J Med Genet 2001;105:675–85.
79. Browne CE, Dennis NR, Maher E, et al. Inherited interstitial duplications of proximal 15q: genotype-phenotype correlations. Am J Hum Genet 1997;61:1342–52.
80. Battaglia A, Parrini B, Tancredi R. The behavioral phenotype of the idic(15) syndrome. Am J Med Genet C Semin Med Genet 2010;154C:448–55.
81. Germain ND, Chen PF, Plocik AM, et al. Gene expression analysis of human induced pluripotent stem cell-derived neurons carrying copy number variants of chromosome 15q11-q13.1. Mol Autism 2014;5:44.

Diagnosis and Management of Autism Spectrum Disorder in the Era of Genomics

⬤ CrossMark

Rare Disorders Can Pave the Way for Targeted Treatments

Elizabeth Baker, BA, Shafali Spurling Jeste, MD*

KEYWORDS

- Neurodevelopmental disorders • Autism spectrum disorders • Genetics
- Copy number variants • Chromosomal microarray • Whole-exome sequencing

KEY POINTS

- Like all neurodevelopmental disorders, ASD is a heterogeneous group of disorders characterized by a constellation of symptoms and behaviors that occur in early development.
- Genetic testing is the only standard medical workup recommended for all children diagnosed with ASD; more than 25% of children with ASD have an identified genetic cause.
- Clinical features, particularly presence of intellectual disability, epilepsy, motor impairment, or certain dysmorphic features, support a likely underlying genetic etiology.
- The comorbidity of intellectual disability and ASD requires that future studies carefully examine early developmental trajectories and cognitive abilities in these genetic variants and syndromes, so as to confirm the diagnostic specificity of ASD.
- Common phenotypes and natural history studies within genetic syndromes can help to inform prognosis and treatment targets.

INTRODUCTION

Autism spectrum disorder (ASD) is a heterogeneous group of disorders defined by impaired social communication function and the presence of restricted, repetitive patterns of behavior or interests.[1] Although the diagnosis of ASD is based on

Disclosures: None.
Department of Psychiatry and Biobehavioral Sciences, Semel Institute for Neuroscience and Human Behavior, David Geffen School of Medicine, UCLA, 760 Westwood Plaza, Los Angeles, CA 90095, USA
* Corresponding author.
E-mail address: sjeste@mednet.ucla.edu

Pediatr Clin N Am 62 (2015) 607–618
http://dx.doi.org/10.1016/j.pcl.2015.03.003
0031-3955/15/$ – see front matter © 2015 Elsevier Inc. All rights reserved.

behavioral signs and symptoms, the evaluation of a child with ASD has become increasingly focused on the identification of the genetic etiology of the disorder. With the advances made in genetic testing over the past decade, more than 25% of children with ASD have an identifiable, causative genetic variant or syndrome, and this rate continues to increase with improved methods in genetic testing. In fact, the term "idiopathic autism" has become increasingly obsolete in this era of genomics, sometimes replaced by the descriptor of "nonsyndromic autism" for cases without a defined genetic etiology. The identification of genetic variants has been accompanied by a concerted effort to define more homogeneous clinical syndromes that are informed by the underlying genetic etiology of a child's ASD. In the future, such characterization will facilitate targeted treatments based on mechanisms of disease and common clinical features. Here we present the clinical phenomenology of ASD, including evaluation and treatment, in the context of our growing appreciation of the genetic basis of this neurodevelopmental disorder.

DIAGNOSIS OF AUTISM SPECTRUM DISORDER IS NOT ETIOLOGY-BASED

As with all the neurodevelopmental disorders, the diagnosis of ASD is based on a collection of behavioral and developmental features, not on presumed or known etiology. However, specific clinical characteristics may provide useful clues for the identification of the underlying etiology. Therefore, the diagnostic evaluation of a child with known ASD, as will be outlined in later sections, is motivated by a search for causative or associated genetic variants and syndromes.

ASD is defined by a dyad of impairments in social communication skills and the presence of repetitive patterns of behavior or restricted interests in the early developmental period, with deficits leading to functional impairment in a variety of domains. The diagnosis must be made by an experienced clinician, using a combination of parent report, direct examination of the child, and standardized developmental and behavioral testing when needed. The combination of these tools can then be assimilated into a "best clinical estimate" based on diagnostic criteria established in the *Diagnostic and Statistical Manual of Mental Disorders* (DSM). In May 2013, the revised DSM-5 was published, and in it significant revisions were made to the diagnostic conceptualization of ASD (**Box 1**). Two fundamental changes were made. First, the separate categories of social function and communication in DSM-IV were merged into one category of social communication impairment. This change shows that deficits in communication, both verbal and nonverbal, are intimately linked to social deficits, particularly early in development. Second, the diagnostic categories (autistic

---

Box 1
Changes from *Diagnostic and Statistical Manual of Mental Disorders, 4th Edition, Text Revision* (DSM-IV-TR) to DSM-5 for autism spectrum disorder

1. Broad category of autism spectrum disorder (ASD) replaces discrete diagnostic categories (autistic disorder, pervasive developmental disorder, not otherwise specified, Asperger disorder)

2. Separate domains of social and language impairment merged into one domain of social communication function

3. Symptom severity ratings generated for the 2 domains based on functional impairment

4. Sensory sensitivities added into repetitive behaviors/restricted interests domain

5. Although symptoms must begin in early childhood, age 3 is no longer a strict age of onset

disorder, Asperger disorder, and pervasive developmental disorder, not otherwise specified [PDD-NOS]) were removed and, instead, one umbrella diagnosis of ASD was created. This change from categories to a continuum better captures the true spectrum of symptom severity of this disorder and shows that often the separate diagnostic categories were not consistently applied across clinical or research centers.

The changes in DSM-5 raised concerns that previously diagnosed children would lose services because of changes in nomenclature and a resulting loss of diagnosis. Since then, several studies have compared DSM-IV and DSM-5 diagnoses with structured diagnostic assessments, such as the Autism Diagnostic Observation Schedule (ADOS) with mixed results. Some studies demonstrate very high consistency, whereas others demonstrate more discrepancy, particularly in those previously given a PDD-NOS diagnosis.[2,3] Of note, from a clinical perspective, a child diagnosed through DSM-IV need not be reevaluated for diagnostic purposes simply because of the changes in DSM-5.

Like most neurodevelopmental disorders, ASD has a strong male predominance.[4] There are 2 primary reasons for this uneven gender distribution. First, there exists a diagnostic bias, as boys tend to exhibit more externalizing and disruptive symptoms that facilitate referrals for diagnosis, and girls manifest symptoms such as anxiety and depression that may delay the diagnosis.[5–7] Second, specific genetic factors may protect girls from developing ASD ("female protective effect").[8,9] Support for this theory comes from studies demonstrating a greater ASD-related genetic load in female individuals with ASD compared with male individuals with ASD, and in clinically unaffected female relatives compared with unaffected male relatives of individuals with ASD. Further substantiation of the greater genetic load in female individuals is found by the higher rate of ASD in siblings of female individuals with ASD compared with male individuals with ASD.

CLINICAL HETEROGENEITY

Variability in clinical presentation is rooted in severity of impairment and comorbidities. Intellectual disability, ranging from mild to severe, occurs in 70% of children.[10] Language impairment can range from deficits in pragmatic use of language to complete lack of spoken language, with 30% of children with ASD remaining minimally verbal despite intensive intervention.[11] Other sources of heterogeneity result from neurologic comorbidities (epilepsy, sleep impairment, motor delays and deficits) and psychiatric disorders (depression, anxiety, irritability, attention deficit hyperactivity disorder). This heterogeneity in clinical presentation requires that treatments, both pharmacologic and behavioral, move away from a "one-size-fits-all" approach and, rather, become tailored to a child's individual clinical profile. As discussed in the following sections, the identification of causative genetic variants can facilitate the characterization of more homogeneous clinical subgroups that, in turn, can guide more targeted therapies.

HERITABILITY OF AUTISM SPECTRUM DISORDER

ASD is one of the most heritable neuropsychiatric disorders, as recognized from the earliest twin studies,[12] with concordance rates in monozygotic twins approaching 70%. Recurrence rates in siblings of children with ASD range from 5% to 20%, with higher rates if the proband is a female. In large prospective cohort studies of infants with older siblings with ASD, the rate of developing ASD has been reported in 18% of infants.[13] The recurrence rate increases to 33% if a family has 2 children with ASD. These heritability estimates can be useful when counseling patients about family planning based on family history of ASD.[14] Considerable research efforts have been dedicated to prospective studies of infant siblings of children with ASD, with the goal of identifying early risk markers and predictors of ASD in this high-risk cohort. Because of the genetic heterogeneity of the sample, no single developmental trajectory or clinical predictor of ASD has been discovered. In fact, these studies have been most successful in identifying overall differences between high-risk and low-risk infants, thus reflecting an endophenotype of elevated risk rather than specific predictors of ASD. By 12 months of age, high-risk infants demonstrate more atypical behaviors, such as reduced social interest and affect, social smiling, orienting to name, imitation, and atypical eye contact. Earlier in infancy, prebehavioral biomarkers of risk include differences in resting state electroencephalogram (EEG) patterns and face processing.[15] These studies have been instrumental in reinforcing that atypical patterns of both brain development and behavior can be quantified early in the developmental period, before formal clinical diagnoses can be made, which, in turn, has justified continued research in early risk markers for ASD.

ADVANCES IN GENETIC TESTING

In part because of the well-established heritability of the disorder, genetic testing for children with ASD has been routinely performed for decades. Initially, the standard test in children was composed of karyotyping alone, which could identify abnormalities only larger than approximately 3 to 5 million base pairs, visible under a light microscope. However, recent advances in genetic methods have led to the identification of contributory mutations in up to 30% of children with ASD.[16,17] The first breakthrough technology was the chromosomal microarray analysis (CMA).[18] Any structural chromosomal duplication or deletion that is larger than 1 kB and causes a deviation from the control copy number is considered a copy number variant (CNV). CNVs can be inherited or sporadic (de novo), with the latter type of mutation considered more likely to be pathogenic. The 2 types of CMA technologies that are most widely used include the array-based comparative genomic hybridization (aCGH) and the single nucleotide polymorphism (SNP) array, both of which permit high-resolution molecular analysis of chromosome copy number. The SNP array has the advantage of being able to detect specific inheritance patterns, such as uniparental disomy, which cannot be detected by aCGH.[19] Both aCGH and SNP arrays provided the first opportunity to perform relatively unbiased genome-wide surveys of chromosomal deletions and duplications with much greater resolution.

However, there are limits to the resolution of CMA testing, and point mutations and microdeletions cannot be identified using these methods. More recently, whole-exome and whole-genome sequencing technology has facilitated investigations at the level of the single base pair, allowing for analysis of single gene defects and for the identification of partial loss of gene function.[16,17,20,21] Most large-scale exome-sequencing studies have been based on data from simplex families, or families with only one affected child (such as the Simons Simplex Collection, a registry of simplex families funded by the Simons Foundation), leading to a growing appreciation of the role of de novo mutations in the pathogenesis of ASD. From these large cohorts of thousands of children, more than 500 candidate genes have been identified, each with 50% chance of being contributory or causative. Network analyses of the functions of the potentially causative genes finds genes implicated in synaptic formation and integrity and in chromatin modulation.[22,23]

GUIDELINES FOR GENETIC TESTING IN AUTISM SPECTRUM DISORDER

The guidelines for genetic testing for ASD have been revised to reflect the advances in methods, which, in turn, have led to larger populations of individuals with known genetic syndromes and variants associated with ASD. In 2000, the American Academy of Neurology and Child Neurology Society published guidelines on the screening and diagnosis of autism, stating that "high-resolution chromosome studies (karyotype) and DNA analysis for fragile X should be performed in the presence of mental retardation...or if dysmorphic features are present."[24] Revised guidelines for testing were published by the American College of Medical Genetics (ACMG) in 2013 (**Fig. 1**).[25] After a comprehensive 3-generation family history, ACMG recommends a CMA for all children. Additionally, fragile X testing should be performed in boys and MECP2 testing (for Rett syndrome) in girls. Children with macrocephaly (head circumference >2 SDs above mean for age) should be tested for phosphatase and tensin homolog (PTEN) gene mutations. A positive test result should be followed by testing of parents for the determination of heritability of the variant. After testing is complete, genetic counseling should be provided regardless of results, as there are risks to future siblings regardless of genetic etiology, as described previously.

Of note, no other neuroimaging or medical testing is routinely recommended for children with ASD. However, certain clinical features may prompt further testing (**Box 2**). Although debate does exist about the implications of the baseline EEG abnormalities found in up to 60% of children with ASD, routine EEG testing is not recommended for all children with an ASD diagnosis. Instead, overnight EEG investigation should be performed in children with a high clinical suspicion for epilepsy or with clear

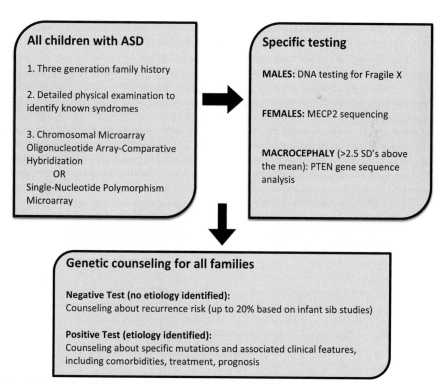

Fig. 1. Recommendations for clinical genetic testing in children with ASD. (*Data from* Schaefer GB, Mendelsohn NJ. Clinical genetics evaluation in identifying the etiology of autism spectrum disorders: 2013 guideline revisions. Genet Med 2013;15:404.)

Box 2
Medical workup for ASD

Genetic testing: indicated for all individuals with ASD, see **Fig. 1**.

Metabolic testing: not indicated routinely, consider if multisystem involvement (cardiac, hepatic, renal), lactic acidosis, severe anemia

MRI: perform if focal neurologic examination, macrocephaly, genetic syndromes associated with structural brain abnormalities

Electroencephalogram: perform for episodes concerning for seizure, language regression, specific genetic syndromes associated with epilepsy

Polysomnograph: May be useful for diagnosing treatable sleep disorders (insomnia) and for diagnosing nocturnal seizures.

---

evidence of language regression that would suggest electrical status epilepticus of sleep.[26,27] Several genetic syndromes, such as tuberous sclerosis complex (TSC), Rett syndrome, fragile X, and Dup15q syndrome are characterized by a high rate of early-onset epilepsy and ASD. In nonsyndromic ASD, the risk of epilepsy seems to increase with age. The largest cross-sectional study of almost 6000 children with ASD and epilepsy found that epilepsy in ASD was associated with lower cognitive, adaptive, and language ability, as well as greater autism severity, with peak prevalence of epilepsy occurring at age 10.[28]

MORE THAN 25% OF INDIVIDUALS WITH AUTISM SPECTRUM DISORDER HAVE AN IDENTIFIABLE GENETIC CAUSE

With genetic testing now routinely recommended and performed, a growing number of individuals are diagnosed with genetic etiologies for their ASD. Two primary categories of genetic etiologies of ASD exist: single gene disorders and CNVs. Single gene disorders are detected in 3% to 5% of children with ASD, and include syndromes such as fragile X, TSC, Rett syndrome, and neurofibromatosis. At least 20% of individuals with ASD have identifiable, causative de novo copy number variations and single gene mutations that are identifiable by using current genetic testing. No single variation, however, accounts for more than 1% of ASD cases, consistent with the phenotypic heterogeneity of the disorder.[29]

CLINICAL RELEVANCE OF GENETIC TESTING: MOVING TOWARD TARGETED PHENOTYPING AND TREATMENT

Parents often voice skepticism about the utility of genetic testing of their child with ASD, highlighting the concern that the knowledge about a causative variant will not actually benefit or inform their child's management and treatment. In the past, knowledge about an associated genetic syndrome or variant did hold more scientific promise than clinical significance. However, recent research efforts have bolstered the clinical impact of the diagnosis of a genetic syndrome or variant associated with ASD, and these advances in the clinical phenomenology of autism genetics are described in the next sections. First, widespread genetic testing has led to the diagnosis of larger cohorts of children with similar variants, which facilitates the identification of common clinical features that can inform more behavioral intervention targets. Second, advances in the identification of causative genes and pathogenic mechanisms associated with these genes have led to molecular treatment targets that, ultimately, may prevent the development of ASD in certain disorders.

COMMON CLINICAL FEATURES: SYMPTOM CLUSTERS

The level of precision in genetic testing still exceeds the precision in clinical phenotyping of the identified genetic syndromes (**Table 1**). However, definite symptom clusters, or clinical features, have been identified that are highly associated with genetic etiologies of ASD, leading to the commonly used term "syndromic autism."[30] These clinical features include intellectual disability (ID), epilepsy, and motor impairment (particularly hypotonia or delay in achieving motor milestones). The presence of macrocephaly or microcephaly (defined by head circumference >2.5 SDs from the mean) can greatly narrow the differential diagnosis. Of each of these comorbidities, ID certainly is the most prevalent, and its presence can reinforce the need for genetic testing. A recent report from the Simons Simplex Collection found that the mean IQ of affected female individuals with de novo mutations was 78, whereas the mean IQ of affected male individuals with de novo mutations was 90.[22] Symptom clusters hold clinical utility in that they may strengthen the argument for genetic testing in children with comorbid ID or epilepsy, and they can guide the need for screening and management of comorbidities, particularly seizures.

INTELLECTUAL DISABILITY AND AUTISM SPECTRUM DISORDER IN GENETIC SYNDROMES

The comorbidity of ID and ASD requires that future studies carefully examine early developmental trajectories and cognitive abilities in these genetic variants and syndromes to confirm the diagnostic specificity of ASD. In DSM-5 it is clearly articulated

Table 1
Common clinical features in genetic variants and syndromes associated with ASD

ID and ASD		
Epilepsy	**Motor Impairment**	**Macro/Microcephaly**
TSC (TSC1 and TSC2)	Hypotonia	Microcephaly
Rett syndrome (MECP2)	Rett Syndrome	Rett syndrome or MECP2 mutations
CNTNAP2	NRXN1 deletion	Angelman syndrome
SYN1	2q23.1 deletion	Cornelia de Lange syndrome
Fragile X syndrome	15q11.2-q13 duplication	16p11.2 duplication syndrome
UBE3a (Angelman syndrome)	22q13.3 deletion (SHANK3) (Phelan-McDermid syndrome)	17q21.31 duplication syndrome
1q21.1 deletion	Severe stereotypes	Macrocephaly
7q11.23 duplication	Rett syndrome	PTEN mutations
15q11.1q13.3 deletion and duplication	Motor delays	Fragile X
16p11.2 deletion	AUTS2	1q21.1 duplication syndrome
17q12 deletion	Fox1 (A2BP1)	
18q12.1 duplication	2q23.1 deletion and duplication	
22q11.2 deletion		

Abbreviations: ASD, autism spectrum disorder; ID, intellectual disability; PTEN, phosphatase and tensin homolog; TSC, tuberous sclerosis complex.

that "to make comorbid diagnoses of ASD and ID, social communication should be below that expected for general developmental level." In other words, clinicians must consider a child's mental age, not chronologic age, when evaluating his or her social, language, and behavioral abilities, as the use of chronologic age may lead to an overdiagnosis of ASD. For instance, in a recently published study of developmental trajectories in infants with TSC, cognitive impairment by age 12 months (based on a standardized scale of development: the Mullen Scales of Early Learning) was strongly associated with social communication impairments at age 3, as quantified by ADOS. The confirmation of ASD in these children with elevated ADOS scores required additional evaluation by an experienced clinician to determine if the scores were secondary to overall delay or specific to ASD.[31] Disentangling ID from ASD holds implications for intervention. For instance, social communication impairment secondary to global developmental delay may improve with interventions targeting cognitive and, perhaps, motor skills, whereas social communication deficits rooted in limited social motivation or attention may respond better to targeted social skills, play-based, therapies. As another example, language impairment in ASD can result from deficits in low-level auditory processing, processing of speech sounds, attention to speech cues necessary for language learning, social motivation, or motor impairment that can undermine the production of words. Identification of the specific pathway will facilitate the choice of intervention most effective for the language impairment in subgroups of children.

Overall, future efforts in clinical characterization of children with genetic syndromes may be better served by placing greater emphasis on core deficits, such as social communication skills or language, rather than on categorical clinical diagnoses, to then design and direct interventions toward the specific areas of impairment.

TREATMENT OF AUTISM SPECTRUM DISORDER IS NOT YET ETIOLOGY-BASED

Behavioral intervention is the mainstay of treatment for core deficits in ASD, with structured, high-intensity, and autism-directed interventions associated with better outcomes.[32] Under the umbrella term of "ABA" or applied behavioral analysis, falls several effective and distinct methods.[33] The traditional ABA program, based on the work of Lovaas and colleagues,[34] is intensive and individualized, with the use of discrete trials to teach simple skills that then can build to more complex skills. Discrete trial therapy is particularly effective for modifying problem behaviors and for teaching specific cognitive and academic skills. More naturalistic and play-based treatments include pivotal response treatment and Floortime. The only medications approved by the Food and Drug Administration (FDA) for ASD are the atypical antipsychotics risperidone and aripiprazole. Both are approved for the treatment of irritability, defined by physical aggression and tantrum behavior. Their primary, sometimes dose-limiting, side effects include weight gain and sedation. Recent guidelines published by Volkmar and colleagues[35] emphasize that pharmacologic treatment can, particularly by reducing comorbidities and aberrant behaviors, "increase the ability of persons with ASD to profit from interventions and to remain in less restrictive environments." In other words, by improving intrusive or maladaptive behaviors, pharmacotherapy can facilitate a child's ability to engage in and learn from educational and behavioral interventions for their core ASD symptoms.

With the advances in our knowledge about genetic etiologies of ASD and the identification of molecular pathways that may be aberrant in these disorders, there is hope for pharmacologic and behavioral targets that may prevent the development of, or attenuate the impact of, the disease. Two such examples of such treatment targets are provided in the following sections.

TARGETED TREATMENT EXAMPLE 1: TUBEROUS SCLEROSIS COMPLEX

The genes responsible for TSC (*TSC 1* and *2*) encode for proteins that regulate the mTORC1 protein complex. Mammalian target of rapamycin (mTOR) is critical for protein synthesis, cell growth, and axon formation. Inactivation of the TSC genes causes an upregulation of this mTORC1 pathway, resulting in an increase in protein synthesis, aberrant axon formation, and tumor growth. In the past 5 years, based on the known mechanisms of *TSC1/2* regulation of the mTOR pathway, mTOR inhibitors have been studied extensively in mouse models of TSC. These studies have revealed that mTOR inhibitors can reverse the cognitive and social impairments found in adult mouse models after surprisingly short courses of treatment.[36,37] In turn, these promising findings have inspired the investigation of mTOR inhibitors, such as rapamycin, in patients with TSC. Everolimus, an mTOR inhibitor, is now FDA approved for reduction of subependymal giant cell astrocytomas (SEGAs) in children with TSC.[38] Now, with safety profiles established, several international studies are investigating the use of mTOR inhibitors for improving the cognitive delays and behavioral deficits found in children with TSC.[39]

Additionally, because TSC is often diagnosed in utero due to cardiac rhabdomyomas or SEGAs, these infants can be studied prospectively for the evaluation of early developmental trajectories and risk markers for ASD, providing an opportunity to identify common behavioral and developmental characteristics within TSC that could serve as targets for behavioral intervention. In the first large-scale prospective study of development in TSC, infants demonstrated delays in visually mediated behaviors (visual attention, disengagement of attention) in the first year of life. Furthermore, declines in nonverbal cognition in the second year of life predicted symptoms of ASD at 24 and 36 months. This developmental slowing in nonverbal cognition is a trajectory that has not been previously reported in other high-risk groups and, in turn, may represent a TSC-specific developmental trajectory.[31] Based on this finding, the group is now investigating whether a behavioral intervention that targets nonverbal communication (such as visual attention to social information) in the second year of life can prevent the development of ASD in TSC. Ultimately, for infants with TSC, a combination of targeted molecular and behavioral treatments may attenuate or even prevent the neurodevelopmental disabilities that occur early in development.

TARGETED TREATMENT EXAMPLE 2: DUP15Q SYNDROME

Duplication of 15q11.2-q13, or Dup15q syndrome, provides another timely example of the clinical utility of genetic testing for targeted management and, eventually, treatment. Duplications of the 15q11.2-q13 region of maternal origin were first associated with ASD more than 15 years ago, and now these duplications are among the most common CNVs associated with ASD and related neurodevelopmental disorders. Duplication of this region leads to the overexpression of several genes, most notably UBE3A (E3 ubiquitin ligase gene) and a cluster of receptor subunits for the neurotransmitter $GABA_A$. There are 2 major structural versions of this CNV: isodicentric chromosome 15 (idic[15]) and interstitial duplication of chromosome 15 (int.dup[15]). Over the past several years, a national alliance of families affected by this CNV, known as the Dup15q Alliance, has been collecting a registry of patients with the goal of advancing both clinical care and scientific investigation of the disorder. There are now more than 400 patients with clinical data entered into the registry with varying duplication types. Through collaborative efforts, studies have identified neurobiological, developmental, and behavioral features of Dup15q syndrome.

In addition to ASD, this CNV is characterized by early onset of epilepsy, profound hypotonia in early infancy, moderate to severe ID, and, in a subgroup of children, excessive beta-range activity (15–30 Hz) on clinical EEG, with overall clinical severity greater in the idic(15) cases.[40–42] The excessive beta oscillations likely represent an electrophysiological signature of the upregulation of GABA$_A$ receptor genes contained in the duplicated chromosomal region.

As a result of data gathered from the national Dup15q syndrome registry, a recent large cohort study of 95 children with Dup15q syndrome sought to identify common characteristics and potential treatments for epilepsy in this population.[43] Investigators found that epilepsy was much more prevalent in the idic(15) cases than in the int.dup15 cases, multiple seizure types (both generalized and focal) were identified, and that infantile spasms were common, reported in 42% of cases. Both broad-spectrum and focal antiepileptic medications (such as carbamazepine) demonstrated efficacy for seizure reduction, suggesting a multifocal etiology to the epilepsy. Importantly, GABAergic medications, such as benzodiazepines, were relatively ineffective, likely because of abnormalities in gamma-aminobutyric acid (GABA) transmission in the setting of overexpression of GABA-A receptor genes in the 15q region. This key discovery led to the recommendation that benzodiazepine medications, which are commonly used in the epilepsy population as a whole, be avoided in this genetic subgroup.

In parallel to the efforts in epilepsy, investigators have begun to better characterize the social communication phenotype in Dup15q syndrome. Given the significant hypotonia present in these children, there is particular interest in the effects of motor delays on social communication development, particularly eye contact, nonverbal communication, expressive language, and play. Elucidation of the nature of the core deficits of ASD in Dup15q syndrome will facilitate the design and implementation of targeted behavioral interventions that will specifically benefit this subgroup within the autism spectrum.

SUMMARY

Genetic testing for children with ASD is no longer confined to the realm of academia. As cohorts of children with genetic variants and syndromes associated with ASD are identified, common themes across disorders and unique features within disorders can be identified that will ultimately guide targeted interventions rooted in both biological mechanisms and behavior.

REFERENCES

1. American Psychiatric Association. Diagnostic and statistical manual of mental disorders: DSM-5. 5th edition. Washington, DC: American Psychiatric Association; 2013.
2. Mazefsky CA, McPartland JC, Gastgeb HZ, et al. Brief report: comparability of DSM-IV and DSM-5 ASD research samples. J Autism Dev Disord 2013;43: 1236–42.
3. McPartland JC, Reichow B, Volkmar FR. Sensitivity and specificity of proposed DSM-5 diagnostic criteria for autism spectrum disorder. J Am Acad Child Adolesc Psychiatry 2012;51:368–83.
4. Fombonne E. Epidemiology of pervasive developmental disorders. Pediatr Res 2009;65:591–8.

5. Bolte S, Duketis E, Poustka F, et al. Sex differences in cognitive domains and their clinical correlates in higher-functioning autism spectrum disorders. Autism 2011; 15:497–511.

6. Hattier MA, Matson JL, Tureck K, et al. The effects of gender and age on repetitive and/or restricted behaviors and interests in adults with autism spectrum disorders and intellectual disability. Res Dev Disabil 2011;32:2346–51.

7. Szatmari P, Liu XQ, Goldberg J, et al. Sex differences in repetitive stereotyped behaviors in autism: implications for genetic liability. Am J Med Genet B Neuropsychiatr Genet 2012;159B:5–12.

8. Dworzynski K, Ronald A, Bolton P, et al. How different are girls and boys above and below the diagnostic threshold for autism spectrum disorders? J Am Acad Child Adolesc Psychiatry 2012;51:788–97.

9. Solomon M, Miller M, Taylor SL, et al. Autism symptoms and internalizing psychopathology in girls and boys with autism spectrum disorders. J Autism Dev Disord 2012;42:48–59.

10. Baird G, Simonoff E, Pickles A, et al. Prevalence of disorders of the autism spectrum in a population cohort of children in South Thames: the special needs and autism project (SNAP). Lancet 2006;368:210–5.

11. Kasari C, Brady N, Lord C, et al. Assessing the minimally verbal school-aged child with autism spectrum disorder. Autism Res 2013;6:479–93.

12. Smalley SL, Asarnow RF, Spence MA. Autism and genetics. A decade of research. Arch Gen Psychiatry 1988;45:953–61.

13. Ozonoff S, Young GS, Carter A, et al. Recurrence risk for autism spectrum disorders: a baby siblings research consortium study. Pediatrics 2011;128:e488–95.

14. Sandin S, Lichtenstein P, Kuja-Halkola R, et al. The familial risk of autism. JAMA 2014;311:1770–7.

15. Zwaigenbaum L. Advances in the early detection of autism. Curr Opin Neurol 2010;23:97–102.

16. Neale BM, Kou Y, Liu L, et al. Patterns and rates of exonic de novo mutations in autism spectrum disorders. Nature 2012;485:242–5.

17. O'Roak BJ, Vives L, Girirajan S, et al. Sporadic autism exomes reveal a highly interconnected protein network of de novo mutations. Nature 2012;485:246–50.

18. Malhotra D, Sebat J. CNVs: harbingers of a rare variant revolution in psychiatric genetics. Cell 2012;148:1223–41.

19. Heil KM, Schaaf CP. The genetics of autism spectrum disorders—a guide for clinicians. Curr Psychiatry Rep 2013;15:334.

20. Sanders SJ, Murtha MT, Gupta AR, et al. De novo mutations revealed by whole-exome sequencing are strongly associated with autism. Nature 2012;485:237–41.

21. Yu TW, Chahrour MH, Coulter ME, et al. Using whole-exome sequencing to identify inherited causes of autism. Neuron 2013;77:259–73.

22. Ronemus M, Iossifov I, Levy D, et al. The role of de novo mutations in the genetics of autism spectrum disorders. Nat Rev Genet 2014;15:133–41.

23. Pinto D, Delaby E, Merico D, et al. Convergence of genes and cellular pathways dysregulated in autism spectrum disorders. Am J Hum Genet 2014;94:677–94.

24. Filipek PA, Accardo PJ, Ashwal S, et al. Practice parameter: screening and diagnosis of autism: report of the Quality Standards Subcommittee of the American Academy of Neurology and the Child Neurology Society. Neurology 2000;55: 468–79.

25. Schaefer GB, Mendelsohn NJ. Clinical genetics evaluation in identifying the etiology of autism spectrum disorders: 2013 guideline revisions. Genet Med 2013;15: 399–407.

26. Ekinci O, Arman AR, Isik U, et al. EEG abnormalities and epilepsy in autistic spectrum disorders: clinical and familial correlates. Epilepsy Behav 2010;17: 178–82.

27. Spence SJ, Schneider MT. The role of epilepsy and epileptiform EEGs in autism spectrum disorders. Pediatr Res 2009;65:599–606.

28. Viscidi EW, Triche EW, Pescosolido MF, et al. Clinical characteristics of children with autism spectrum disorder and co-occurring epilepsy. PLoS One 2013;8: e67797.

29. Iossifov I, Ronemus M, Levy D, et al. De novo gene disruptions in children on the autistic spectrum. Neuron 2012;74:285–99.

30. Rosti RO, Sadek AA, Vaux KK, et al. The genetic landscape of autism spectrum disorders. Dev Med Child Neurol 2014;56:12–8.

31. Jeste SS, Wu JY, Senturk D, et al. Early developmental trajectories associated with ASD in infants with tuberous sclerosis complex. Neurology 2014;83:160–8.

32. National Research Council (U.S.). Committee on Educational Interventions for Children with Autism. Educating children with autism. Washington, DC: National Academy Press; 2001.

33. Vismara LA, Rogers SJ. Behavioral treatments in autism spectrum disorder: what do we know? Annu Rev Clin Psychol 2010;6:447–68.

34. Lovaas OI, Schreibman L, Koegel RL. A behavior modification approach to the treatment of autistic children. J Autism Child Schizophr 1974;4:111–29.

35. Volkmar F, Siegel M, Woodbury-Smith M, et al. Practice parameter for the assessment and treatment of children and adolescents with autism spectrum disorder. J Am Acad Child Adolesc Psychiatry 2014;53:237–57.

36. Tsai PT, Greene-Colozzi E, Goto J, et al. Prenatal rapamycin results in early and late behavioral abnormalities in wildtype C57BL/6 mice. Behav Genet 2013;43: 51–9.

37. Ehninger D, Han S, Shilyansky C, et al. Reversal of learning deficits in a Tsc2+/− mouse model of tuberous sclerosis. Nat Med 2008;14:843–8.

38. Jozwiak J, Sontowska I, Ploski R. Frequency of TSC1 and TSC2 mutations in American, British, Polish and Taiwanese populations. Mol Med Rep 2013;8: 909–13.

39. Sahin M. Targeted treatment trials for tuberous sclerosis and autism: no longer a dream. Curr Opin Neurobiol 2012;22:895–901.

40. Urraca N, Cleary J, Brewer V, et al. The interstitial duplication 15q11.2-q13 syndrome includes autism, mild facial anomalies and a characteristic EEG Signature. Autism Res 2013;6:268–79.

41. Battaglia A. The inv dup (15) or idic (15) syndrome (Tetrasomy 15q). Orphanet J Rare Dis 2008;3:30.

42. Bolton PF, Park RJ, Higgins JN, et al. Neuro-epileptic determinants of autism spectrum disorders in tuberous sclerosis complex. Brain 2002;125:1247–55.

43. Conant KD, Finucane B, Cleary N, et al. A survey of seizures and current treatments in 15q duplication syndrome. Epilepsia 2014;55:396–402.

Comparative Analysis of Self-Injury in People with Psychopathology or Neurodevelopmental Disorders

Liam Crapper, BSc[a,b], Carl Ernst, PhD[a,b,c,d],*

KEYWORDS

- Self-injurious behavior • Neurodevelopmental disorders
- Borderline personality disorder • Opioids • Dopamine

KEY POINTS

- Self-injury (SI) is a harmful behavior present in persons with neurodevelopmental disorders (NDDs) such as Lesch-Nyhan syndrome, and those with psychopathological conditions such as major depressive disorder or borderline personality disorder.
- There appears to be a genetic underpinning to SI, given its prevalence in monogenic disorders and heritable psychiatric conditions.
- There is convergent evidence regarding the functions of SI in NDD and psychopathology.
- Between NDD and psychopathology, the roles of neurotransmitter systems in self-injurious behaviors (SIBs) converge on the opioid signaling system, diverge with respect to serotonergic signaling, and show mixed effects on dopaminergic and nucleoside signaling.
- Further study of commonalities between SI in psychopathology and NDDs will increase our understanding of this challenging behavior and may lead to improved treatment of SIBs.

INTRODUCTION

Self-injurious behaviors (SIBs) are observed in people with neurodevelopmental disorders (NDDs) and those with psychopathological conditions, although it is unclear

Conflict of interest statement: The authors have nothing to disclose.
[a] Integrated Program in Neuroscience, McGill University, Montreal, Quebec H3A 0G4, Canada; [b] McGill Group for Suicide Studies, Douglas Mental Health University Institute, Montreal, Quebec H4H 1R3, Canada; [c] Department of Psychiatry, McGill University, Montreal, Quebec H3A 0G4, Canada; [d] Department of Human Genetics, McGill University, Montreal, Quebec H3A 0G4, Canada
* Corresponding author. Douglas Hospital Research Institute, 6875 LaSalle Boulevard, Frank Common Building, Room 2101.2, Verdun, Quebec H4H 1R3, Canada.
E-mail address: carl.ernst@mcgill.ca

Pediatr Clin N Am 62 (2015) 619–631
http://dx.doi.org/10.1016/j.pcl.2015.03.001
0031-3955/15/$ – see front matter Crown Copyright © 2015 Published by Elsevier Inc. All rights reserved.

pediatric.theclinics.com

whether the biological bases of SIBs in these 2 populations are similar. Evidence of similarities between the SIBs observed in patients with psychopathology and NDDs at the behavioral and molecular level, reviewed and analyzed here, suggests that the 2 fields of research could establish a synergistic relationship. Results from defined molecular models of genetic disorders could inform drug development and the basic biology of self-injury (SI) in psychiatric populations, while results from clinical research taking advantage of the larger populations with psychopathological disorders could inform behavioral and pharmacological treatment of NDD patients.

Why might SI in the NDD population inform the underlying causes of SI in a psychiatric, nonintellectually disabled population? SIB in NDDs is often associated with particular syndromes,[1] many of which are linked to disorders caused by mutations in single genes or deletions of small parts of a chromosome, and can be studied in animal models or in vitro. The best example of this is Lesch-Nyhan disease (LND) whereby mutations in *HPRT1* are associated with SIBs in almost all cases.[2] As genetics are likely an important part of the complex etiology of SIBs in psychiatric populations,[3] investigating the genes and molecular pathways that are altered in disorders like LND may reveal important information about molecular biology of SIBs in psychiatric populations.

SIBs are broadly defined as any nonnormative behavior performed with the intent of causing physical self-harm without the intent to die.[4] Although diverse terminology is used to describe these behaviors, SIB is often used when describing NDD populations, whereas nonsuicidal self-injury (NSSI) is used when describing behaviors in psychiatric or community samples.[5] For simplicity, SIB is used throughout this article when referring to SI in either population. A wide variety of definitions of SIBs are also used, and behaviors considered self-injurious in some studies are not in others. In part this accounts for the wide diversity of prevalence estimates observed, discussed in greater detail later. The *Diagnostic and Statistical Manual of Mental Disorders* (5th edition) (DSM-5) defines NSSI in part as "intentional self-inflicted damage to the surface of his or her body of a sort likely to induce bleeding, bruising, or pain (eg, cutting, burning, stabbing, hitting, excessive rubbing), with the expectation that the injury will lead to only minor or moderate physical harm."[6] This definition is used in this review.

There is not always a clear diagnostic boundary between NDD and psychopathology, in that persons with NDDs may have comorbid psychiatric disorders and subjects presenting primarily with psychopathology may have undiagnosed mild or moderate intellectual disability (ID). For example, a large population-based study in Scotland found that 40.9% of patients with ID met clinical diagnostic criteria for mental illness, and 15.7% met DSM-IV-TR (DSM 4th edition, text revision) diagnostic criteria.[7] In addition, patients presenting with SI or other related behavioral problems are more likely to have psychiatric conditions than controls matched for level of disability.[8] In other words, not all subjects with SIB have a diagnosed psychopathology.[9]

EPIDEMIOLOGY OF SELF-INJURIOUS BEHAVIORS

Prevalence estimates of SIBs vary widely within and between psychopathology and NDD populations. In persons with NDDs the prevalence of SIB is disorder dependent, and estimates from populations with mixed NDD diagnoses range from 1.7% to 41%.[10] In some forms of NDD (see later discussion), nearly 100% of patients show SIB. However, a 2003 meta-analysis examining risk factors for SIB in NDD suggested that degree of ID, autism, and deficiencies in communication are the strongest risk markers of SI,[11] and are thus more prevalent in NDD populations with these attributes.

A second meta-analysis found that SIBs were increased in NDD subjects with urinary incontinence, pain related to cerebral palsy, chronic sleep problems, or visual impairment.[12] SIBs can be documented as early as 6 months, and tend to be fully expressed by 5 years of age.[13] It is interesting that unlike other measures of aggression, SIBs do not decline with age in NDD populations.[14]

In the non-NDD population, SIB appears to be particularly prevalent in younger people. In a random sample of American adults, Klonsky[15] reported a lifetime prevalence of SIB of 4.8% in those older than 30, and of 18.9% in those 30 years or younger, while the Child & Adolescent Self-harm in Europe (CASE) Study[16] reported an 8% lifetime incidence of SI in a random sample of the population. Longitudinal studies in youth[17,18] and college students[19] have shown that current or prior depression and parental depression are strong predictors of SIB in both age groups. Current depressive symptoms, diagnosis with an internalizing disorder (such as depression or borderline personality disorder), and diagnosis with an eating disorder were significantly associated with SIBs in another large cohort of university undergraduates.[20]

DESCRIPTION OF SELF-INJURIOUS BEHAVIORS IN SPECIFIC DISORDERS
Lesch-Nyhan Disease

LND is caused by a mutation in *HPRT1*, which encodes hypoxanthine-guanine phosphoribosyltransferase (HPRT), an enzyme required for the salvage of the purines hypoxanthine and guanine, and is estimated to occur in 1 in 380,000 live births.[21] The amount of functional HPRT protein varies depending on the type of mutation (eg, a single DNA base change or a complete deletion of the gene) seen in LND patients, and a strong correlation exists between residual HPRT activity and disease severity. NDD without SIB generally occurs in between 1.5% and 8% HPRT1 activity, and SI occurs in nearly 100% of patients with less than 1.5% activity.[22] Of note, there is variation in disease expression including SIBs, even in members of the same family with the identical *HPRT1* mutation, suggesting environmental effects and an interaction with genetic background.[23]

Patients with LND demonstrate a wide variety of SIBs. Among the most common are biting of the lips and fingers, sticking out an arm, leg, or head when passing through a doorway, and head banging, but people with LND appear to use whatever form of SIB is available to them.[24] LND is also associated with increased aggression toward others, expressed through hitting, spitting, scratching, and swearing.[2] Parents of LND patients report that SIBs increase during times of stress and boredom, and independent observation of boys younger than 5 years with LND documented increased SIBs during times of reduced social contact.[25] An immediate prophylactic measure for children with LND is thus to increase social contact and reduce boredom.

Smith-Magenis Syndrome

Smith-Magenis syndrome (SMS) is a developmental disorder associated with abnormal facial development, hearing loss, expressive speech delay, short stature, brachydactyly, sleep disturbances, and variable levels of ID, believed to occur in from 1:15,000 to 1:25,000 live births.[26] SMS is usually caused by deletions in the 17p11.2 region. However, mutation of the gene RAI1, a transcription factor whose function remains largely unknown, is sufficient to cause most of the observed phenotypes, including SIBs.[27] Similarly to LND, the prevalence of SIB approaches 100%.[28] The forms of SIB most commonly demonstrated in SMS are biting, hitting, picking at fingers or toenails (onychotillomania), and the insertion of foreign objects into body orifices (polyembolokoilamania).[29] SMS patients also demonstrate a characteristic "self-hugging," tightly wrapping their arms around their torso and squeezing, which appears to be benign and exacerbated by happiness.[30]

Cri du Chat Syndrome

Cri du chat syndrome (CdCS) is a developmental disorder named for a distinctive cat-like cry observed in many infants with the disorder. It is caused by a large deletion on chromosome 5p, although the genes responsible for the behavioral symptoms have not yet been confirmed.[31] CdCS is characterized by intellectual disability, limited language development, sleep disturbances, hypersensitivity to auditory stimuli, and SIB,[32] with prevelance estimates ranging from 1:15,000 to 1:50,000 live births.[33,34]

SIB occurs in 76.8%[1]–92%[35] of patients with CdCS, and is predominantly expressed as hitting the head with another body part, hitting the head with an object, vomiting and rumination, scratching, and self-biting. CdCS patients also display aggressive behaviors toward others, including hair pulling, hitting, and throwing objects, as is seen in LND.[35]

Borderline Personality Disorder

Borderline personality disorder (BPD) is a psychopathology characterized by pervasive instability of affect, interpersonal relationships, identity, and self-image,[6] and is a significant risk factor for SIB.[36] Indeed one of the diagnostic criteria for BPD is SI or attempted suicide, and prevalence estimates for these behaviors are 17% to 80% and 46% to 92%, respectively, in this population. People with BPD engage in self-cutting and burning at a higher rate than other populations engaging in SIB but also use biting, banging, and needle sticking, and are more likely to endorse suicide prevention and self-punishment as reasons for SIB.[37]

Major Depressive Disorder

Major depressive disorder (MDD) is strongly associated with SIBs, and is the risk factor most consistently associated with SIB in both referred and community samples of adolescents and adults.[38] Studies of depression have observed rates of SIBs (recorded as NSSI) of between 9%[39] and 30%,[40] while another study found that more than 70% of hospitalized self-injurers had depression.[41] In the context of depression, SIB most commonly expresses as cutting, scratching, and burning,[39] and has been associated with negative self-esteem and heightened emotional reactivity.[38,42]

CONCEPTUALIZATION OF SELF-INJURIOUS BEHAVIORS

SIB in non-NDD populations is predominantly conceptualized using the 4-factor model proposed by Nock and Prinstein.[43] In this model, SIB is thought of along 2 dichotomous scales: automatic (ie, intrapersonal) versus social (ie, interpersonal), and positive (ie, increasing a desired stimulus) or negative (ie, decreasing an aversive stimulus); thus, stopping negative emotions is an example of an automatic negative function, whereas increasing attention from others would be a social positive function. Results from studies using interviews and surveys have largely supported this framework, although it has been debated whether these functional groups delineate distinct clinical populations.[44,45] The most common motivation for SIBs in community samples and patients with psychopathologies appears to be autonomic negative, but most people endorse multiple reasons for SIBs. Some commonly cited reasons are "to cope with feelings of depression" (83%) or "distraction from unwanted memories" (62%), "expressing frustration" (73%), and "self-punishment" (50%).[46] Following SIB participants tend to report relief, or a decrease in negative emotions, but an increase in self-aware emotions such as shame and guilt.[38,46]

Several studies have suggested that non-NDD people with SIB have a heightened response to stressful situations,[47] which can be reduced by imagining SI.[48,49] Interestingly this stress reduction has also been observed in self-injuring macaques, in which self-biting was seen to significantly reduce an accelerated heartbeat in a subpopulation of monkeys.[50] Not all studies have supported these findings. Kaess and colleagues[51] did not see evidence of increased heart rate in a sample of 14 self-injuring patients compared with 14 normal controls when subjected to standard psychosocial stressors. However, self-injuring populations self-report greater psychological stress from these tests, even without an increase in physiological response.[52]

The operant model of SIB, which is commonly used for subjects with NDDs, classifies the rationale for SIBs along similar axes to the 4-factor model proposed for subjects without an NDD; however, the autonomic positive and negative categories are collapsed into one. In one large study, 152 NDD patients were assessed for social positive, social negative, and autonomic reinforcement of SIBs. Behavioral therapy using one or all of these models reduced SIB in 95% of patients, and suggested that 38% of subjects used SIB for social negative reasons, 26% for social positive, and 25% for autonomic.[53] A more recent review of research has supported the idea that social functions are the predominant mode of reinforcement for SIB.[54]

SIB functions also correlate with the severity of disability, with people with a mild to moderate NDD exhibiting more outwardly directed aggression and challenging behaviors, and people with more severe NDD exhibiting more self-directed aggression and SIB.[55] Subsequent research has suggested that people with severe NDD are more likely to use SIBs to obtain tangible items and escape social demands more often than people with mild to moderate ID.[56]

Fig. 1 provides a summary of some differences between NDD SIB and psychiatric NSSI.

	NDD-SIB	Psychiatric-NSSI
Prevalence	1.7-41% Up to 100% in Lesch-Nyhan Syndrome	4.8-18.9% Up to 80% in Borderline Personality Disorder
Risk factors	Degree of ID Autism Communication problems	Young age Internalizing disorder Parental depression
Specific disorders	Lesch-Nyhan Disease Smith Magenis Syndrome Cri du Chat Syndrome	Major Depressive Disorder Borderline Personality Disorder
Functions	64% social reinforcement 25% autonomic enforcement	Decreases negative emotions increase self-aware emotions

Fig. 1. Comparison of clinical factors for self-injurious behaviors (SIB) and nonsuicidal self-injury (NSSI) in persons with a neurodevelopmental disorder (NDD) and those with a psychiatric disorder. ID, intellectual disability.

NEUROTRANSMITTERS IMPLICATED IN SELF-INJURIOUS BEHAVIORS
Dopamine

The involvement of the dopamine (DA) system has been most strongly implicated in SIB through its role in the pathogenesis of LND. Postmortem brains from patients with LND show up to a 60% decrease in DA concentrations compared with controls.[57] This decrease seems to be the result of a deficiency in DA synthesis rather than decrease in the number of dopaminergic neurons.[58,59] These reductions in DA synthesis are accompanied by large increases in cell-surface expression of D1 and D2 receptors in the putamen and caudate.[60]

Direct evidence for the involvement of the dopaminergic system in psychopathology-associated SIB has been limited.[61] However, depressed suicide attempters, some of whom had the intent to die and so do not fall into strict SIB criteria used here, have significantly lower levels of homovanillic acid (HVA), one of the primary metabolites of DA, in their cerebrospinal fluid[62] and urine[63] than normal controls or affective controls. These findings and others have led to the proposal of an addiction model of SIB, which suggests that SI leads to the release of DA and the stimulation of the reward system. SIB has several characteristics of dependent behavior, including a requirement of increased severity or frequency to achieve the same effect and perseverance despite negative consequences[46]; however, cravings for SIB seem to be more context dependent than the cravings observed in substance addiction.[64]

Serotonin

The serotonin (5-HT) pathway has been suspected to play a role in SIB, largely because of its involvement in impulsivity and aggression, which have been associated with SIB,[65] and its well-established connection to depression and suicide.[66] However, the relevance of self-report impulsivity has been questioned, and findings on experimental measures of impulsivity have been inconsistent.[67,68] Patients receiving treatment with selective serotonin reuptake inhibitors (SSRIs) show little change in SIBs.[69]

Trials using SSRIs to limit SIBs in NDD have yielded mixed results. Fluoxetine has been demonstrated to reduce SIB in autism but citalopram has not, raising questions of off-target effects.[70] Risperidone, an atypical antipsychotic that antagonizes DA and 5-HT receptors, has also been repeatedly shown to reduce challenging behaviors, including SIB in patients with NDDs, autism,[71] or LND.[72]

Nucleoside Signaling

Signaling by the neuromodulatory purine nucleoside adenosine (Ade) has been hypothesized to play in important role in the pathology of LND. Ade receptors are decreased in lymphoblasts from LND patients, and the elevated hypoxanthine concentrations present in these cells have been shown to interfere with the normal transport of adenosine.[73] Although HPRT dysfunction disrupts many neurological pathways, the lack of HPRT function seems to be requisite for the SIB phenotype. For instance, although the dopaminergic system has been implicated in SIBs in LND, dopaminergic dysfunction may not suffice to cause SI, as is evidenced by the absence of SIBs in patients with tyrosine hydroxylase deficiencies or mutations in dopamine receptors.

Ade has not been studied in SIB in the context of psychopathology per se; however, adenosine signaling though the A1 and A2A receptors has been associated with depression and anxiety,[74] and regular consumption of caffeine, an adenosine receptor antagonist, has been associated with increased anxiety but a reduction in depression and suicide attempts.[75] Adenosine antagonists might provide an intriguing avenue for the treatment of SIBs in both psychiatric and NDD populations.[76]

Endogenous Opioids

Reduction in pain sensitivity, which is frequently reported by people engaging in SIB, implies involvement of the endogenous opioid (EO) system.[77] One model suggests that people who engage in SIBs have lower baseline levels of EOs, and that SIB causes the activation of the EO system. This process leads to relief from negative emotions,[78] which is the most common reason reported for engaging in the SIB.[46] Consistent with this hypothesis, patients with BPD were shown to have increased μ-opioid receptor availability during a baseline state and increased occupancy during induced sadness.[79] In a second study, cerebrospinal fluid from group of subjects who repeatedly engaged in SIBs was compared to that of a diagnostically matched control group, and was found to contain significantly lower levels of the EOs β-endorphin and met-enkephalin.[80] Together, these studies support the idea that people with psychopathology show low baseline levels of EO and may engage in SIB, in part to stimulate this system.

Reduced pain sensitivity is less consistent in patients with NDD,[81] in whom SIBs may in fact be associated with increased nociception.[82] A systematic review of 10 randomized controlled trials of opioid antagonists to treat SIB in patients with NDD (where ID ranged from mild to profound, with 40% having an autism diagnosis)[83] revealed that 8 of the 10 reported positive results and opioid antagonist treatments reduced episodes of SI in 50% of the subjects. Opioid signaling may be a convergence point for SIBs for persons with an NDD or psychopathology; however, the dynamics of this signaling, and the baseline states, may differ between these populations.

Interactions Between Signaling Pathways

When considering complex behaviors such as SIB it is important to remember that the neurotransmitter systems do not act independently, but interact with each other in a myriad of ways, many of which we do not yet fully understand. For instance adenosine A2A receptors form heterodimers with DA D2 receptors, and they reciprocally oppose each other's functions, including D2-mediated enkephalin release.[84] Adenosine signaling through both the A1 and A2A receptors is analgesic[85] and reduces symptoms of opiate withdrawal,[86] while opiates may increase the degradation of adenosine.[87] Meanwhile the EO system bidirectionally modulates the dopaminergic system (**Fig. 2**).[88] This level of interconnectivity indicates that one neurotransmitter system may alter its signaling to compensate for another. Although this is likely to be beneficial in many instances it is possible that overcompensation, perhaps caused by genetic predisposition, or deficits in multiple systems, could drive the SIB phenotype, which would suggest that combinations of pharmacological treatments may be more effective than any one alone.

DISCUSSION

The authors have reviewed the literature on SIB in populations with NDDs or psychopathologies, both of which are at heightened risk for SI. Some of the features of SI in these 2 populations were compared and contrasted, and a cursory analysis of the molecules that might underlie them was performed. The authors suggest that studying both the behavior and biology of SI in either population may inform the other and may help to prevent the development of SIBs in children who display them. There remain several caveats, however, as outlined here.

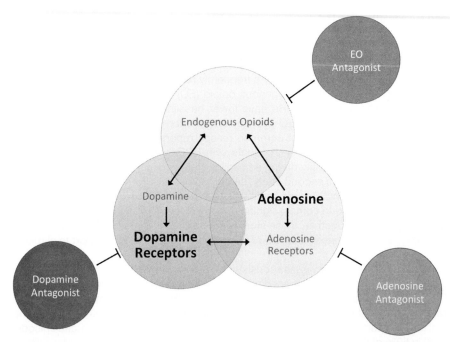

Fig. 2. Possible interaction of neurotransmitter systems in the context of self-injury. The Endogenous opioid (EO), adenosine, and dopamine systems are tightly intertwined with one another. Red typeface indicates elements of a system that are hypofunctional in the context of SIB, while systems in black are overactive. Arrows indicate the most likely directions of causation. Outer circles indicate possible therapeutic options.

Caveat 1

Our understanding of the epidemiology of SIB is lacking. The ranges of estimates for the prevalence or comorbidities of SIBs vary widely. This variation stems in part from the differences in definitions used, which will hopefully be resolved by the inclusion of NSSI in the DSM-5, and in part from the range of populations used, for instance studies performed on psychiatric outpatients or community samples. Accurate information on SIB epidemiology will require prospective longitudinal studies in clearly defined populations.

Caveat 2

We have a poor understanding of the reasons people self-injure. SIBs seem to serve several functions, such as increasing and decreasing autonomic or social factors.[43] In the context of psychopathology, subjects often self-report several reasons for SIB, but this form of reporting requires that participants have the insight to understand their true motivations for engaging in SIB. Given, for example, the discrepancies between self-reported and experimental impulsivity,[67] the reliability of these data are questionable. Evidence from studies in NDDs, on the other hand, have shown that behavioral therapy can be an effective means of reducing SIB once reinforcing factors have been identified,[53] and it is likely that this is true in persons with psychopathologies. Future studies should attempt to experimentally determine the triggering factors in individuals with psychopathology beyond simply "anxiety," with the aim of improving the efficacy of behavioral treatments in persons with psychopathology who self-injure.

Caveat 3

Studies attempting to use nonbehavioral treatments based on the suspected biological underpinnings of SIB show little efficacy. Dopamine and serotonin, which are among the most studied systems in MDD and BPD, have the least consistent evidence connecting them to SIB for these 2 psychiatric disorders. DA has been implicated in SIB through its connections to LND and "reward" in depression, but treatments targeting DA systems have not prevented SIBs in these or other disorders. Similarly, 5-HT was suspected to be involved in SIBs because of its well-established connection to risk factors for SIBs such as impulsivity and aggression; however, treatment with SSRIs does not reduce SIBs in people with depression or NDDs.[69] The most promising biological basis for SIB would seem to be the EO system. EOs might explain the analgesia and affect changes seen during SIB,[78] and treatments targeting EOs have been shown to reduce SIBs in NDDs.[83] The authors suggest that future work might focus on further characterization of the EO system in SIB, and on the utility of EO antagonists in the treatment of SIB in persons with psychopathologies.

SIB remains poorly understood, but collaboration between researchers studying NDDs and others studying psychopathologies may be a worthwhile avenue moving forward.

REFERENCES

1. Arron K, Oliver C, Moss J, et al. The prevalence and phenomenology of self-injurious and aggressive behaviour in genetic syndromes. J Intellect Disabil Res 2011;55(2):109–20.
2. Schretlen DJ, Ward J, Meyer SM, et al. Behavioral aspects of Lesch-Nyhan disease and its variants. Dev Med Child Neurol 2005;47:673–7.
3. Ernst C, Morton CC, Gusella JF. Self-injurious behaviours in people with and without intellectual delay: implications for the genetics of suicide. Int J Neuropsychopharmacol 2010;13:527–8.
4. Nock M. Self-injury. Annu Rev Clin Psychol 2010;6:339–402.
5. Bloom C, Holly S, Miller A. Self-injurious behavior vs. nonsuicidal self-injury. Crisis 2012;33:106–18.
6. American Psychiatric Association. Diagnostic and statistical manual of mental disorders: DSM-5. Washington (DC): American Psychiatric Association; 2013. Available at: http://dsm.psychiatryonline.org/book.aspx?bookid=556.
7. Cooper SA, Smiley E, Morrison J, et al. Mental ill-health in adults with intellectual disabilities: prevalence and associated factors. Br J Psychiatry 2007;190(1):27–35.
8. Myrbakk E, von Tetzchner S. Psychiatric disorders and behavior problems in people with intellectual disability. Res Dev Disabil 2008;29(4):316–32.
9. Davies LE, Oliver C. The purported association between depression, aggression, and self-injury in people with intellectual disability: a critical review of the literature. Am J Intellect Dev Disabil 2014;119(5):452–71.
10. Cooper SA, Smiley E, Allan LM, et al. Adults with intellectual disabilities: prevalence, incidence and remission of self-injurious behaviour, and related factors. J Intellect Disabil Res 2009;53(3):200–16.
11. McClintock K, Hall S, Oliver C. Risk markers associated with challenging behaviours in people with intellectual disabilities: a meta-analytic study. J Intellect Disabil Res 2003;47(6):405–16.
12. de Winter CF, Jansen AA, Evenhuis HM. Physical conditions and challenging behaviour in people with intellectual disability: a systematic review. J Intellect Disabil Res 2011;55(7):675–98.

13. Schroeder SR, Marquis JG, Reese RM, et al. Risk factors for self-injury, aggression, and stereotyped behavior among young children at risk for intellectual and developmental disabilities. Am J Intellect Dev Disabil 2014;119(4):351–70.

14. Cohen IL, Tsiouris JA, Flory MJ, et al. A large scale study of the psychometric characteristics of the IBR modified overt aggression scale: findings and evidence for increased self-destructive behaviors in adult females with autism spectrum disorder. J Autism Dev Disord 2010;40:599–609.

15. Klonsky ED. Non-suicidal self-injury in United States adults: prevalence, sociodemographics, topography and functions. Psychol Med 2011;41:1981–6.

16. Madge N, Hewitt A, Hawton K, et al. Deliberate self-harm within an international community sample of young people: comparative findings from the Child & Adolescent Self-harm in Europe (CASE) Study. J Child Psychol Psychiatry 2008;49:667–77.

17. Hankin BL, Abela JR. Nonsuicidal self-injury in adolescence: prospective rates and risk factors in a 2 $\frac{1}{2}$ year longitudinal study. Psychiatry Res 2011;186(1): 65–70.

18. Marshall S, Tilton-Weaver L, Stattin H. Non-suicidal self-injury and depressive symptoms during middle adolescence: a longitudinal analysis. J Youth Adolesc 2013;42(8):1234–42.

19. Wilcox HC, Arria AM, Caldeira KM, et al. Longitudinal predictors of past-year nonsuicidal self-injury and motives among college students. Psychol Med 2012; 42(04):717–26.

20. Taliaferro LA, Muehlenkamp JJ. Risk factors associated with self-injurious behavior among a national sample of undergraduate college students. J Am Coll Health 2015;63(1):40–8.

21. Crawhall JC, Henderson JF, Kelley WN. Diagnosis and treatment of the Lesch-Nyhan syndrome. Pediatr Res 1972;6:504–13.

22. Fu R, Jinnah HA. Genotype-phenotype correlations in Lesch-Nyhan disease. J Biologic Chem 2012;287(5):2997–3008.

23. Hladnik U, Nyhan WL, Bertelli M. Variable expression of HPRT deficiency in 5 members of a family with the same mutation. Arch Neurol 2008;65:1240–3.

24. Anderson LT, Ernst M. Self-injury in Lesch-Nyhan disease. J Autism Dev Disord 1994;24:67–81.

25. Hall S, Oliver C, Murphy G. Self-injurious behaviour in young children with Lesch-Nyhan syndrome. Dev Med Child Neurol 2001;43:745–9.

26. Vlangos CN, Yim DK, Elsea SH. Refinement of the Smith-Magenis syndrome critical region to ~950 kb and assessment of 17p11.2 deletions. Are all deletions created equally? Mol Genet Metab 2003;79(2):134–41.

27. Elsea SH, Williams SR. Smith–Magenis syndrome: haploinsufficiency of RAI1 results in altered gene regulation in neurological and metabolic pathways. Expert Rev Mol Med 2011;13:e14.

28. Sloneem J, Oliver C, Udwin O, et al. Prevalence, phenomenology, aetiology and predictors of challenging behaviour in Smith-Magenis syndrome. J Intellect Disabil Res 2011;55(2):138–51.

29. Finucane B, Dirrigl KH, Simon EW. Characterization of self-injurious behaviors in children and adults with Smith-Magenis syndrome. Am J Ment Retard 2001; 106(1):52–8.

30. Finucane BM, Konar D, Givler BH, et al. The spasmodic upper-body squeeze: a characteristic behavior in Smith-Magenis syndrome. Dev Med Child Neurol 1994; 36(1):78–83.

31. Cerruti Mainardi P. Cri du chat syndrome. Orphanet J Rare Dis 2006;1:33.

32. Rodriguez-Caballero A, Torres-Lagares D, Rodriguez-Perez A, et al. Cri du chat syndrome: a critical review. Med Oral Patol Oral Cir Bucal 2010;15(3):e473–8.

33. Higurashi M, Oda M, Iijima K, et al. Livebirth prevalence and follow-up of malformation syndromes in 27,472 newborns. Brain Dev 1990;12(6):770–3.

34. Niebuhr E. The Cri du chat syndrome: epidemiology, cytogenetics, and clinical features. Hum Genet 1978;44(3):227–75.

35. Collins MS, Cornish K. A survey of the prevalence of stereotypy, self-injury and aggression in children and young adults with Cri du chat syndrome. J Intellect Disabil Res 2002;46(Pt):133–40.

36. Muehlenkamp JJ, Ertelt TW, Miller AL, et al. Borderline personality symptoms differentiate non-suicidal and suicidal self-injury in ethnically diverse adolescent outpatients. J Child Psychol Psychiatry 2011;52(2):148–55.

37. Bracken-Minor KL, McDevitt-Murphy ME. Differences in features of non-suicidal self-injury according to borderline personality disorder screening status. Arch Suicide Res 2013;18(1):88–103.

38. Jacobson CM, Gould M. The epidemiology and phenomenology of non-suicidal self-injurious behavior among adolescents: a critical review of the literature. Arch Suicide Res 2007;11(2):129–47.

39. Brent DA, Emslie GJ, Clarke GN, et al. Predictors of spontaneous and systematically assessed suicidal adverse events in the treatment of SSRI-resistant depression in adolescents (TORDIA) study. Am J Psychiatry 2009;166(4):418–26.

40. Wilkinson P, Kelvin R, Roberts C, et al. Clinical and psychosocial predictors of suicide attempts and nonsuicidal self-injury in the Adolescent Depression Antidepressants and Psychotherapy Trial (ADAPT). Am J Psychiatry 2011;168(5):495–501.

41. Haw C, Hawton K, Houston K, et al. Psychiatric and personality disorders in deliberate self-harm patients. Br J Psychiatry 2001;178(1):48–54.

42. Watters AJ, Williams LM. Negative biases and risk for depression; integrating self-report and emotion task markers. Depress Anxiety 2011;28(8):703–18.

43. Nock MK, Prinstein MJ. A functional approach to the assessment of self-mutilative behavior. J Consult Clin Psychol 2004;72(5):885–90.

44. Klonsky ED, Olino TM. Identifying clinically distinct subgroups of self-injurers among young adults: a latent class analysis. J Consult Clin Psychol 2008;76(1):22–7.

45. Whitlock J, Muehlenkamp J, Eckenrode J. Variation in nonsuicidal self-injury: identification and features of latent classes in a college population of emerging adults. J Clin Child Adolesc Psychol 2008;37(4):725–35.

46. Nixon MK, Cloutier PF, Aggarwal S. Affect regulation and addictive aspects of repetitive self-injury in hospitalized adolescents. J Am Acad Child Adolesc Psychiatry 2002;41(11):1333–41.

47. Nock MK, Mendes WB. Physiological arousal, distress tolerance, and social problem-solving deficits among adolescent self-injurers. J Consult Clin Psychol 2008;76(1):28–38.

48. Brain KL, Haines J, Williams CL. The psychophysiology of self-mutilation: evidence of tension reduction. Arch Suicide Res 1998;4(3):227–42.

49. Haines J, Williams CL, Brain KL, et al. The psychophysiology of self-mutilation. J Abnorm Psychol 1995;104(3):471–89.

50. Novak MA. Self-injurious behavior in rhesus monkeys: new insights into its etiology, physiology, and treatment. Am J Primatol 2003;59(1):3–19.

51. Kaess M, Hille M, Parzer P, et al. Alterations in the neuroendocrinological stress response to acute psychosocial stress in adolescents engaging in nonsuicidal self-injury. Psychoneuroendocrinology 2012;37:157–61.

52. Glenn C, Blumenthal T, Klonsky E, et al. Emotional reactivity in nonsuicidal self-injury: divergence between self-report and startle measures. Int J Psychophysiol 2011;80:166–236.

53. Iwata BA, Pace GM, Dorsey MF, et al. The functions of self-injurious behavior: an experimental-epidemiological analysis. J Appl Behav Anal 1994;27(2):215–40.

54. Furniss F, Biswas AB. Recent research on aetiology, development and phenomenology of self-injurious behaviour in people with intellectual disabilities: a systematic review and implications for treatment. J Intellect Disabil Res 2012; 56(5):453–75.

55. Witwer AN, Lecavalier L. Psychopathology in children with intellectual disability: risk markers and correlates. J Ment Health Res Intellect 2008;1(2):75–96.

56. Medeiros K, Rojahn J, Moore LL, et al. Functional properties of behaviour problems depending on level of intellectual disability. J Intellect Disabil Res 2014; 58(2):151–61.

57. Lloyd KG, Hornykiewicz O, Davidson L, et al. Biochemical evidence of dysfunction of brain neurotransmitters in the Lesch-Nyhan syndrome. N Engl J Med 1981; 305(19):1106–11.

58. Jinnah H, Wojcik B, Hunt M, et al. Dopamine deficiency in a genetic mouse model of Lesch-Nyhan disease. J Neurosci 1994;14:1164–239.

59. Gottle M, Prudente CN, Fu R, et al. Loss of dopamine phenotype among midbrain neurons in Lesch-Nyhan disease. Ann Neurol 2014;76(1):95–107.

60. Saito Y, Ito M, Hanaoka S, et al. Dopamine receptor upregulation in Lesch-Nyhan syndrome: a postmortem study. Neuropediatrics 1999;30:66–71.

61. Groschwitz RC, Plener PL. The neurobiology of non-suicidal self-injury (NSSI): a review. Suicidol Online 2012;3:24–32.

62. Sher L, Mann JJ, Traskman-Bendz L, et al. Lower cerebrospinal fluid homovanillic acid levels in depressed suicide attempters. J Affect Disord 2006;90(1):83–9.

63. Roy A, Karoum F, Pollack S. Marked reduction in indexes of dopamine metabolism among patients with depression who attempt suicide. Arch Gen Psychiatry 1992;49(6):447–50.

64. Victor S, Glenn C, Klonsky E. Is non-suicidal self-injury an "addiction"? A comparison of craving in substance use and non-suicidal self-injury. Psychiatry Res 2012;197(1–2):73–7.

65. Herpertz S, Steinmeyer SM, Marx D, et al. The significance of aggression and impulsivity for self-mutilative behavior. Pharmacopsychiatry 1995;28(Suppl 2): 64–72.

66. Ernst C, Mechawar N, Turecki G. Suicide neurobiology. Prog Neurobiol 2009; 89(4):315–33.

67. Janis IB, Nock MK. Are self-injurers impulsive?: results from two behavioral laboratory studies. Psychiatry Res 2009;169(3):261–7.

68. McCloskey MS, Look AE, Chen EY, et al. Nonsuicidal self-injury: relationship to behavioral and self-rating measures of impulsivity and self-aggression. Suicide Life Threat Behav 2012;42(2):197–209.

69. Miller M, Pate V, Swanson SA, et al. Antidepressant class, age, and the risk of deliberate self-harm: a propensity score matched cohort study of SSRI and SNRI users in the USA. CNS Drugs 2014;28(1):79–88.

70. Canitano R, Scandurra V. Psychopharmacology in autism: an update. Prog Neuropsychopharmacol Biol Psychiatry 2011;35(1):18–28.

71. McDougle CJ, Scahill L, Aman MG, et al. Risperidone for the core symptom domains of autism: results from the study by the autism network of the research units on pediatric psychopharmacology. Am J Psychiatry 2005;162(6):1142–8.

72. Allen SM, Rice SN. Risperidone antagonism of self-mutilation in a Lesch-Nyhan patient. Prog Neuropsychopharmacol Biol Psychiatry 1996;20(5):793–800.

73. Torres RJ, Prior C, Garcia MG, et al. HPRT deficiency in Spain: what have we learned in the past 30 years (1984-2013)? Nucleosides Nucleotides Nucleic Acids 2014;33(4–6):223–32.

74. Yamada K, Kobayashi M, Kanda T. Involvement of adenosine A2A receptors in depression and anxiety. Int Rev Neurobiol 2014;119:373–93.

75. Sperlagh B, Csolle C, Ando RD, et al. The role of purinergic signaling in depressive disorders. Neuropsychopharmacol Hung 2012;14(4):231–8.

76. Randall PA, Nunes EJ, Janniere SL, et al. Stimulant effects of adenosine antagonists on operant behavior: differential actions of selective A2A and A1 antagonists. Psychopharmacology 2011;216(2):173–86.

77. Sher L, Stanley BH. The role of endogenous opioids in the pathophysiology of self-injurious and suicidal behavior. Arch Suicide Res 2008;12(4):299–308.

78. Bresin K, Gordon KH. Endogenous opioids and nonsuicidal self-injury: a mechanism of affect regulation. Neurosci Biobehav Rev 2013;37(3):374–83.

79. Prossin AR, Love TM, Koeppe RA, et al. Dysregulation of regional endogenous opioid function in borderline personality disorder. Am J Psychiatry 2010;167(8):925–33.

80. Stanley B, Sher L, Wilson S, et al. Non-suicidal self-injurious behavior, endogenous opioids and monoamine neurotransmitters. J Affect Disord 2010;124:134–40.

81. Courtemanche A, Schroeder S, Sheldon J, et al. Observing signs of pain in relation to self-injurious behaviour among individuals with intellectual and developmental disabilities. J Intellect Disabil Res 2012;56(5):501–15.

82. Symons FJ. Self-injurious behavior in neurodevelopmental disorders: relevance of nociceptive and immune mechanisms. Neurosci Biobehav Rev 2011;35(5):1266–74.

83. Roy A, Roy M, Deb S, et al. Are opioid antagonists effective in reducing self-injury in adults with intellectual disability? A systematic review. J Intellect Disabil Res 2015;59(1):55–67.

84. Chen JF, Moratalla R, Impagnatiello F, et al. The role of the D2 dopamine receptor (D2R) in A2A adenosine receptor (A2AR)-mediated behavioral and cellular responses as revealed by A2A and D2 receptor knockout mice. Proc Natl Acad Sci U S A 2001;98(4):1970–5.

85. Gan TJ, Habib AS. Adenosine as a non-opioid analgesic in the perioperative setting. Anesth Analg 2007;105(2):487–94.

86. Stella L, De Novellis V, Vitelli MR, et al. Interactive role of adenosine and dopamine in the opiate withdrawal syndrome. Naunyn Schmiedebergs Arch Pharmacol 2003;368(2):113–8.

87. Amanlou M, Saboury AA, Bazl R, et al. Adenosine deaminase activity modulation by some street drug: molecular docking simulation and experimental investigation. Daru 2014;22:42.

88. Spanagel R, Herz A, Shippenberg TS. Opposing tonically active endogenous opioid systems modulate the mesolimbic dopaminergic pathway. Proc Natl Acad Sci U S A 1992;89(6):2046–50.

Tuberous Sclerosis Complex

Francis J. DiMario Jr, MD[a],*, Mustafa Sahin, MD[b], Darius Ebrahimi-Fakhari, MD[c]

KEYWORDS

- Neurocutaneous • Neurogenetic • Tuberous sclerosis complex
- Subependymal giant cell astrocytoma • Epilepsy • Autism
- Mechanistic target of rapamycin (mTOR) • Rapamycin

KEY POINTS

- Hypopigmented macules in the skin coupled with either epilepsy or autism are important diagnostic findings.
- Prenatal identification of a cardiac rhabdomyoma is a common early presenting manifestation.
- Hyperactivity of the mechanistic target of rapamycin complex 1 (mTORC1) constitutes the molecular basis of tuberous sclerosis complex (TSC).
- Symptomatic treatments as well as molecular-targeted therapy with current mTORC1 inhibitors are treatment options.
- The mTORC1 inhibitor, everolimus, is approved by the US Food and Drug Administration for the treatment of renal angiomyolipomas that do not require immediate surgery in adults with TSC and subependymal giant cell astrocytomas that cannot be surgically resected in adults or children with TSC.

Disclosures: F.J. DiMario has received research grant support from Novartis; Research in the Sahin laboratory is supported by the NIH (U01 NS082320, P20 NS080199, P30 HD018655), Department of Defense (W81XWH-13-1-0040), Tuberous Sclerosis Alliance (2013DB17Y2), Autism Speaks (8703), Nancy Lurie Marks Family Foundation (88736), Simons Foundation, Boston Children's Hospital Translational Research Program (96854), Novartis, Roche, and Shire (73403) (M. Sahin); D. Ebrahimi-Fakhari acknowledges support from the Graduate Academy of the University of Heidelberg, the Young Investigator Award Program at Ruprecht-Karls-University Heidelberg Faculty of Medicine, the Daimler and Benz Foundation (Daimler und Benz Stiftung, Ladenburg, Germany), and the Reinhard-Frank Foundation (Reinhard-Frank-Stiftung, Hamburg, Germany) and has received financial support from Actelion Pharmaceuticals for attending an international scientific meeting in 2014.
[a] Department of Pediatrics, Neurogenetics–Tuberous Sclerosis Clinic, Connecticut Children's Medical Center, 282 Washington Street, Hartford, CT 06070, USA; [b] Multidisciplinary Tuberous Sclerosis Program, Department of Neurology, Boston Children's Hospital, 300 Longwood Avenue, Boston, MA 02115, USA; [c] Department of Neurology, Boston Children's Hospital, Harvard Medical School, 300 Longwood Avenue, Boston, MA 02115, USA
* Corresponding author.
E-mail address: fdimari@connecticutchildrens.org

Pediatr Clin N Am 62 (2015) 633–648
http://dx.doi.org/10.1016/j.pcl.2015.03.005
0031-3955/15/$ – see front matter Published by Elsevier Inc.
pediatric.theclinics.com

INTRODUCTION

Tuberous sclerosis complex (TSC) is an autosomal-dominant, neurocutaneous, multi-system disorder characterized by cellular hyperplasia and tissue dysplasia.[1,2] The disease has 2 known genetic loci: *TSC1*, found on chromosome 9q34; and *TSC2*, found on chromosome 16p13.[2–4] Clinical phenotypes resulting from mutations in either of these genes are variable.[5–9]

EPIDEMIOLOGY

TSC can be identified in all ethnic groups and is equally identified in both sexes. Population studies have estimated a prevalence of 1 in 6000 to 9000 people. Although TSC is an autosomal-dominant inherited disorder, up to 65% to 75% of people affected with TSC have had spontaneous mutations. An estimated 40,000 Americans and at least 2 million people worldwide are affected with TSC.[2]

CAUSE

TSC can be caused by mutations in 2 different genes: the *TSC1* gene, found on chromosome 9q34; and the *TSC2* gene, found on 16p13.[2–4] The *TSC2* gene accounts for as many as 90% of the clinical cases; however, mutations in both TSC1 and TSC2 may produce the same phenotype, varying from individual to individual.[5–7] This genetic heterogeneity is made more complex by variable clinical expression even with the same genetic mutation within a given family (**Figs. 1–12**).[7]

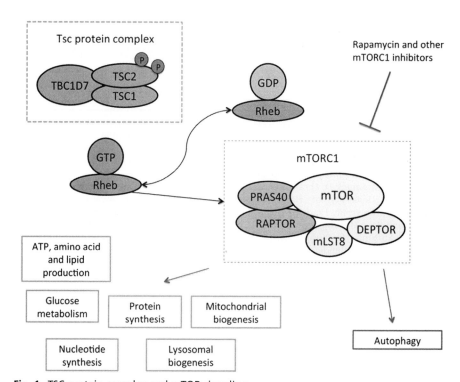

Fig. 1. TSC protein complex and mTOR signaling.

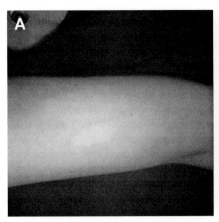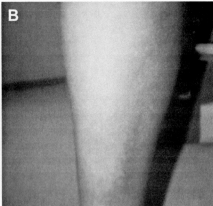

Fig. 2. (*A, B*) Hypopigmented macules.

The *Tuberous Sclerosis Complex Variation Database* (http://chromium.liacs.nl/ LOVD2/TSC/home) of small mutations, small and large deletions, and rearrangements for both genes has compiled more than 500 different mutations.[7] The *TSC1* gene incorporates mainly small mutations that result in nonsense or frameshifts, which lead to protein truncation, whereas most *TSC2* mutations involve missense mutations (25% to 32%) and large deletions or rearrangements (12% to 17%).[5–7] *TSC2* gene mutations are more common whether in familial patients (about 65%) or in sporadic patients (about 75%), accounting for a ratio of TSC2:TSC1 of almost 2:1 in familial patients and 3.5:1 in sporadic cases.

Clinical differences between individuals who harbor the *TSC2* versus the *TSC1* mutation indicate that more severe clinical manifestations often occur in those with *TSC2* mutations. These individuals tend to have more hypomelanotic macules and learning disabilities, with more frequent neurologic and ophthalmologic signs, renal cysts, and ungual fibromas in male individuals.[7]

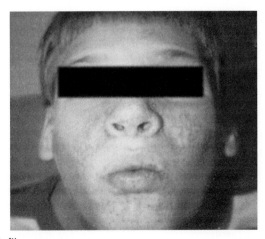

Fig. 3. Facial angiofibromas.

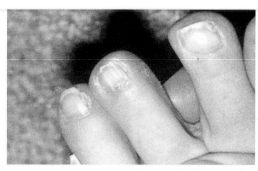

Fig. 4. Ungual fibromas.

PATHOPHYSIOLOGY

The pathologic condition of TSC is characterized by cellular hyperplasia and tissue dysplasia affecting multiple organs.[1,2] Following the discovery of the *TSC1* and *TSC2* genes and their respective protein product (hamartin and tuberin), subsequent genetic and functional studies have identified several downstream targets and signaling cascades (**Fig. 1**). Tsc1 and Tsc2, together with a third protein, TBC1D7,[10] form the TSC protein complex, which regulates multiple cellular processes and importantly acts as a critical negative regulator of the mechanistic target of rapamycin (mTOR) complex 1 (mTORC1),[8,11,12] a serine/threonine kinase that is central to many cell functions including cell growth and proliferation. Rheb (Ras homolog enriched in brain) is a specific GTPase downstream of the TSC protein complex that functionally links TSC1/TSC2 to mTORC1 (see **Fig. 1**). The TSC1/TSC2 complex functions as a GTPase-activating protein (GAP) for Rheb and stimulates the conversion of Rheb-GTP to a GDP-bound state, thereby inactivating Rheb signaling and thus removing its stimulatory effect on mTORC1. Conversely, loss-of-function mutations in either TSC1 or TSC2 lead to enhanced Rheb-GTP signaling and mTORC1 activation (see **Fig. 1**). Constitutively active mTORC1 signaling thus constitutes the molecular basis of TSC.

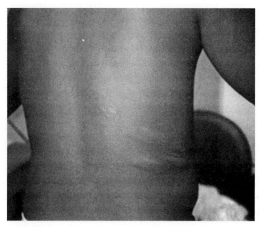

Fig. 5. Shagreen patches.

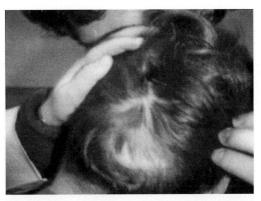

Fig. 6. Fibrous plaque.

mTORC1 has emerged as a central regulator of cell growth and metabolism. Not surprisingly, derangement in the mTOR pathway has been linked to the process of aging and a myriad of human diseases, including neurodegenerative, neurodevelopmental, and psychiatric diseases, epilepsy, cancer, obesity, type 2 diabetes, and others.[13–15] When in its active state, mTORC1 phosphorylates the translational regulators 4E-BP1 (eukaryotic translation initiation factor 4E-binding protein 1) and S6K1 (S6 kinase 1), which, in turn, stimulate protein synthesis. Through other direct and secondary downstream targets, mTORC1 critically regulates anabolic pathways that enable an adaptation to various external stimuli and lead to an increase in cell size and growth. Active mTORC1 stimulates the biosynthesis of ribosomes, lipid biogenesis, glucose metabolism, nucleotide synthesis, mitochondrial and lysosomal biogenesis, ATP, and amino acid production (see **Fig. 1**). mTORC1 also functions as a negative regulator for autophagy, another key cellular pathway that has been implicated in many diseases including neurodegenerative and neurodevelopmental diseases (see **Fig. 1**).[16–18]

Important to clinical practice, the activity of mTORC1 is very sensitive to the macrolide antibiotic rapamycin and related compounds. When bound to the adapter protein

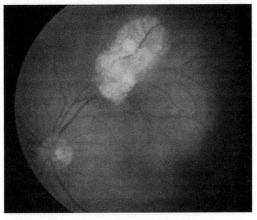

Fig. 7. Retinal hamartoma.

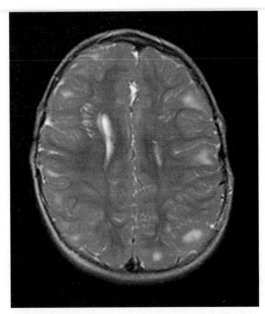

Fig. 8. Cortical dysplasias (dysplasia, tubers, and migration lines).

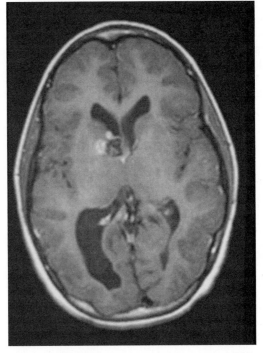

Fig. 9. Subependymal giant cell astrocytoma.

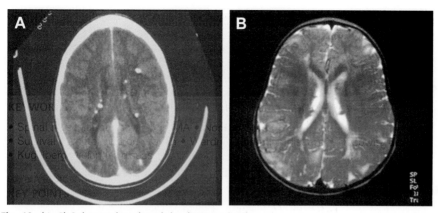

Fig. 10. (*A, B*) Subependymal nodules (MRI and CT).

FKBP12, rapamycin physically binds and blocks mTOC1 kinase activity.[19–21] The pivotal role of deregulated mTORC1 signaling in the pathogenesis of TSC and associated conditions with hyperactive mTORC1 has provided a strong molecular basis for the use of mTORC1 inhibitors, such as rapamycin, as a targeted therapy. Indeed, derivatives of rapamycin have successfully entered the clinic as discussed later. By bridging decades of basic research into the molecular basis of TSC to a successful clinical application, the development of mTORC1 inhibitors can be viewed as a model for the bench-to-beside paradigm of translation research.[22–24]

Diagnostic Approach

Box 1 describes the clinical features of each diagnostic approach.

The diagnosis of TSC is made by careful clinical examination and is supported by selective organ imaging and laboratory testing, including genetic evaluation.[1,2,25] Additional investigations are used primarily to confirm the diagnosis, determine the extent of disease by identifying which organs are involved, and clarify parental recurrence risks.

There are no symptoms that are specific for TSC. However, there are several common presentations that should prompt consideration of TSC and further investigation.[1,2,25] First and foremost is the identification of a family member with TSC. If the

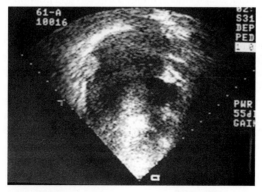

Fig. 11. Cardiac rhabdomyoma.

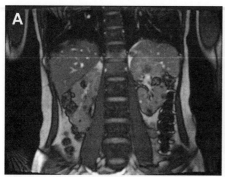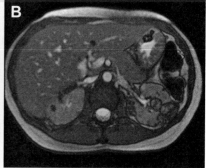

Fig. 12. (*A, B*) Renal angiomyolipomas.

family member is a first-degree relative (ie, a parent or siblings), there is an up to 50% chance for the patient under evaluation to have the disorder. This 50% risk remains when multiple siblings are affected and may even occur when the affected parent is unaware of his or her diagnostic status. A gonadal mosaicism in a clinically unaffected parent is an additional, albeit rare, cause.[1] TSC is a condition whereby the only organ affected with the TSC mutation is the gonads and their affected gametes, thus allowing the potential for multiple affected children from an otherwise unaffected parent. This risk is estimated to be less than 2% for all parents with an affected child.[1]

The recognition of diagnostic hallmarks should prompt further consideration of an underlying diagnosis of TSC (see **Box 1**). Patients commonly come to medical attention through one of several ways: prenatal identification of cardiac rhabdomyomas, postnatal identification of hypopigmented macules on the skin, or the development of seizures, especially with infantile spasms and during an evaluation for autism with or without cognitive impairment. Under these specific clinical scenarios, a heightened suspicion for underlying diagnosis of TSC is warranted.

Among infants with multiple cardiac rhabdomyomas, 80% or more are ultimately diagnosed with TSC. These lesions may be identified at 22 weeks of gestation. Most patients have an average of 3 lesions, 3 to 25 mm in size, but isolated lesions are also of diagnostic significance. Cardiac rhabdomyomas are most commonly located within the ventricles along the septum rather than within the walls or atria.[1,2]

Hypopigmented macules spots are identifiable in the vast majority of patients and approaches 90% to 95%. The classic ash leaf spot, while not diagnostic, characteristically has a pyramidal shape with a rounded bottom and pointed end. Most macules can be seen under ambient light but visualization can be enhanced with the use of a Wood lamp.[1,2]

Up to 90% of patients with TSC will experience epilepsy in their lifetime. All seizure types may develop, with the possible exception of pure absence epilepsy. Seizures are most often manifest in childhood with infantile spasms as the presenting feature in one-third of patients.[1,2]

Autism spectrum disorders (ASD) among other behavioral problems can be identified in 40% to 50% of patients with TSC.[26,27] Patients affected with ASD have a 75% prevalence of coexisting cognitive impairment and an additional 75% to 100% prevalence of concurrent epilepsy.[1,2]

Practical Management, Follow-up, and Surveillance

Box 2 provides resources for TSC patients and caregivers.

Box 1
Diagnostic criteria according to the International Tuberous Sclerosis Complex Consensus Conference

Definite diagnosis: 2 major features or 1 major feature with greater than 2 minor features or the presence of a TSC1 or TSC2 mutation of confirmed pathogenicity[a]

Possible diagnosis: Either 1 major feature or greater than 2 minor features

Major criteria:

Skin/oral cavity

- Hypomelanotic macules (n>3, at least 5 mm diameter)
- Angiofibromas (n>3) or fibrous cephalic plaque
- Ungual fibromas (n>2)
- Shagreen patch

Central nervous system

- Cortical dysplasias (includes tubers and cerebral white matter radial migration lines)
- Subependymal nodules
- Subependymal giant cell astrocytoma

Heart

- Cardiac rhabdomyoma

Lungs

- Lymphangioleiomyomatosis[b]

Kidney

- Angiomyolipomas (n>2)[b]

Eyes

- Multiple retinal hamartomas

Minor criteria:

Skin/oral cavity

- "Confetti" skin lesions
- Dental enamel pits (n>3)
- Intraoral fibromas (n>2)

Kidney

- Multiple renal cysts

Eyes

- Retinal achromic patch

Other organs

- Nonrenal hamartomas

Genetics: identification of either a TSC1 or a TSC2 pathogenic[a] mutation in DNA from normal tissue is sufficient to make a definite diagnosis

[a] A pathogenic mutation is defined as a mutation that clearly inactivates the function of the TSC1 or TSC2 proteins, prevents protein synthesis, or is a missense mutation whose effect on protein function has been established by functional assessment (www.lovd.nl/TSC1, www.lovd/TSC2)

[b] A combination of the 2 major clinical features (lymphangioleiomyomatosis and angiomyolipomas) without other features does not meet criteria for a definite diagnosis.

> **Box 2**
> **Resources for tuberous sclerosis complex patients and caregivers**
>
> - Tuberous Sclerosis Complex International: http://www.tscinternational.org
> - Tuberous Sclerosis Alliance: http://www.tsalliance.org
> - Tuberous Sclerosis Canada: http://www.tscanada.ca
> - OrphaNet: http://www.orpha.net
> - Autism Society: http://www.autism-society.org
> - The LAM Foundation: http://www.thelamfoundation.org

Novel Treatment Approaches

It is encouraged that children with TSC be referred to specialized TSC clinics for inter-disciplinary management, support, and follow-up.[25,27] Updated recommendations for surveillance and management of TSC manifestations have been published by the *International Tuberous Sclerosis Complex Consensus Conference*.[25] In recent years, increased understanding of the molecular biology of TSC has led to a paradigm shift.[14,16,17] Historically, the treatment of TSC-related organ manifestations and complications has been mostly symptomatic, but the advent of mTORC1 inhibitors as a targeted therapy has, for the first time, opened the opportunity for treating the underlying pathophysiology of TSC.[22]

mTORC1 inhibitors, such as rapamycin or everolimus, have successfully undergone clinical trials for the treatment of TSC-related subependymal giant cell astrocytoma (SEGA) and renal angiomyolipomas, leading to regulatory approval in many countries, including the United States, Canada, and Europe. Following these encouraging results, mTORC1 inhibitors are currently in clinical trials for TSC-related refractory epilepsy, neurocognitive manifestations, and facial angiofibromas.

Neurologic sequelae of TSC are among the greatest challenges, but new and promising therapeutic avenues are becoming available. As an example, treatment modalities for SEGA now include surgical therapy and medical therapy with mTORC1 inhibitors. Surgical resection with or without placement of a ventriculoperitoneal shunt is often necessary in acutely symptomatic SEGA. Definite indications for surgical resection include obstructive hydrocephalus with secondary complications such as increased intracranial pressure, focal neurologic deficits, and an increase in seizure frequency. For cases of symptomatic SEGA that are not amenable to surgery, initial therapy with mTORC1 inhibitors can be considered.

Early surgical resection and medical therapies are options for growing, asymptomatic SEGA.[12,13] Treatment decisions in this scenario should be made on a shared decision-making basis with the patient or parents and require integrating the most recent evidence. Potential adverse events, possible beneficial effects on other TSC manifestations, the patient's resources, and environment have to be evaluated in each individual case. Timing of the intervention for asymptomatic SEGA remains controversial. Limited evidence exists that early surgical resection might have a superior outcome compared with surgery at a later symptomatic stage.[28,29] Important evidence for the use of mTORC1 inhibitors in SEGA has been provided by the EXIST-1 trial, a randomized double-blind placebo-controlled multicenter study, which randomly assigned pediatric and adult TSC patients with growing SEGA to receive everolimus or placebo.[21,30] After a mean follow-up of 10 months, patients in the everolimus group showed a significantly higher reduction in SEGA volume (defined as a reduction $\geq$50%).[30,31] In addition, no patient in the everolimus group showed tumor progression, whereas 15% of placebo-treated patients met criteria for tumor progression. As a potential caveat, the response to mTORC1 inhibition seems to depend on continuous therapy,[30,31] and data on long-term safety and efficiency have only recently become available.[32]

Based on these positive results, the US Food and Drug Administration has approved everolimus for the treatment of TSC-related SEGA in patients that require treatment but are not candidates for surgical resection. The starting dose for everolimus is based on body surface area and subsequent doses are titrated to reach a serum trough concentration of 5 to 10 ng/mL. Monitoring for potential adverse events, such as stomatitis, common infections, and dyslipidemia, is required.

Seizures in TSC are often difficult to control and may become refractory to medical treatment.[33] Infantile spasms are a particular challenge and affect cognitive outcome significantly. Although evidence is limited given the lack of large randomized clinical trials, the recommended first-line treatment in TSC-related infantile spasms is vigabatrin.[34–40] Potential adverse events, most importantly retinal toxicity, have to be discussed with the patient, parents, and caregivers. Second-line options consist of hormonal therapy (ACTH, prednisolone, and others) similar to recommendations for infantile spasms of other causes.[40] Recommendations for other types of seizures are unfortunately limited. Vigabatrin may be particularly effective in treating focal-onset seizures before the age of 1 year, and there is evidence that supports the use of antiepileptic drugs that enhance GABAergic inhibition such as topiramate or carbamazepine.[41] Importantly, early treatment with antiepileptic drugs may benefit children with ictal discharges before the age of 2 years even if electrographic seizures do not show a clinical correlate.[41] However, this should not be confused with preemptive antiepileptic therapy, for which supporting evidence does not yet exist. Invasive treatment modalities for refractory seizures consist of epilepsy surgery and vagus nerve stimulation.[41] Patients with medically refractory seizures are best evaluated at epilepsy centers with expertise in TSC to identify individuals that might benefit from these invasive procedures. A ketogenic diet or related variants are additional alternatives that have been effective in a small number of cases.[42–44] Perhaps most encouraging, anecdotal reports[45,46] and a first open-label study[47] found a significant reduction in seizure frequency in cases of refractory focal-onset seizures treated with an mTORC1 inhibitor. Following these promising results, a randomized, controlled double-blind phase 3 multicenter study is currently underway (clinicaltrials.gov, NCT01713946).

Neuropsychiatric manifestations of TSC are among the most burdensome for patients, parents, and caregivers and are often difficult to manage.[26,48] In addition to a detailed assessment on diagnosis, routine assessments for neuropsychiatric symptoms can be performed on regular office visits, with a minimum frequency of once per year.[26,27] Comprehensive, formal evaluations by specialists are recommended at key developmental time points (during the first 3 years of life, preschool [3–6 years], before middle school entry [6–9 years], during adolescence [12–16 years], and early adulthood [18–25 years]).[26,27] These assessments serve to identify individuals who might benefit from early interventions and supportive therapy for individual disorders such as ASD, anxiety, or attention-deficit hyperactivity disorder.[26,27] Although no TSC-specific treatment modalities for TSC-associated neuropsychiatric manifestations are currently available, several current clinical trials are looking to assess the benefit of mTORC1 inhibition on behavioral and cognitive outcomes (clinicaltrials.gov, NCT01289912; NCT01954693; NCT01730209; NCT01929642). It is hoped that these and future clinical trials will inform treatment decisions for neuropsychiatric manifestations of TSC and provide new therapeutic avenues. With the results of current trials pending however, there is currently insufficient evidence to support the routine use of mTORC1 inhibitors in the treatment of TSC-associated neuropsychiatric disorders.

Renal complications of TSC require interdisciplinary assessment and management.[27,49,50] Current guidelines recommend treatment with mTORC1 inhibitors for asymptomatic growing angiomyolipomas larger than 3 cm in diameter.[27] These current guidelines are based on evidence from several clinical trials that found a significant reduction in tumor size under treatment with mTORC1 inhibitors and a tolerability that seems superior compared with surgical or ablative interventions.[51–54] It should be cautioned, however, that no randomized trials have directly compared these therapeutic interventions. As with the treatment of SEGA, mTORC1 inhibitors have to be continued long term and studies assessing the long-term benefits and safety are not yet available. Second-line therapies for asymptomatic angiomyolipomas include selective interventional embolization followed by corticosteroids, nephron-sparing resection, or ablation of exophytic lesions.[27] "Neoadjuvant" treatment of large angiomyolipomas with mTORC1 inhibitors to reduce tumor volume and to facilitate nephron-sparing surgery has been a successful approach in a small number of patients.[55] Acutely hemorrhaging angiomyolipomas are a life-threatening condition that can be best treated with selective arterial embolization, allowing a rapid stabilization and often omitting the need for more invasive interventions. Complete nephrectomy should be avoided because of potential secondary complications, and the associated increased risk of renal failure, chronic kidney disease, and end-stage renal failure, which impact prognosis significantly.[47]

mTORC1 inhibitors have also entered clinical trials for pulmonary lymphangioleiomyomatosis. Patients with moderate to severe lung disease and/or rapid progression may benefit from mTORC1 inhibitors to stabilize pulmonary function, quality of life, and functional performance.[27] Evidence is again derived from several studies that reported a favorable outcome,[51–54,56–59] including a phase 3 clinical trial.[59] Interestingly, serum VEGF-D levels seem to be a good biomarker that correlates with disease severity and a response to treatment with mTORC1 inhibitors.[60] Bronchodilators, oxygen, and estrogen antagonists are supportive therapies. Lung transplantation remains an option of last resort for patients who are suitable candidates.

Cardiac rhabdomyomas usually regress spontaneously and interventions are rarely necessary. Fetal echocardiography may be helpful in identifying patients with a high risk of heart failure after birth. Until regression is documented, follow-up with echocardiography and electrocardiography studies is recommended.[27] Symptomatic lesions may require surgical resection.

Ophthalmic manifestations of TSC require close monitoring. Periodic ophthalmologic examinations are advised, particularly in patients receiving vigabatrin. Retinal hamartomas, although found in 30% to 50% of TSC patients, rarely become symptomatic.[61] Laser photocoagulation and photodynamic therapies are the treatment options. Decision for either therapy is tailored to the individual case, because no general treatment guidelines are available.[61]

TSC-associated skin lesions are very common and may require treatment when prominent or disfiguring.[62] Established treatment options include laser therapy or surgical excision.[62] Recently, mTORC1 inhibitors have shown very promising results.[63] For example, in the above-mentioned phase 2 trial of oral rapamycin for renal angiomyolipomas, secondary benefits, namely subjective improvement, was noted in 57% of patients with facial angiofibromas, 18% with hypomelanotic macules, 29% with shagreen patches or with ungual fibromas, and 21% with forehead plaques.[53] Similarly, phase 3 trials of everolimus for SEGA or renal angiomyolipomas reported secondary benefits on skin manifestations.[30,51] Small case series have documented benefits for topical preparations of rapamycin on facial angiofibromas, leading to a flattening and sometimes even a complete resolution of lesions.[63] Long-term safety and outcome data are lacking, but a phase 2 clinical trial for topical rapamycin is underway (clinicaltrials.gov, NCT01526356). Current guidelines limit the use of oral mTORC1 inhibitors for the management of TSC skin lesions to individuals who are not candidates for surgical approaches and whose skin lesions pose serious medical risk, such as angiofibromas causing recurrent extensive bleeding.[62] TSC manifestations in the oral cavity necessitate close monitoring, and oral hygiene is imperative. Treatment options for symptomatic lesions include various surgical approaches.[62] Topical application of mTORC1 inhibitors to subungual fibromas has been successful in anecdotal reports.[64]

Despite the fact that TSC pathophysiology emanates directly from intracellular signaling pathways, which when impaired result in cellular proliferation and poorly differentiated tissues, the development of overt malignancy is very infrequent.[1] The risk for malignancy in unaffected relatives of patients with TSC is not known to be elevated.[1,2]

SUMMARY

TSC is a commonly recognized autosomal-dominant neurocutaneous disorder that exemplifies both genetic heterogeneity and phenotypic variability. The underlying pathophysiology of TSC involves critical intracellular signaling cascades that regulate many cellular functions, including intermediary metabolism, cell growth, and proliferation. TSC serves as a model for other neurodevelopmental and neurodegenerative conditions, which result from parallel and overlapping molecular mechanisms. The therapeutic targeting of mTORC1 has been demonstrated to reverse some of the clinical phenotype of TSC and heralds the possibility of even more effective interventions in the future.

REFERENCES

1. Gomez M, Sampson J, Whittemore V, editors. The tuberous sclerosis complex. Oxford (UK): Oxford University Press; 1999.
2. Hyman MH, Whittemore VH. National Institutes of Health consensus conference: tuberous sclerosis complex. Arch Neurol 2000;57:662–5.
3. European Chromosome 16 Tuberous Sclerosis Consortium. Identification and characterization of the tuberous sclerosis gene on chromosome 16. Cell 1993; 75:1305–15.
4. van Slegtenhorst M, de Hoogt R, Hermans C, et al. Identification of the tuberous sclerosis gene TSC1 on chromosome 9q34. Science 1997;277:805–8.
5. Dabora SL, Joswiak S, Franz DN, et al. Mutational analysis in a cohort of 224 tuberous sclerosis patients indicates increased severity of TSC2, compared to TSC1, disease in multiple organs. Am J Hum Genet 2001;68:64–80.
6. Cheadle J, Reeve M, Samson J, et al. Molecular genetic advances in tuberous sclerosis. Hum Genet 2000;62:345–57.
7. Au KS, Williams AT, Roach ES, et al. Genotype/phenotype correlation in 325 individuals referred for a diagnosis of tuberous sclerosis complex in the United States. Genet Med 2007;9:88–100.
8. Tee AR, Fingar DC, Manning BD, et al. Tuberous sclerosis complex-1 and -2 gene products function together to inhibit mammalian target of rapamycin (mTOR)-mediated downstream signaling. Proc Natl Acad Sci U S A 2002;99:13571–6.

9. Mak BC, Yeung RS. The tuberous sclerosis complex genes in tumor development. Cancer Invest 2004;22:588–603.

10. Dibble CC, Elis W, Menon S, et al. TBC1D7 is a third subunit of the TSC1-TSC2 complex upstream of mTORC1. Mol Cell Biol 2012;47(4):535–46.

11. Gao X, Zhang Y, Arrazola P, et al. Tsc tumour suppressor proteins antagonize amino-acid-TOR signalling. Nat Cell Biol 2002;4(9):699–704.

12. Inoki K, Li Y, Zhu T, et al. TSC2 is phosphorylated and inhibited by Akt and suppresses mTOR signalling. Nat Cell Biol 2002;4(9):648–57.

13. Mannaa M, Kramer S, Boschmann M, et al. mTOR and regulation of energy homeostasis in humans. J Mol Med 2013;91(10):1167–75.

14. Laplante M, Sabatini DM. mTOR signaling in growth control and disease. Cell 2012;149(2):274–93.

15. Lipton JO, Sahin M. The neurology of mTOR. Neuron 2014;84(2):275–91.

16. Ebrahimi-Fakhari D, Wahlster L, Hoffmann GF, et al. Emerging role of autophagy in pediatric neurodegenerative and neurometabolic diseases. Pediatr Res 2014; 75(1–2):217–26.

17. Ebrahimi-Fakhari D, Wahlster L, McLean PJ. Protein degradation pathways in Parkinson's disease: curse or blessing. Acta Neuropathol 2012;124(2):153–72.

18. Schneider JL, Cuervo AM. Autophagy and human disease: emerging themes. Curr Opin Genet Dev 2014;26C:16–23.

19. Sabatini DM, Erdjument-Bromage H, Lui M, et al. RAFT1: a mammalian protein that binds to FKBP12 in a rapamycin-dependent fashion and is homologous to yeast TORs. Cell 1994;78(1):35–43.

20. Brown EJ, Albers MW, Shin TB, et al. A mammalian protein targeted by G1-arresting rapamycin-receptor complex. Nature 1994;369(6483):756–8.

21. Sabers CJ, Martin MM, Brunn GJ, et al. Isolation of a protein target of the FKBP12-rapamycin complex in mammalian cells. J Biol Chem 1995;270(2): 815–22.

22. Sahin M. Targeted treatment trials for tuberous sclerosis and autism: no longer a dream. Curr Opin Neurobiol 2012;22(5):895–901.

23. Julich K, Sahin M. Mechanism-based treatment in tuberous sclerosis complex. Pediatr Neurol 2014;50(4):290–6.

24. Kohrman MH. Emerging treatments in the management of tuberous sclerosis complex. Pediatr Neurol 2012;46(5):267–75.

25. Northrup H, Kruger DA, on behalf of the International Tuberous Sclerosis Complex Consensus Group. Tuberous Sclerosis Complex Diagnostic Criteria Update: Recommendations of the 2012 International Tuberous Sclerosis Complex Consensus Conference. Pediatr Neurol 2013;49:243–54.

26. de Vries P, Humphrey A, McCartney D, et al. TSC Behaviour Consensus Panel. Consensus clinical guidelines for the assessment of cognitive and behavioural problems in tuberous sclerosis. Eur Child Adolesc Psychiatry 2005;14:183–90.

27. Kruger DA, Northrup H, on behalf of the International Tuberous Sclerosis Complex Consensus Group. Tuberous sclerosis complex surveillance and management: recommendations of the 2012 International Tuberous Sclerosis Complex Consensus Conference. Pediatr Neurol 2013;49:255–65.

28. de Ribaupierre S, Dorfmuller G, Bulteau C, et al. Subependymal giant-cell astrocytomas in pediatric tuberous sclerosis disease: when should we operate? Neurosurgery 2007;60(1):83–9 [discussion: 89–90].

29. Berhouma M. Management of subependymal giant cell tumors in tuberous sclerosis complex: the neurosurgeon's perspective. World J Pediatr 2010;6(2): 103–10.

30. Franz DN, Belousova E, Sparagana S, et al. Efficacy and safety of everolimus for subependymal giant cell astrocytomas associated with tuberous sclerosis complex (EXIST-1): a multicentre, randomised, placebo-controlled phase 3 trial. Lancet 2013;381(9861):125–32.

31. Krueger DA, Care MM, Holland K, et al. Everolimus for subependymal giant-cell astrocytomas in tuberous sclerosis. N Engl J Med 2010;363(19):1801–11.

32. Krueger DA, Care MM, Agricola K, et al. Everolimus long-term safety and efficacy in subependymal giant cell astrocytoma. Neurology 2013;80(6):574–80.

33. Chu-Shore CJ, Major P, Camposano S, et al. The natural history of epilepsy in tuberous sclerosis complex. Epilepsia 2010;51(7):1236–41.

34. Camposano SE, Major P, Halpern E, et al. Vigabatrin in the treatment of childhood epilepsy: a retrospective chart review of efficacy and safety profile. Epilepsia 2008;49(7):1186–91.

35. Chiron C, Dumas C, Jambaque I, et al. Randomized trial comparing vigabatrin and hydrocortisone in infantile spasms due to tuberous sclerosis. Epilepsy Res 1997;26(2):389–95.

36. Elterman RD, Shields WD, Bittman RM, et al. Vigabatrin for the treatment of infantile spasms: final report of a randomized trial. J Child Neurol 2010;25(11):1340–7.

37. Parisi P, Bombardieri R, Curatolo P. Current role of vigabatrin in infantile spasms. Eur J Paediatr Neurol 2007;11(6):331–6.

38. Bombardieri R, Pinci M, Moavero R, et al. Early control of seizures improves long-term outcome in children with tuberous sclerosis complex. Eur J Paediatr Neurol 2010;14(2):146–9.

39. Jozwiak S, Kotulska K, Domanska-Pakiela D, et al. Antiepileptic treatment before the onset of seizures reduces epilepsy severity and risk of mental retardation in infants with tuberous sclerosis complex. Eur J Paediatr Neurol 2011;15(5):424–31.

40. Hancock EC, Osborne JP, Edwards SW. Treatment of infantile spasms. Cochrane Database Syst Rev 2013;(6):CD001770.

41. Curatolo P, Jozwiak S, Nabbout R, et al. Management of epilepsy associated with tuberous sclerosis complex (TSC): clinical recommendations. Eur J Paediatr Neurol 2012;16(6):582–6.

42. Coppola G, Klepper J, Ammendola E, et al. The effects of the ketogenic diet in refractory partial seizures with reference to tuberous sclerosis. Eur J Paediatr Neurol 2006;10(3):148–51.

43. Kossoff EH, Thiele EA, Pfeifer HH, et al. Tuberous sclerosis complex and the ketogenic diet. Epilepsia 2005;46(10):1684–6.

44. Larson AM, Pfeifer HH, Thiele EA. Low glycemic index treatment for epilepsy in tuberous sclerosis complex. Epilepsy Res 2012;99(1–2):180–2.

45. Muncy J, Butler IJ, Koenig MK. Rapamycin reduces seizure frequency in tuberous sclerosis complex. J Child Neurol 2009;24(4):477.

46. Wiegand G, May TW, Ostertag P, et al. Everolimus in tuberous sclerosis patients with intractable epilepsy: a treatment option? Eur J Paediatr Neurol 2013;17(6):631–8.

47. Krueger DA, Wilfong AA, Holland-Bouley K, et al. Everolimus treatment of refractory epilepsy in tuberous sclerosis complex. Ann Neurol 2013;74(5):679–87.

48. Tsai P, Sahin M. Mechanisms of neurocognitive dysfunction and therapeutic considerations in tuberous sclerosis complex. Curr Opin Neurol 2011;24(2):106–13.

49. Rakowski SK, Winterkorn EB, Paul E, et al. Renal manifestations of tuberous sclerosis complex: incidence, prognosis, and predictive factors. Kidney Int 2006;70(10):1777–82.

50. Dixon BP, Hulbert JC, Bissler JJ. Tuberous sclerosis complex renal disease. Nephron Exp Nephrol 2011;118(1):e15–20.

51. Bissler JJ, Kingswood JC, Radzikowska E, et al. Everolimus for angiomyolipoma associated with tuberous sclerosis complex or sporadic lymphangioleiomyomatosis (EXIST-2): a multicentre, randomised, double-blind, placebo-controlled trial. Lancet 2013;381(9869):817–24.

52. Bissler JJ, McCormack FX, Young LR, et al. Sirolimus for angiomyolipoma in tuberous sclerosis complex or lymphangioleiomyomatosis. N Engl J Med 2008; 358(2):140–51.

53. Dabora SL, Franz DN, Ashwal S, et al. Multicenter phase 2 trial of sirolimus for tuberous sclerosis: kidney angiomyolipomas and other tumors regress and VEGF- D levels decrease. PLoS One 2011;6:e23379.

54. Davies DM, de Vries PJ, Johnson SR, et al. Sirolimus therapy for angiomyolipoma in tuberous sclerosis and sporadic lymphangioleiomyomatosis: a phase 2 trial. Clin Cancer Res 2011;17(12):4071–81.

55. Staehler M, Sauter M, Helck A, et al. Nephron-sparing resection of angiomyolipoma after sirolimus pretreatment in patients with tuberous sclerosis. Int Urol Nephrol 2012;44(6):1657–61.

56. Ando K, Kurihara M, Kataoka H, et al. Efficacy and safety of low-dose sirolimus for treatment of lymphangioleiomyomatosis. Respir Investig 2013;51(3):175–83.

57. Taveira-DaSilva AM, Hathaway O, Stylianou M, et al. Changes in lung function and chylous effusions in patients with lymphangioleiomyomatosis treated with sirolimus. Ann Intern Med 2011;154(12):797–805 W-292-3.

58. Neurohr C, Hoffmann AL, Huppmann P, et al. Is sirolimus a therapeutic option for patients with progressive pulmonary lymphangioleiomyomatosis? Respir Res 2011;12:66.

59. McCormack FX, Inoue Y, Moss J, et al. Efficacy and safety of sirolimus in lymphangioleiomyomatosis. N Engl J Med 2011;364(17):1595–606.

60. Young L, Lee HS, Inoue Y, et al. Serum VEGF-D a concentration as a biomarker of lymphangioleiomyomatosis severity and treatment response: a prospective analysis of the Multicenter International Lymphangioleiomyomatosis Efficacy of Sirolimus (MILES) trial. Lancet Respir Med 2013;1(6):445–52.

61. Agrawal S, Fulton AB. Ophthalmic manifestations. In: Kwiatkowski DJ, Whittemore VH, Thiele E, editors. Tuberous sclerosis complex: genes, clinical features, and therapeutics. Weinheim (Germany): WILEY-VCH Verlag GmbH & Co; 2010. p. 271–84 KGaA.

62. Teng JM, Cowen EW, Wataya-Kaneda M, et al. Dermatologic and dental aspects of the 2012 International tuberous sclerosis complex consensus statements. JAMA Dermatol 2014;150(10):1095–101.

63. Balestri R, Neri I, Patrizi A, et al. Analysis of current data on the use of topical rapamycin in the treatment of facial angiofibromas in tuberous sclerosis complex. J Eur Acad Dermatol Venereol 2015;29:14–20.

64. Muzic JG, Kindle SA, Tollefson MM. Successful treatment of subungual fibromas of tuberous sclerosis with topical rapamycin. JAMA Dermatol 2014;150(9): 1024–5.

Emerging Treatments for Pediatric Leukodystrophies

Guy Helman, BS[a,b], Keith Van Haren, MD[c], Maria L. Escolar, MD[d],
Adeline Vanderver, MD[a,b,e],*

KEYWORDS

- Leukodystrophy • Genomics • Therapy • Symptomatic • Disease modifying
- Stem cell • Gene therapy

KEY POINTS

- Although leukodystrophies remain incurable, they are uniformly treatable disorders.
- Next-generation sequencing technologies have enhanced the ability to detect the underlying cause of disease and have permitted identification of pathologic mechanisms in many disorders.
- Several pilot and phase I, II, or III clinical trials are currently in progress for patients with leukodystrophy covering various disorders.
- Awareness and early recognition of the signs and symptoms of patients with leukodystrophy is of utmost importance for the small number with existing therapies.

Disclosures: G. Helman has received support from the Myelin Disorders Bioregistry Project. K. Van Haren has received grants from the Lucile Packard Foundation (salary support), and the Child Neurology Foundation (research and salary support). K. Van Haren also receives salary support as a site coinvestigator on clinical studies funded by Edison Pharmaceuticals (Mountain View, CA) and Bluebird Bio (Cambridge, MA). M.L. Escolar has no relevant disclosures. A. Vanderver has received grants from the National Institutes of Health, National Institute of Neurologic Disorders and Stroke (1K08NS060695), and the Myelin Disorders Bioregistry Project.

[a] Department of Neurology, Children's National Health System, 111 Michigan Avenue, Northwest, Washington, DC 20010, USA; [b] Center for Genetic Medicine Research, Children's National Health System, 111 Michigan Avenue, Northwest, Washington, DC 20010, USA; [c] Department of Neurology, Lucile Packard Children's Hospital, Stanford University School of Medicine, 730 Welch Rd, Palo Alto, CA 94304, USA; [d] Department of Integrated Systems Biology, George Washington University School of Medicine, 2150 Pennsylvania Ave NW, Washington, DC 20037, USA; [e] Department of Integrated Systems Biology, George Washington University School of Medicine, 2150 Pennsylvania Ave NW, Washington, DC 20037, USA
* Corresponding author. Children's National Health System, 111 Michigan Avenue, Northwest, Washington, DC 20010.
E-mail address: avanderv@childrensnational.org

The leukodystrophies are a heterogeneous group of inherited disorders with broad clinical manifestations and variable pathologic mechanisms.[1,2] Although these disorders are individually rare, an incidence of 1 in 7000 suggests that these disorders are collectively more common than was once thought.[1,3–5] In many cases, patients with leukodystrophy remain in the diagnostic category of unsolved disorders, despite significant improvements in diagnostic approaches.[6,7] Even more important, only a few of these disorders have well-established treatments or therapies readily available to the leukodystrophy population.[8] With this in mind, this article provides an update on the emerging treatments available to patients with leukodystrophy and the prospect for future therapies based on new molecular understanding of these conditions in the context of next-generation sequencing.

THE LEUKODYSTROPHIES: CLINICAL BACKGROUND

Although a comprehensive and disease-specific overview of clinical features of the leukodystrophies is beyond the scope of this article, important neurologic and extra-neurologic features are described (**Table 1**). The early clinical course for patients with leukodystrophy is most commonly marked by motor symptoms, manifesting as delayed development of motor skills, a plateau in development, or regression in motor skills.[6] Although patients typically present with acute or subacute onset of neurologic symptoms, a few of these disorders have such a slowly progressive course that they seem more like static encephalopathy until their course is considered over a long span of time.[9] Although marked spasticity and pyramidal motor symptoms are prominent features, leukodystrophies are often associated with rigidity, dystonia, ataxia, and bulbar symptoms.

Although cognition may be spared in the early stages of disease, it is almost invariably affected in the more advanced stages of most leukodystrophies. The nature and severity of cognitive impairment is most likely based on the neural networks affected because of neuronal and axonal dysfunction secondary to myelin disturbances. In childhood this dysfunction is often initially categorized as developmental delay or intellectual disability, and may progress, in some patients, to dementia. However, testing cognitive skills by standard diagnostic tools becomes a challenge as the motor disease progresses and the level of patient cognitive function is often underestimated. In adult-onset leukodystrophies the dysfunction and decline commonly include signs and symptoms of dementia, sometimes accompanied by comorbid psychiatric features.[6]

Other neurologic features may also be present and can help streamline diagnostic efforts. These features include nystagmus, irritability, titubation, autonomic dysfunction, and encephalopathy (with or without autistic features). Macrocephalies and microcephalies are associated with a few leukodystrophies.

Several extraneurologic features in a broad range of categories may indicate specific disorders. These clinical features are particularly useful for guiding the diagnostic evaluation of patients who are initially found to have white matter disease. Endocrine dysfunction may be present as adrenal insufficiency (Addison disease), manifested by fatigue; hypotension; hyponatremia; cutaneous hyperpigmentation; and, sporadically, hypoglycemia. Hypothyroidism, hypogonadotropic hypogonadism, and growth failure are other prominent endocrine abnormalities associated with specific leukodystrophies. Ophthalmologic abnormalities are present in many disorders and may include congenital cataracts or cataract development, retinitis pigmentosa, retinal cherry red macula, optic atrophy, and retinal vascular defects. Dysmorphic physical features, bony abnormalities, hearing impairment, cutaneous abnormalities, and ovarian

Table 1
Common neurologic symptoms for pediatric leukodystrophies with existing and emerging therapies

Symptoms	Associated Diseases	Prevention/Treatment
Adrenal insufficiency	ALD	Annual ACTH screening; corticosteroids. Rare in women with ALD
Inflammatory cerebral demyelination	ALD	Sporadic onset. Highest risk (~40%) of onset occurs in ALD boys 3–12 y old. Also affects 25% of ALD men aged 12–50 y, although comorbid symptoms of AMN in adult men can complicate HSCT. Phenotype is rare among older men as well as women with ALD of any age. Surveillance MRI can detect early demyelination before symptoms appear, thereby enabling HSCT, which effectively halts demyelination, but only if initiated soon after lesion onset
Premature ovarian failure	VWM	None known
Episodic deterioration	VWM, mitochondrial, Pol-III	Avoidance of triggers (eg, head trauma, fevers, severe fright)
Cardiac dysfunction	Mitochondrial	Cardiac evaluation; pacemaker/defibrillator may be appropriate in some patients. Patients should be reevaluated at intervals according to their needs
Deafness	Mitochondrial and 18q− in early stages; many leukodystrophies in later stages	Auditory evaluation; treatments limited
Hypogonadotropic hypogonadism, growth hormone deficiency	Pol-III	Supplemental hormonal therapies
Dental anomalies	Pol-III, ODDD, Cockayne	Dental care to prevent caries, consultation with an orthodontist as necessary. General anesthesia should be used with caution if procedure is nonessential
Hypercholesterolemia xanthoma formation, cataracts, psychomotor decline	CTX	Daily supplementation with chenodeoxycholic acid normalizes cholestanol levels and may prevent and/or improve other disease manifestations, statins

This list is not exhaustive and the remaining leukodystrophies without current therapeutic options are covered elsewhere.
Abbreviations: ACTH, adrenocorticotropic hormone; ALD, adrenoleukodystrophy; AMN, advanced mucosal neoplasia; CTX, cerebrotendinous xanthomatosis; HSCT, hematopoietic stem cell transplant; ODDD, oculo-dento-digital dysplasia; VWM, vanishing white matter disease.
From Parikh S, Bernard G, Leventer R, et al. A clinical approach to the diagnosis of patients with leukodystrophies and genetic leukoencephalopathies. Mol Genet Metab 2014. [pii:S1096-7192(14)00827-0]; with permission.

dysgenesis are other common extraneurologic manifestations of specific white matter disorders. These symptoms are well covered by the work of Parikh and colleagues.[6]

DIAGNOSTIC STRATEGY

Historically, characterization of leukodystrophies has been based on gross pathology and microscopy, identifying common glial cell or myelin sheath abnormalities. More recently, disease characterization has been supplemented by MRI pattern recognition.[10–12] Improved MRI technology is now able to explore abnormalities of myelin in these disorders without neuropathologic correlation.[13] Characterization of MRI patterns has facilitated diagnosis in patients who present on neuroimaging with abnormalities of the cerebral white matter suspicious for a leukodystrophy.[3,12] More recently, diagnosis of patients with leukodystrophies has been successfully enhanced by next-generation sequencing technologies, decreasing the number of unsolved cases from nearly half to approximately 20%.[2]

Several recent publications discuss the diagnostic approach in patients with abnormal white matter on neuroimaging,[2,6] which consists of detailed clinical and neurologic evaluations, review of the MRI to identify disease-specific patterns followed by either targeted genetic or biochemical testing, or, if no disease-specific MRI pattern is found, rapid advance to broad genetic testing strategies.

EXISTING AND EMERGING THERAPIES

A small number of therapies are established in the leukodystrophies. Hematopoietic stem cell therapy (HSCT) is a therapy currently in use for a restricted number of leukodystrophies including X-linked adrenoleukodystrophy (X-ALD) and Krabbe disease, and is still being evaluated as a viable therapy in the case of metachromatic leukodystrophy (MLD). For patients with cerebrotendinous xanthomatosis (CTX), supplementation with chenodeoxycholic acid may provide some neurologic benefits. In all cases, patients benefit most if intervention occurs early in the course of disease, making prompt recognition of the disorders of utmost importance.[14–17]

In addition, an increased understanding of the mechanisms of disease in leukodystrophies has provided a molecular framework for developing potential therapeutic strategies. As such, there are a variety of promising, disease-specific therapies currently in or on the verge of human trials for several leukodystrophies, including Aicardi-Goutières syndrome (AGS), adult polyglucosan body disease (APBD), X-ALD, Krabbe disease, MLD, peroxisomal biogenesis disorders, and Pelizaeus-Merzbacher disease (PMD). Of the 29 active leukodystrophy studies that are listed on clinicaltrials.gov, 16 of these are listed as phase I, II, or III trials (**Table 2**). Covering a broad spectrum of modalities, these studies include traditional pharmaceutical practices as well as the manipulation of stem cells, genes, and enzymes.

Although improved therapeutic strategies and advanced research trials in specific disorders provide long-term hope to patients, clinicians must also attend to the more immediate goals of daily patient care. Leukodystrophies as a group of disorders are symptomatically treatable and require thorough management by the caregiver and responsible clinician to address the complex array of symptoms. As such, this article describes existing and emerging therapies for individual leukodystrophies and highlights several important complications associated with select leukodystrophies as a tool for clinicians encountering a patient with leukodystrophy.

X-ALD is the most common leukodystrophy with disease-specific management and therapeutic guidelines.[18] X-ALD is caused by mutations in *ABCD1*, encoding the adrenoleukodystrophy protein (ALDP), and is an X-linked dominant disorder that results

Table 2
Current clinical trials for pediatric leukodystrophies

Associated Diseases	Study Title	Phase	Intervention
All leukodystrophies and genetic leukoencephalopathies	The Nosology and Etiology of Leukodystrophies of Unknown Causes NCT00889174	NA	Biorepository study
X-ALD; globoid cell leukodystrophy; MLD; PMD	UCB Transplant of Inherited Metabolic Diseases With Administration of Intrathecal UCB Derived Oligodendrocyte-Like Cells NCT02254863	Phase I	Biological: DUOC-01
Globoid cell leukodystrophy; MLD; X-ALD; PMD	Phase I/II Pilot Study of Mixed Chimerism to Treat Inherited Metabolic Disorders NCT01372228	Phase I	Biological: enriched HSCT/novel platform technology
X-ALD; MLD; globoid cell leukodystrophy	Human Placental-Derived Stem Cell Transplantation NCT01586455	Phase I	Drug: human placental-derived stem cell
X-ALD; MLD; globoid cell leukodystrophy	HSCT for High Risk Inherited Inborn Errors NCT00383448	Phase II	Drug: clofarabine Procedure: total body irradiation Drug: melphalan Biological: HSCT Drug: alemtuzumab Drug: mycophenolate mofetil Device: cyclosporine A Drug: hydroxyurea
X-ALD; peroxisomal biogenesis disorders; globoid cell leukodystrophy; MLD; fucosidosis	MT2013-31:Allo BMT for Metabolic Disorders, Osteopetrosis and Males With Rett Syndrome NCT02171104	Phase II	Procedure: blood stem cell transplant Drug: rabbit antithymocyte globulin Drug: fludarabine Drug: busulfan Drug: cyclophosphamide Drug: cyclosporine A Drug: methylprednisolone Drug: mycophenolate mofetil Drug: granulocyte colony-stimulating factor Drug: granulocyte-macrophage colony-stimulating factor Drug: N-acetylcysteine Drug: celecoxib Drug: vitamin E Drug: alpha lipoic acid

(continued on next page)

Table 2
(continued)

Associated Diseases	Study Title	Phase	Intervention
X-ALD; MLD; globoid cell leukodystrophy; peroxisomal biogenesis disorders	Allogeneic Bone Marrow Transplant for Inherited Metabolic Disorders NCT01043640	Phase II	Drug: campath-1H Drug: cyclophosphamide Drug: busulfan Procedure: allogeneic stem cell transplantation Drug: cyclosporine A Drug: mycophenolate mofetil
X-ALD	Exercise Study of Function and Pathology for Women With X-linked Adrenoleukodystrophy NCT01594853	NA	Behavioral: exercise training
	Expanded Access for Lorenzo's Oil (GTO/GTE) in Adrenoleukodystrophy NCT02233257	NA	Drug: Lorenzo's oil
	Safety and Pharmacodynamic Study of Sobetirome in X-ALD NCT01787578	Phase I	Drug: sobetirome
	A Phase 2/3 Study of the Efficacy and Safety of Hematopoietic Stem Cells Transduced With Lenti-D Lentiviral Vector for the Treatment of Childhood Cerebral Adrenoleukodystrophy NCT01896102	Phase II/III	Genetic: Lenti-D drug product Drug: busulfan Drug: cyclophosphamide Drug: filgrastim
APBD	Triheptanoin Treatment Trial for Patients With Adult Polyglucosan Body Disease NCT01971957	Phase II	Drug: triheptanoin Dietary supplement: vegetable oil
Canavan disease	Oral GTA in Newborns With Canavan NCT00724802	NA	Dietary supplement: GTA Drug: GTA
CTX	Evaluation of Carotid IMT and Atherogenic Risk Factors in Patients With Cerebrotendinous Xanthomatosis NCT01613898	NA	Biological: blood tests
	Phase II Study of Cholesterol- and Cholestanol-Free Diet, Lovastatin, and Chenodeoxycholic Acid for Cerebrotendinous Xanthomatosis NCT00004346	Phase II	Drug: chenodeoxycholic acid Drug: lovastatin

Disease	Study	Phase	Intervention
Krabbe disease	The Natural History of Infantile Globoid Cell Leukodystrophy NCT00983879	NA	NA
	Biomarker for Krabbe Disease NCT01425489	NA	NA
	Lysosomal Storage Disease: Health, Development, and Functional Outcome Surveillance in Preschool Children NCT01938014	NA	NA
MLD	Biomarker for Metachromatic Leukodystrophy NCT01536327	NA	NA
	Imaging Study of the White Matter Lesions in Children With Metachromatic Leukodystrophy NCT01325025	NA	High-field MRI
	Natural History Study of Children With Metachromatic Leukodystrophy NCT01963650	NA	Natural history study
	The Natural History of Infantile Metachromatic Leukodystrophy NCT00639132	NA	—
	Intracerebral Gene Therapy for Children With Early Onset Forms of Metachromatic Leukodystrophy NCT01801709	Phase I/II	Genetic: intracerebral administration of AAVrh.10cuARSA
	Gene Therapy for Metachromatic Leukodystrophy NCT01560182	Phase I/II	Genetic: autologous CD34+ stem cells transduced with ARSA encoding lentiviral vector
	Multicenter Study of HGT-1110 Administered Intrathecally in Children With MLD NCT01510028	Phase I/II	Biological: recombinant human arylsulfatase A
	Open-Label Extension Study Evaluating Safety and Efficacy of -1110 in Patients With Metachromatic Leukodystrophy NCT01887938	Phase I/II	Biological: recombinant human arylsulfatase A
Peroxisomal biogenesis disorders	Betaine and Peroxisome Biogenesis Disorders NCT01838941	Phase III	Drug: betaine
Sjögren-Larsson syndrome	Sjögren-Larsson Syndrome: Natural History, Clinical Variation and Evaluation of Biochemical Markers NCT01971957	Phase III	NA
18q deletion syndrome	Growth Hormone and Chromosome 18q⁻ and Abnormal Growth NCT00134420	Phase III	Drug: Nutropin AQ; Procedure: arginine and clonidine stimulation testing; Procedure: growth factors laboratory testing; Procedure: neuropsychological testing

Abbreviations: APBD, adult polyglucosan body disease; ARSA, arylsulfatase A; BMT, bone marrow transplantation; DUOC, UCB-derived oligodendrocyte-like cells; GTA, glyceryl triacetate; HGT, horizontal genet transfer; IMT, intima-media thickness; MLD, metachromatic leukodystrophy; NA, not applicable; PMD, Pelizaeus-Merzbacher disease; UCB, umbilical cord blood; X-ALD, X-linked adrenoleukodystrophy.

from a deficient very-long-chain fatty acid transport protein on the surface of the peroxisome. Four primary phenotypes (asymptomatic, adrenal insufficiency, cerebral ALD, and adrenomyeloneuropathy) have been identified in patients with X-ALD, which may overlap during the lifespan. All patients begin life asymptomatic and, in rare cases, may remain asymptomatic into the fourth decade in the case of men or the sixth decade in the case of women. However, all men and most women who carry an aberrant copy of the X-ALD gene eventually manifest the spastic paraparesis and sphincter dysfunction that is characteristic of adrenomyeloneuropathy. Women are generally spared from adrenal insufficiency and cerebral ALD, which are the most dangerous forms of ALD. The adrenal insufficiency phenotype is life threatening if undiagnosed, but is also easily treatable with a daily, oral corticosteroid supplementation. Diagnosis is made via clinical history and cortisol stimulation testing. All men with X-ALD should be screened via cortisol stimulation testing every 6 to 9 months for adrenal insufficiency. Endocrinology follow-up and a corticosteroid regime should be considered in patients who show an inadequate response to cortisol stimulation testing.

As for the cerebral ALD phenotype, HSCT is highly effective at arresting the otherwise relentless progression of the brain lesion if administered during the early stages of cerebral demyelination when the lesion is still small. However, HSCT has no therapeutic effect if administered in the later stages of disease,[14,15,17] highlighting the importance of early diagnosis. Surveillance MRI studies can help identify early brain lesions, before clinical symptoms appear and in time for HSCT. When a suspicious brain lesion is identified in an individual with X-ALD, it is imperative that they be promptly evaluated using established clinical and radiologic criteria that have been established for triaging candidates for HSCT.[15] In general, lower levels of pretransplant neurologic morbidity (ie, low MRI severity score,[19] low degree of neurologic disability, and a high neuropsychometric measures) predict favorable HSCT outcomes.[14,15] The therapeutic benefits of HSCT in patients with X-ALD are thought to arise, at least in part, through the replacement of the patient's genetically deficient brain microglia with genetically competent microglial progenitor cells arising from the donor blood.[20]

Newborn screening for X-ALD is being implemented in a growing number of US states. Boys with X-ALD, aged 3 to 12 years, identified through newborn screening or as relatives of a proband, should undergo gadolinium-enhanced MRI of the brain every 6 months to screen for early signs of cerebral demyelination in order to establish the need for early intervention. Annual MRI studies should be considered for adolescent boys and adults, who are at slightly lower risk for developing the cerebral ALD phenotype (**Fig. 1**). Among men with X-ALD more than 50 years of age and women with X-ALD (heterozygotes) of any age, the onset of the cerebral and/or adrenal insufficiency phenotypes is uncommon, suggesting that routine surveillance screening for these individuals is probably unnecessary.

The risk of developing cerebral X-ALD, the most serious phenotype, may be mitigated by daily consumption of Lorenzo's oil, which is a mixture of oleic and erucic acid, in combination with dietary restriction of very-long-chain fatty acids.[21] The oil acts as a competitive inhibitor of enzymes involved in endogenous production of very-long-chain fatty acids.[22] Use of Lorenzo's oil does not affect the progression of cerebral X-ALD once the disease course has begun,[21] and it has not been proved to mitigate the onset or progression of adrenomyeloneuropathy. Its consumption carries health risks[23] and its availability in the United States is currently restricted to boys with X-ALD aged 3 to 10 years under an expanded access trial (ClinicalTrials.gov, NCT02233257). A pilot phase trial using thyromimetics, synthetic structural analogues of thyroid hormone that mimic tissue-restricted thyroid hormone actions,[24] is in

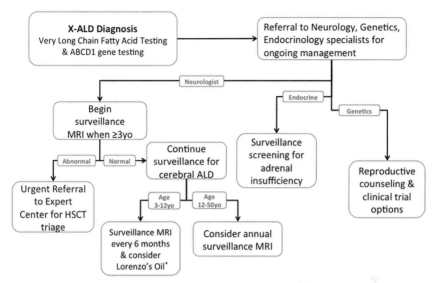

Fig. 1. X-ALD outpatient care management flow diagram. Note the emphasis on identification of a treatable disorder if recognized early in the clinical course. Routine evaluations for any clinical changes are of utmost importance. The asterisk designates therapies in clinical trial stages. (*Adapted from* Engelen M, Kemp S, de Visser M, et al. X-linked adrenoleukodystrophy (X-ALD): clinical presentation and guidelines for diagnosis, follow-up and management. Orphanet J Rare Dis 2012;7:51.)

preparatory phases using soberitome (ClinicalTrials.gov identifier NCT01787578). They can distinctly regulate subsets of thyroid hormone–responsive genes by mimicking subtype-selective thyroid hormone receptor agonists. Sobetirome, a thyroid hormone receptor beta agonist,[25] has had promising results in cholesterol metabolism. It is thought that sobetirome can also activate the production of ATP-binding cassette, subfamily D (ALD), member 2 (ABCD2), closely related to ATP-binding cassette, subfamily D (ALD), member 1 (ABCD1) protein. The work of Weber and colleagues[26] has shown that ABCD2 can compensate for defective ABCD1, providing support for its targeting in therapeutic measures.

Lentiviral-based gene therapy has shown early promise in X-ALD.[27] This technology relies on ex vivo transduction of autologous hematopoietic stem cells encoding wild-type ABDC1 complementary DNA by a human immunodeficiency virus type 1–derived vector that targets microglial precursors. The therapy performed in 2 young male patients resulted in polyclonal hematopoietic repopulation and stable lentivirally encoded ALD protein expression.[20] In addition, stabilization of cerebral demyelination was noted on MRI after reinfusion of the genetically modified cells. To date, there have been no reported cases of insertional mutagenesis or malignancy. This treatment is now entering phase II/III clinical trials (ClinicalTrials.gov identifier NCT01896102).

Despite the potential for overlap between the 4 recognized phenotypes, each has its own distinct management strategies.[18] Adrenal insufficiency is life threatening in most cases of X-ALD but can be treatable if identified in a timely fashion. Although symptoms may not be present, extenuating circumstances, such as an affected relative, may allow early diagnosis of the X-ALD genotype.

AGS is an inherited leukodystrophy characterized by a calcifying microangiopathy and increased cerebrospinal fluid (CSF) interferon alfa levels. There are now 7 known AGS causative genes (*TREX1, RNASEH2A/B/C, SAMHD1, ADAR1*, and *IFIH1*), all of which are associated with genome surveillance, integrity, damage repair, and DNA sensing. Mutations in these genes seem to result in the irregular accumulation of RNA/DNA hybrids and other immunogenic nucleic acid structures within the cell.[28–31] Experiments in the murine model of AGS have shown this overaccumulation of endogenous retroelements,[32,33] whereas sterile alpha motif (SAM) domain and histidine-aspartic domain–containing protein 1 (SAMHD1) has been shown to be a dominant suppressor of long interspersed element 1 (LINE-1). AGS-related mutations compromise the potency of SAMHD1 against LINE-1 retrotransposition.[34] Within the murine model of AGS, the use of reverse transcriptase inhibitors presumably targeting production of endogenous retroelements has been studied with promising results.[35] Significant work is still necessary to better understand the mechanisms of this disorder but efforts are underway to test the use of antiretroviral therapy in patients with AGS.

Patients with AGS are susceptible to autoimmune complications as a result of possible accumulated immunogenic nucleic acids. Increased CSF interferon alfa level has been an important marker in patient diagnosis as well as prompting investigation into these autoimmune complications. Patients may manifest features that overlap with those shown by patients affected by systemic lupus erythematosus (SLE), and rare cases of SLE have been found to be associated with *TREX1* mutations. Patients with AGS have persistent induced immune system activation with autoinflammation and cytokine production causing an accumulation of cytokines.[36] Symptom management has involved corticosteroid and other immunosuppressive regimens but definite improvements in neurologic symptoms have not been observed.[36] Patients with AGS require monitoring for chilblains and other skin inflammation, arthritis, inflammatory bowel disease, hematologic complications, and cardiomyopathy.[37] In addition, patients with AGS may manifest other autoimmune, thyroid, and endocrine conditions, and should be screened and treated appropriately. For patients with mutations in *SAMHD1* causative of AGS, a potential life-threatening complication is large vessel vasculitis, which requires screening.

Alexander disease (AxD) is a leukodystrophy with distinct early-onset and late-onset forms, named type I and type II, respectively. Patients present with common leukodystrophy symptoms, such as motor deficits and, in type I AxD, seizures. More specific to type I AxD is the accumulation of mutated glial fibrillary acidic protein, which can result in obstruction of CSF pathways and hydrocephalus.[38] Patients require routine monitoring for this complication and attention to complaints of headache, changes in vision, or abrupt changes in behavior should help detect this complication. Consultation and intervention by neurosurgical teams maybe warranted depending on severity. Patients with late-onset (older child or adult), type II AxD may show symptoms such as obstructive sleep apnea, which if untreated can result in encephalopathy, as well as significant bulbar dysfunction, with the characteristic dysphonia and palatal myoclonus.[38]

APBD is an adult-onset leukodystrophy manifesting with peripheral neuropathy and progressive spasticity. It is thought that these symptoms arise from neuronal damage and dysfunction caused by accumulated intracellular polyglucosan bodies throughout the peripheral nerves and central nervous system (CNS). Mutated *GBE1* causes deficient glycogen brancher enzyme activity and, in combination with accumulated polyglucosan bodies, is hypothesized to lead to an energy-deficient state after deficient glycogen degradation. The implementation of triheptanoin, a 7-carbon triglyceride, is suspected to provide an efficient substrate to the citric acid cycle to correct the resultant energy deficit.[39] The use of triheptanoin in anaplerotic therapy may prove beneficial in slowing the clinical course of these patients (ClinicalTrials.gov identifier NCT00947960).

Canavan disease is caused by a deficiency of the aspartoacylase, which is required for *N*-acetylaspartic acid (NAA) metabolism in the brain.[40] Onset is usually in the first year of life and neuropathology is characterized by progressive spongiform degeneration of the brain. Initial results from the first gene therapy trial showed that intraventricular delivery of liposome-encapsulated plasmid DNA produced a transient decrease in NAA accumulation, with neuroimaging suggestive of new myelination in 50% of patients.[41] Subsequent phase I/II clinical trials used intraparenchymal gene delivery and a recombinant adeno-associated virus serotype 2 vector. Magnetic resonance spectroscopy revealed decreased brain NAA concentrations and MRI changes suggesting more normal myelination and stabilization of brain atrophy with reduced disease symptoms on long-term follow-up.[42]

Patients with CTX may benefit from chenodeoxycholic acid therapy by oral supplementation. CTX is an autosomal recessive inherited lipid storage disorder that results from a genetic mutation causing a deficiency in 27-hydroxylase. This mitochondrial enzyme is responsible for an early step in bile acid synthesis. High levels of serum cholestanol and bile acids deposit in the brain, lens, and tendons as features of this disorder. Patients show symptoms of cataracts and diarrhea in early childhood, progressing to psychomotor decline and tendon xanthomas in late adulthood. Daily oral supplementation with 750 mg of chenodeoxycholic acid, a bile salt, typically corrects the biochemical abnormalities and may reverse some clinical symptoms.[43,44] Earlier treatment initiation may lead to better outcomes; reversibility of existing neurologic injury is limited.[16] Oral statins are often included in the CTX treatment regimen, although their clinical benefit is unknown.

Krabbe or globoid cell leukodystrophy results in deficiency in galactosylceramidase (GALC). Patients with Krabbe disease have severe neurologic symptoms caused by mutations in *GALC*, the gene encoding GALC. Patients have had beneficial results from HSCT, in particular in the presymptomatic infantile-onset forms. HSCT can arrest CNS deterioration and cognitive ability has been well preserved based on clinical follow-up.[45–47] However, several patients have experienced progressive motor difficulties despite early intervention. Clinical staging criteria have been proposed for Krabbe disease[48] and are useful in evaluating potential outcomes of HSCT.[49] Newborn screening for Krabbe disease is also available in a select number of US states, providing a basis for presymptomatic treatment. HSCT may also prove beneficial to patients with later disease onset, such as late-infantile, juvenile-onset, and adult-onset cases, although it has not been well studied.[46,47]

More than 60% of patients with Krabbe have missense mutations in *GALC*. These mutations are predicted to generate misfolded proteins[50] that can be mislocalized, prematurely degraded, accumulate intracellularly, or trigger an unfolded protein response.[51–53] The neurologic consequences of this disorder are hypothesized to be potentially avoidable with even 10% of normal GALC function.[54] Orally administered pharmacologic chaperones can rescue the function of mutant proteins by directing proper folding or cellular localization, or protecting them from degradation.[55–57] α-Lobeline and 3′,4′,7-trihydroxyisoflavone are two pharmacologic agents that are currently being studied for their utility in improving the function of GALC after initial misfolding.[58,59]

Hypomyelination with brain stem and spinal cord abnormalities and leg spasticity (HBSL) is the result of mutations in *DARS*, a cytoplasmic transfer RNA (tRNA) synthetase gene for aspartate. Patients with HBSL present with a broad phenotypic spectrum characterized by focal cerebral white matter abnormalities and spinal cord signal abnormalities.[60] Responsiveness to steroids in several patients with HBSL with subacute disease onset suggests that steroids may be an appropriate treatment modifying approach in mutation-positive patients.[60] Certain tRNA synthetases have noncanonical functions in biological processes such as angiogenesis, regulation of gene transcription, and RNA splicing.[61] These noncanonical tRNA synthetase functions are conserved across the complete phylogeny of animals, and are now established as playing key roles in several pathophysiologic processes.[61] Aspartyl-tRNA synthetase (DARS) is one of 9 cytoplasmic tRNA synthetases that make up the multisynthetase complex, which facilitates gene-specific translational silencing of inflammation-related mRNAs. Although these mechanisms and functions must be studied further to elucidate why individuals seem responsive to steroids and what their clinical response is, it provides an interesting basis for compassionate care treatment in these patients.

Metachromatic leukodystrophy (MLD) has been treated with HSCT,[47,62–64] although its use has been widely debated within the MLD community. Because of the phenotypic variability seen, the use of HSCT has proved particularly complex. The posttransplant patients with late-infantile-onset forms have been found to have poor motor skills and variable cognitive outcomes, resulting in some doubt over the utility of transplant.[15] Other factors, such as transplant-refractory peripheral neuropathy, significant morbidity and mortality risks, and a lack of long-term outcome data have hindered its use. Symptomatic children with the late-infantile form of MLD are poor candidates for these therapies, as are individuals with later onset forms of the disease who have already accrued cognitive morbidity.[15,47,65,66] Bone marrow transplantation has been shown to halt demyelination in asymptomatic patients diagnosed because of family history of late-infantile-onset disease, and in minimally symptomatic patients with juvenile or adult MLD.[67]

Although there is still disagreement about the viability of transplants for some forms of MLD, morbidity rates for HSCT have decreased and treatment regimens have been improved.[15] Patient outcomes of minimally symptomatic patients with late-infantile and juvenile MLD have also been improved by the use of umbilical cord blood, which has decreased the time between diagnosis and transplantation. Patients with the minimally symptomatic juvenile disease form have reported the most favorable outcomes, although there is still substantial variability with regard to clinical status, MRI severity score, peripheral nerve disease, and neurologic examination.[68–71]

Treatment recommendations are based on the limited long-term longitudinal outcome data currently available, as is the case of allogeneic HSCT for Krabbe and MLD.[63,69,72] The decision to pursue transplantation among patients with these disorders can be complex and as a result must be evaluated on an individual basis by a specialized and experienced center, prepared to provide the most up-to-date information and support patients with complex neurologic and systemic manifestations.

Because therapy with HSCT has resulted in variable outcomes, enzyme replacement therapy (ERT) is currently being studied internationally. ERT replaces the deficient or missing enzyme with an active enzyme through a recombinant human protein produced by gene activation technology. Although data are currently being collected, therapeutic efficacy of ERT seems to depend on factors such as enzyme dose, frequency, and the disease stage at which treatment is initiated. A regular repeated intravenous delivery of recombinant human arylsulfatase A used in previous clinical trials had limited efficacy in permeating the blood-brain barrier,[73] thus current phase I/II studies use an intrathecal delivery and a different enzyme doses (ClinicalTrials.gov identifier NCT01510028).

As a result of lentiviral gene therapy, there was greater than normal enzyme activity in the CNS and arrested disease progression in 3 presymptomatic patients with MLD as part of a phase I/II clinical trial. There are efforts ongoing to prepare for phase II/III studies (ClinicalTrials.gov identifier NCT01560182).[27]

In patients with MLD, deficient arylsulfatase A results in accumulated sulfatides, with significant complications. The gallbladder is especially affected, and patients may present with enlarged gallbladder, cholecystitis, sludge, gallstone, papillomatosis, wall thickening, and more rarely polyposis. Special monitoring is required for these patients whereas gallbladder complications preceding neurologic symptom onset may provide an opportunity for early detection and management to stall the neurologic consequences associated with MLD.[74]

Peroxisomal biogenesis disorders or Zellweger spectrum disorders (ZSDs) result from mutations in at least 13 peroxisomal (*PEX*) genes that aid in peroxisome assembly[75] and is inherited in autosomal recessive fashion. The resulting defects result in a heterogenous clinical picture with peroxisomal enzyme deficiencies caused by a diminished number of peroxisomes, enlarged peroxisomes for those that are formed, and loss of enzyme import functions. Although there is multisystem involvement in almost all patients, those with mutations that entirely annul PEX protein function cause Zellweger syndrome, which is the most severe form of the disorder. Patients with Zellweger syndrome are born with neuronal migration defects, and typically do not survive past 1 to 2 years of age. In contrast, most patients with ZSD do not show similar migration defects. MRI may initially be normal, but patients are at risk of developing white matter changes over time. About 30% of patients have a PEX1-Gly843Asp common mutation, caused by a founder effect in persons of European ancestry.[76] The resultant protein is misfolded and open to degradation but was notably receptive to stabilizing cell-level interventions.[77] Zhang and colleagues[78] used a phenotype-based assay with PEX1-Gly843Asp cell lines expressing a GFP-PTS1 reporter to test the utility of chaperone compounds in recovering peroxisome enzyme import as part of a drug library screen. This work has been ongoing in a phase III clinical trial, based on the nonspecific chemical chaperone betaine, to determine whether there is improvement in key peroxisome functions and patient growth/development (ClinicalTrials.gov identifier NCT01838941).

PMD results from mutations in *PLP1*. *PLP1* encodes proteolipid protein, which comprises a large percentage of myelin sheath proteins and promotes stability within the sheath, but also plays a role in oligodendrocyte development and axonal survival.[79] The resultant phenotype is a severe hypomyelinating leukodystrophy characterized by early-onset nystagmus, hypotonia, and cognitive impairment progressing to ataxia and spasticity. The connatal form is more severe, with onset within the first 2 weeks of life and symptoms commonly including seizures and stridor. Preclinical studies with human CNS stem cell (HuCNS-SC) showed that transplantation in hypomyelinated *shiverer* mice generated new oligodendrocytes with myelin production.[80] Phase I safety studies have been pursued in the use of HuCNS-SC transplant for patients with the connatal form of PMD. The phase I trial at the University of California, San Francisco, in conjunction with StemCells, Inc (Newark, CA), transplanted HuCNS-SC directly into subcortical white matter tracts of 4 children with connatal PMD. MRI studies showed evidence for qualitative changes on T_1-weighted and T_2-weighted imaging and progressive increases in fractional anisotropy on diffusion tensor imaging (DTI).[81] Moreover, such DTI signal changes persisted after stopping immunosuppressive therapies. This approach has established a potentially safe methodology for other leukodystrophies and leukoencephalopathies that may benefit from the application of HuCNS-SCs, or other CNS cell types (eg, oligodendrocyte precursors), through direct transplantation into the brain.[82]

Polymerase III-related leukodystrophies typically present with some sort of hormonal deficiency, most notably hypogonadotropic hypogonadism, which presents as delayed puberty, requiring input and follow-up with an endocrinologist. Treatment of hormonal deficiency should be evaluated on a case-by-case basis, weighing the risk of disease against potential treatment benefits with the input of the clinician and family. Other manifestations commonly seen are growth hormone failure and/or hypothyroidism, which should be screened for in routine follow-up.

Dental anomalies are also common manifestations of polymerase III–related leukodystrophies, and are also a common finding in other hypomyelinating leukodystrophies, such as Cockayne syndrome, and oculodentodigital dysplasia. For patients with any of these conditions, dental care is of utmost importance and regular visits to the dentist are recommended. Regular dental care and hygiene are important for all patients with leukodystrophy because cavities and abscesses may go unnoticed in routine medical care and can result in severe medical morbidity. Thus, regular dental visits are recommended for all patients with leukodystrophy.

SUMMARY

Current treatment of most patients with leukodystrophy is based on symptomatic management and supportive care. Leukodystrophies are complex, serious disorders that provide challenges for families and clinicians alike. The severe complications that can arise for these patients should be addressed proactively and follow a plan that is well communicated between the clinician and the family with the ultimate goals of maximizing patient quality of life and prevention of other serious complications. With this in mind, the number of disorders on the verge of phase I/II clinical trials is especially promising for treatment of patients with leukodystrophy, who after a long diagnostic journey frequently encounter a disorder with limited treatment prospects. Although there is still much work to be done, the growth of clinical research networks in leukodystrophies and the alliance of these consortiums with patient advocacy groups is an important step for the advancement and prioritization of care for patients with leukodystrophy.

REFERENCES

1. Vanderver A, Hussey H, Schmidt JL, et al. Relative incidence of inherited white matter disorders in childhood to acquired pediatric demyelinating disorders. Semin Pediatr Neurol 2012;19:219–23.
2. Vanderver A, Prust M, Tonduti D, et al. Case definition and classification of leukodystrophies and leukoencephalopathies. Mol Genet Metab 2014 [pii:S1096–7192(15)00028-1].
3. Bonkowsky JL, Nelson C, Kingston JL, et al. The burden of inherited leukodystrophies in children. Neurology 2010;75:718–25.
4. Brimley CJ, Lopez J, van Haren K, et al. National variation in costs and mortality for leukodystrophy patients in US children's hospitals. Pediatr Neurol 2013;49:156–62.e1.
5. Nelson C, Mundorff MB, Korgenski EK, et al. Determinants of health care use in a population-based leukodystrophy cohort. J Pediatr 2013;162:624–8.e1.
6. Parikh S, Bernard G, Leventer R, et al. A clinical approach to the diagnosis of patients with leukodystrophies and genetic leukoencephalopathies. Mol Genet Metab 2014 [pii:S1096–7192(14)00827-0].
7. Vanderver A, Simons C, Helman G, et al. Whole exome sequencing in a cohort of patients with unresolved white matter abnormalities, in press.
8. Helman G, Van Haren K, Bonkowsky J, et al. Targeted disease specific and emerging therapeutics in leukodystrophies and leukoencephalopathies. 2015 [pii:S1096-7192(15)00036-0].

9. Vanderver A, Tonduti D, Schiffmann R, et al. Leukodystrophy overview. In: Pagon RA, Adam MP, Bird TD, et al, editors. GeneReviews(R). Seattle (WA): University of Washington; Seattle University of Washington; 2014.
10. Schiffmann R, van der Knaap MS. Invited article: an MRI-based approach to the diagnosis of white matter disorders. Neurology 2009;72:750–9.
11. Steenweg ME, Vanderver A, Blaser S, et al. Magnetic resonance imaging pattern recognition in hypomyelinating disorders. Brain 2010;133:2971–82.
12. Van der Knaap M, editor. Magnetic resonance of myelination and myelin disorders. Berlin: Springer-Verlag; 2005.
13. Pouwels PJ, Vanderver A, Bernard G, et al. Hypomyelinating leukodystrophies: translational research progress and prospects. Ann Neurol 2014;76:5–19.
14. Miller WP, Rothman SM, Nascene D, et al. Outcomes after allogeneic hematopoietic cell transplantation for childhood cerebral adrenoleukodystrophy: the largest single-institution cohort report. Blood 2011;118:1971–8.
15. Peters C, Charnas LR, Tan Y, et al. Cerebral X-linked adrenoleukodystrophy: the international hematopoietic cell transplantation experience from 1982 to 1999. Blood 2004;104:881–8.
16. Pilo-de-la-Fuente B, Jimenez-Escrig A, Lorenzo JR, et al. Cerebrotendinous xanthomatosis in Spain: clinical, prognostic, and genetic survey. Eur J Neurol 2011; 18:1203–11.
17. Shapiro E, Krivit W, Lockman L, et al. Long-term effect of bone-marrow transplantation for childhood-onset cerebral X-linked adrenoleukodystrophy. Lancet 2000; 356:713–8.
18. Engelen M, Kemp S, de Visser M, et al. X-linked adrenoleukodystrophy (X-ALD): clinical presentation and guidelines for diagnosis, follow-up and management. Orphanet J Rare Dis 2012;7:51.
19. Thibert KA, Raymond GV, Nascene DR, et al. Cerebrospinal fluid matrix metalloproteinases are elevated in cerebral adrenoleukodystrophy and correlate with MRI severity and neurologic dysfunction. PLoS One 2012;7:e50430.
20. Cartier N, Hacein-Bey-Abina S, Bartholomae CC, et al. Hematopoietic stem cell gene therapy with a lentiviral vector in X-linked adrenoleukodystrophy. Science 2009;326:818–23.
21. Moser HW, Raymond GV, Lu SE, et al. Follow-up of 89 asymptomatic patients with adrenoleukodystrophy treated with Lorenzo's oil. Arch Neurol 2005;62:1073–80.
22. Sassa T, Wakashima T, Ohno Y, et al. Lorenzo's oil inhibits ELOVL1 and lowers the level of sphingomyelin with a saturated very long-chain fatty acid. J Lipid Res 2014;55:524–30.
23. Semmler A, Kohler W, Jung HH, et al. Therapy of X-linked adrenoleukodystrophy. Exp Rev Neurother 2008;8:1367–79.
24. Hirano T, Kagechika H. Thyromimetics: a review of recent reports and patents (2004–2009). Expert Opin Ther Pat 2010;20:213–28.
25. Scanlan TS. Sobetirome: a case history of bench-to-clinic drug discovery and development. Heart Fail Rev 2010;15:177–82.
26. Weber FD, Wiesinger C, Forss-Petter S, et al. X-linked adrenoleukodystrophy: very long-chain fatty acid metabolism is severely impaired in monocytes but not in lymphocytes. Hum Mol Genet 2014;23:2542–50.
27. Biffi A, Montini E, Lorioli L, et al. Lentiviral hematopoietic stem cell gene therapy benefits metachromatic leukodystrophy. Science 2013;341:1233158.
28. Crow YJ, Hayward BE, Parmar R, et al. Mutations in the gene encoding the 3'-5' DNA exonuclease TREX1 cause Aicardi-Goutieres syndrome at the AGS1 locus. Nat Genet 2006;38:917–20.

29. Crow YJ, Leitch A, Hayward BE, et al. Mutations in genes encoding ribonuclease H2 subunits cause Aicardi-Goutieres syndrome and mimic congenital viral brain infection. Nat Genet 2006;38:910–6.

30. Rice GI, Bond J, Asipu A, et al. Mutations involved in Aicardi-Goutieres syndrome implicate SAMHD1 as regulator of the innate immune response. Nat Genet 2009; 41:829–32.

31. Rice GI, Kasher PR, Forte GM, et al. Mutations in ADAR1 cause Aicardi-Goutieres syndrome associated with a type I interferon signature. Nat Genet 2012;44: 1243–8.

32. Stetson DB. Endogenous retroelements and autoimmune disease. Curr Opin Immunol 2012;24:692–7.

33. Stetson DB, Ko JS, Heidmann T, et al. Trex1 prevents cell-intrinsic initiation of autoimmunity. Cell 2008;134:587–98.

34. Zhao K, Du J, Han X, et al. Modulation of LINE-1 and Alu/SVA retrotransposition by Aicardi-Goutieres syndrome-related SAMHD1. Cell Rep 2013;4:1108–15.

35. Beck-Engeser GB, Eilat D, Wabl M. An autoimmune disease prevented by antiretroviral drugs. Retrovirology 2011;8:91.

36. Chahwan C, Chahwan R. Aicardi-Goutieres syndrome: from patients to genes and beyond. Clin Genet 2012;81:413–20.

37. Crow YC, Chase D, Lowenstein Schmidt J, et al. Characterization of human disease phenotypes associated with mutations in TREX1, RNASEH2A, RNASEH2B, RNASEH2C, SAMHD1, ADAR and IFIH1. Am J Med Genet A 2015;167:296–312.

38. Prust M, Wang J, Morizono H, et al. GFAP mutations, age at onset, and clinical subtypes in Alexander disease. Neurology 2011;77:1287–94.

39. Roe CR, Bottiglieri T, Wallace M, et al. Adult polyglucosan body disease (APBD): anaplerotic diet therapy (Triheptanoin) and demonstration of defective methylation pathways. Mol Genet Metab 2010;101:246–52.

40. Matalon R, Michals K, Sebesta D, et al. Aspartoacylase deficiency and N-acetylaspartic aciduria in patients with Canavan disease. Am J Med Genet 1988;29: 463–71.

41. Leone P, Janson CG, Bilaniuk L, et al. Aspartoacylase gene transfer to the mammalian central nervous system with therapeutic implications for Canavan disease. Ann Neurol 2000;48:27–38.

42. Leone P, Shera D, McPhee SW, et al. Long-term follow-up after gene therapy for Canavan disease. Sci Transl Med 2012;4:165ra163.

43. Berginer VM, Salen G, Shefer S. Long-term treatment of cerebrotendinous xanthomatosis with chenodeoxycholic acid. N Engl J Med 1984;311:1649–52.

44. Tokimura Y, Kuriyama M, Arimura K, et al. Electrophysiological studies in cerebrotendinous xanthomatosis. J Neurol Neurosurg Psychiatry 1992;55:52–5.

45. Escolar ML, Poe MD, Provenzale JM, et al. Transplantation of umbilical-cord blood in babies with infantile Krabbe's disease. N Engl J Med 2005;352:2069–81.

46. Krivit W. Allogeneic stem cell transplantation for the treatment of lysosomal and peroxisomal metabolic diseases. Springer Semin Immunopathol 2004;26:119–32.

47. Krivit W, Peters C, Shapiro EG. Bone marrow transplantation as effective treatment of central nervous system disease in globoid cell leukodystrophy, metachromatic leukodystrophy, adrenoleukodystrophy, mannosidosis, fucosidosis, aspartylglucosaminuria, Hurler, Maroteaux-Lamy, and Sly syndromes, and Gaucher disease type III. Curr Opin Neurol 1999;12:167–76.

48. Escolar ML, Poe MD, Martin HR, et al. A staging system for infantile Krabbe disease to predict outcome after unrelated umbilical cord blood transplantation. Pediatrics 2006;118:e879–89.

49. Escolar ML, Poe MD, Smith JK, et al. Diffusion tensor imaging detects abnormalities in the corticospinal tracts of neonates with infantile Krabbe disease. AJNR Am J Neuroradiol 2009;30:1017–21.

50. Wenger DA, Rafi MA, Luzi P. Molecular genetics of Krabbe disease (globoid cell leukodystrophy): diagnostic and clinical implications. Hum Mutat 1997;10: 268–79.

51. Bueter W, Dammann O, Leviton A. Endoplasmic reticulum stress, inflammation, and perinatal brain damage. Pediatr Res 2009;66:487–94.

52. D'Antonio M, Feltri ML, Wrabetz L. Myelin under stress. J Neurosci Res 2009;87: 3241–9.

53. Herczenik E, Gebbink MF. Molecular and cellular aspects of protein misfolding and disease. FASEB J 2008;22:2115–33.

54. Conzelmann E, Sandhoff K. Partial enzyme deficiencies: residual activities and the development of neurological disorders. Dev Neurosci 1983;6:58–71.

55. Boyd RE, Lee G, Rybczynski P, et al. Pharmacological chaperones as therapeutics for lysosomal storage diseases. J Med Chem 2013;56:2705–25.

56. Chaudhuri TK, Paul S. Protein-misfolding diseases and chaperone-based therapeutic approaches. FEBS J 2006;273:1331–49.

57. Valenzano KJ, Khanna R, Powe AC, et al. Identification and characterization of pharmacological chaperones to correct enzyme deficiencies in lysosomal storage disorders. Assay Drug Dev Technol 2011;9:213–35.

58. Berardi AS, Pannuzzo G, Graziano A, et al. Pharmacological chaperones increase residual beta-galactocerebrosidase activity in fibroblasts from Krabbe patients. Mol Genet Metab 2014;112:294–301.

59. Ribbens J, Whiteley G, Furuya H, et al. A high-throughput screening assay using Krabbe disease patient cells. Anal Biochem 2013;434:15–25.

60. Wolf NI, Toro C, Kister I, et al. "Hypomyelination with brain stem and spinal cord involvement and leg spasticity" can mimic a steroid responsive inflammatory condition. Neurology 2015;84(3):226–30.

61. Yao P, Poruri K, Martinis S, et al. Non-catalytic regulation of gene expression by aminoacyl-tRNA synthetases. In: Kim S, editor. Aminoacyl-tRNA synthetases in biology and medicine. Netherlands: Springer; 2014. p. 167–87.

62. Bredius RG, Laan LA, Lankester AC, et al. Early marrow transplantation in a presymptomatic neonate with late infantile metachromatic leukodystrophy does not halt disease progression. Bone Marrow Transpl 2007;39:309–10.

63. Duffner PK, Caviness VS Jr, Erbe RW, et al. The long-term outcomes of presymptomatic infants transplanted for Krabbe disease: report of the workshop held on July 11 and 12, 2008, Holiday Valley, New York. Genet Med 2009;11:450–4.

64. Malm G, Ringden O, Winiarski J, et al. Clinical outcome in four children with metachromatic leukodystrophy treated by bone marrow transplantation. Bone Marrow Transpl 1996;17:1003–8.

65. Krivit W, Lockman LA, Watkins PA, et al. The future for treatment by bone marrow transplantation for adrenoleukodystrophy, metachromatic leukodystrophy, globoid cell leukodystrophy and Hurler syndrome. J Inherit Metab Dis 1995;18: 398–412.

66. Weinberg KI. Early use of drastic therapy. N Engl J Med 2005;352:2124–6.

67. Sevin C, Aubourg P, Cartier N. Enzyme, cell and gene-based therapies for metachromatic leukodystrophy. J Inherit Metab Dis 2007;30:175–83.

68. Cable C, Finkel RS, Lehky TJ, et al. Unrelated umbilical cord blood transplant for juvenile metachromatic leukodystrophy: a 5-year follow-up in three affected siblings. Mol Genet Metab 2011;102:207–9.

69. Martin HR, Poe MD, Provenzale JM, et al. Neurodevelopmental outcomes of umbilical cord blood transplantation in metachromatic leukodystrophy. Biol Blood Marrow Transpl 2013;19:616–24.

70. Pierson TM, Bonnemann CG, Finkel RS, et al. Umbilical cord blood transplantation for juvenile metachromatic leukodystrophy. Ann Neurol 2008;64:583–7.

71. van Egmond ME, Pouwels PJ, Boelens JJ, et al. Improvement of white matter changes on neuroimaging modalities after stem cell transplant in metachromatic leukodystrophy. JAMA Neurol 2013;70:779–82.

72. Kohlschutter A. Lysosomal leukodystrophies: Krabbe disease and metachromatic leukodystrophy. Handb Clin Neurol 2013;113:1611–8.

73. Matthes F, Stroobants S, Gerlach D, et al. Efficacy of enzyme replacement therapy in an aggravated mouse model of metachromatic leukodystrophy declines with age. Hum Mol Genet 2012;21:2599–609.

74. Agarwal A, Shipman PJ. Gallbladder polyposis in metachromatic leukodystrophy. Pediatr Radiol 2013;43:631–3.

75. Braverman NE, D'Agostino MD, Maclean GE. Peroxisome biogenesis disorders: biological, clinical and pathophysiological perspectives. Dev Disabil Res Rev 2013;17:187–96.

76. Collins CS, Gould SJ. Identification of a common PEX1 mutation in Zellweger syndrome. Hum Mutat 1999;14:45–53.

77. Walter C, Gootjes J, Mooijer PA, et al. Disorders of peroxisome biogenesis due to mutations in PEX1: phenotypes and PEX1 protein levels. Am J Hum Genet 2001; 69:35–48.

78. Zhang R, Chen L, Jiralerspong S, et al. Recovery of PEX1-Gly843Asp peroxisome dysfunction by small-molecule compounds. Proc Natl Acad Sci U S A 2010;107: 5569–74.

79. Appikatla S, Bessert D, Lee I, et al. Insertion of proteolipid protein into oligodendrocyte mitochondria regulates extracellular pH and adenosine triphosphate. Glia 2014;62:356–73.

80. Uchida N, Chen K, Dohse M, et al. Human neural stem cells induce functional myelination in mice with severe dysmyelination. Sci Transl Med 2012;4:155ra136.

81. Trepanier A, Bennett L, Garbern J, editors. Paper Presented at the American College of Medical Genetics. Albuquerque (NM), 2010.

82. Gupta N, Henry RG, Strober J, et al. Neural stem cell engraftment and myelination in the human brain. Sci Transl Med 2012;4:155ra137.

Autoimmune Encephalopathies

Ming Lim, MRCP, PhD[a,b,*], Yael Hacohen, MRCPCH[a], Angela Vincent, FMedSci, FRS[a,*]

KEYWORDS

- Autoimmunity • Antibody • Encephalitis • Immune-mediated • Immunotherapy
- N-methyl D-aspartate receptor • VGKC-complex • Limbic • AQP4 • MOG

KEY POINTS

- There are several antibody-mediated central nervous system diseases that need to be recognized in children.
- These diseases are identified by the clinical features, paraclinical findings, and presence of serum/cerebrospinal fluid antibodies to cell-surface proteins, such as the N-methyl D-aspartate receptor.
- Early recognition and institution of treatment can optimize outcomes in some but not all patients with autoimmune encephalopathy.
- Despite some very characteristic and easily recognizable features of certain antibody-mediated syndromes, significant phenotypic overlap exists between children with different antibodies.
- The lack of detection of an established cell-surface antibody should not dissuade clinicians from early initiation of immune therapy.

Conflict of interest: See last page of article.

Author contributions: The review was planned by Y. Hacohen, M. Lim, and A. Vincent. Y. Hacohen and M. Lim performed the literature review. M. Lim prepared early drafts of the article, and all authors contributed to the revisions of the article.

Funding: This work was supported by Oxford University Clinical Academic Graduate School, Oxford (Y. Hacohen) and the National Institute for Health Research (NIHR) Oxford Biomedical Research Centre based at Oxford University Hospitals NHS Trust and the University Of Oxford (Y. Hacohen and A. Vincent).

[a] Nuffield Department of Clinical Neurosciences, John Radcliffe Hospital, University of Oxford, Level 6, West Wing, Oxford 3 9DU, UK; [b] Children's Neurosciences, Evelina Children's Hospital @ Guy's and St Thomas' NHS Foundation Trust, King's Health Partners Academic Health Science Centre, Lambeth Palace Road, London SE1 7EH, UK

* Corresponding authors. Nuffield Department of Clinical Neurosciences, John Radcliffe Hospital, University Of Oxford, Level 6, West Wing, Oxford 3 9DU, UK.

E-mail addresses: ming.lim@gstt.nhs.uk; angela.vincent@ndcn.ox.ac.uk

0031-3955/15/$ – see front matter © 2015 Elsevier Inc. All rights reserved.

INTRODUCTION

The immune response within the brain depends on interactions between the immune and nervous systems, complicated by the blood-brain barrier.[1] Neuroinflammation, involving the innate (glial cells) and/or components of the adaptive (lymphocytes) immune system infiltrating the central nervous system (CNS), is observed in a range of neurologic disorders and may represent the primary pathology in an autoimmune condition like multiple sclerosis but can also represent a secondary response to biological processes, such as neurodegeneration.[2]

Over the last few years, a more specific form of CNS autoimmunity has been recognized, identified mainly by the presence of antibodies binding to neuronal synaptic receptors and ion channel–related proteins, and found in both adults and children.[3] These cell-surface antigens are important for cellular function or neurotransmission and are generally expressed at different levels throughout the CNS, with patients demonstrating either focal or more generalized clinical signs, probably depending on the extent of brain regions targeted.[4] Some of these disorders are associated with tumors and are, therefore, paraneoplastic; but the frequency of malignancies differs depending on the identity of the antigen and the age of the patients.[5] By contrast to classic paraneoplastic syndromes that are associated with antibodies against intracellular antigens, these conditions frequently respond to immunotherapy; although some have a monophasic illness, both a protracted period for recovery and/or a relapsing course can occur in adults[5,6] and children.[7]

In a large multicenter UK encephalitis study of acute or subacute encephalitis presenting to general hospitals, 21% patients without a detected infection were found retrospectively to have a specific antibody to N-methyl D-aspartate receptor (NMDAR) or to the voltage-gated potassium channel (VGKC) complex, a frequency that surpassed that of any single virus identified.[8] This finding was mirrored in the California Encephalitis project, whereby the frequency of NMDAR antibody encephalitis surpassed that of any of the individual viral encephalitides.[9] The discovery that several forms of encephalitis result from neuronal antibodies, and are immunotherapy responsive, has led to a paradigm shift in the diagnostic and management approach to all forms of encephalitis. Here, the authors review the important developments in characterizing the autoimmune encephalopathies in children, particularly when antibodies targeting neuronal cell-surface antigens have been implicated, with a focus on how to recognize and treat these conditions early.

CLINICAL AND PARACLINICAL FEATURES OF AUTOIMMUNE ENCEPHALOPATHIES

The key clinical feature is that children and adolescents present with encephalopathy, a clinical description of an altered mental state that can manifest as confusion, disorientation, behavioral changes, or other cognitive impairments (**Box 1**). This condition is often preceded by a less specific prodrome composed of a viral illness with headaches and fever. However, at the early stage of illness, an autoimmune cause cannot be distinguished from the many conditions that cause encephalopathy, such as infections, parainfectious, metabolic, genetic, traumatic, malignant, or toxic disorders. The clinical features of these disorders overlap; in many cases, the cause will not be apparent from the initial history and examination. Rigorous clinical observations and extensive investigations, with empirical treatments for multiple, potentially life-threatening causes, are often started simultaneously in patients presenting with encephalopathy.[10]

Seizures occur in most autoimmune encephalopathies, indicating an encephalitic process; but the clinical evidence of inflammation of brain parenchyma may not

> **Box 1**
>
> **Working definition of encephalopathy and encephalitis. This is a working definition of encephalopathy and encephalitis based on Granerod and colleagues,[8] 2010. The diagnosis of encephalopathy relies on the clinical observation of behavioral change or altered level of consciousness. Care should be given when a child has a fever or is post ictal when interpreting behavioral change. A diagnosis of encephalitis requires a child to have encephalopathy and additional features of inflammation either from the clinical presentation or investigations**
>
> Encephalopathy
>
> - Behavioral change (eg, confusion, excessive irritability)
> - Or alteration in consciousness (eg, lethargy, coma)
>
> Encephalitis
>
>   Encephalopathy was present with 2 or more of the following:
>
> - Fever or history of fever ($\geq 38°C$)
> - Seizures and/or focal neurologic findings (with evidence of brain parenchyma involvement)
> - Cerebrospinal fluid pleocytosis (>4 white blood cells per microliter)
> - Electroencephalogram findings indicating encephalitis
> - Neuroimaging in keeping with encephalitis (computed tomography or MRI)

always be accompanied by radiological or biological evidence of inflammation, such as a reactive cerebrospinal fluid (CSF), as reviewed in the adult[5,6] and pediatric[11] literature. Hence, *autoimmune encephalopathy* is the more accurate term to describe these disorders but is often used interchangeably with *autoimmune encephalitis* (see **Box 1**; Granerod and colleagues,[8] 2010).

The presence of seizures, movement disorders, autonomic dysfunction, and sleep disorders, alongside more specific neuroimaging and electrophysiological features, may indicate a specific antibody-mediated disorder (see **Table 1**) as described in more detail later. However, despite the recognizable features of some antibody-mediated diseases, there are emerging phenotypic overlaps between children with different antibodies and conversely phenotypic differences in children with the same detected antibody.

ANTIBODY DETECTION METHODS

Methods such as immunohistochemistry on brain tissue are useful to demonstrate regional-specific binding but often identify intracellular proteins (eg, paraneoplastic antigens) that may not be disease causative. The denaturation of proteins for immuno-blotting often destroys the conformationally dependent antigenic targets and is seldom helpful for the antibodies discussed here. Radioimmunoprecipitation assays are highly sensitive but not suitable for most of the CNS antigens and can detect antibodies to intracellular as well as extracellular epitopes on the precipitated proteins. These techniques may be of help, but the specific and most appropriate tests are currently the cell-based assays (CBAs). These assays allow optimal detection of antibodies binding extracellular epitopes of the neuronal surface antigens in a manner that would occur when antigen is exposed to circulating antibodies (in tissue fluids). Each CBA relies on introducing, by transfection, the DNA for the specific antigen into a suitable human cell line. Many clinical laboratories use a commercial mosaic of fixed cells expressing different antigens. Although this allows greater accessibility to testing, the fixation of the cells, required for transportation may obscure some epitopes and reduce sensitivities. Alternatively, live cell assays can be developed in-house but are much more time consuming.[6,12]

These assays can be designed for use with either serum or CSF. The CSF, usually tested at a high concentration, can be surprisingly strongly positive (given the normal ratio of serum to CSF immunoglobulin G [IgG] levels of around 400), which indicates intrathecal synthesis of the specific antibody. Some laboratories prefer CSF because the results can be easier to assess than using serum with its greater stickiness even after dilution. An additional test of binding of antibody to the surface of live neurons in culture, usually from the hippocampus, can be undertaken to confirm the relevance of the antibody detected but is not yet available commercially. An understanding of the assays used, and communication with the clinical laboratory, can be very helpful to the clinician in assessing the results of these tests.

SPECIFIC ANTIBODY-MEDIATED SYNDROMES
N-Methyl D-Aspartate Receptor Antibody Encephalitis

NMDAR antibody encephalitis was first characterized in young girls presenting with severe encephalopathy, psychiatric features, movement disorder, and autonomic dysfunction associated with an ovarian teratoma.[13] Historical cases of sudden catastrophic encephalopathy in children with relatively good outcomes likely represent the same condition.[14] Patients are found to have antibodies in serum and CSF targeting the extracellular epitopes of the NR1 subunit of the NMDAR.[15,16] In children, the presence of an underlying tumor is uncommon, but 30% of girls younger than 18 years and 9% of girls younger than 14 years are reported to have an associated ovarian teratoma.[17] The characteristic clinical syndrome of a poly-symptomatic encephalopathy affects both adults and children, with around 40% of the patients presenting at less than 18 years of age.[16–18]

Most patients develop at least 3 of the following groups of symptoms within 1 month of disease onset: psychiatric features, memory disturbance, speech disorder, seizures, dyskinesias, decreased level of consciousness, autonomic instability, or hypoventilation.[18] There may be seasonal variability in non–tumor-related pediatric NMDAR antibody encephalitis, with 78% presenting in the warmer months of April to September.[19]

The behavioral changes are age dependent; younger children develop new-onset temper tantrums, whereas agitation, aggression, and changes in mood or personality predominate in older children. Many parents also report changes in speech, including reduced speech, mutism, echolalia, or perseveration.[17] On occasions, the cognitive regression may be accompanied by a loss of social and communication skills, mimicking an autistic spectrum disorder.[20] Infants and young children may present with more neurologic (eg, seizures, movement disorder) than psychiatric symptoms, but psychiatric symptoms may go under recognized in the young. Autonomic features and hypoventilation are less frequently reported in children.[18]

Despite the severity of the encephalopathy, with 69% of the patients being admitted to intensive care,[18] the neuroimaging is normal in most patients. When abnormal, MRI usually reveals discrete lesions in white and/or gray matter that are predominantly subtle (see **Fig. 1**), nonenhancing, and often reverse spontaneously.[21] Similarly, the CSF analysis reveals only moderate lymphocytic pleocytosis, with normal protein concentration, but can be normal. Intrathecal oligoclonal bands are present in up to 60% of patients[21] but not necessarily at the onset of the disease.[16]

The electroencephalogram (EEG) is encephalopathic in the majority, with generalized rhythmic delta activity with or without epileptic discharges.[21] Extreme delta brush is a continuous EEG pattern that may be unique to some patients with NMDAR anti-body encephalitis[22] and, when found, can be a clue to the diagnosis. Early electro-clinical features may also correlate with severity; persistence of normal physiologic background activity in at least one hemisphere is suggestive of moderate severity and better outcomes, whereas diffuse abnormalities, with lack of physiologic background activity, indicate severe neurologic impairment and poor prognosis.[23]

Despite the widely reported initial excellent response to immunotherapy,[17] children are often left with residual deficits. Of the 211 children reported in a comprehensive mainly retrospective multicenter study of 577 patients with NMDAR antibody encephalitis, only 60% made a full recovery at the 2-year follow-up.[18] In that study, concomitant and early use of intravenous steroids and intravenous immunoglobulins and/or plasmapheresis (deemed first-line therapy) was effective in achieving control of symptoms and remission, with additional benefits of second-line therapy, such as rituximab and cyclophosphamide, when first-line therapy failed or was partially effective. Additionally, in a recent international study on the utility and safety of rituximab in pediatric autoimmune and inflammatory CNS disease, the prompt use of second-line therapy (rituximab) within 4 weeks of diagnosis was found to be beneficial in NMDAR antibody encephalitis.[24] Relapses were noted in 12% to 25% of patients, with risk factors including lack of immunotherapy at the first episode and absence of a tumor diagnosis. Predictors of a good outcome included early administration of therapy and avoidance of an intensive care admission.[18] Thus, it seems that early diagnosis and immunotherapy at first presentation reduces the chance of relapses and improves neurologic outcomes.

N-METHYL D-ASPARTATE RECEPTOR ANTIBODY MEDIATES NEUROLOGIC RELAPSE FOLLOWING HERPES SIMPLEX ENCEPHALITIS

Neurologic relapse in the weeks or months following primary herpes simplex encephalitis (HSVE) is well described in children and adults as reviewed by Hacohen and colleagues.[25] In a subset of children presenting with biphasic illness, the second stage was characterized by predominant movement disorder but negative CSF herpes simplex virus polymerase chain reaction and stable brain MRI findings.[26] The clinical characteristics of these relapses resembled the acute stages of NMDAR antibody encephalitis and were associated with NMDAR antibodies[25,27,28] and, less commonly, dopamine-2 receptor[27,28] and other unidentified neuronal surface targets.[28] Importantly, in the handful of previous cases of relapsing HSVE, when the immunotherapy used was of adequate intensity and duration, a benefit was reported.[25] However, the eventual outcomes are likely to be confounded by the sequelae of the initial infective encephalitis. Intriguingly, the immune response to NMDAR may preexist or begin very early in the HSVE; variable classes (IgG, IgA, and IgM) and levels of NMDAR antibodies were reported in 13 out of 44 (30%) adults with HSVE.[29]

Limbic Encephalitis

Voltage-gated potassium channel–complex antibody-mediated encephalopathy

VGKC-complex antibody-associated CNS diseases, as measured by antibodies that immunoprecipitate 125I-α-dendrotoxin-labeled VGKC extracted from mammalian brain tissue, have been detected in patients with limbic encephalitis (LE), Morvan syndrome, neuromyotonia, and cases of adult-onset epilepsy.[6] Associated neoplasms have been found in less than 10% (most often thymomas); patients respond well to immunotherapy, with substantial and sometimes complete recovery.[30] However, it is now clear that the VGKC-complex antibodies in LE are mainly directed at neuronal proteins that are complexed with the VGKCs in situ. These proteins include the

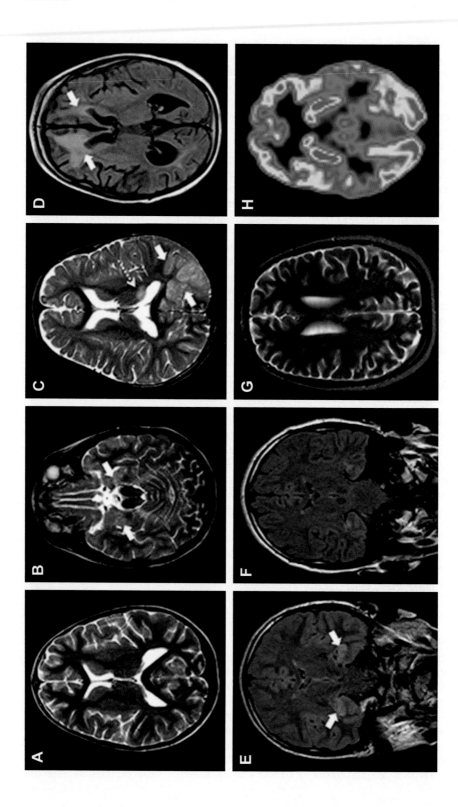

secreted synaptic protein leucine-rich glioma inactivated 1 (LGI1) and the transmembrane axonal protein contactin-associated protein 2 (CASPR2).[6] Antibodies to LGI1 (LGI1-Abs) are frequent in adult limbic encephalitis,[31,32] and CASPR2-antibodies (CASPR2-Abs) are more common in patients with peripheral nerve hyperexcitability,[31,33] including the rare Morvan syndrome.[34]

In adults the most commonly associated phenotype is LE, presenting with seizures, amnesia, limbic changes on MRI imaging (**Fig. 1**), and frequently low sodium levels.[6] Children with VGKC-complex antibodies can present with limbic encephalitis[35] but much less frequently than adults. The clinical phenotypes associated with VGKC-complex antibodies in children are very broad and includes both epilepsies (summarized in Hacohen and colleagues,[11] 2013; see also **Table 1**) and some children with acute demyelination syndromes.[36] In most pediatric cases, the antibodies to the recognized VGKC-complex proteins are not found[7,37] (Hacohen, Lim, and Vincent, submitted for publication, 2015), suggesting that most of the sera bind to novel autoreactive targets within the VGKC-complex. These targets could include intracellular epitopes on the VGKC subunits or other components of the complexes, and may sometimes be secondary to other disease mechanisms. For instance, in a study of 39 children with a range of different presentations, high levels of VGKC-complex antibodies were only found in children with neuroinflammatory diseases, suggesting that they may occur secondary to other inflammatory CNS mechanisms (Hacohen, Lim, and Vincent, submitted for publication, 2015).

Other antibody-mediated limbic encephalitides Three other neuronal cell-surface antibodies have been associated with limbic encephalitis. Antibodies to the α-amino-3-hydroxy-5-methyl-4-isoxazolepropionic acid receptor (AMPAR), γ-aminobutyric acid B receptor (GABAbR) or GABAaR, and metabotropic glutamate receptors (mGluR), are briefly described focusing on the pediatric aspect of presentation (**Table 1**). Antibodies against intracellular antigen, such as thyroid peroxidase (TPO) and the intracellular synaptic proteins glutamic acid decarboxylase (GAD65) and amphyphysin, have also been reported in patients with LE; but the pathogenic potential of the antibodies is not established, and most adult patients with these antibodies do not show good immunotherapy responses. There are occasional case reports of children with GAD65 antibodies who benefit from immunotherapies.[35] These forms of LE are also briefly outlined in **Table 1**.

◄───

Fig. 1. Neuroimaging in autoimmune encephalopathy (*A–G*). The imaging features in NMDAR antibody encephalitis are varied (*A–D*) and may often be normal (not shown). (*B*) Axial T2 images in a 7 year old with classic NMDAR antibody encephalitis demonstrating only subtle cortical enhancement in the temporal lobes (*arrows*). (*C*) By contrast, T2 axial images of a similarly affected 2 year old reveal significant parenchymal involvement in the parieto-occipital lobe (*arrow*) and posterior thalamus (*dashed arrow*). (*D*) On occasion, and more commonly in children, a leukoencephalopathy is observed, as seen here on the T2 fluid-attenuated inversion recovery (FLAIR) images of a 4 year old with relapsing NMDAR antibody encephalitis (*arrows*). (*E*) Coronal T2 FLAIR images of a 15-year-old girl with seizures and a subacute memory loss demonstrating high signal changes in the hippocampus (*arrows*). Her clinical and radiological features are that of an LE; but despite an exhaustive evaluation of CNS-directed autoantibodies, none were identified. On repeat imaging at 6 months, coronal T2 FLAIR (*F*) later demonstrated resolution of her imaging changes, mirroring the clinical improvement. In a 12-year-old boy presenting with seizures, dyskinesia and psychiatric symptoms with normal imaging (*G*), PET revealed a reduced uptake in the frontal, temporal, and parietal cortex, with normal activity within the basal ganglia and occipital lobes (*H*). This child also had no identifiable antibody and made a good recovery following steroid and IVIG therapy.

Table 1
Cell-surface autoantibodies and the associated phenotypes

Antibody	Clinical Presentations	Specific Features	Disease Course
NMDAR	• Encephalopathy • Psychosis • Movement disorder • Seizures • Dysautonomia	• Mutism or language regression can occur • Lower risk of associated malignancies in children	• Prolonged disease course • 75% admitted to ICU • Immunotherapy responsive • Full recovery in 60% • Relapse seen in 12%
	• Preceding HSV encephalitis	• More common in children • NMDAR antibodies are negative at time of HSV encephalitis • HSV PCR negative at the time of NMDAR antibody encephalitis	• Response to immunotherapy • No reports of recurrence of HSV infection during treatment
	White matter syndromes • Brain stem encephalitis • Optic neuritis • ADEM or ADEM plus ON • NMOSD	• May or may not have clinical NMDAR antibody encephalitis • Demyelinating presentations may follow or precede the NMDAR encephalopathy • Some patients have MOG Abs • The frequency of NMDAR antibodies in children with CNS demyelination is likely low	• More frequent relapses of neurologic deficits than is seen in typical NMDAR encephalitis
AQP4	• NMO • NMOSD (CRITERIA)	• ADEM-like attacks may occur, particularly in younger children • Oligoclonal bands found in fewer than 20% • Apparent worsening of disease or at least failure to respond to MS-specific immunomodulatory therapies	• Typically relapsing disease, although patients with a single episode of ON and TM are reported • Recovery from attacks may be poor • Relapse frequency reduced by immuno-suppressive therapies
MOG	• ON • ON and TM • ADEM • ADEM plus recurrent ON	• Likely predictor of non-MS disease course • OCB negative	• Monophasic or relapsing course • Persistent of antibodies in relapsing demyelin-ation and normaliza-tion in monophasic diseases

(continued on next page)

Table 1
(continued)

Antibody	Clinical Presentations	Specific Features	Disease Course
VGKC-complex	• LE • Neuromyotonia • Morvan syndrome	• Rare in children	• See specific associated proteins
LGI1	• LE	• Not reported in children	• Often monophasic • Clinical response to immunotherapy • Persistent memory deficits may be noted
CASPR2	• Peripheral nerve hyperexcitability	• Guillain-Barre syndrome	• Chronic disease • Symptomatic therapy • For GBS monophasic
Contactin-2	• LE • Neuromyotonia • Morvan syndrome	• Not reported in children	• Found in association with VGKC, LGI1, and CASPR2 antibodies
D2R	• Basal ganglia encephalitis • Sydenham chorea • Tourette syndrome	• Not reported in adults	• Full recovery in 42% • Clinical improvement with immunotherapy in some
GlyR	• PERM • SPS	• Rare	• Immunotherapy responsive
GABAbR	• Encephalitis with prominent seizures	• Associated with small-cell lung cancer in adults • Only 2 children reported	• One child died with refractory seizures • Some response to immunotherapy
GABAaR	• Encephalopathy with refractory seizures and status epilepticus	• 3 of 6 Patients reported are <18 y	• Extensive cortical and subcortical MRI abnormalities • Positive TPO and GAD65 antibodies • Immunotherapy may be beneficial • Long-term outcome is poor
DPPX	• Cognitive dysfunction, psychiatric features, resting tremor and myoclonus • PERM	• One adolescent patient reported • Associated with diarrheal illness	• Immunotherapy responsive (aggressive)
mGluR1	• Cerebellar ataxia • Hodgkin lymphoma	• Not reported in children	
mGluR5	• LE and Hodgkin lymphoma (Ophelia syndrome)	• Rare	• Improvement with resection • Immunotherapy responsive
AMPAR	• LE	• Not reported in children	• Frequently relapse • Response to immunotherapy

(continued on next page)

Table 1 (continued)			
Antibody	Clinical Presentations	Specific Features	Disease Course
GAD65	• SPS	• Very rare in children but have been reported in patients with LE and refractory seizures	• Usually chronic disorders but some do respond to immunotherapy

Abbreviations: Abs, antibodies; ADEM, acute disseminated encephalomyelitis; AMPAR, α-amino-3-hydroxy-5-methyl-4-isoxazolepropionic acid receptor; AQP4, aquaporin-4; CASPR2, contactin-associated protein 2; DPPX, dipeptidyl-peptidase–like protein-6; D2R, dopamine receptor 2; GABAaR, g-aminobutyric acid A receptor; GABAbR, g-aminobutyric acid B receptor; GAD65, glutamic acid decarboxylase; GBS, Guillain Barre syndrome; GlyR, glycine receptor; HSV, herpes simplex virus; ICU, intensive care unit; LE, limbic encephalitis; LGI1, leucine-rich glioma inactivated 1; mGluR, metabotropic glutamate receptors; MOG, myelin oligodendrocyte glycoprotein; MS, multiple sclerosis; NMOSD, neuromyelitis optica spectrum disorder; OCB, oligoclonal bands; ON, optic neuritis; PCR, polymerase chain reaction; PERM, progressive encephalomyelitis with rigidity and myoclonus; SPS, stiff-person syndrome; TM, transverse myelitis; TPO, thyroid peroxidase.

Antibodies to AMPARs have been reported in adult patients with otherwise typical LE often associated with relapses,[38] seen more commonly in female patients with different tumors who respond well to tumor treatment and immunotherapies. To date, no pediatric cases of AMPAR antibodies associated with LE have been reported. Earlier reports of antibodies to the AMPAR (GluR3) subunits in pediatric patients with Rasmussen encephalitis[39] have not been replicated originally, although a recent study identified antibodies to AMPAR (Glu2/3) in 2 of more than 50 children with Rasmussen encephalitis (Nibber, Vincent, and Lang, submitted for publication).

Patients with antibodies to the GABAbR receptor most frequently present with LE.[40] Although initially thought to be a paraneoplastic syndrome with strong association with small cell lung cancer, it seems that around half of the patients have a nonparaneoplastic syndrome and show complete or partial improvement following immunotherapy.[41] These antibodies are typically seen in adult patients with a median age of 60 years; but they were also reported in a 16-year-old boy presenting with LE who made a complete recovery following treatment with steroids, intravenous immunoglobulin (IVIG), and plamapheresis[41] and more recently in a 3-year-old boy with a mixed movement disorder (opsoclonus, ataxia, and chorea) and refractory seizures who was treated with intravenous corticosteroids and IVIG but died of overwhelming sepsis.[42]

Antibodies to the mGluR are found in patients with Hodgkin lymphoma (HL). MGluR5 antibody is strongly associated with limbic encephalitis (which when seen in association with HL is termed *Ophelia syndrome*),[43] whereas mGluR1 antibody is seen in patients with cerebellar ataxia.[44] These patients are often young, and pediatric presentations have been reported.[43] Patients respond to tumor resection and immunotherapy.

Progressive Encephalomyelitis with Rigidity and Myoclonus

Antibodies to the glycine receptor (GlyR) are now recognized to be associated with progressive encephalomyelitis with rigidity and myoclonus (PERM), also known as stiff-person syndrome (SPS) plus. Patients present with rigidity, excessive startle response, and brain stem involvement with oculomotor dysfunction and potentially life-threatening respiratory arrests[45] and can have co-occurrence of GAD65 antibodies.[46] GlyR antibodies are rare in children but reported in a 14 month old girl who developed startle-induced episodes of generalized rigidity and myoclonus and axial hyperextension, without impairment of consciousness[47]; and in a few children with SPS.[48] In a recently characterized cohort of 45 patients, 2 children presented with an epileptic encephalopathy or encephalopathy associated with demyelination.[45]

Other encephalitis/encephalopathy associated with neuronal cell surface antibodies
Dipeptidyl-peptidase–like protein-6 Antibodies to dipeptidyl-peptidase–like protein-6 were reported in 4 adult patients with encephalopathy, cognitive dysfunction, psychiatric features, resting tremor, and myoclonus who responded to intensive immunotherapy, 3 of whom had concurrent diarrheal illness.[49] However, these antibodies have also been reported in 3 patients with PERM, presenting with a distinct syndrome of subacute onset hyperekplexia, abnormal eye movements, and variable trunk stiffness; one was aged 15 years and another responded to aggressive immunotherapy.[50] These antibodies have also been reported in 20 patients with multifocal CNS presentations, with or without encephalopathy, with predominant brain stem signs, of which 2 (10%) were children.[51] This finding illustrates the often-widening phenotypes associated with any single antibody when antibody testing becomes more widespread.

γ-Aminobutyric acid A receptor These antibodies were recently identified in 6 patients (3 children) with encephalitis with predominant seizures who showed specific immunostaining patterns on rat brain sections, similar to those seen in patients with GABAbR antibodies.[52] Patients presented with refractory seizures and status epilepticus and had extensive cortical and subcortical MRI abnormalities; interestingly some patients had other markers of autoimmunity with positive TPO antibody and GAD65 antibodies. Although immunotherapy was beneficial, the long-term outcome was poor; 1 out of 6 reported patients died. GABAaR antibodies have also been identified in a UK cohort whereby a more heterogeneous clinical presentation and variable response to immunotherapy were observed.[53]

Dopamine Receptor 2 in Basal Ganglia Encephalitis

Basal ganglia encephalitis is a focal autoimmune encephalitic syndrome whereby patients demonstrate isolated subcortical features, including movement disorders, such as parkinsonism, dystonia, or chorea. They also exhibit hypersomnolence and psychiatric features, such as attention deficit, emotional lability, obsessive-compulsive disorder, and psychosis. Antibodies to the dopamine receptor 2 (D2R) were recently described in children with basal ganglia encephalitis.[54] Although the antibodies bind to the extracellular domain of D2R, the antibody levels were low. D2R antibodies were also identified in other groups of patients with postinfectious conditions frequently associated with streptococcal infections that target the basal ganglia, such as in Sydenham chorea and Tourette syndrome,[54] and by a different group in pediatric autoimmune neuropsychiatric disorders associated with streptococcal infection.[55] Currently, the clinical relevance of these antibodies requires further study.

Antibodies Associated with Encephalopathy and White Matter Syndromes

Aquaporin-4 and myelin oligodendrocyte glycoprotein antibodies in childhood demyelination syndromes

There is a growing interest in the role of B cells and CNS antibodies in demyelination.[56] Antibodies against the astrocyte water channel protein, aquaporin-4 (AQP4), were first described in 2004 in patients with the rare inflammatory demyelinating disease, neuromyelitis optica (NMO).[57] The clinical features, imaging abnormalities, and AQP4-Ab seropositivity reported in children with NMO are similar to the adult phenotype,[58] although permanent visual disturbance was more common in children than in adults in a UK/Japanese study.[59]

Myelin oligodendrocyte glycoprotein (MOG) is exclusively expressed in the CNS. Although only a minor component (0.05%) of the myelin sheath, its location on the outermost lamellae[5] and on the cell surface of oligodendrocytes makes it available for antibody binding.[60] Using a full-length MOG protein bell-based assay, antibodies are found in 30% to 50% of children at first presentation of demyelination syndromes, including acute disseminated encephalomyelitis,[60] and in 4 AQP4-negative NMO adult and children.[61] These antibodies have been reported in both monophasic and relapsing diseases,[60] with persistence of antibodies in relapsing demyelination, including multiple sclerosis, and normalization in monophasic diseases.[62] Currently, it remains unclear if the presence of these antibodies requires a different therapeutic approach to that used in patients with AQP4 antibodies.

N-methyl D-aspartate receptor antibody associated with distinct white matter syndromes

In the study of 691 patients with NMDAR encephalitis, 23 (3%) patients were identified with clinical or radiological features of a demyelinating disorder at some time, with about half having both neurologic syndromes concurrently.[58,63] In another study,10 of 46 (22%) consecutive children from 6 centers in the United Kingdom in whom NMDAR antibodies were detected had clinical and/or radiological white matter involvement, brain stem encephalitis, or leukoencephalopathy following HSVE. In all 3 groups of patients with these distinct white matter syndromes, a response to immunotherapy was found, particularly when treated in the acute phase of neurologic presentation.[64] When observed, this clinical improvement was often mirrored by reduction in NMDAR antibody levels, suggesting that these antibodies may mediate the white matter disease.

WHEN TO SUSPECT AN AUTOIMMUNE CAUSE?

Laboratory[3] and clinical[65] criteria have been proposed to help identification of an autoimmune cause. Most clinical recommendations rely on an algorithm based on clinical and paraclinical parameters purported to support an autoimmune or immune cause, although their specificity and sensitivity have not been systematically evaluated. Furthermore, some considerations are required when applying such criteria to a pediatric cohort,[66] whereby certain investigations are less accessible (such as PET) or the indications need to be balanced with the probability of identifying a cause (such as tumor screening). Crucially, as timely treatment has been shown to be beneficial in a range of autoimmune encephalopathies,[18,67] the threshold for considering empirical immunotherapy becomes important. Here, the authors provide a simple clinical algorithm largely adapted from the previous proposed criteria to aid with this decision making (**Fig. 2**).

Currently, the final clinical diagnosis of autoimmune encephalopathy, as applied to adult cohorts, relies on either identification of neuronal autoantibodies and/or a positive response to immunotherapy, 2 criteria that pragmatically combine the specificity of the antibody, using available detection assays, and the sensitivity of an immunotherapy response. Attempts have been made to categorize the likelihood of an autoimmune cause to definite, probably, or possible categories.[65,66]

CASES WHEREBY NO ANTIBODY CAN BE IDENTIFIED

The physician should consider the following:

1. *Were samples taken at the time when patients were symptomatic or maximally affected?* Samples taken outside the acute clinical event may simply reflect a decreasing monophasic course of antibody positivity. Additional effort is often required to source an acute sample, such as retrieval of serum initially sent for virological testing.
2. *Were samples taken after immunotherapy?* A false negative following initiation of immunotherapy remains predominantly a theoretic consideration; but one cause is sampling soon after patients have undergone a cycle of plasmapheresis or significantly later, particularly when patients have recovered symptomatically. Conversely, treatment after IVIG, which substantially raises circulating IgG levels, may induce a false-positive result. Prior treatments must be made clear on the referral form so that these confounding factors can be taken into account.
3. *Was CSF measured for additional sensitivity?* Compared with serum measurement of NMDAR antibodies, an additional 15% sensitivity of CSF has recently been reported,[68] although it is unclear if this would translate to commercial tests, across centers, or for other antibodies. These authors' suggestion would be that CSF testing, if unavailable initially, should be performed if the serum is negative with a strongly suggestive clinical phenotype or, conversely, it can be used to provide further support for the clinical relevance of the serum antibodies in patients in whom the clinical features are less typical.

Nevertheless, there are a group of patients with suspected autoimmune encephalopathy who are antibody negative or whereby the precise antigenic target has yet to be identified. The authors have recently found no significant differences in the clinical presentation between antibody-positive and antibody-negative groups or in the response to immunotherapy. Thus the absence on identification of a known antibody should not exclude the diagnosis of autoimmune encephalopathy or preclude initiation of treatment.[11]

TREATMENT STRATEGIES IN AUTOIMMUNE ENCEPHALOPATHY

Although there are no definitive therapeutic guidelines for most of the autoimmune encephalopathies, current immune therapeutic strategies seek to (1) remove or suppress the production of circulating antibodies (plasma exchange or IVIGs) and (2) attenuate the autoimmune production of pathogenic antibodies (steroids and other immunosuppressive agents). To date no controlled trial has been conducted to provide high-quality evidence on the optimal therapeutic strategy for any of these conditions. The treatment recommendation, such as in NMDAR encephalitis in children is based on an authoritative review[7] supported by large cohort analysis[18] suggests that the concomitant and early use of intravenous steroids and IVIGs and/or plasmapheresis are often effective in achieving control of symptoms and remission, with additional benefits of rituximab and/or cyclophosphamide, when initial therapy fails. Importantly, patients may remain symptomatic despite first- and second-line treatment, prompting physicians to repeat (and combine) therapeutic cycles. This decision to escalate immune treatment is primarily reliant on the clinical syndrome, as there remains no radiological or immunologic biomarker that can reliably inform on this decision making, although, in individual cases, quantitative antibody testing over time can be helpful. These aspects need to be explored further.

CLINICALLY SUSPECTED AUTOIMMUNE ENCEPHALOPATHY

1. Acute or sub acute (<12 weeks) onset of a recognizable syndrome:
   Antibody specific presentation (NMDAR, VGKC, GlycineR, D2R)
2. If partial syndrome[a], one additional supportive clinical feature required:
   Previously normal
   Viral or fever prodrome
   History of autoimmunity
   Or evidence of CNS inflammation (imaging and CSF)

INVESTIGATIONS

START TREATMENT
Once excluded infective and life-threatening metabolic causes

Serum studies
- Neuronal surface antibody studies[b]
  NMDAR; VGKC and associated proteins
  LGI1, CASPR2, Contactin; AMPAR;
  GABA(a+b)R; GlycineR; D2R
- Other antibodies
  GAD, Thyroid antibodies
- Onconeural if concerned
- *Exclude other infective,*
  inflammatory and metabolic
  disorders

EEG

Imaging studies
- MRI
- PET
- *Exclude tumours*

CSF studies
- Microscopy and infective
  investigations
- Oligoclonal bands and IgG Index
- Antibody studies (store and perform
  following discussion)
- Neopterins

ACUTE TREATMENT 1st line immunotherapy
High dose intravenous steroids 3-5 days then oral steroids
IVIG

Responds

ACUTE TREATMENT Additional 1st line immunotherapy
Plasma Exchange

Responds

ACUTE TREATMENT 2nd line immunotherapy[c]
Cyclophosphamide and/or Rituximab

Responds

MAINTENANCE IMMUNOTHERAPY
Treatment may include:-
- Long term oral steroid therapy
- Repeated IVIG
- Steroid sparing agent such as
  mycophenolate mofetil or
  azathioprine
- Repeated use of 2nd line agents

Duration is tailored according to
antibody identified and response
to immunotherapy

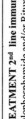

IF NO RESPONSE AND/OR NO ANTIBODY IDENTIFIED EVALUATE DIAGNOSIS AGAIN

When considering if therapy is adequate, in the future the multitude of pathomechanisms contributing to CNS dysfunction, such as receptor internalization,[69] recycling, and secondary effects on synaptic remodeling, may require consideration.[70] Ultimately the strategy producing optimal outcomes may not solely rely on escalating immunotherapy but include targeting these biological perturbations.

FUTURE DIRECTIONS

The discovery that several forms of encephalitis result from neuronal antibodies, which are immunotherapy responsive, has led to a paradigm shift in the diagnostic approach. However, despite the many advances in clinically characterizing autoimmune encephalopathy and understanding of the biological mechanism contributing to disease pathogenesis, there remain many challenges.

Efforts should be made to develop treatment pathways with consistent definitions of adequate and insufficient therapeutic responses, alongside development of rigorous clinical and biological outcome measures that can be used in clinical trials. Therefore, these are key factors that will facilitate the translation of any current knowledge to optimizing patient outcomes.

CONFLICT OF INTEREST

Y. Hacohen has no financial disclosures. M. Lim receives research grants from Action Medical Research (SP4472), DES society (A20249PID10583), GOSH charity (V1214), NIHR (HTA11/129/148; EME12/212/15), MS Society (893/08), SPARKS charity (11OUH01; 12KCL02), London Clinical Research Network (2011FSF; 2014FSF), Evelina Appeal (X141005); has received consultation fees from CSL Behring; received travel grants from Merck Serono; and awarded educational grants to organize meetings by Novartis, Biogen Idec, Merck Serono, and Bayer. A. Vincent serves/has served on scientific advisory boards for the Patrick Berthoud Trust, the Brain Research Trust, and the Myasthenia Gravis Foundation of America; has received funding for travel and a speaker honorarium from Baxter International and Biogen; receives royalties from the publication of Clinical Neuroimmunology (Blackwell Publishing, 2005) and Inflammatory and Autoimmune Disorders of the Nervous System in Children (Mac Keith Press, 2010); receives/has

---

Fig. 2. Clinical algorithm for the management of autoimmune encephalopathy. The diagnosis of autoimmune encephalopathy may be suspected if the child has a recognizable syndrome. In the absence of a full syndrome, additional clinical features as suggested by Zuliani and colleagues[65] (2012) and Suleiman and colleagues[66] (2013) are required to trigger the threshold for investigations and empirical treatment before results of antibody testing being available. The timeline between first-line treatments are often pragmatically decided, with the decision to proceed to plasma exchange usually taken 7 to 10 days after failure of response following high-dose intravenous steroids and IVIG. In a very sick child requiring intensive care support, plasma exchange is often considered before IVIG. [a] An encephalopathy is required. [b] The range and sequence performed may be modified depending on antibody testing assays offered locally, where a less selective strategy is used if commercially available multiple antigen assay is used. [c] The threshold to escalate to second-line therapy may differ between physicians, with some preferring to have an identifiable antibody result, whereas others proceed largely based on clinical grounds. Importantly, the absence of a response to immune treatment or the inability to identify an antibody should always prompt repeated evaluation of the diagnosis and may include further and more extensive neurometabolic investigations. In italics are investigations that may be performed at different stages, particularly if repeated evaluations are required.

received research support from the European Union, NIHR Biomedical Research Centre Oxford, Euroimmun AG, and the Sir Halley Stewart Trust; has received Musk antibody royalties and consulting fees from Athena Diagnostics Inc; and holds patents and/or receive royalties and payments for antibody assays in neurologic diseases.

REFERENCES

1. Ransohoff RM, Engelhardt B. The anatomical and cellular basis of immune surveillance in the central nervous system. Nat Rev Immunol 2012;12:623–35.
2. Lim M. Treating inflammation in childhood neurodegenerative disorders. Dev Med Child Neurol 2011;53:298–304.
3. Lancaster E, Dalmau J. Neuronal autoantigens–pathogenesis, associated disorders and antibody testing. Nat Rev Neurol 2012;8(7):380–90.
4. Irani SR, Gelfand JM, Al-Diwani A, et al. Cell-surface central nervous system autoantibodies: clinical relevance and emerging paradigms. Ann Neurol 2014; 76(2):168–84.
5. Leypoldt F, Armangue T, Dalmau J. Autoimmune encephalopathies. Ann N Y Acad Sci 2014. http://dx.doi.org/10.1111/nyas.12553.
6. Vincent A, Bien CG, Irani SR, et al. Autoantibodies associated with diseases of the CNS: new developments and future challenges. Lancet Neurol 2011;10(8): 759–72.
7. Armangue T, Petit-Pedrol M, Dalmau J. Autoimmune encephalitis in children. J Child Neurol 2012;27(11):1460–9.
8. Granerod J, Ambrose HE, Davies NW, et al. Causes of encephalitis and differences in their clinical presentations in England: a multicentre, population-based prospective study. Lancet Infect Dis 2010;10(12):835–44.
9. Gable MS, Sheriff H, Dalmau J, et al. The frequency of autoimmune N-methyl-D-aspartate receptor encephalitis surpasses that of individual viral etiologies in young individuals enrolled in the California Encephalitis Project. Clin Infect Dis 2012;54(7):899–904.
10. Davies E, Connolly DJ, Mordekar SR. Encephalopathy in children: an approach to assessment and management. Arch Dis Child 2012;97(5):452–8.
11. Hacohen Y, Wright S, Waters P, et al. Paediatric autoimmune encephalopathies: clinical features, laboratory investigations and outcomes in patients with or without antibodies to known central nervous system autoantigens. J Neurol Neurosurg Psychiatry 2013;84(7):748–55.
12. Waters P, Vincent A. Detection of anti-aquaporin-4 antibodies in neuromyelitis optica: current status of the assays. Int MS J 2008;15(3):99–105.
13. Dalmau J, Tuzun E, Wu HY, et al. Paraneoplastic anti-N-methyl-D-aspartate receptor encephalitis associated with ovarian teratoma. Ann Neurol 2007;61(1): 25–36.
14. Sebire G. In search of lost time from "Demonic Possession" to anti-N-methyl-D-aspartate receptor encephalitis. Ann Neurol 2010;67:141–2.
15. Dalmau J, Gleichman AJ, Hughes EG, et al. Anti-NMDA-receptor encephalitis: case series and analysis of the effects of antibodies. Lancet Neurol 2008;7(12): 1091–8.
16. Irani SR, Bera K, Waters P, et al. N-methyl-D-aspartate antibody encephalitis: temporal progression of clinical and paraclinical observations in a predominantly non-paraneoplastic disorder of both sexes. Brain 2010;133(Pt 6):1655–67.
17. Florance NR, Davis RL, Lam C, et al. Anti-N-methyl-D-aspartate receptor (NMDAR) encephalitis in children and adolescents. Ann Neurol 2009;66(1):11–8.

18. Titulaer MJ, McCracken L, Gabilondo I, et al. Treatment and prognostic factors for long-term outcome in patients with anti-NMDA receptor encephalitis: an observational cohort study. Lancet Neurol 2013;12(2):157–65.

19. Adang LA, Lynch DR, Panzer JA. Pediatric anti-NMDA receptor encephalitis is seasonal. Ann Clin Transl Neurol 2014;1:921–5.

20. Creten C, van der Zwaan S, Blankespoor RJ, et al. Late onset autism and anti-NMDA-receptor encephalitis. Lancet 2011;378:98.

21. Dalmau J, Lancaster E, Martinez-Hernandez E, et al. Clinical experience and laboratory investigations in patients with anti-NMDAR encephalitis. Lancet Neurol 2011;10(1):63–74.

22. Schmitt SE, Pargeon K, Frechette ES, et al. Extreme delta brush: a unique EEG pattern in adults with anti-NMDA receptor encephalitis. Neurology 2012;79(11):1094–100.

23. Gitiaux C, Simonnet H, Eisermann M, et al. Early electro-clinical features may contribute to diagnosis of the anti-NMDA receptor encephalitis in children. Clin Neurophysiol 2013;124:2354–61.

24. Dale RC, Brilot F, Duffy LV, et al. Utility and safety of rituximab in pediatric autoimmune and inflammatory CNS disease. Neurology 2014;83:142–50.

25. Hacohen Y, Deiva K, Pettingill P, et al. N-methyl-D-aspartate receptor antibodies in post-herpes simplex virus encephalitis neurological relapse. Mov Disord 2014;29(1):90–6.

26. De Tiege X, Rozenberg F, Des Portes V, et al. Herpes simplex encephalitis relapses in children: differentiation of two neurologic entities. Neurology 2003;61:241–3.

27. Mohammad SS, Sinclair K, Pillai S, et al. Herpes simplex encephalitis relapse with chorea is associated with autoantibodies to N-methyl-D-aspartate receptor or dopamine-2 receptor. Mov Disord 2014;29(1):117–22.

28. Armangue T, Leypoldt F, Malaga I, et al. Herpes simplex virus encephalitis is a trigger of brain autoimmunity. Ann Neurol 2014;75(2):317–23.

29. Pruss H, Finke C, Holtje M, et al. N-methyl-D-aspartate receptor antibodies in herpes simplex encephalitis. Ann Neurol 2012;72(6):902–11.

30. Vincent A, Buckley C, Schott JM, et al. Potassium channel antibody-associated encephalopathy: a potentially immunotherapy-responsive form of limbic encephalitis. Brain 2004;127:701–12.

31. Irani SR, Alexander S, Waters P, et al. Antibodies to Kv1 potassium channel-complex proteins leucine-rich, glioma inactivated 1 protein and contactin-associated protein-2 in limbic encephalitis, Morvan's syndrome and acquired neuromyotonia. Brain 2004;127(Pt 3):701–12.

32. Lai M, Huijbers MG, Lancaster E, et al. Investigation of LGI1 as the antigen in limbic encephalitis previously attributed to potassium channels: a case series. Lancet Neurol 2010;9(8):776–85.

33. Lancaster E, Huijbers MG, Bar V, et al. Investigations of caspr2, an autoantigen of encephalitis and neuromyotonia. Ann Neurol 2011;69(2):303–11.

34. Irani SR, Pettingill P, Kleopa KA, et al. Morvan syndrome: clinical and serological observations in 29 cases. Ann Neurol 2012;72(2):241–55.

35. Haberlandt E, Bast T, Ebner A, et al. Limbic encephalitis in children and adolescents. Arch Dis Child 2011;96(2):186–91.

36. Hacohen Y, Absoud M, Woodhall M, et al. Autoantibody biomarkers in childhood-acquired demyelinating syndromes: results from a national surveillance cohort. J Neurol Neurosurg Psychiatry 2014;85(4):456–61.

37. Wong-Kisiel LC, McKeon A, Wirrell EC. Autoimmune encephalopathies and epilepsies in children and teenagers. Can J Neurol Sci 2012;39(2):134–44.

38. Lai M, Hughes EG, Peng X, et al. AMPA receptor antibodies in limbic encephalitis alter synaptic receptor location. Ann Neurol 2009;65(4):424–34.

39. Rogers SW, Andrews PI, Gahring LC, et al. Autoantibodies to glutamate receptor GluR3 in Rasmussen's encephalitis. Science 1994;265(5172):648–51.

40. Lancaster E, Lai M, Peng X, et al. Antibodies to the GABA(B) receptor in limbic encephalitis with seizures: case series and characterisation of the antigen. Lancet Neurol 2010;9(1):67–76.

41. Hoftberger R, Titulaer MJ, Sabater L, et al. Encephalitis and GABAB receptor antibodies: novel findings in a new case series of 20 patients. Neurology 2013; 81(17):1500–6.

42. Kruer MC, Hoeftberger R, Lim KY, et al. Aggressive course in encephalitis with opsoclonus, ataxia, chorea, and seizures: the first pediatric case of gamma-aminobutyric acid type b receptor autoimmunity. JAMA Neurol 2014;71(5): 620–3.

43. Lancaster E, Martinez-Hernandez E, Titulaer MJ, et al. Antibodies to metabotropic glutamate receptor 5 in the Ophelia syndrome. Neurology 2011;77: 1698–701.

44. Marignier R, Chenevier F, Rogemond V, et al. Metabotropic glutamate receptor type 1 autoantibody-associated cerebellitis: a primary autoimmune disease? Arch Neurol 2010;67(5):627–30.

45. Carvajal-Gonzalez A, Leite MI, Waters P, et al. Glycine receptor antibodies in PERM and related syndromes: characteristics, clinical features and outcomes. Brain 2014;137(Pt 8):2178–92.

46. McKeon A, Martinez-Hernandez E, Lancaster E, et al. Glycine receptor autoimmune spectrum with stiff-man syndrome phenotype. JAMA Neurol 2013;70: 44–50.

47. Damasio J, Leite MI, Coutinho E, et al. Progressive encephalomyelitis with rigidity and myoclonus: the first pediatric case with glycine receptor antibodies. JAMA Neurol 2013;70(4):498–501.

48. Clardy SL, Lennon VA, Dalmau J, et al. Childhood onset of stiff-man syndrome. JAMA Neurol 2013;70(12):1531–6.

49. Boronat A, Gelfand JM, Gresa-Arribas N, et al. Encephalitis and antibodies to dipeptidyl-peptidase-like protein-6, a subunit of Kv4.2 potassium channels. Ann Neurol 2013;73:120–8.

50. Balint B, Jarius S, Nagel S, et al. Progressive encephalomyelitis with rigidity and myoclonus: a new variant with DPPX antibodies. Neurology 2014;82:1521–8.

51. Tobin WO, Lennon VA, Komorowski L, et al. DPPX potassium channel antibody: frequency, clinical accompaniments, and outcomes in 20 patients. Neurology 2014;83:1797–803.

52. Petit-Pedrol M, Armangue T, Peng X, et al. Encephalitis with refractory seizures, status epilepticus, and antibodies to the GABAA receptor: a case series, characterisation of the antigen, and analysis of the effects of antibodies. Lancet Neurol 2014;13:276–86.

53. Petttingill P, Kramer H, Coebergh J, et al. Antibodies to GABAA receptor alpha and gamma2 subunits: clinical and serological characterization. Neurology 2015;84(12):1233–41.

54. Dale RC, Merheb V, Pillai S, et al. Antibodies to surface dopamine-2 receptor in autoimmune movement and psychiatric disorders. Brain 2012;135(Pt 11): 3453–68.

55. Brimberg L, Benhar I, Mascaro-Blanco A, et al. Behavioral, pharmacological, and immunological abnormalities after streptococcal exposure: a novel rat model of

Sydenham chorea and related neuropsychiatric disorders. Neuropsychopharmacology 2012;37(9):2076–87.

56. Krumbholz M, Derfuss T, Hohlfeld R, et al. B cells and antibodies in multiple sclerosis pathogenesis and therapy. Nat Rev Neurol 2012;8(11):613–23.

57. Lennon VA, Wingerchuk DM, Kryzer TJ, et al. A serum autoantibody marker of neuromyelitis optica: distinction from multiple sclerosis. Lancet 2004;364(9451):2106–12.

58. McKeon A, Lennon VA, Lotze T, et al. CNS aquaporin-4 autoimmunity in children. Neurology 2008;71:93–100.

59. Kitley J, Leite MI, Nakashima I, et al. Prognostic factors and disease course in aquaporin-4 antibody-positive patients with neuromyelitis optica spectrum disorder from the United Kingdom and Japan. Brain 2012;135(Pt 6):1834–49.

60. Reindl M, Di Pauli F, Rostasy K, et al. The spectrum of MOG autoantibody-associated demyelinating diseases. Nat Rev Neurosci 2002;3(4):291–301.

61. Kitley J, Waters P, Woodhall M, et al. Neuromyelitis optica spectrum disorders with aquaporin-4 and myelin-oligodendrocyte glycoprotein antibodies: a comparative study. JAMA Neurol 2014;71:276–83.

62. Probstel AK, Dornmair K, Bittner R, et al. Antibodies to MOG are transient in childhood acute disseminated encephalomyelitis. Neurology 2011;77(6):580–8.

63. Titulaer MJ, Hoftberger R, Iizuka T, et al. Overlapping demyelinating syndromes and anti-NMDA receptor encephalitis. Ann Neurol 2014;75(3):411–28.

64. Hacohen Y, Absoud M, Hemingway C, et al. NMDA receptor antibodies associated with distinct white matter syndromes. Neurol Neuroimmunol Neuroinflamm 2014;1:e2.

65. Zuliani L, Graus F, Giometto B, et al. Central nervous system neuronal surface antibody associated syndromes: review and guidelines for recognition. J Neurol Neurosurg Psychiatry 2012;83(6):638–45.

66. Suleiman J, Brilot F, Lang B, et al. Autoimmune epilepsy in children: case series and proposed guidelines for identification. Epilepsia 2013;54:1036–45.

67. Irani SR, Stagg CJ, Schott JM, et al. Faciobrachial dystonic seizures: the influence of immunotherapy on seizure control and prevention of cognitive impairment in a broadening phenotype. Brain 2013;136:3151–62.

68. Gresa-Arribas N, Titulaer MJ, Torrents A, et al. Antibody titres at diagnosis and during follow-up of anti-NMDA receptor encephalitis: a retrospective study. Lancet Neurol 2014;13:167–77.

69. Moscato EH, Peng X, Jain A, et al. Acute mechanisms underlying antibody effects in anti-NMDA receptor encephalitis. Ann Neurol 2014;76(1):108–19.

70. Mikasova L, De RP, Bouchet D, et al. Disrupted surface cross-talk between NMDA and Ephrin-B2 receptors in anti-NMDA encephalitis. Brain 2012;135:1606–21.

Advances in Tourette Syndrome
Diagnoses and Treatment

Fatema J. Serajee, MD[a,b], A.H.M. Mahbubul Huq, MD, PhD[a,b],*

KEYWORDS

- Tourette • Tics • ADHD • OCD

KEY POINTS

- Tourette syndrome (TS) is a childhood-onset neurodevelopmental disorder characterized by multiple motor tics and at least one vocal or phonic tic, and often one or more comorbid psychiatric disorders.
- Premonitory sensory urges before tic execution and desire for "just-right" perception are central features.
- The pathophysiology involves cortico-striato-thalamo-cortical circuits and possibly dopaminergic system.
- TS is considered a genetic disorder but the genetics is complex and likely involves rare mutations, common variants, and environmental and epigenetic factors.
- Treatment is multimodal and includes education and reassurance, behavioral interventions, pharmacologic, and rarely, surgical interventions.

INTRODUCTION

The prevalence of Tourette syndrome (TS) is approximately 0.3% to 1% with a male to female ratio of 4:1.[1,2]

TS is considered a disorder of cortico-striato-thalamo-cortical circuits that is involved in motor, cognitive, and motivational aspects of behavior.[3] Direct striatonigral (dopamine D1 receptor) and indirect striatopallidal (dopamine D2 receptor) pathways are parallel loops in this circuit that provide excitatory and inhibitory feedback.[4] Tics

Disclosure: The authors have nothing to disclose.
[a] Department of Pediatrics, Children's Hospital of Michigan, Wayne State University, 3901 Beaubien Street, Detroit, MI 48201, USA; [b] Department of Neurology, Children's Hospital of Michigan, Wayne State University, 3901 Beaubien Street, Detroit, MI 48201, USA
* Corresponding author. Department of Pediatrics, Children's Hospital of Michigan, Wayne State University, 3901 Beaubien Street, Detroit MI 48201.
E-mail address: ahuq@med.wayne.edu

0031-3955/15/$ – see front matter © 2015 Elsevier Inc. All rights reserved.

and unwanted behaviors can result from reduced activity of indirect striatopallidal (D2 receptor) pathway leading deficient inhibition of unwanted or off-target movements and behavior.

Consistently reported neuroanatomical abnormalities in TS include reduced caudate volumes across the lifespan, thinning of sensorimotor cortices correlating with tic severity in children, hypertrophy of the limbic and prefrontal cortices, and a smaller corpus callosum correlating with fewer symptoms in children.[5] Focal ischemic damage to the striatum can produce tics.[6] Similarly, tics and TS-like behavior abnormalities are elicited by local striatal disinhibition in monkeys.[7]

Disruption of dopaminergic modulation in basal ganglia is implicated in TS, although other neurotransmitters are likely involved.[7,8] The dopamine D2 receptor antagonists haloperidol and pimozide are among the most effective used to treat severe tics.[9]

Although the evidence for a genetic contribution in TS is strong, its exact nature is not known. Monozygotic twins are concordant for TS approximately 50% of the time compared with 10% for dizygotic twins. When all tic disorders are considered, the concordance rate for monozygotic twins is 77% compared with 23% for dizygotic twins; studies estimate a sibling relative risk of 6 to 8.[10]

Segregation analyses suggest that the transmission of TS and related phenotypes within families is complex, and likely involves many genetic loci.[11] Up to 40% of pedigrees with multiple affected children have bilineal inheritance of tics and obsessive-compulsive disorder (OCD).

Linkage analyses results have been inconsistent; however, a locus on chromosome 2p was detected that achieved genome-wide significance ($p = 9.8 \times 10^{-8}$).[12]

The genetic risks for TS include both common and rare variants and may involve complex multigenic inheritance or, in rare cases, a single major gene.[13–17]

Cytogenetic abnormalities involving inner mitochondrial membrane protein 2L (IMMP2L), contactin-associated protein-like 2 (CNTNAP2), neuroligin 4, X-linked (NGLN4X), and Slit and Trk-like, Family Member 1 (SLITRK1) genes have been identified in rare patients with TS.[18]

Chromosome microarray studies have suggested common copy number variants (CNVs) in TS and other neurodevelopmental disorders (eg, CNVs involving neurexins, neuroligins, and genes from the histaminergic and glutamatergic pathways).[14,18] Several studies implicated CNVs that are seen in autism such as neurexin 1 (NRXN1), catenin, alpha 3 (CTNNA3); and 16p13.11deletions.[13,14,19,20] Enrichment of genes involved in histamine signaling within CNVs, an excess of large (>500 Kb) CNVs compared with controls, and a higher burden of large deletions within regions previously known to harbor recurrent pathogenic CNVs in subjects with other neurodevelopmental disorders, have been reported.[13,20]

A rare coding mutation in the gene ʟ-histidine decarboxylase, which is the rate-limiting enzyme in histamine biosynthesis, has been described.[21]

A genome-wide association study (GWAS) with 1285 TS European ancestry cases and 4964 ancestry-matched controls[22] with a parallel GWAS of OCD[23] demonstrated that the most TS heritability could be explained by common polymorphisms rather than rare mutations. In addition, TS and OCD had an estimated genetic correlation of 0.41, confirming the presence of shared genetic variation between the disorders.

Nongenetic factors, including perinatal complications, maternal smoking, and maternal stress during pregnancy, may play a role.[24,25]

Whether the generation of tics in some individuals involves a postinfectious autoimmune component remains controversial.[26]

PATIENT HISTORY

Clinical history is of utmost importance in establishing the diagnosis.

Cardinal features of TS are vocal and phonic tics. Tics are unwanted, brief, repetitive, nonrhythmic motor movements and vocalizations. Tics that involve a single muscle or a small group of muscles are considered simple; those that include a coordinated pattern of movement or sound and resemble purposeful action or speech are considered complex (**Table 1**).

Involuntary expression of socially unacceptable words (coprolalia) or gestures (copropraxia) and nonobscene socially inappropriate behaviors are present in a small minority of individuals.[27] Coprolalia and copropraxia appear when tics are most severe, and are positively associated with psychiatric comorbidity and more severe form of disease.

The typical age of onset for TS is between 3 and 8 years (mean age ~7 years) with motor tics most often preceding vocal tics.

Tics have a waxing and waning course, suppressibility followed by rebound, and suggestibility.[28] Tics tend to be aggravated by anxiety and stress and alleviated by physical and mental tasks requiring concentration. In adults and older children, tics are often preceded by premonitory sensations, a sense of inner tension that is reduced or relieved by the performance of the tic, and they may occur in orchestrated sequences.[28]

Comorbid psychiatric disorders are present in 90% of individuals with TS both in clinical and community cohorts. The most common comorbidities are attention-deficit hyperactivity disorder (ADHD), OCD, autistic spectrum disorders, depression, anxiety, and behavioral disorders such as oppositional defiant and conduct disorder (**Table 2**).[29,30]

The onset of ADHD typically precedes the onset of tics and may be associated with academic, social, and family difficulties.[31] ADHD symptoms often persist into adulthood despite the tendency for tics to diminish.

OCD is also commonly observed in individuals with TS[32] and in family members.[33] Tic-related OCD may represent a subtype of OCD comprising concerns about symmetry, evening-up behaviors, obsessional counting, and "just-right" perceptions; whereas patients with pure OCD have higher rate of cleaning rituals, compulsive washing, and fears of contamination.[33] Tic-related OCD also has an earlier age of

Table 1 Common motor and phonic tics		
	Motor	**Phonic**
Simple	Eye blinking	Throat clearing
	Shoulder shrugging	Cough
	Eye rolling	Gulping
	Nose twitching	Snorting
	Mouth pouting	Sniffing
	Head jerking	Grunting
	Muscle tensing	Barking
	Finger flexing	Belching
		Hiccough
Complex	Touching	Coprolalia
	Flexing of abdomen	Echolalia
	Kissing	Palilalia
	Squatting	
	Jumping	
	Copropraxia	
	Echopraxia	

Table 2 Prevalence of comorbid disorders	
Condition	Prevalence in TS
Any neurobehavioral problem[29,30]	85%–90%
ADHD[32]	Clinical setting[32]: 50%–90% Community-ascertained[30,34]: 20%–50%
OCD[32]	50%
Behavior, conduct problems[35]	26%
Mood disorders[36]	Depressive symptoms: 76% Major depression: 13% Bipolar disorder: 7%–28%
Autism[35]	35%
Personality disorder[37]	64%
Learning disability[34]	47%
Speech and language disorder[35]	29%
Intellectual disability[35]	12%
Anxiety[38]	49%
Trichotillomania[39]	4%
Pathologic nail biting[39]	25%
Sleep disorders[40]	65%

onset, is more common in males, and is associated with higher rate of ADHD and disruptive behaviors.

Difficulties with learning are common in children and adolescents with TS.[34] Specific cognitive deficits in TS consist of visuomotor integration problems, impaired fine motor skill, and executive dysfunction.[41] The presence of comorbid conditions, notably ADHD and OCD, seems to significantly increase the likelihood that an individual with TS will also have learning problems or some demonstrable cognitive impairment. Parents of children with TS and ADHD also have an elevated rate of language-based learning problems.

Mood disorders are common in individuals with TS.[36] Dysthymia, major depressive disorder, and depressive illness occur in 13% to 76% of persons with TD who attend specialty clinics.[36] Bipolar disorder has been reported in 7% to 28% of the TS population.[42]

Individuals with TS have significantly elevated rates of anxiety disorders, including separation anxiety, simple phobia, social phobia, and agoraphobia, compared with those who do not have TS in both community-based studies and clinically ascertained samples.[38,43]

Impulse control disorders, including intermittent, explosive disorder, self-injurious behavior, trichotillomania, and impulsive-compulsive sexual behavior, are more common in clinic populations with TS than in the general population.[44]

PHYSICAL EXAMINATION

Physical examination is usually not very helpful; however, a careful neurologic examination should be performed to exclude secondary causes.

DIAGNOSIS

The diagnosis of TD is made clinically based on the history, pattern, and intensity of the symptoms. The standard diagnostic criteria for Tourette disorder in the United

States are defined by the *American Psychiatric Association Manual of Psychiatric Diseases, 5th edition* (DSM V) (**Table 3**).[45]

Other movement disorders, including Huntington disease, Wilson disease, chorea, dystonia, myoclonus, dyskinesia, or stereotypies and dissociative disorders, may mimic TS. Complex motor tics may be difficult to distinguish from compulsive rituals. The early onset and waxing, waning, and fluctuating symptoms of tics, co-occurrence of simple and complex tics, normal neurologic examination, suppressibility, the premonitory sensation, and "just-right" perception are all highly suggestive of TS. Late onset of tics or the presence of complex tics in the absence of a history of simple tics should warrant further investigation.

IMAGING AND ADDITIONAL TESTING

Imaging, electrophysiology, biochemical, and molecular genetic testing are of little clinical relevance currently and cannot confirm the presence of TS; however, rarely, they may be needed to establish alternative diagnoses.

A neuropsychological evaluation is helpful for assessing comorbid cognitive deficits and emotional problems. Several standardized instruments may be useful for research, establishing severity, and assessing the response to medication. These include the Yale Global Tic Severity Scale,[46] the Yale-Brown Obsessive Compulsive Scale,[47] or the Children's Yale-Brown Obsessive Compulsive Scale.[48]

PHARMACOLOGIC TREATMENT OPTIONS

- Only few large double-blind clinical trials are available for TS patients. Treatment decisions are often guided by individual needs and the personal experience of treating clinicians.
- The treatment of TS should address both tics and psychiatric comorbidities, including ADHD, OCD, depression, and anxiety, which are often of greater clinical concern than the tics.

Table 3 Diagnostic criteria	
Diagnosis	**DSM V Criteria**
Tourette syndrome	• 2 or more motor tics and at least 1 vocal tic, not necessarily concurrent • Tics present for at least 1 y • Onset before age 18 y • Tics not due to direct physiologic effects of a substance (eg, cocaine) or a general medical condition
Persistent (chronic) motor or vocal tic	• Single or multiple motor or vocal tics, not both • Tics present for at least 1 y • Onset before age 18 y • Tics not due to direct physiologic effects of a substance (eg, cocaine) or a general medical condition
Provisional tic disorder	• Single or multiple motor and/or vocal tics • Tics present for <1 y since first onset • Onset before age 18 y • Disturbance not attributable to the physiologic effects of a substance (eg, cocaine) or another medical condition (eg, Huntington disease, postviral encephalitis) • Criteria never met for Tourette disorder or persistent (chronic) motor or vocal tic disorder

- Tics show significant improvement around middle to late adolescence. Not all patients with tics need pharmacologic treatment (**Box 1**). Common drugs used to treat tics are shown in **Table 4**.
- Consensus guidelines are available (**Box 2**).
- The pharmacologic treatment of tics is significantly complicated by the waxing, waning, and fluctuating course of the illness.

Both typical and atypical antipsychotics have demonstrated efficacy in double-blind or open-label clinical trials.[49–58] Although the only 2 formally approved medications in the United States are haloperidol and pimozide, these treatments are generally not used as first-line interventions due to their significant potential for adverse effects of sedation, weight gain, dysphoria, and cognitive dulling. The risk of tardive dyskinesia may be less with fluphenazine.[59] The efficacy of atypical antipsychotics may be related to the relative efficacy of dopamine blockade.

The α-adrenoceptor agonists guanfacine and clonidine have demonstrated efficacy in double-blind or open-label clinical trials.[51,54,60–64] Percentage improvement in tics from clonidine or guanfacine is between 30% to 35% compared with 39% to 58% for pimozide, 66% for haloperidol, or 35% to 50% for risperidone.

Alpha-2 agonists, such as clonidine and guanfacine, are less effective than antipsychotics but are usually recommended as initial pharmacotherapy due to low side effects. Atypical neuroleptics, such as aripiprazole or risperidone, are typically used if the α-adrenoceptor agonists are ineffective or intolerable.

Additional treatment options, such as tetrabenazine, may be useful if patients do not respond to the primary agents.[65,66] Benzodiazepines, baclofen, and tetrabenazine would benefit from additional controlled trials.

Levetiracetam was not effective in recent trials. One trial suggested potential efficacy and tolerability of topiramate for tics.[67]

Single clinical trials of metoclopramide, atomoxetine, and ondansetron were of limited quality, and these would benefit from additional controlled trials.[68]

Botulinum toxins showed a roughly 40% reduction in tics in a placebo-controlled trial.[69] It may be considered for a single interfering tic but dose and frequency of injection remain uncertain. Adverse effects include weakness of the injected muscle, including the vocal cords.[70]

Methylphenidate and clonidine (particularly in combination) are effective for ADHD in children with comorbid tics.[60] Prior recommendations to avoid methylphenidate in these children because of concerns of worsening tics are not currently supported. Atomoxetine or risperidone[71–73] may also be tried.

OCD can be treated with cognitive behavioral therapy, selective serotonin reuptake inhibitors (SSRIs), and atypical antipsychotics. Deep brain stimulation (DBS) is a treatment option for patients with disabling OCD despite other therapies.[74]

Box 1
Indications for drug treatment of tics

- Tics that cause subjective discomfort, pain, or injury
- Sustained social problems such as isolation or bullying
- Social and emotional problems (eg, reactive depressive symptoms)
- Functional interference (eg, impairment of academic performance).

Table 4
Commonly used agents in Tourette syndrome

Drug	Evidence[a]	Comments
Clonidine	A	6 double-blind clinical trials showing superiority compared with placebo[51,54,60–64]
		Side effects include sedation, light-headedness, and irritability
Guanfacine	B	1 randomized trial showing efficacy compared with placebo[77]
		Side effects include lightheadedness due to orthostatic hypotension
Haloperidol	A	4 double-blind trials showing efficacy compared with placebo[49,56,58,78]
Pimozide	A	Multiple double-blind trials showing efficacy[49,52,56–58]
Fluphenazine	C	Risk of tardive dyskinesia may be less than other antipsychotics[59]
Risperidone	A	4 randomized trials showing efficacy compared with placebo[52–55]
		Weight gain, metabolic syndrome, tardive dyskinesia
Aripiprazole[79]	B	1 randomized trial showing efficacy compared with placebo[80]
Ziprasidone	B	1 randomized trial showing efficacy compared with placebo[81]
Tetrabenazine	C	Risk of tardive dyskinesia may be less than other antipsychotics[82]
Botulinum toxin	B	Several open studies and 1 double-blind study[69]
		May be considered for single disabling tic

[a] A, 2 or more randomized placebo-controlled clinical trials; B, 1 randomized placebo-controlled clinical trial; C, case series or open-label trial.

However, it is not clear if usual treatment of OCD, including SSRIs and atypical antipsychotics, are similarly effective in the treatment of tics-related OCD, especially in children.[75,76]

NONPHARMACOLOGIC TREATMENT OPTIONS
Behavior Therapy

- Habit reversal therapy[83,84] encourages patients to be aware of their premonitory sensations and tics and substitute a competing response that is inconsistent with performance of the unwanted tic so that tic expression is delayed and ultimately

Box 2
Canadian guidelines for treatment of tic disorders

Strong recommendations

- Clonidine

- Guanfacine (children only)

Weak recommendations

- Pimozide, haloperidol, fluphenazine, metoclopramide (children only), risperidone, aripiprazole, olanzapine, quetiapine, ziprasidone, topiramate, baclofen (children only), botulinum toxin injections, tetrabenazine, and cannabinoids (adults only)

Data from Pringsheim T, Doja A, Gorman D, et al. Canadian guidelines for the evidence-based treatment of tic disorders: pharmacotherapy. Can J Psychiatry 2012;57:133–43.

abolished. A cooperative patient, the presence of a premonitory urge, and a committed family are essential ingredients for success.
- Results have been promising for comprehensive behavioral intervention for tics, which involves a combination of habit reversal therapy, education, relaxation techniques, symptom analysis, and social support.[85–87]
- Other cognitive behavioral approaches, such as exposure with response inhibition, seems to be effective.[83,88] Relaxation therapy was not effective when used alone.[89] However, it may be beneficial when used in combination with other behavioral approaches (**Table 5**).[83]

Repetitive Transcranial Magnetic Stimulation

- Repetitive transcranial magnetic stimulation is a noninvasive therapy in which targeted regions of the brain are stimulated using rapidly changing magnetic fields. Both positive and negative results have been reported.[90,91] Further clinical studies are required to address questions regarding optimal approach to treatment and efficacy.

Combination Therapies

Only anecdotal are available regarding combination therapy for tics.[92]

Surgical Treatment Options

- Surgical intervention, specifically DBS, has been used for a small subset of individuals with intractable TS in whom conventional therapy has been unsuccessful and in whom the tics have been harmful.
- DBS sends out electrical impulses through implanted electrodes in specific targeted regions in the brain, altering brain activity in that region. Fewer than 5% of cases are estimated to be suitable for DBS in a tertiary specialized clinic cohort.[93]
- Various structures in the cortico-striato-thalamo-cortical pathway have been targeted in DBS, including thalamus, globus pallidus pars interna, globus pallidus externus, anterior limb of the internal capsule or nucleus accumbens, and subthalamic nucleus.[94–96]
- Overall, individuals treated with DBS have experienced a reduction in tic frequency and intensity, without major side effects.
- Although persistent serious adverse effects are few, surgery-related effects (eg, bleeding, infection) as well as stimulation-related effects (eg, sedation, anxiety, altered mood, changes in sexual function) may occur.
- The optimal surgical target regions for TS and eligibility criteria are still being debated.

Table 5	
European guidelines for behavioral treatment of tic disorders	
First-line treatment	Habit reversal training
	Exposure with response prevention
Second-line treatment	Contingency management
	Function-based interventions
	Relaxation training
Experimental	Neurofeedback

Data from Verdellen C, van de Griendt J, Hartmann A, et al. European clinical guidelines for Tourette syndrome and other tic disorders. Part III: behavioural and psychosocial interventions. Eur Child Adolesc Psychiatry 2011;20:197–207.

TREATMENT RESISTANCE OR COMPLICATIONS

- Factors associated with treatment resistance are not well understood. Patients with severe tics or comorbid psychiatric disorders tend to have poor response to medications.[97]
- DBS seems to be effective in most treatment-resistant cases but, so far, only a small number of individuals with TS have undergone DBS.

EVALUATION OF OUTCOME AND LONG-TERM RECOMMENDATIONS

- Tics typically have an onset between the ages of 4 and 6 years and reach their worst-ever severity between the ages of 10 and 12 years. On average, tic severity declines during adolescence. By early adulthood, roughly three-quarters of children with TS will have greatly diminished tic symptoms and more than one-third will be tic free.
- Approximately 10% of patients with TS only have tics and they did not differ from unaffected controls on many ratings, including aggression, delinquency, or conduct difficulties.[98,99]
- Co-occurrence of ADHD and TS is associated with increased risk of disruptive behaviors.[98,99]
- Predictors of increased tic severity in adulthood include higher childhood tic severity, smaller caudate volumes, and poorer fine motor control.[100]
- OCD symptoms in children with TS become more severe at a later age and are more likely to persist than tic symptoms.[101]
- About 5% of patients referred to a specialty clinic have life-threatening symptoms due to tic-related injuries, self-injurious behavior, uncontrollable violence and temper, and suicidal ideation or attempts.[97] Malignant TS is associated with greater severity of motor symptoms and the presence of 2 or more behavioral comorbidities. Those with malignant TS were significantly more likely to have a personal history of obsessive-compulsive behavior or OCD, complex phonic tics, coprolalia, copropraxia, self-injurious behavior, mood disorder, suicidal ideation, and poor response to medications.

GENETIC COUNSELING

At present, genetic counseling based on empiric familial risk is the only available strategy for the families of children with TS (**Table 6**).

- A Japanese population study reported much lower risk for family members compared with those listed in **Table 6**. The empiric risk for tics in a Japanese cohort was lower (2.3%) than in other studies.[102]

Table 6	
Empiric risk to family members	
Relation To Proband	**Risk**
Father	Tourette, 11.9%–23.1%; chronic tics, 11.5% to 21%; OCD, 10% to 23.1%
Mother	Tourette, 1%–9.6%; chronic tics, 11.5% to 21%; OCD, 10% to 23.1%
Siblings	Tourette, 8%; chronic tics, 0%–11%; OCD, 9.7%–22%
Offspring	Tourette, 22%; chronic tics, 50%; OCD, 9.7%–22%

Data from Refs.[102–105]

- In bilineal families, the risk of TS for offspring increases to 42.8% compared with 15% for unilineal families. Additionally, rates of any tic diagnosis, OCD, and ADHD are increased.[105]

REFERENCES

1. Centers for Disease Control and Prevention (CDC). Prevalence of diagnosed Tourette syndrome in persons aged 6-17 years - United States, 2007. MMWR Morb Mortal Wkly Rep 2009;58:581–5.
2. Robertson MM, Eapen V, Cavanna AE. The international prevalence, epidemiology, and clinical phenomenology of Tourette syndrome: a cross-cultural perspective. J Psychosom Res 2009;67:475–83.
3. Neuner I, Werner CJ, Arrubla J, et al. Imaging the where and when of tic generation and resting state networks in adult Tourette patients. Front Hum Neurosci 2014;8:362.
4. Grillner S, Robertson B, Stephenson-Jones M. The evolutionary origin of the vertebrate basal ganglia and its role in action selection. J Physiol 2013;591: 5425–31.
5. Draganski B, Martino D, Cavanna AE, et al. Multispectral brain morphometry in Tourette syndrome persisting into adulthood. Brain 2010;133:3661–75.
6. Kwak CH, Jankovic J. Tourettism and dystonia after subcortical stroke. Mov Disord 2002;17:821–5.
7. Worbe Y, Sgambato-Faure V, Epinat J, et al. Towards a primate model of Gilles de la Tourette syndrome: anatomo-behavioural correlation of disorders induced by striatal dysfunction. Cortex 2013;49:1126–40.
8. Jankovic J, Kurlan R. Tourette syndrome: evolving concepts. Mov Disord 2011; 26:1149–56.
9. Kurlan RM. Treatment of Tourette syndrome. Neurotherapeutics 2014;11:161–5.
10. Price RA, Kidd KK, Cohen DJ, et al. A twin study of Tourette syndrome. Arch Gen Psychiatry 1985;42:815–20.
11. Pauls DL. An update on the genetics of Gilles de la Tourette syndrome. J Psychosom Res 2003;55:7–12.
12. Tourette Syndrome Association International Consortium for Genetics. Genome scan for Tourette disorder in affected-sibling-pair and multigenerational families. Am J Hum Genet 2007;80:265–72.
13. McGrath LM, Yu D, Marshall C, et al. Copy number variation in obsessive-compulsive disorder and tourette syndrome: a cross-disorder study. J Am Acad Child Adolesc Psychiatry 2014;53:910–9.
14. Sundaram SK, Huq AM, Wilson BJ, et al. Tourette syndrome is associated with recurrent exonic copy number variants. Neurology 2010;74:1583–90.
15. Sundaram SK, Huq AM, Sun Z, et al. Exome sequencing of a pedigree with Tourette syndrome or chronic tic disorder. Ann Neurol 2011;69:901–4.
16. Abe K, Oda N. Contributions of genetic studies to clinical psychiatry. Jpn J Psychiatry Neurol 1991;45:819–23.
17. Paschou P, Yu D, Gerber G, et al. Genetic association signal near NTN4 in Tourette syndrome. Ann Neurol 2014;76:310–5.
18. Pauls DL, Fernandez TV, Mathews CA, et al. The Inheritance of Tourette Disorder. A review. J Obsessive Compuls Relat Disord 2014;3:380–5.
19. Fernandez TV, Sanders SJ, Yurkiewicz IR, et al. Rare copy number variants in tourette syndrome disrupt genes in histaminergic pathways and overlap with autism. Biol Psychiatry 2012;71:392–402.

20. Nag A, Bochukova EG, Kremeyer B, et al. CNV analysis in Tourette syndrome implicates large genomic rearrangements in COL8A1 and NRXN1. PLoS One 2013;8:e59061.
21. Ercan-Sencicek AG, Stillman AA, Ghosh AK, et al. L-histidine decarboxylase and Tourette's syndrome. N Engl J Med 2010;362:1901–8.
22. Scharf JM, Yu D, Mathews CA, et al. Genome-wide association study of Tourette's syndrome. Mol Psychiatry 2013;18:721–8.
23. Stewart SE, Yu D, Scharf JM, et al. Genome-wide association study of obsessive-compulsive disorder. Mol Psychiatry 2013;18:788–98.
24. Mathews CA, Bimson B, Lowe TL, et al. Association between maternal smoking and increased symptom severity in Tourette's syndrome. Am J Psychiatry 2006; 163:1066–73.
25. Mathews CA, Scharf JM, Miller LL, et al. Association between pre- and perinatal exposures and Tourette syndrome or chronic tic disorder in the ALSPAC cohort. Br J Psychiatry 2014;204:40–5.
26. Macerollo A, Martino D. Pediatric autoimmune neuropsychiatric disorders associated with streptococcal infections (PANDAS): an evolving concept. Tremor Other Hyperkinet Mov (N Y) 2013;3 [pii: tre-03-167-4158-7].
27. Freeman RD, Zinner SH, Muller-Vahl KR, et al. Coprophenomena in Tourette syndrome. Dev Med Child Neurol 2009;51:218–27.
28. Banaschewski T, Woerner W, Rothenberger A. Premonitory sensory phenomena and suppressibility of tics in Tourette syndrome: developmental aspects in children and adolescents. Dev Med Child Neurol 2003;45:700–3.
29. Freeman RD, Fast DK, Burd L, et al. An international perspective on Tourette syndrome: selected findings from 3,500 individuals in 22 countries. Dev Med Child Neurol 2000;42:436–47.
30. Khalifa N, von Knorring AL. Tourette syndrome and other tic disorders in a total population of children: clinical assessment and background. Acta Paediatr 2005;94:1608–14.
31. Sukhodolsky DG, Landeros-Weisenberger A, Scahill L, et al. Neuropsychological functioning in children with Tourette syndrome with and without attention-deficit/hyperactivity disorder. J Am Acad Child Adolesc Psychiatry 2010;49: 1155–64.
32. Ghanizadeh A, Mosallaei S. Psychiatric disorders and behavioral problems in children and adolescents with Tourette syndrome. Brain Dev 2009;31:15–9.
33. Worbe Y, Mallet L, Golmard JL, et al. Repetitive behaviours in patients with Gilles de la Tourette syndrome: tics, compulsions, or both? PLoS One 2010;5:e12959.
34. Scahill L, Sukhodolsky DG, Williams SK, et al. Public health significance of tic disorders in children and adolescents. Adv Neurol 2005;96:240–8.
35. Bitsko RH, Holbrook JR, Visser SN, et al. A national profile of Tourette syndrome, 2011–2012. J Dev Behav Pediatr 2014;35:317–22.
36. Robertson MM. Mood disorders and Gilles de la Tourette's syndrome: an update on prevalence, etiology, comorbidity, clinical associations, and implications. J Psychosom Res 2006;61:349–58.
37. Robertson MM, Banerjee S, Hiley PJ, et al. Personality disorder and psychopathology in Tourette's syndrome: a controlled study. Br J Psychiatry 1997;171:283–6.
38. Kurlan R, Como PG, Miller B, et al. The behavioral spectrum of tic disorders: a community-based study. Neurology 2002;59:414–20.
39. Lochner C, Hemmings SM, Kinnear CJ, et al. Cluster analysis of obsessive-compulsive spectrum disorders in patients with obsessive-compulsive disorder: clinical and genetic correlates. Compr Psychiatry 2005;46:14–9.

40. Ghosh D, Rajan PV, Das D, et al. Sleep disorders in children with Tourette syndrome. Pediatr Neurol 2014;51:31–5.

41. Como PG. Neuropsychological function in Tourette syndrome. Adv Neurol 2001; 85:103–11.

42. Kerbeshian J, Burd L, Klug MG. Comorbid Tourette's disorder and bipolar disorder: an etiologic perspective. Am J Psychiatry 1995;152:1646–51.

43. Coffey BJ, Biederman J, Smoller JW, et al. Anxiety disorders and tic severity in juveniles with Tourette's disorder. J Am Acad Child Adolesc Psychiatry 2000;39: 562–8.

44. Wright A, Rickards H, Cavanna AE. Impulse-control disorders in gilles de la tourette syndrome. J Neuropsychiatry Clin Neurosci 2012;24:16–27.

45. American Psychiatric Association. Diagnostic and statistical manual of mental disorders. 5th edition. Washington; 2013.

46. Leckman JF, Riddle MA, Hardin MT, et al. The Yale Global Tic Severity Scale: initial testing of a clinician-rated scale of tic severity. J Am Acad Child Adolesc Psychiatry 1989;28:566–73.

47. Goodman WK, Price LH, Rasmussen SA, et al. The Yale-Brown Obsessive Compulsive Scale. I. Development, use, and reliability. Arch Gen Psychiatry 1989;46:1006–11.

48. Scahill L, Riddle MA, McSwiggin-Hardin M, et al. Children's Yale-Brown Obsessive Compulsive Scale: reliability and validity. J Am Acad Child Adolesc Psychiatry 1997;36:844–52.

49. Ross MS, Moldofsky H. A comparison of pimozide and haloperidol in the treatment of Gilles de la Tourette's syndrome. Am J Psychiatry 1978;135:585–7.

50. Shapiro AK, Shapiro E, Eisenkraft GJ. Treatment of Gilles de la Tourette syndrome with pimozide. Am J Psychiatry 1983;140:1183–6.

51. Shapiro AK, Shapiro E, Eisenkraft GJ. Treatment of Gilles de la Tourette's syndrome with clonidine and neuroleptics. Arch Gen Psychiatry 1983;40: 1235–40.

52. Bruggeman R, van der Linden C, Buitelaar JK, et al. Risperidone versus pimozide in Tourette's disorder: a comparative double-blind parallel-group study. J Clin Psychiatry 2001;62:50–6.

53. Dion Y, Annable L, Sandor P, et al. Risperidone in the treatment of tourette syndrome: a double-blind, placebo-controlled trial. J Clin Psychopharmacol 2002;22:31–9.

54. Gaffney GR, Perry PJ, Lund BC, et al. Risperidone versus clonidine in the treatment of children and adolescents with Tourette's syndrome. J Am Acad Child Adolesc Psychiatry 2002;41:330–6.

55. Scahill L, Leckman JF, Schultz RT, et al. A placebo-controlled trial of risperidone in Tourette syndrome. Neurology 2003;60:1130–5.

56. Sallee FR, Nesbitt L, Jackson C, et al. Relative efficacy of haloperidol and pimozide in children and adolescents with Tourette's disorder. Am J Psychiatry 1997; 154:1057–62.

57. Shapiro AK, Shapiro E. Controlled study of pimozide vs. placebo in Tourette's syndrome. J Am Acad Child Psychiatry 1984;23:161–73.

58. Shapiro E, Shapiro AK, Fulop G, et al. Controlled study of haloperidol, pimozide and placebo for the treatment of Gilles de la Tourette's syndrome. Arch Gen Psychiatry 1989;46:722–30.

59. Wijemanne S, Wu LJ, Jankovic J. Long-term efficacy and safety of fluphenazine in patients with Tourette syndrome. Mov Disord 2014;29:126–30.

60. Tourette's Syndrome Study Group. Treatment of ADHD in children with tics: a randomized controlled trial. Neurology 2002;58:527–36.

61. Du YS, Li HF, Vance A, et al. Randomized double-blind multicentre placebo-controlled clinical trial of the clonidine adhesive patch for the treatment of tic disorders. Aust N Z J Psychiatry 2008;42:807–13.
62. Goetz CG, Tanner CM, Wilson RS, et al. Clonidine and Gilles de la Tourette's syndrome: double-blind study using objective rating methods. Ann Neurol 1987;21:307–10.
63. Leckman JF, Hardin MT, Riddle MA, et al. Clonidine treatment of Gilles de la Tourette's syndrome. Arch Gen Psychiatry 1991;48:324–8.
64. Singer HS, Brown J, Quaskey S, et al. The treatment of attention-deficit hyperactivity disorder in Tourette's syndrome: a double-blind placebo-controlled study with clonidine and desipramine. Pediatrics 1995;95:74–81.
65. Jankovic J, Glaze DG, Frost JD Jr. Effect of tetrabenazine on tics and sleep of Gilles de la Tourette's syndrome. Neurology 1984;34:688–92.
66. Porta M, Sassi M, Cavallazzi M, et al. Tourette's syndrome and role of tetrabenazine: review and personal experience. Clin Drug Investig 2008;28:443–59.
67. Jankovic J, Jimenez-Shahed J, Brown LW. A randomised, double-blind, placebo-controlled study of topiramate in the treatment of Tourette syndrome. J Neurol Neurosurg Psychiatry 2010;81:70–3.
68. Rajapakse T, Pringsheim T. Pharmacotherapeutics of Tourette syndrome and stereotypies in autism. Semin Pediatr Neurol 2010;17:254–60.
69. Marras C, Andrews D, Sime E, et al. Botulinum toxin for simple motor tics: a randomized, double-blind, controlled clinical trial. Neurology 2001;56:605–10.
70. Scahill L, Erenberg G, Berlin CM Jr, et al. Contemporary assessment and pharmacotherapy of Tourette syndrome. NeuroRx 2006;3:192–206.
71. Allen AJ, Kurlan RM, Gilbert DL, et al. Atomoxetine treatment in children and adolescents with ADHD and comorbid tic disorders. Neurology 2005;65:1941–9.
72. Bloch MH, Panza KE, Landeros-Weisenberger A, et al. Meta-analysis: treatment of attention-deficit/hyperactivity disorder in children with comorbid tic disorders. J Am Acad Child Adolesc Psychiatry 2009;48:884–93.
73. Spencer TJ, Sallee FR, Gilbert DL, et al. Atomoxetine treatment of ADHD in children with comorbid Tourette syndrome. J Atten Disord 2008;11:470–81.
74. Kurlan R, Kersun J, Ballantine HT Jr, et al. Neurosurgical treatment of severe obsessive-compulsive disorder associated with Tourette's syndrome. Mov Disord 1990;5:152–5.
75. Kurlan R, Como PG, Deeley C, et al. A pilot controlled study of fluoxetine for obsessive-compulsive symptoms in children with Tourette's syndrome. Clin Neuropharmacol 1993;16:167–72.
76. Geller DA, Biederman J, Stewart SE, et al. Impact of comorbidity on treatment response to paroxetine in pediatric obsessive-compulsive disorder: is the use of exclusion criteria empirically supported in randomized clinical trials? J Child Adolesc Psychopharmacol 2003;13(Suppl 1):S19–29.
77. Cummings DD, Singer HS, Krieger M, et al. Neuropsychiatric effects of guanfacine in children with mild tourette syndrome: a pilot study. Clin Neuropharmacol 2002;25:325–32.
78. Silver AA, Shytle RD, Philipp MK, et al. Transdermal nicotine and haloperidol in Tourette's disorder: a double-blind placebo-controlled study. J Clin Psychiatry 2001;62:707–14.
79. Liu ZS, Chen YH, Zhong YQ, et al. A multicenter controlled study on aripiprazole treatment for children with Tourette syndrome in China. Zhonghua Er Ke Za Zhi 2011;49:572–6 [in Chinese].

80. Yoo HK, Joung YS, Lee JS, et al. A multicenter, randomized, double-blind, placebo-controlled study of aripiprazole in children and adolescents with Tourette's disorder. J Clin Psychiatry 2013;74:e772–80.

81. Sallee FR, Kurlan R, Goetz CG, et al. Ziprasidone treatment of children and adolescents with Tourette's syndrome: a pilot study. J Am Acad Child Adolesc Psychiatry 2000;39:292–9.

82. Jankovic J. Tetrabenazine in the treatment of hyperkinetic movement disorders. Adv Neurol 1983;37:277–89.

83. Wilhelm S, Deckersbach T, Coffey BJ, et al. Habit reversal versus supportive psychotherapy for Tourette's disorder: a randomized controlled trial. Am J Psychiatry 2003;160:1175–7.

84. Himle MB, Woods DW, Piacentini JC, et al. Brief review of habit reversal training for Tourette syndrome. J Child Neurol 2006;21:719–25.

85. Wile DJ, Pringsheim TM. Behavior therapy for Tourette Syndrome: a systematic review and meta-analysis. Curr Treat Options Neurol 2013;15:385–95.

86. Wilhelm S, Peterson AL, Piacentini J, et al. Randomized trial of behavior therapy for adults with Tourette syndrome. Arch Gen Psychiatry 2012;69:795–803.

87. O'Connor KP, Laverdure A, Taillon A, et al. Cognitive behavioral management of Tourette's syndrome and chronic tic disorder in medicated and unmedicated samples. Behav Res Ther 2009;47:1090–5.

88. Verdellen CW, Keijsers GP, Cath DC, et al. Exposure with response prevention versus habit reversal in Tourettes's syndrome: a controlled study. Behav Res Ther 2004;42:501–11.

89. Bergin A, Waranch HR, Brown J, et al. Relaxation therapy in Tourette syndrome: a pilot study. Pediatr Neurol 1998;18:136–42.

90. Mantovani A, Lisanby SH, Pieraccini F, et al. Repetitive transcranial magnetic stimulation (rTMS) in the treatment of obsessive-compulsive disorder (OCD) and Tourette's syndrome (TS). Int J Neuropsychopharmacol 2006;9:95–100.

91. Orth M, Kirby R, Richardson MP, et al. Subthreshold rTMS over pre-motor cortex has no effect on tics in patients with Gilles de la Tourette syndrome. Clin Neurophysiol 2005;116:764–8.

92. Alessi NE, Walden M, Hsieh PS. Nifedipine-haloperidol combination in the treatment of Gilles de la Tourette's syndrome: a case study. J Clin Psychiatry 1989; 50:103–4.

93. Colquhoun M, Stern J, Collicott N, et al. Severe refractory tourette syndrome. J Neurol Neurosurg Psychiatry 2014;85:e3.

94. Flaherty AW, Williams ZM, Amirnovin R, et al. Deep brain stimulation of the anterior internal capsule for the treatment of Tourette syndrome: technical case report. Neurosurgery 2005;57:E403.

95. Ackermans L, Duits A, van der Linden C, et al. Double-blind clinical trial of thalamic stimulation in patients with Tourette syndrome. Brain 2011;134: 832–44.

96. Cannon E, Silburn P, Coyne T, et al. Deep brain stimulation of anteromedial globus pallidus interna for severe Tourette's syndrome. Am J Psychiatry 2012; 169:860–6.

97. Cheung MY, Shahed J, Jankovic J. Malignant Tourette syndrome. Mov Disord 2007;22:1743–50.

98. Robertson MM. Attention deficit hyperactivity disorder, tics and Tourette's syndrome: the relationship and treatment implications. A commentary. Eur Child Adolesc Psychiatry 2006;15:1–11.

99. Robertson MM. Gilles de la Tourette syndrome: the complexities of phenotype and treatment. Br J Hosp Med (Lond) 2011;72:100–7.
100. Hassan N, Cavanna AE. The prognosis of Tourette syndrome: implications for clinical practice. Funct Neurol 2012;27:23–7.
101. Bloch MH, Peterson BS, Scahill L, et al. Adulthood outcome of tic and obsessive-compulsive symptom severity in children with Tourette syndrome. Arch Pediatr Adolesc Med 2006;160:65–9.
102. Kano Y, Ohta M, Nagai Y, et al. A family study of Tourette syndrome in Japan. Am J Med Genet 2001;105:414–21.
103. Pauls DL, Raymond CL, Stevenson JM, et al. A family study of Gilles de la Tourette syndrome. Am J Hum Genet 1991;48:154–63.
104. Walkup JT, LaBuda MC, Singer HS, et al. Family study and segregation analysis of Tourette syndrome: evidence for a mixed model of inheritance. Am J Hum Genet 1996;59:684–93.
105. McMahon WM, Carter AS, Fredine N, et al. Children at familial risk for Tourette's disorder: Child and parent diagnoses. Am J Med Genet B Neuropsychiatr Genet 2003;121B:105–11.

Genetics of Pediatric Epilepsy

Abeer J. Hani, MD[a], Husam M. Mikati, RA[b], Mohamad A. Mikati, MD[a],*

KEYWORDS

- Genetics • Epilepsy • Children • Epilepsy syndromes

KEY POINTS

- Epilepsy can be secondary to single gene, or much more commonly, to multifactorial and remote symptomatic etiologies, such as stroke or hypoxia.
- Causative single gene mutations have been identified that result in multiple genetic, often overlapping, epilepsy syndromes each with distinctive clinical phenotypes.
- Causative mutations causing epilepsy have either been in ion channel genes, neurotransmitter receptor genes, structural genes, or signal transduction pathway genes.
- Discovery of the causative mutations is allowing for investigation of more targeted and precision individualized therapies of patients with epilepsy owing to such mutations.

INTRODUCTION AND GENERAL PRINCIPLES

The role of genetics in epilepsy has been contemplated since the time of Hippocrates. Subsequently, twin studies, family studies, linkage studies, and more recently copy number variation and whole exome sequencing studies on larger populations have provided modern added evidence for the role of genetics in epilepsy.[1] Whereas the role of genetic factors in idiopathic epilepsies has long been suspected, the role of these factors in cryptogenic and symptomatic epilepsies has been demonstrated in a number of other studies.[2,3] It is now thought that genetic factors account for about 40% of the etiologic causes of epilepsy.[4] Mendelian epilepsies, which can be demonstrated to have such inheritance, however, account only for 1% of epilepsies. Epidemiologic studies have estimated the risk of epilepsy for offsprings and siblings of patients with epilepsy of any cause to be about 2% to 5%.[3,5] Twin studies continue to show higher concordance in monozygotic compared with than dizygotic pairs

Disclosures: None.
[a] Division of Pediatric Neurology, Department of Pediatrics, Duke Children's Hospital and Health Center, Suite T0913J, 2301 Erwin Road, Durham, NC 27710, USA; [b] Center of Human Genome Variation, LSRC, Duke University School of Medicine, 201 Trent Drive, Durham, NC 27710, USA
* Corresponding author.
E-mail address: mohamad.mikati@duke.edu

0031-3955/15/$ – see front matter © 2015 Elsevier Inc. All rights reserved.

(case-wise concordance of 0.62 vs 0.18, respectively).[6] With the recent advance in modalities of genetic testing, multiple gene mutations have been discovered to be the cause of a wide spectrum of genetic epilepsies.[7] The term 'genetic epilepsies' has expanded to include conditions caused by a genetic defect where seizures are the core manifestation.[8] It has been hard to parcel out the role of environmental factors in such epilepsies, but it is thought that the genetic defect is the major determinant of the phenotype in such entities.[9] While sorting out the interplay of environmental and genetic factors, the following 2 types of epilepsies have been recognized. The Mendelian epilepsies, which are often "monogenic, simple, and rare" epilepsies account for about 1% of all epilepsy cases.[10] These epilepsies include monogenic syndromes where single gene mutations produce the specific phenotype,[7] including, for example, benign familial neonatal epilepsy syndrome. Monogenic epilepsies, however, may show variable penetrance and variable degrees of severity of the epilepsy and some could be owing to de novo mutations like the majority of cases of Dravet syndrome.[11] On the other hand, the majority of epilepsy patients have what is referred to as "complex epilepsy," which are common and multigenic. It is believed that genetic and environmental factors interact to various degrees to play a role in the susceptibility to epilepsy.[2,7] The genetic alterations in these complex epilepsies are being identified using collaborative, multicenter, and multinational projects like the Epilepsy Genome Phenome Program, EPICURE Consortium, EuroEPINOMICS consortium, EMINet Consortium, and the Epi4K consortium.[12,13] These and similar projects have permitted the identification of specific and recurrent copy number variants (which are deletions or duplications of the genetic information in excess of a kilobase) that occur at genomic hot spots and that increase likelihood of certain epilepsies.[7] These copy number variants tend to occur in genes that are intolerant to mutations, which are also phylogenetically preserved. Continued research shows also that a monogenic etiology could not be established for most of the generalized idiopathic epilepsies, including childhood absence epilepsies and most cases of juvenile myoclonic epilepsies, so susceptibility genes are being investigated.[14] Ongoing studies are also starting to concentrate on whole genome sequencing, because this may identify possible contribution of intronic mutations to the occurrence of epilepsy. All this constitutes a rapidly growing body of knowledge that is compiled in the Online Mendelian Inheritance in Man database (OMIM).[15] To start to address some of these questions, experimental research on animal models of epilepsy has been able to identify the additive effects of genetic mutations to environmental insults and the complex interaction between different genes resulting in different epilepsy phenotypes. The combination of 2 mild alleles of monogenic epilepsy genes in mutant mice, namely in sodium and potassium channel genes, can lead to a much more severe phenotype,[16] whereas in other situations combining 2 genetic mutations that predispose to epilepsy does not necessarily enhance epileptogenicity, but actually ameliorates it.[17] Additionally, it has been demonstrated that mouse strain can influence seizure threshold.[18,19] Finally, we have recently shown that the presence of an epilepsy predisposing gene mutation (in the potassium channel KCN1a) and of mild hypoxia can result in spontaneous seizures and in predisposition to other consequences when either one of these insults alone was not sufficient to result in either.[20]

The clinical utility of genetic testing in pediatric epilepsy is an important issue. The yield from genetic testing of the usual cases is so low that it is not justifiable to do such testing unless there is family history to suggest it, or if there is drug resistance or developmental delay and an abnormal neurologic examination not explained by other findings. In such situations, genetic testing is justifiable because the yield is relatively high (as high as 34.5%) and there is more of a chance of uncovering potentially treatable genetic conditions, such as vitamin-responsive genetic epilepsies.[21–27] Genetic testing in patients with intractable epilepsy and developmental delay usually involves, in addition to metabolic testing for inborn errors of metabolism and vitamin dependent conditions, 1 or more of the following: karyotype, chromosomal micro-array, specific gene or gene panel sequencing, or whole exome sequencing. This testing often leads to closure of the search for an underlying etiology and helps physicians to better prognosticate and families to better accept and deal with the problem. However, such genetic testing also often raises many other questions, such as dealing with the uncertainty of variants of unknown significance, which is seen in at least one-third of patients tested with gene panels or whole exome sequencing, not to mention the often very high cost of the testing and the need to decide how to deal with possible incidental unrelated findings.[27] In some situations, finding the underlying etiology may help in the choice of therapy, such as in the case of Dravet syndrome, the avoidance of use of valproate in patients with polymerase G mutations to avoid risk of hepatotoxicity, and the diagnosis of glucose transporter deficiency in rare patients with normal cerebrospinal fluid glucose levels, leading to initiation of the ketogenic diet.[27] Such testing can also help to detect and confirm the diagnosis of vitamin-responsive (B_6, folinic acid, biotin) epilepsies suspected clinically or on metabolic testing. Such testing may also, at times, lead to the investigation of novel therapies (**Fig. 1**; see **Fig. 3**).[16]

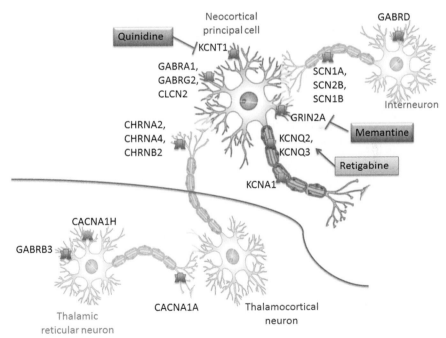

Fig. 1. Epileptic channelopathies. The tentative roles of some ion channels that play a role in genetic epilepsy are indicated schematically, with gain-of-function mutations shown in red and loss-of-function mutations in blue. The various genes are detailed in the associated tables and text. Memantine and quinidine are being investigated as potential therapies for GRIN2A and KCNT1-related epilepsies respectively that may ameliorate the gain of function in the respective channels as discussed in the text. Retigabine, which opens potassium channels, is being investigated as a potential therapy for loss-of-function mutations related KCNQ2 and KCNQ3 epilepsies.

Although faced with a widening spectrum of genetic epilepsies, these epilepsies could be stratified into 2 groups: syndromic (defined here as per Rees in 2010 as the presence of epilepsy as a comorbidity part of an independent disorder such as brain malformation or well-defined dysmorphic syndromes such as Down syndrome or tuberous sclerosis).[28] This should not be confused with the different epilepsy syndromes that constitute different phenotypes of the idiopathic or "nonsyndromic" epilepsies. Thus, nonsyndromic epilepsies are defined herein as the presence of epilepsy as the core manifestations of the disorder.[28] This article presents the range of nonsyndromic genetic epilepsies only with only a brief mention of the syndromic epilepsies, because describing syndromic epilepsies in detail is beyond the goals of this review. As will be illustrated, causative gene mutations can either be in ion channel genes like sodium or potassium channel genes, in neurotransmitter receptor genes like GABA, acetylcholine, or N-methyl-D-aspartate (NMDA) receptors, in structural genes or in signal transduction pathway genes (see **Fig. 1**).[29] These discoveries are now allowing for investigation of more targeted and precision individualized therapies of patients with epilepsy owing to such mutations such as the targeting the use of quinidine for certain potassium channel mutation and of memantine for NMDA receptor mutations.

NONSYNDROMIC GENETIC EPILEPSIES

The spectrum of nonsyndromic genetic epilepsies continues to expand and may be stratified based on age of onset of the seizures in the neonatal, infantile, childhood, adolescence, or adulthood period.[8]

Epilepsies of Neonatal Onset

Benign familial neonatal seizures
Benign familial neonatal seizures (BFNS) is an autosomal-dominant focal idiopathic epilepsy syndrome. Multifocal clonic or focal seizures typically start on the second day of life but could be delayed up to 1 to 3 months of life. Seizures often spontaneously remit within weeks to months and patients tend to have normal psychomotor development.[30] Mutations in KCNQ2 and KCNQ3 have been identified as causes of BFNS (**Table 1**) with the recent discovery that certain mutations of KCQ2 may be associated with severe epileptic encephalopathy.[31] In these severe cases, the use of retigabine, a neuronal potassium channel enhancer, is being investigated as a potential for therapy in these patients.[32,33]

Benign familial neonatal–infantile seizures
Benign familial neonatal–infantile seizures (BFNIS) presents as afebrile, secondary, generalized, partial seizures between day 2 and 7 months of age and tend to remit by 1 year of age. BFNIS has autosomal-dominant inheritance and is often caused by missense mutation of KCNQ2 (see **Table 1**).[34]

Neonatal epileptic encephalopathies
The neonatal epileptic encephalopathies include the early infantile epileptic encephalopathy (EIEE)/Ohtahara syndrome and the early infantile myoclonic epilepsy (EIME). Both are severe neonatal and early infantile epilepsy syndromes characterized by frequent tonic seizures and spasms (Ohtahara) or myoclonic seizures (EIME) with electroencephalographic findings of burst suppression in both.[35] They constitute a genetically heterogeneous disease group with multiple gene mutations identified and many disease subclasses (see **Table 1**).

Table 1
Genetics of nonsyndromic epilepsies of neonatal onset

Epilepsy Syndrome	Epilepsy Syndrome Subgroup	Inheritance	Locus	Gene	Gene Product	Gene Function
BFNS	BFNS	AD	20q13.33	KCNQ2	Subunit voltage-gated K channel	Subunit voltage-gated K channel activity
		AD	8q24.22	KCNQ3	Subunit voltage-gated K channel	Subunit voltage-gated K channel activity
BFNIS	BFNIS	AD	2q24.3	SCN2A	Alpha subunit voltage-gated Na channel	Alpha subunit voltage-gated Na channel activity
EIEE	EIEE1	X-linked recessive	Xp21.3	ARX	Aristaless-related homeobox	Homeobox transcription factor
	EIEE2	X-linked dominant	Xp22.13	CDKL5	Cyclin-dependent kinase-like 5	Regulation of other gene function (MECP2)
	EIEE3	AR	11p15.5	SLC25A22	Solute carrier family 25, member 22	Mitochondrial carrier of L-glutamate
	EIEE4	AD	9q34.11	STXBP1	Syntaxin-binding protein 1	Synaptic vesicles docking and fusion
	EIEE5	AD	9q34.11	SPTAN1	Spectrin, alpha, nonerythrocytic 1	Regulation of receptor binding and actin cross-linking
	EIEE6/Dravet syndrome	AD	2q24.3	SCN1A SCN9A	Alpha subunit voltage-gated Na channel	Subunit voltage-gated Na channel activity
		AD	5q34	GABRG2	GABA-A receptor, gamma-2 polypeptide	GABA-A receptor activity
	EIEE7	AD	20q13.33	KCNQ2	Subunit voltage-gated K channel	Subunit voltage-gated K channel activity

(continued on next page)

Table 1
(continued)

Epilepsy Syndrome	Epilepsy Syndrome Subgroup	Inheritance	Locus	Gene	Gene Product	Gene Function
	EIEE8	X-linked recessive	Xq11.1-q11.2	ARHGEF9	Rho guanine nucleotide exchange factor 9	Formation of postsynaptic glycine and GABA receptor clusters
	EIEE9	X-linked	Xq22.1	PCDH19	Protocadherin 19	Cell signaling and adhesion
	EIEE10	AR	19q13.33	PNKP	Polynucleotide kinase 3-prime phosphatase	DNA repair
	EIEE11	AD	2q24.3	SCN2A	Alpha subunit voltage-gated Na channel	Subunit voltage-gated Na channel activity
	EIEE12	AR	20p12.3	PLCB1	Phospholipase C, beta-1	Signal transduction
	EIEE13	AD	12q13.13	SCN8A	Alpha subunit voltage-gated Na channel	Subunit voltage-gated Na channel activity
	EIEE14	AD	9q34.3	KCNT1 (gain of function)	Subunit voltage-gated K channel	Subunit voltage-gated K channel activity
	EIEE15	AR	1p34.1	ST3GAL3	ST3 beta-galactoside alpha-2,3-sialyltransferase 3	Glycosylation of proteins
	EIEE16	AR	16p13.3	TBC1D24	Tre2-Bub2-Cdc16- domain family, member 24	Intracellular vesicular transport
	EIEE17	AD	16q12.2	GNAO1	Guanine nucleotide-binding protein, alpha-activating polypeptide O gene	Signal transduction
	EIEE18	AR	1p34.2	SZT2	Mouse seizure threshold 2 gene	Induction of superoxide dismutase

Name	Inheritance	Locus	Gene	Protein	Function
EIEE19	—	5q34	GABRA1	GABA receptor, alpha-1	GABA-A receptor function
EIEE20	X-linked recessive	Xp22.2	PIGA	Phosphatidylinositol glycan, class A	Anchoring proteins to cell surface
EIEE 21	AR	12p13.31	NECAP1	NECAP Endocytosis-associated protein 1	Clathrin-mediated endocystosis in synapses
EIEE22 congenital disorder of glycosylation, type IIm	X-linked dominant	Xp11.23	SLC35A2	Solute carrier family 35, member 2	UDP-galactose transporter
EIEE23	AR	1p31.3	DOCK7	Dedicator of cytokinesis 7	Guanine-nucleotide exchange factor, role in neurogenesis
EIEE24	AD	5p12	HCN1	Hyperpolarization-activated cyclic nucleotide-gated potassium channel 1	Function of this subset of K channels
EIEE25	AR	17p13.1	SLC13A5	Solute carrier family 13, member 5	Sodium-dependent citrate transporter
SRGAP2-associated EIEE	—	1q32.1	SRGAP2	Slit-Robo Rho GTP-ase activation protein 2	Neuronal migration and differentiation
MEF2C-associated EIEE	—	5q14.3	MEF2C	MADs Box transcription enhancer factor 2, polypeptide C	Neuronal migration

Abbreviations: AD, autosomal dominant; AR, autosomal recessive; BFNIS, benign familial neonatal infantile seizures; BFNS, benign familial neonatal seizures; EIEE, early infantile epileptic encephalopathy; GABA, Gamma-aminobutyric acid; UDP, uridine-5-prime-diphosphate.
Adapted from OMIM database. Available at: http://www.ncbi.nlm.nih.gov/omim/. Accessed September 1, 2014.

Epilepsies of Infantile Onset

Benign familial infantile seizures

Benign familial infantile seizures is an autosomal-dominant epilepsy with onset between 4 and 8 months of age. Seizures are partial and may cluster with good response to treatment and good prognosis for remission.[36] There have been multiple mutations associated with this syndrome (**Table 2**).

Dravet syndrome

Dravet syndrome is also known as severe myoclonic epilepsy of infancy. It was described first by Charlotte Dravet in 1978 as an epileptic encephalopathy that starts at the age of 6 months, typically with prolonged generalized febrile seizures with evolution into other seizure types (myoclonic, complex partial seizures, atypical absence) later in the course of the disease.[37] The syndrome is also associated with cognitive and behavioral deterioration that tend to correlate with the frequency of convulsive seizures.[38] In 2001, the association of this disease with SCN1A gene mutations was described.[39] Since then, more than 600 mutations have been described and a website exists to track the newly discovered mutations (http://www.scn1a.info). This SCN1A gene (**Fig. 2**) encodes for the alpha subunit of voltage-gated sodium channels that are concentrated in the brain and are important in regulating the excitability of neurons and neuronal networks.[40] The mutations are present in 85% of patients with Dravet syndrome and are commonly de novo truncations, but missense mutations may also occur.[41] Other SCN1A gene mutations have also been implicated in other benign epilepsies and other epileptic syndromes, the most notable of which is generalized epilepsy with febrile seizures plus.[42] It has been found that SCN1A mutations with more severe loss of function cause more severe epilepsy syndromes.[43] Treatment of Dravet syndrome continues to be challenging, with some benefit seen with the use of stiripentol, topiramate, valproate, clobazam, clonazepam, and levetiracetam, as well as a ketogenic diet.[44,45] Certain anticonvulsants including lamotrigine and carbamazepine may exacerbate seizures in these patients. Recently, the use of cannabidiol in refractory Dravet syndrome patients has been suggested; however, confirmatory clinical trials are lacking at this stage.[46]

West syndrome

West syndrome is another severe epileptic encephalopathy syndrome of infantile onset. It is characterized by a triad of infantile spasms, developmental delay or regression, and a characteristic electroencephalographic pattern called hypsarrhythmia.[47] Many of the early infantile epileptic encephalopathy syndromes detailed in **Table 1** may progress into a West syndrome phenotype. The most notable of these are EIEE caused by mutations in ARX and CDKL5 genes, del 1p36 and inv dup (15).[48,49] Treatment of West syndrome is rather challenging and includes adrenocorticotrophic hormone and vigabatrin as primary drugs, and often also the ketogenic diet, topiramate, felbamate, zomisamide, and valproate.[47]

Generalized epilepsy with febrile seizures plus

Patients typically present first with febrile seizure and often continue to have seizures with or without fever beyond 6 years of age. The other seizure types include myoclonic, absence, and partial seizures.[50] They usually remit by 11 years of age. Development is usually unaffected and the inheritance is typically autosomal dominant. Multiple mutations in the sodium channel genes have been identified and are detailed in **Table 2**.

Table 2
Genetics of nonsyndromic epilepsies of infantile onset

Epilepsy Syndrome	Epilepsy Syndrome	Inheritance	Locus	Gene	Gene Name/Product	Gene Function
BFIS	BFIS1	AD	19q	BFIS1	Benign familial infantile seizure 1	—
	BFIS2	AD	16p11.2	PRRT2	Proline-rich transmembrane protein 2	Transport of synaptic vesicles
	BFIS3	AD	2q24.3	SCN2A	Sodium channel, voltage-gated type II, alpha subunit	Sodium channel activity
	BFIS4	AD?	1p36.12-p35.1	—	—	—
Dravet Syndrome (EIEE6), SMEI	Dravet syndrome	AD	2q24.3	SCN1A	Alpha subunits of voltage-gated Na channel	Subunit voltage-gated Na channel activity
				SCN9A		Na channel activity
		AD	5q34	GABRG2	GABA-A receptor, Gamma-2 polypeptide	GABA-A receptor activity
West syndrome	Please refer to EIEE section in **Table 1**					
Generalized epilepsy with febrile seizures plus	GEFSP type 1 (GEFSP1)	AD	19q13.2	SCN1B	Beta subunits of voltage-gated Na channel	Subunit voltage-gated Na channel activity
	GEFSP2,	AD	2q24.3	SCN1A	Alpha subunits of voltage-gated Na channel	Subunit voltage-gated Na channel activity
	GEFSP3	AD	5q34	GABRG2	GABA-A receptor, gamma-2 polypeptide	GABA-A receptor activity
	GEFSP4	AD	2p24	—	—	—
	GEFSP5	AD	1p36.3	GABRD	GABA receptor, delta subunit	GABA-A receptor activity
	GEFSP6	AD	8p23-p21	—	—	—
	GEFSP7	AD	2q24.3	SCN9A	Alpha subunits of voltage-gated Na channel	Subunit voltage-gated Na channel activity
	GEFSP8	AD	6q16.3-q22.31	—	—	—
EIMFS	Please refer to EIEE6, EIEE16, and EIEE14 in **Table 1** for possible causative genes.					
	EIMFS	AR	11p15.5	SLC25A22	Solute carrier family 25, member 22	Mitochondrial carrier of L-glutamate
	EIMFS	AR	20p12.3	PLCB1	Phospholipase C, beta-1	Signal transduction
Familial infantile myoclonic epilepsy	FIME	AR	16p13.3	TBC1D24	Tre2-Bub2-Cdc16- domain family, member 24	Intracellular vesicular transport

Abbreviations: BFIS, Benign familial infantile seizures; EIEE, early infantile epileptic encephalopathy; EIMFS, Epilepsy of infancy with migrating focal seizures; SMEI, severe myoclonic epilepsy of infancy.
Adapted from OMIM database. Available at: http://www.ncbi.nlm.nih.gov/omim/. Accessed September 1, 2014.

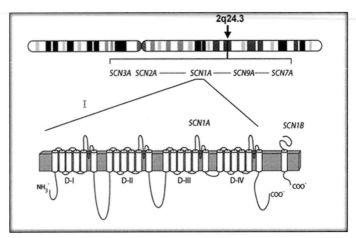

Fig. 2. SCN1A channel is shown in the bottom row, where the 4 protein domains (D-I to D-IV) form a central pore to allow the sodium passage. The SCN1A location in the genome is shown in the upper panel at 2q24.3. Mutations and deletions of the SCN1A gene is present throughout the gene. (*From* Williams CA, Battaglia A. Molecular biology of epilepsy genes. Exp Neurol 2013;244:54; with permission.)

Epilepsy of infancy with migrating focal seizures

Epilepsy of infancy with migrating focal seizures is also known as malignant migrating partial epilepsies in infancy. This rare syndrome is characterized by onset in the first 6 months of life of several refractory seizure types independently migrating from 1 cortical area to another. The seizure frequency and severity typically improves with age, although patients usually end with often severe degrees of developmental delay.[51] This syndrome is associated with multiple mutations (see **Table 2**), of which KCNT1 mutations are the most common.[52] KCNT1 encodes for a sodium-activated potassium channel and is highly expressed in neurons and cardiomyocytes. KCNT1 mutations are typically gain-of-function mutations causing activation of the channel and subsequent pathologic potassium conductance. Selective targeting of this KCNT1 channel using antiarrhythmic drugs like quinidine is now being investigated as potential therapy for such patients.[53,54] Other, more rare gene mutations include SLC25A22 homozygous mutations causing impaired mitochondrial glutamate transport and those of phospholipase C beta-1 (PLCB1) genes causing impaired intracellular second messenger systems.[55,56]

Benign myoclonic epilepsy of infancy

Benign myoclonic epilepsy of infancy is regarded as a benign epilepsy syndrome that starts in infancy in the form of myoclonic seizures. Patients may have reflex myoclonus and one-fifth may have photosensitivity. The etiology of this syndrome has not been determined yet, but 50% of patients have a family history of epilepsy or febrile seizures.[50]

Familial infantile myoclonic epilepsy

Familial infantile myoclonic epilepsy is another idiopathic familial epilepsy syndrome that starts in early infancy in the form of myoclonic seizures, febrile seizures, and tonic–clonic seizures. Patients have normal psychomotor development.[57] Familial infantile myoclonic epilepsy is thought to be caused by a homozygous loss-of-function mutation in the TBC1D24 gene that regulates neurotransmitter release at the synaptic level (see **Table 2**).

Epilepsies of Childhood Onset

Early- and late-onset childhood occipital epilepsy
The early-onset childhood occipital epilepsy, also known as Panayiotopoulos syndrome, is a benign epilepsy syndrome with the hallmark of autonomic seizures including vomiting that often may not require treatment. On the other hand, late-onset childhood occipital epilepsy described first by Gastaut is characterized by visual seizures that often warrant anticonvulsants. Both syndromes are associated with normal intellectual abilities. The etiology of both syndromes is thought to be partly genetic given the increased incidence of epilepsy in first-degree members of patients with epilepsy.[58]

Benign epilepsy with centrotemporal spikes
Benign epilepsy with centrotemporal spikes (BECTS) is the most common benign focal epilepsy of childhood. Seizures are typically unilateral sensorimotor involving face with speech arrest and hypersalivation and present between 7 and 10 years of age. The genetics of this syndrome remains to be well-characterized. Genome wide analysis showed linkage to a region on chromosome 11p13.[59] Some cases have also been linked to GRIN2A mutations also (see section on Landau–Kleffner Syndrome) and to DEPDC5 mutations (see section on Familial Focal Epilepsy with Variable Foci).

Childhood absence epilepsy
Childhood absence epilepsy is a common, usually benign epilepsy syndrome of childhood with seizures marked by brief alteration of consciousness for an average of 10 seconds followed by rapid return to baseline mental status within 2 to 3 seconds. The genetics of this epilepsy is thought to be polygenic with multiple susceptibility genes identified (**Table 3**). Mutations in various genes encoding the various subunits of the GABA-A receptor and mutations in the voltage-gated calcium channel subunits have been described as contributing to the features of this epilepsy syndrome.[60,61]

Landau–Kleffner syndrome
Landau–Kleffner syndrome (LKS) belongs to the group of focal epilepsies with speech disorder with or without mental retardation and is marked by epileptic aphasia. Both this group of focal epilepsies, including some cases of BECTS, and LKS may be caused by mutations of GRIN2A gene that cause an increase in open time and decrease in the closed time of NMDA channels. This has raised the possibility of investigating the use memantine, which blocks this channel in such patients.[62]

Epilepsy with myoclonic atonic (astatic) seizures
Also known as Doose syndrome, the hallmark of epilepsy with myoclonic atonic (astatic) seizures is onset in early childhood of atonic or astatic seizures that may be preceded by myoclonic jerking. The etiology of this syndrome is thought to be a multifactorial polygenic trait with no specific genes identified, but with correlations suggested to generalized epilepsy with febrile seizure plus syndrome where SCN1A, SCN1B, and GABRG2 mutations may play a causative role.[63]

Lennox–Gastaut syndrome
Lennox–Gastaut syndrome is a severe epileptic encephalopathy that starts between 2 and 10 years of age. About two-thirds of the children with this syndrome have a history of infantile spasms.[64] This syndrome is usually owing to the various etiologies that cause West syndrome and EIEE in infancy.

Table 3
Genetics of nonsyndromic epilepsies of childhood onset

Epilepsy Syndrome	Epilepsy Syndrome	Inheritance	Locus	Gene	Gene Product	Gene Function
Early-onset childhood occipital epilepsy	Panayiatopoulos syndrome[a]					
LOCOE	LOCOE- described by Gastaut[a]					
Benign epilepsy with centrotemporal spikes	BECTS = Rolandic epilepsy	AD	11p13			
CAE	CAE susceptibility gene 1	AD	8q24			
	CAE susceptibility gene 2	AD	5134	GABRG2	GABA-A receptor, gamma-2 polypeptide	GABA-A receptor activity
	CAE susceptibility gene 5	AD	15q12	GABRB3	GABA-A receptor, beta-3 polypeptide	GABA-A receptor activity
	CAE susceptibility gene 6	AD	16p13.3	CACNA1H	Alpha-1-subunit of voltage-gated calcium channel	Voltage-gated Ca channel function
	CAE susceptibility gene 4	AD	5q34	GABRA1	GABA-A receptor, alpha-1 polypeptide	GABA-A receptor activity
LKS: subset of focal epilepsy with speech disorder	LKS	AD	16p13.2	GRIN2A	Glutamate receptor, ionotropic, NMDA, subunit 2A	Regulates NMDA receptor excitatory properties
Epilepsy with myoclonic-atonic seizures	Possible association with GEFSP 1, 2 and 3 (see **Table 2**).					
Lennox–Gastaut syndrome	Please refer to EIEE genes in **Table 1**.					
Epileptic encephalopathy with continuous spike-wave during sleep	Please refer to LKS gene GRIN2A detailed above in this table.					

Abbreviations: BECTS, benign epilepsy with centrotemporal spikes; CAE, childhood absence epilepsy; LKS, Landau-Kleffner syndrome; LOCOE, late-onset childhood occipital epilepsy; NMDA, N-methyl-D-aspartate.
[a] These syndromes are presumed to have a genetic etiology, but no definite mutations have been identified.
Adapted from OMIM database. Available at: http://www.ncbi.nlm.nih.gov/omim/. Accessed September 1, 2014.

Epileptic encephalopathy with continuous spike-and-wave during sleep
Epileptic encephalopathy with continuous spike-and-wave during sleep is characterized by clinical seizures and neurocognitive regression with characteristic electroencephalographic pattern of continuous spike wave during non-REM sleep. Heterozygous mutations in the GRIN2A gene that regulate the excitatory currents of NMDA receptors were found to be a major genetic determinant of this syndrome.[62]

Epilepsies of Adolescent Onset

Juvenile absence epilepsy
Juvenile absence epilepsy is characterized by onset of absence seizures at an average age of 12 years with 80% of adolescents also having generalized tonic–clonic (GTC) seizures.[50] The study of the genetics of this syndrome has revealed several susceptibility genes (**Table 4**).

Juvenile myoclonic epilepsy
Juvenile myoclonic epilepsy is determined genetically. Clinically, patients present with morning myoclonic jerks, GTC seizures, and at times absence seizures. Susceptibility to this syndrome is caused by mutations of the GABRA1, CACNB4, GABRD, EFHC1, and CLCN2 genes (see **Table 4**).

Autosomal-dominant nocturnal frontal lobe epilepsy
Autosomal-dominant nocturnal frontal lobe epilepsy (ADNFLE) starts in late childhood or adolescence and is characterized by nocturnal frontal lobe seizures as the name implies. It is caused mostly by mutations involving the alpha and beta (α4, α2, and β2 subunits) of the nicotinic acetylcholine receptors. These mutations seem to modify the kinetics of the receptor and paradoxically increase excitability through increasing nicotine-induced GABAergic inhibition.[65] Heterozygous gain-of-function mutations in the KCNT1 gene have also been found to cause severe ADNFLE.[66]

Autosomal-dominant partial epilepsy with auditory features
Autosomal-dominant partial epilepsy with auditory features (ADPEAF) is also known as autosomal dominant, familial lateral temporal lobe epilepsy (FLTLE). ADPEAF starts between second and fourth decades with presence of focal seizures and predominant auditory auras. Truncations, deletions and single amino acid substitutions of the LGI1 (leucine-rich glioma inactivated 1 protein) have been found to be the causative agents in more than one-half of patients with ADPEAF.[67] Although LGI1 is not part of an ion channel, it is thought that the mutant protein loses its ability to regulate AMPA-receptor mediated synaptic transmission.[67]

Epilepsies of Variable Age of Onset

Familial focal epilepsy with variable foci
Familial focal epilepsy with variable foci (FFEVF) is an autosomal-dominant epilepsy type that starts in the first or second decade. The hallmark of this condition is the presence of usually daytime focal seizures that arise from different foci in different family members. The prognosis is usually favorable. Recently, it was discovered that heterozygous mutations in DEPDC5 (DEP domain-containing protein 5 involved in G-protein signaling pathways) gene on chromosome 22q12 may cause this syndrome.[68] DEPDC5 has also been reported in a broad spectrum of inherited focal epilepsies including (BECTS, ADNFLE, and FLTLE, FFEVF) as well as brain malformations ranging from relatively subtle bottom of sulcus focal cortical dysplasia to subcortical gray matter heterotopia (**Fig. 3**).[69]

Table 4
Genetics of nonsyndromic epilepsies of adolescent onset

Epilepsy Syndrome	Epilepsy Syndrome	Inheritance	Locus	Gene	Gene Product	Gene Function
JAE	JAE susceptibility gene 1	AD	6p12.2	EFHC1	EF-hand domain containing protein 1	Enhances calcium influx
	JAE susceptibility gene 2	AD	3q27.1	CLCN2	Chloride-channel 2	Regulates activity of the chloride channel
JME	JME susceptibility gene 1	AD	6p12.2	EFHC1	EF-hand domain containing protein 1	Enhances calcium influx
	JME susceptibility gene 3	AR	6p21			
	JME susceptibility gene 4	AD	5q12-q14			
	JME susceptibility gene 5	AD	5q34	GABRA1	GABA-A receptor, alpha-1 polypeptide	GABA-A receptor activity
	JME susceptibility gene 6	AD	2q23.3	CACNB4	Voltage-gated Ca channel, beta-4 subunit	Voltage-gated Ca channel activity
	JME susceptibility gene 7	AD	1p36.33	GABRD	GABA receptor, delta subunit	GABA-A receptor activity
	JME susceptibility gene 8	AD	3q27.1	CLCN2	Chloride-channel 2	Regulates activity of the chloride channel
	JME susceptibility gene 9	AD	2q33-q36			
ADNFLE	ADNFLE 1	AD	20q13.33	CHRNA4	Alpha-4 subunit of nAch receptor	Regulates nAch receptor GABAergic inhibition
	ADNFLE 2	AD	15q24			
	ADNFLE 3	AD	1q21.3	CHRNB2	Beta-2 nAch receptor	Regulates nAch receptor GABAergic inhibition
	ADNFLE 4	AD	8p21.2	CHRNA2	Alpha-2 subunit of nAch receptor	Regulates nAch receptor GABAergic inhibition
	ADNFLE 5	AD	9q34.3	KCNT1	subunit voltage-gated K channel	Subunit voltage-gated K channel activity
Autosomal-dominant partial epilepsy with auditory features	Also known as AD lateral temporal lobe epilepsy	AD	10q23.33	LGI1	Leucine-rich, glioma-inactivated protein	Regulates glutamatergic synapse development

Abbreviations: Ach, acetylcholine; AD, autosomal dominant; ADNFLE, autosomal-dominant nocturnal frontal lobe epilepsy; Ca, calcium; GABA, gamma-aminobutyric acid; JAE, juvenile absence epilepsy; JME, Juvenile myoclonic epilepsy; Na, sodium; nAch, nicotinic acetylcholine.
Adapted from OMIM database. Available at: http://www.ncbi.nlm.nih.gov/omim/. Accessed September 1, 2014.

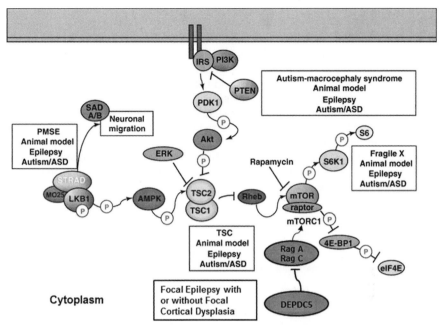

Fig. 3. Mammalian target of rapamycin (mTOR) pathway, which is involved in a number of syndromic (eg, tuberous sclerosis [TSC]) and nonsyndromic (focal epilepsy of various types) epilepsies and is now target for investigation for novel therapies that could modify the dysregulation in this pathway (such as the use of inhibitors of the pathway like everolimus to treat not only TSC-related tumors but possibly also the epilepsy associated with that). (*Adapted from* Crino PB. mTOR: a pathogenic signaling pathway in developmental brain malformations. Trends Mol Med 2011;17(12):740; with permission.)

Progressive myoclonic epilepsies

Progressive myoclonic epilepsies (PME) include a group of mostly autosomal-recessive disorders characterized by epileptic and nonepileptic myoclonus, generalized tonic–clonic seizures, and progressive neurologic deterioration, with subsequent development of cerebellar signs and dementia. There are multiple types of PME, the details of which are beyond the scope of this review.[70] Unverricht–Lundborg disease is the most common PME, presents between 6 and 15 years of age, and is characterized by stimulus-sensitive or action myoclonus. It is linked to an autosomal-recessive mutation in cystatin B gene that is thought to be important in regulating apoptosis.[71] Lafora disease, which starts in adolescence, causes severe early dementia and is caused in 90% of cases by autosomal recessively inherited mutations in EPM2A (laforin that regulates protein folding) or EPM2B (NHLRC1, malin that regulates dendritic transport in neurons) genes.[72] Other causes include neuronal ceroid lipofuscinosis, which comprises several subtypes, each of which presents at a specific age, the 2 subtypes of sialidosis (early onset with coarse facial features and late onset), dentatorubral–pallidoluysian atrophy, mitochondrial disease such as myoclonic epilepsy with ragged-red fibers, PME with or without renal failure owing to mutations in the SCARB2 gene, Gaucher disease, Niemann–Pick disease type C, juvenile-onset Huntington disease, rare type of spinal muscular atrophy, central nervous system celiac disease, and recently described rare familial PME caused by mutations in the following genes: SCARB2, PRICKLE1, or GOSR2, CARS2, CERS2, and KCTD7.[73–77]

Reflex epilepsies

These include epilepsies where seizures are triggered reproducibly and instantaneously by a well-defined stimulus. The best studied variants of this condition at present include photosensitivity, language-induced orofacial reflex myoclonic, and musicogenic seizures.[78] Recently, CHD2 gene mutations have been associated with epilepsy the phenotypes of Dravet-like and Lennox-Gastaut–like epileptic encephalopathies with myoclonic photosensitive seizures.[79] Hyperekplexia or startle disease is not strictly an epileptic syndrome because it is associated with increased startle response, but epilepsy often occurs owing to hypoxic injury. It manifests both dominant and recessive inheritance of mutations in presynaptic and postsynaptic glycinergic genes (GLRA1, SLC6A5/GlyT2, and GLRB).[80] There have been a number of other suspected gene loci associated with other reflex epilepsies, but definitive confirmation of such loci remains the subject of ongoing research.

Table 5
Genetics of some syndromic epilepsies

Syndrome	Genes	Mode of Inheritance	Clinical Features
Rett syndrome	MECP2	X-linked dominant	Ataxia, postnatal microcephaly, severe neurodevelopmental problems, especially with movement and absent or deficient speech, regression and breathing abnormalities
Angelman syndrome	UBE3A	Uniparental disomy, maternal deletion	Severe cognitive disability, absent speech, periods of inappropriate laughter, postnatal microcephaly, ataxic gait, jerky movements, and epilepsy
Tuberous sclerosis	TSC1 TSC2	Autosomal dominant	Skin (ie, hypomelanotic macules, facial angiofibromas, shagreen patches, fibrous facial plaques, ungual fibromas), central nervous system (ie, cortical tubers, subependymal nodules, subependymal giant cell astrocytoma), kidney (ie, angiomyolipomas, cysts), and heart (ie, rhabdomyomas, arrhythmias).
Mowat–Wilson syndrome	ZEB2	Autosomal dominant	Microcephaly, agenesis of the corpus callosum, cognitive disability with severe speech impairment, and seizures
Pitt–Hopkins syndrome	MBD5 TCF4	Autosomal dominant	Intellectual disability with severe speech impairment, motor incoordination, postnatal microcephaly, breathing anomalies, and seizures

Data from Noh GJ, Jane Tavyev Asher Y, Graham JM Jr. Clinical review of genetic epileptic encephalopathies. Eur J Med Genet 2012;55(5):281–98.

SYNDROMIC GENETIC EPILEPSIES

Syndromic genetic epilepsies include entities where epilepsy is part of a constellation of symptoms that determine the clinical phenotype.[81] A detailed discussion of these syndromes is beyond the scope of this review. **Table 5** summarizes some common syndromic epilepsy syndromes and **Fig. 3** the pathways involved in tuberous sclerosis and related syndromes.[82]

SUMMARY

As the genetic etiology of many of the familial and inherited epilepsy syndromes is revealed, the complexity of the phenotype–genotype correlation increases. Multiple gene mutations can cause different epilepsy syndromes of variable severity and prognosis, thus identification of the specific mutation may allow for more directed treatment and better prognostication. This would also permit more targeted drug trials and design of knockout animal models that help us to better define and study the various epilepsy syndromes. The need to avoid specific seizure medications in Dravet syndrome and the potential use of retigabine in KCNQ2-related epilepsies, quinidine in KCNT1-related epilepsies, and memantine in GRIN2A-related epilepsies proves the potential for more targeted therapeutics once these genetic causes are revealed.

REFERENCES

1. Mefford HC. CNVs in epilepsy. Curr Genet Med Rep 2014;2:162–7.
2. Choueiri RN, Fayad MN, Farah A, et al. Classification of epilepsy syndromes and role of genetic factors. Pediatr Neurol 2001;24(1):37–43.
3. Peljto AL, Barker-Cummings C, Vasoli VM, et al. Familial risk of epilepsy: a population-based study. Brain 2014;137(Pt 3):795–805.
4. Guerrini R, Noebels J. How can advances in epilepsy genetics lead to better treatments and cures? Adv Exp Med Biol 2014;813:309–17.
5. Winawer MR, Shinnar S. Genetic epidemiology of epilepsy or what do we tell families? Epilepsia 2005;46(Suppl 10):24–30.
6. Berkovic SF, Howell RA, Hay DA, et al. Epilepsies in twins: genetics of the major epilepsy syndromes. Ann Neurol 1998;43(4):435–45.
7. Thomas RH, Berkovic SF. The hidden genetics of epilepsy-a clinically important new paradigm. Nat Rev Neurol 2014;10(5):283–92.
8. Berg AT, Berkovic SF, Brodie MJ, et al. Revised terminology and concepts for organization of seizures and epilepsies: report of the ILAE Commission on Classification and Terminology, 2005–2009. Epilepsia 2010;51(4):676–85.
9. Scheffer IE. Epilepsy genetics revolutionizes clinical practice. Neuropediatrics 2014;45(2):70–4.
10. Tripathi M, Jain S. Genetics in epilepsy: transcultural perspectives. Epilepsia 2003;44(Suppl 1):12–6.
11. Novarino G, Baek ST, Gleeson JG. The sacred disease: the puzzling genetics of epileptic disorders. Neuron 2013;80(1):9–11.
12. EPGP Collaborative, Abou-Khalil B, Alldredge B, et al. The epilepsy phenome/ genome project. Clin Trials 2013;10(4):568–86.
13. Epi KC. Epi4K: gene discovery in 4,000 genomes. Epilepsia 2012;53(8):1457–67.
14. Hildebrand MS, Dahl HH, Damiano JA, et al. Recent advances in the molecular genetics of epilepsy. J Med Genet 2013;50(5):271–9.
15. Online Mendelian Inheritance in Man (OMIM). Available at: http://www.ncbi.nlm.nih.gov/omim/. Accessed September 1, 2014.

16. Kearney JA, Yang Y, Beyer B, et al. Severe epilepsy resulting from genetic interaction between Scn2a and Kcnq2. Hum Mol Genet 2006;15(6):1043–8.
17. Glasscock E, Qian J, Yoo JW, et al. Masking epilepsy by combining two epilepsy genes. Nat Neurosci 2007;10(12):1554–8.
18. McKhann GM 2nd, Wenzel HJ, Robbins CA, et al. Mouse strain differences in kainic acid sensitivity, seizure behavior, mortality, and hippocampal pathology. Neuroscience 2003;122(2):551–61.
19. Papandrea D, Anderson TM, Herron BJ, et al. Dissociation of seizure traits in inbred strains of mice using the flurothyl kindling model of epileptogenesis. Exp Neurol 2009;215(1):60–8.
20. Leonard AS, Hyder SN, Kolls BJ, et al. Seizure predisposition after perinatal hypoxia: effects of subsequent age and of an epilepsy predisposing gene mutation. Epilepsia 2013;54(10):1789–800.
21. Veerapandiyan A, Winchester SA, Gallentine WB, et al. Electroencephalographic and seizure manifestations of pyridoxal 5'-phosphate-dependent epilepsy. Epilepsy Behav 2011;20(3):494–501.
22. Naasan G, Yabroudi M, Rahi A, et al. Electroencephalographic changes in pyridoxine-dependant epilepsy: new observations. Epileptic Disord 2009;11(4):293–300.
23. Mikati MA, Zalloua P, Karam P, et al. Novel mutation causing partial biotinidase deficiency in a Syrian boy with infantile spasms and retardation. J Child Neurol 2006;21(11):978–81.
24. Mikati MA, Trevathan E, Krishnamoorthy KS, et al. Pyridoxine-dependent epilepsy: EEG investigations and long-term follow-up. Electroencephalogr Clin Neurophysiol 1991;78(3):215–21.
25. Steele SU, Cheah SM, Veerapandiyan A, et al. Electroencephalographic and seizure manifestations in two patients with folate receptor autoimmune antibody-mediated primary cerebral folate deficiency. Epilepsy Behav 2012;24(4):507–12.
26. El-Hajj TI, Karam PE, Mikati MA. Biotin-responsive basal ganglia disease: case report and review of the literature. Neuropediatrics 2008;39(5):268–71.
27. Ream MA, Mikati MA. Clinical utility of genetic testing in pediatric drug-resistant epilepsy: a pilot study. Epilepsy Behav 2014;37:241–8.
28. Rees MI. The genetics of epilepsy–the past, the present and future. Seizure 2010;19(10):680–3.
29. Kullmann DM. Neurological channelopathies. Annu Rev Neurosci 2010;33:151–72.
30. Deprez L, Jansen A, De Jonghe P. Genetics of epilepsy syndromes starting in the first year of life. Neurology 2009;72(3):273–81.
31. Allen NM, Mannion M, Conroy J, et al. The variable phenotypes of KCNQ-related epilepsy. Epilepsia 2014;55(9):e99–105.
32. Maljevic S, Lerche H. Potassium channel genes and benign familial neonatal epilepsy. Prog Brain Res 2014;213:17–53.
33. Orhan G, Bock M, Schepers D, et al. Dominant-negative effects of KCNQ2 mutations are associated with epileptic encephalopathy. Ann Neurol 2014;75(3):382–94.
34. Berkovic SF, Heron SE, Giordano L, et al. Benign familial neonatal-infantile seizures: characterization of a new sodium channelopathy. Ann Neurol 2004;55(4):550–7.
35. Tavyev Asher YJ, Scaglia F. Molecular bases and clinical spectrum of early infantile epileptic encephalopathies. Eur J Med Genet 2012;55(5):299–306.
36. Vigevano F. Benign familial infantile seizures. Brain Dev 2005;27(3):172–7.
37. Brunklaus A, Zuberi SM. Dravet syndrome–from epileptic encephalopathy to channelopathy. Epilepsia 2014;55(7):979–84.

38. Wolff M, Casse-Perrot C, Dravet C. Severe myoclonic epilepsy of infants (Dravet syndrome): natural history and neuropsychological findings. Epilepsia 2006; 47(Suppl 2):45–8.
39. Claes L, Del-Favero J, Ceulemans B, et al. De novo mutations in the sodium-channel gene SCN1A cause severe myoclonic epilepsy of infancy. Am J Hum Genet 2001;68(6):1327–32.
40. Williams CA, Battaglia A. Molecular biology of epilepsy genes. Exp Neurol 2013; 244:51–8.
41. Stafstrom CE. Severe epilepsy syndromes of early childhood: the link between genetics and pathophysiology with a focus on SCN1A mutations. J Child Neurol 2009;24(8 Suppl):15S–23S.
42. Lossin C. A catalog of SCN1A variants. Brain Dev 2009;31(2):114–30.
43. Catterall WA, Kalume F, Oakley JC. NaV1.1 channels and epilepsy. J Physiol 2010;588(Pt 11):1849–59.
44. Catterall WA. Sodium channels, inherited epilepsy, and antiepileptic drugs. Annu Rev Pharmacol Toxicol 2014;54:317–38.
45. Laux L, Blackford R. The ketogenic diet in Dravet syndrome. J Child Neurol 2013; 28(8):1041–4.
46. Devinsky O, Cilio MR, Cross H, et al. Cannabidiol: pharmacology and potential therapeutic role in epilepsy and other neuropsychiatric disorders. Epilepsia 2014;55(6):791–802.
47. Pavone P, Striano P, Falsaperla R, et al. Infantile spasms syndrome, West syndrome and related phenotypes: What we know in 2013. Brain Dev 2014; 36(9):739–51.
48. Paciorkowski AR, Thio LL, Dobyns WB. Genetic and biologic classification of infantile spasms. Pediatr Neurol 2011;45(6):355–67.
49. Poulat AL, Lesca G, Sanlaville D, et al. A proposed diagnostic approach for infantile spasms based on a spectrum of variable aetiology. Eur J Paediatr Neurol 2014;18(2):176–82.
50. Caraballo RH, Dalla Bernardina B. Idiopathic generalized epilepsies. Handb Clin Neurol 2013;111:579–89.
51. Coppola G. Malignant migrating partial seizures in infancy. Handb Clin Neurol 2013;111:605–9.
52. Barcia G, Fleming MR, Deligniere A, et al. De novo gain-of-function KCNT1 channel mutations cause malignant migrating partial seizures of infancy. Nat Genet 2012;44(11):1255–9.
53. Bearden D, Strong A, Ehnot J, et al. Targeted treatment of migrating partial seizures of infancy with quinidine. Ann Neurol 2014;76(3):457–61.
54. Mikati MA, Jiang Y, Carboni M, et al. Quinidine in the treatment of KCNT1 positive epilepsies. Ann Neurol; in press.
55. Poduri A, Heinzen EL, Chitsazzadeh V, et al. SLC25A22 is a novel gene for migrating partial seizures in infancy. Ann Neurol 2013;74(6):873–82.
56. Poduri A, Chopra SS, Neilan EG, et al. Homozygous PLCB1 deletion associated with malignant migrating partial seizures in infancy. Epilepsia 2012;53(8):e146–50.
57. Striano P, de Falco FA, Minetti C, et al. Familial benign nonprogressive myoclonic epilepsies. Epilepsia 2009;50(Suppl 5):37–40.
58. Vigevano F, Specchio N, Fejerman N. Idiopathic focal epilepsies. Handb Clin Neurol 2013;111:591–604.
59. Strug LJ, Clarke T, Chiang T, et al. Centrotemporal sharp wave EEG trait in rolandic epilepsy maps to Elongator Protein Complex 4 (ELP4). Eur J Hum Genet 2009;17(9):1171–81.

60. Chen Y, Parker WD, Wang K. The role of T-type calcium channel genes in absence seizures. Front Neurol 2014;5:45.

61. Hirose S. Mutant GABAA receptor subunits in genetic (idiopathic) epilepsy. Prog Brain Res 2014;213:55–85.

62. Lesca G, Rudolf G, Bruneau N, et al. GRIN2A mutations in acquired epileptic aphasia and related childhood focal epilepsies and encephalopathies with speech and language dysfunction. Nat Genet 2013;45(9):1061–6.

63. Kelley SA, Kossoff EH. Doose syndrome (myoclonic-astatic epilepsy): 40 years of progress. Dev Med Child Neurol 2010;52(11):988–93.

64. Nordli DR Jr. Epileptic encephalopathies in infants and children. J Clin Neurophysiol 2012;29(5):420–4.

65. Mann EO, Mody I. The multifaceted role of inhibition in epilepsy: seizure-genesis through excessive GABAergic inhibition in autosomal dominant nocturnal frontal lobe epilepsy. Curr Opin Neurol 2008;21(2):155–60.

66. Heron SE, Smith KR, Bahlo M, et al. Missense mutations in the sodium-gated potassium channel gene KCNT1 cause severe autosomal dominant nocturnal frontal lobe epilepsy. Nat Genet 2012;44(11):1188–90.

67. Nobile C, Michelucci R, Andreazza S, et al. LGI1 mutations in autosomal dominant and sporadic lateral temporal epilepsy. Hum Mutat 2009;30(4):530–6.

68. Dibbens LM, de Vries B, Donatello S, et al. Mutations in DEPDC5 cause familial focal epilepsy with variable foci. Nat Genet 2013;45(5):546–51.

69. Poduri A. DEPDC5 does it all: shared genetics for diverse epilepsy syndromes. Ann Neurol 2014;75(5):631–3.

70. Shahwan A, Farrell M, Delanty N. Progressive myoclonic epilepsies: a review of genetic and therapeutic aspects. Lancet Neurol 2005;4(4):239–48.

71. de Siqueira LF. Progressive myoclonic epilepsies: review of clinical, molecular and therapeutic aspects. J Neurol 2010;257(10):1612–9.

72. Girard JM, Turnbull J, Ramachandran N, et al. Progressive myoclonus epilepsy. Handb Clin Neurol 2013;113:1731–6.

73. Hallmann K, Zsurka G, Moskau-Hartmann S, et al. A homozygous splice-site mutation in CARS2 is associated with progressive myoclonic epilepsy. Neurology 2014;83(23):2183–7.

74. Mosbech MB, Olsen AS, Neess D, et al. Reduced ceramide synthase 2 activity causes progressive myoclonic epilepsy. Ann Clin Transl Neurol 2014;1(2):88–98.

75. Farhan SM, Murphy LM, Robinson JF, et al. Linkage analysis and exome sequencing identify a novel mutation in KCTD7 in patients with progressive myoclonus epilepsy with ataxia. Epilepsia 2014;55(9):e106–11.

76. Franceschetti S, Michelucci R, Canafoglia L, et al. Progressive myoclonic epilepsies: definitive and still undetermined causes. Neurology 2014;82(5):405–11.

77. Boisse Lomax L, Bayly MA, Hjalgrim H, et al. 'North Sea' progressive myoclonus epilepsy: phenotype of subjects with GOSR2 mutation. Brain 2013;136(Pt 4):1146–54.

78. Wolf P, Koepp M. Reflex epilepsies. Handb Clin Neurol 2012;107:257–76.

79. Lund C, Brodtkorb E, Oye AM, et al. CHD2 mutations in Lennox-Gastaut syndrome. Epilepsy & behavior: E&B 2014;33:18–21.

80. Chung SK, Bode A, Cushion TD, et al. GLRB is the third major gene of effect in hyperekplexia. Hum Mol Genet 2013;22(5):927–40.

81. Noh GJ, Jane Tavyev Asher Y, Graham JM Jr. Clinical review of genetic epileptic encephalopathies. Eur J Med Genet 2012;55(5):281–98.

82. Crino PB. mTOR: a pathogenic signaling pathway in developmental brain malformations. Trends Mol Med 2011;17(12):734–42.

Genetics and Emerging Treatments for Duchenne and Becker Muscular Dystrophy

CrossMark

Nicolas Wein, PhD[a], Lindsay Alfano, DPT[a,b], Kevin M. Flanigan, MD[a,c,d,*]

KEYWORDS

- Duchenne • Becker • Muscular dystrophy • *DMD* gene • Dystrophin • Gene therapy
- Exon skipping • Nonsense suppression

KEY POINTS

- Duchenne and Becker muscular dystrophy (DMD and BMD) are X-linked disorders that occur because of mutations in the *DMD* gene, encoding the dystrophin protein, which provides an important part of the protein complex that provides a link between the cytoskeleton the extracellular matrix.
- In most cases, DMD occurs because of mutations that result in the production of no dystrophin, and BMD occurs because of mutations that result in the production of partially functional dystrophin; this concept is being used for novel potential therapies directed at DMD.
- DMD typically presents at ages 2 to 5 years with gait abnormalities or motor performance that falls behind peers, but clinicians must be aware it may present with delayed motor milestones, early cognitive impairment, or elevated serum transaminases, any of which should lead to testing serum creatine kinase.
- Treatment with systemic corticosteroids (prednisone and deflazacort) is the only therapy that has definitively been shown to alter the course of DMD; careful monitoring and counseling are required to minimize side effects.
- Promising potential therapies, such as exon skipping or nonsense suppression, are directed toward specific mutations or mutation classes; definitive mutation analysis of the *DMD* gene from genomic DNA is widely available and detects approximately 95% of mutations.

Disclosures: Dr K.M. Flanigan receives research support from the National Institutes of Health (NS085238); the Association Francaise contre les Myopathies; and the CureDuchenne foundation. He has served as a site investigator or subinvestigator on trials funded by Prosensa Therapeutics; Sarepta Therapeutics; PTC Therapeutics; and Akashi Therapeutics. He has served on advisory boards for Prosensa, Sarepta, PTC, and Italofarmaco, Inc. Dr L. Alfano serves as a consultant for PTC Therapeutics, Eli Lilly and Company, and Pfizer Inc. Dr N. Wein has no disclosures.
 a The Center for Gene Therapy, The Research Institute, Nationwide Children's Hospital, 700 Children's Drive, Columbus, OH 43205, USA; b Department of Physical Therapy, Nationwide Children's Hospital, 700 Children's Drive, Columbus, OH 43205, USA; c Department of Pediatrics, Ohio State University, 700 Children's Drive, Columbus, OH 43205, USA; d Department of Neurology, Ohio State University, 700 Children's Drive, Columbus, OH 43205, USA
* Corresponding author. Center for Gene Therapy, Rm 3014, Nationwide Children's Hospital, 700 Children's Drive, Columbus, OH 43205.
E-mail address: kevin.flanigan@nationwidechildrens.org

Pediatr Clin N Am 62 (2015) 723–742
http://dx.doi.org/10.1016/j.pcl.2015.03.008
0031-3955/15/$ – see front matter © 2015 Elsevier Inc. All rights reserved.

pediatric.theclinics.com

The videos, showing a boy with DMD climbing stairs and a boy with DMD arising from the floor, accompany this article at http://www.pediatric. theclinics.com/

INTRODUCTION

Duchenne and Becker muscular dystrophy (DMD and BMD) are related disorders that occur because of mutations in the *DMD* gene, encoding the dystrophin protein. DMD is more severe, and more common, with newborn screening studies showing an incidence ranging from 1:3802 to 1:6291 live male births[1] (rather than the 1:3500 that is commonly cited),[2] and BMD is about one-third as common.[2,3] Because the gene is X-linked, the diseases affect only boys (except in those rare cases explained by unusual genetic mechanisms such as balanced chromosomal translocations).

The dystrophin protein consists of an N-terminal actin-binding domain, a long central rod domain consisting of 24 spectrin-like repeats, and a C-terminal dystroglycan-binding domain. Within the central rod domain is a second actin-binding domain as well as a binding site for neuronal nitric oxide synthase; additional proteins, including dystrobrevin and syntrophin, bind dystrophin distal to the dystroglycan-binding domain. These partners suggest a role for dystrophin in signaling, but it is clear that dystrophin plays a critical role as a structural linker between the cytoskeletal F-actin and β-dystroglycan, one of the proteins of the membrane-bound dystroglycan-associated glycoprotein complex. Another of these proteins, α-dystroglycan, is located externally, where it binds with the extracellular matrix. The deformational forces generated by muscle contraction are significant, and in the absence of dystrophin, which is typically the case with DMD, the muscle membrane is damaged. This damage leads to elevations of creatine kinase (CK) in the serum and to calcium influx within the muscle fiber, leading in turn to activation of calcium-dependent proteases. Cycles of muscle fiber necrosis, degeneration, and regeneration follow, with increasing endomysial fibrosis and fatty replacement of muscle over time, and loss of muscle contractile function. In BMD, a partially functional dystrophin is typically produced, leading to an attenuated clinical course and attenuated muscle pathologic abnormality.

At the level of gene mutations, the difference between an absent or a partially functional dystrophin (and hence DMD or BMD) is explained by the concept of the "reading frame rule."[4] Mutations that ablate the open reading frame (or "out-of-frame" mutations) lead to translation termination and DMD. In contrast, those that maintain an open reading frame (or "in-frame" mutations) lead to BMD, via translation of an internally truncated protein that still has domains critical to binding F-actin and β-dystroglycan. This reading frame rule is generally accurate, being 90% specific in DMD cases,[5] and it is important for the pediatrician ordering and interpreting genetic tests to be familiar with it, but as discussed later exceptions to the rule occur. Nevertheless, restoration of an open reading frame is a key goal of new molecular therapies now in clinical trials.

CLINICAL FEATURES
Duchenne Muscular Dystrophy

Typically, parents of boys with DMD seek attention when their boys are between ages 2 and 5 years old. They frequently describe altered gait, often with toe walking that leads to a referral to a physical therapist or orthopedic surgeon even before a serum CK is tested. Parents frequently describe a diagnostic odyssey, with diagnosis taking more than a year from presentation,[6] but serum CK elevations that are typically 50 to 100 times the normal levels lead quickly to a diagnosis of muscular dystrophy. Gait acquisition and other motor skills may be delayed in comparison with their peers,[7] and the American Academy of Pediatrics recommends testing of serum CK for all cases of motor delay.[8] Language development may similarly be delayed; cognition is affected, and the intelligence quotient (IQ) is diminished by one standard deviation with improvements in verbal IQ with age.[9–11] On examination, proximal weakness is evident even at an early age and can be demonstrated by difficulty in climbing stairs (Video 1), hopping on either foot, or arising from the floor, which is usually performed with the use of the classic Gower maneuver (Video 2). Calf enlargement is usually seen—the classic "pseudohypertrophy" of Duchenne, although true muscle hypertrophy is present—as is tight heel cords and lordosis, both of which may be quite mild at presentation.

Boys with DMD typically improve in strength through the sixth or seventh year, followed by a measurable plateau in function for up to 2 years before a decline leading to wheelchair dependence.[12–15] In historical studies from the presteroid treatment era, the loss of independent ambulation reliably occurred before the age of 12 years. Once in a wheelchair, forced vital capacity begins to decline, leading to ventilatory insufficiency, particularly at night.[15,16] Scoliosis also is frequent and may require surgical correction. The incidence of cardiomyopathy increases with age and arguably has a greater clinical impact now that improvements in noninvasive ventilatory care are improving life expectancy. In the absence of ventilatory intervention, death typically occurs late in the second or early in the third decade.[17]

Becker Muscular Dystrophy

BMD is much more clinically heterogeneous.[18–20] Half of affected boys demonstrate muscle weakness by age 10, typically in a limb-girdle pattern, but many without muscle weakness at that age recall myalgias with exertion and calf hypertrophy.[20] BMD is defined by loss of ambulation by the age of 15 or greater, but most patients with childhood onset of weakness typically lose ambulation in the third or fourth decade. Others, however, have much milder symptoms, including onset of limb-girdle weakness beginning only in mid or late adulthood[21,22]; isolated quadriceps weakness[23]; adult or childhood cramp-myalgia syndromes or exercise-induced myoglobinuria[24]; or (very rarely) asymptomatic hyperCKemia.[25] Cognition is usually normal, although isolated cognitive impairment has been reported.[26,27] Cardiomyopathy is common, although the age at onset may vary depending on the structure of the residual dystrophin protein.[28]

SERUM CHEMISTRIES

The serum CK level is almost always the first diagnostic test performed once the diagnosis of DMD or BMD is suspected. It is always elevated, frequently 50 to 100 times normal in DMD, and lower in BMD, where it peaks around 10 to 15 years of age.[29] It is elevated at birth, leading to its use as a tool for newborn screening[30,31]; both CK level and DNA mutational analysis can be performed from Guthrie card blood spots.[1] Extremely elevated serum CK levels are sometimes observed, associated with myoglobinuria and leading to a diagnosis of rhabdomyolysis; this is more commonly seen in BMD than in DMD, presumably because BMD allows more strenuous activity, which may precipitate such episodes.[24,32–35] Importantly, CK is not the only enzyme elevated in serum. The transaminases aspartate aminotransferase and alanine aminotransferase are elevated and correlate with serum CK[36–38]; in this case, they are derived from muscle, not liver, yet patients occasionally present following extensive workup for hepatic disease, even including liver biopsy. For this reason, γ-glutamyl transferase level should be used as a marker of liver injury in DMD patients.[39] Similarly, renal function may be assessed by use of cystatin C rather than serum creatinine or creatinine clearance, because both of these are routinely decreased in patients with DMD.[40]

MUTATION ANALYSIS

Mutation analysis of the *DMD* gene has largely replaced muscle biopsy as the first diagnostic test performed after serum CK testing. Testing of genomic DNA derived from lymphocytes is readily available. Detailed mutational analysis now represents the standard of care,[41] not only because it may provide prognostic information but also because it facilitates genetic counseling and potentially more importantly may determine suitability for specific novel therapies, as discussed later.

The implications of *DMD* mutations are outlined in **Fig. 1**. The *DMD* gene consists of 79 exons spread over more than 2.4 million nucleotides on the X chromosome, and deletions of one or more these exons account for 65% of cases of dystrophinopathy.[5,42,43] This enormous size of the DMD gene originally precluded detailed mutational analysis, and early clinical diagnostic tests interrogated around 25 exons within the 2 deletion hot-spot regions of the gene by use of a multiplex PCR approach.[44,45] This method frequently did not define the extent of a multiexon deletion, nor could it detect duplications, which represent around 6% of all mutations. It could also not detect point mutations, and sequencing of the entire greater than 11 kilobase cDNA (from muscle-derived RNA) was required. Over the past decade, nearly complete mutational analysis has become possible. Exon copy number can be reliably assessed by a multiplex ligation dependent probe amplification technique,[46,47] or by comparative genomic hybridization array,[48–50] each of which allows determination of exon copy number in both hemizygous men and in carrier women. Sequence analysis is required to detect the remaining mutations, including nonsense, small subexonic insertions or deletions, missense, or splice site mutations. These mutations may be detected by traditional Sanger sequencing or next-generation sequencing methods. For practical purposes in the clinic, the method itself is not important as long as the entire coding region is sequenced, because point mutations are typically "private" mutations.

Mutational analysis of genomic DNA as described above thus detects around 95% of mutations.[42,51] Importantly, one class of mutations is not detected by current genomic DNA approaches. Point mutations that occur deep within the large introns of *DMD* may activate a cryptic splice site; as a result, an intronic fragment may be included in the assembled mature mRNA as a pseudo-exon.[52,53] Such mutations likely account for less than 5% of all dystrophinopathy patients, but are important to be aware of because they can only be diagnosed via muscle biopsy, followed by sequencing of cDNA derived from muscle mRNA.

An additional clinical challenge is presented by patients who represent exceptions to the reading frame rule, which is accurate 90% of the time. At diagnosis, parents typically request prognostic information based on the results of the mutation analysis, and the reading frame rule-based prediction may be misleading. For example, large in-frame deletions affecting the N-terminal dystrophin actin binding domain 1 and extending into the central rod domain may in fact be associated with DMD rather than BMD.[54] Similarly, predicted "nonsense mutations" within exons 23 to 42, a region in which deletion of any single exon maintains the reading frame, may alter splice definition elements such that the exon containing the mutation is not spliced into the mature mRNA, resulted in an open reading frame and a BMD phenotype.[55–57] Therefore, particularly in the absence of an informative family history regarding the implication of a given mutation, prognostication or phenotypic classification cannot rely solely

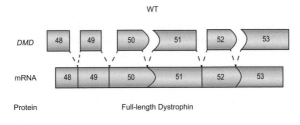

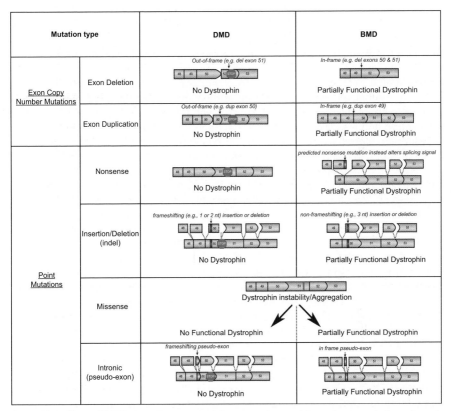

Fig. 1. The effect of *DMD* mutations on protein expression and the subsequent phenotype. In this illustration, only the region from *DMD* exon 48 to 53 has been depicted. Each blue box represents an exon, shaped to indicate the junctions necessary to maintain an open reading frame (ORF). A dystrophin protein is synthesized only if, after intron splicing, exon junctions fit together to maintain the ORF. Exceptions to the reading frame rule can occur when mutations predicted to have a particular effect on translation instead alter mRNA structure to maintain an ORF (for example, with BMD-associated nonsense mutations).

on the results of mutation analysis, but must take into account the entire clinical picture, including age at presentation, consistency of the examination findings with the predicted phenotype, and, if available, the results of any dystrophin expression studies on muscle biopsy.

Families affected by DMD and BMD should be provided with genetic counseling, and carrier testing should be offered to each mother unless there is an extensive

X-linked family history that defines her as an obligate carrier. However, one-third of all cases are de novo, consistent with Haldane's rule, so direct testing of the mother's DNA is warranted. The risk of germline mosaicism, which may be as high as 10%,[58,59] should be addressed with a genetic counselor.

MUSCLE BIOPSY

The role of muscle biopsy in the diagnosis of DMD and BMD has become less important as molecular mutation analysis has improved. However, as previously discussed, muscle biopsy is still required to establish the mutational mechanism in some patients. Furthermore, absent or altered dystrophin expression remains the gold standard of diagnosis of a dystrophinopathy.

The degree of histopathology present in the muscle biopsy depends in part on the age of the patient in the muscle sampled. Absence of dystrophin results in loss of muscle fiber integrity, and a cascade of myofiber necrosis, phagocytosis, and regeneration is associated with fibrosis and fatty replacement. Pathologically, it is these chronic and end-stage pathologic changes that are termed dystrophic. In BMD, the degree of pathologic abnormality may be less severe, with more moderate variation in muscle architecture and less fibrosis, although the degree of these changes may vary.

Dystrophin protein expression can be assessed by either immunofluorescent (IF) or immunohistochemical (IHC) staining of muscle sections, or by immunoblot (Western blot) analysis of homogenized tissue. Clinical laboratories make use of 3 antibodies with one directed toward each of the N-terminal, C-terminal, and central rod domains; in this fashion, if a BMD protein is missing only one of these epitopes, the presence of dystrophin can still be detected. In clinical practice, IF or IHC staining demonstrates localization of dystrophin and allows semiquantitative descriptors of amount (ie, "absent," "reduced," "traces"). As shown in **Fig. 2**A, in normal muscle, dystrophin decorates the sarcolemmal membrane evenly; in BMD muscle, staining is reduced and often patchy, and in DMD, it is absent. However, it is important to note that biopsies from DMD patients can frequently show clusters of fibers with significant dystrophin expression. Termed "revertant fibers," they occur due to secondary alterations in the *DMD* gene—typically, altered mRNA splicing resulting in some mRNA with an open reading frame resulting in the expression of dystrophin—and are found in up to 50% of patient biopsies.[60–63] Immunoblot analysis (see **Fig. 2**B) provides information on protein size and allows more quantitative assessment; values of less than 3% in association with DMD and greater than 20% in association with BMD have been described and are still cited by some diagnostic laboratories.[64] The presence of internal yet in-frame BMD deletions frequently result in abundant dystrophin of diminished size (see **Fig. 2**B).[65]

MANAGEMENT

Although DMD commonly presents because of its effect on skeletal muscle, the disease affects multiple systems. As examples, both cardiac muscle and brain are directly affected by absence or alteration of dystrophin expression; ventilation becomes impaired because of diaphragmatic weakness, and bone density is diminished, a finding compounded by corticosteroid therapy. Once boys are in a wheelchair, cardiac and pulmonary care become increasingly important, and scoliosis is frequent. Nocturnal ventilatory support and assistive cough devices become necessary, and adaptive therapies play an increasingly large role. For this reason, management is frequently provided within a multidisciplinary clinic, making use of specialists from multiple disciplines. Universal care standards have been defined,[41,66] but at a

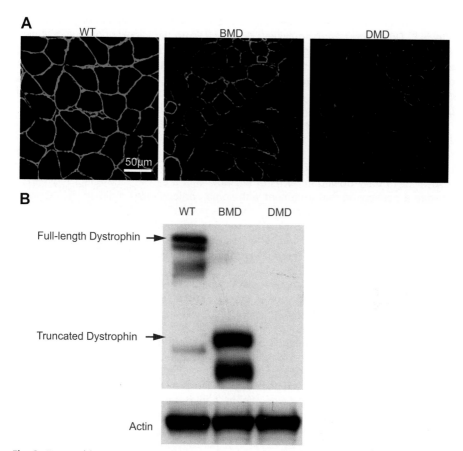

Fig. 2. Dystrophin expression in skeletal muscle in the dystrophinopathies. (*A*) Immunofluorescent analysis of muscle biopsy sections. Dystrophin (C-terminal antibody) is detected at the sarcolemmal membrane of all muscle fibers in control tissue. In BMD, the intensity of staining and the number of dystrophin positive fibers are diminished. In DMD, only rare dystrophin-positive fibers are detected. (*B*) An example of a Western blot using a C-terminal antibody (dys1). In control tissue, full-length (427 kDa) dystrophin is detected. In BMD tissue, an abundant but shortened protein is present, consistent with an internally truncated dystrophin. In DMD, no dystrophin is typically present. Actin is used here as a loading control.

minimum, DMD patients should be seen yearly by a neurologist or rehabilitation physician, a cardiologist, a pulmonologist, physical and occupational therapists, and a nutritionist. Additional input may be required from endocrinologists, orthopedic surgeons, social workers, and palliative care specialists.

Medical Management

Corticosteroids

The corticosteroids prednisone and deflazacort are the only medications that have been shown to affect the clinical course of DMD and, although the precise mechanism of their effect is unknown, their use is considered standard of care. The classic randomized placebo-controlled trial of prednisone demonstrated that treatment of 0.75 mg per kilogram per day resulted in improved muscle strength by 6 months, whereas a dose twice that showed no additional benefit with significantly more side effects.[67] Deflazacort at an equivalent dose of 0.9 mg per kilogram per day has also frequently been used, with a generally equivalent efficacy but a potentially less marked side effect profile, in particular, in relation to weight gain.[68] Nevertheless, the side effects of both drugs are marked. Weight gain often results in obesity. Osteoporosis due to muscle weakness is exacerbated, often leading to long bone and vertebral body fracture. Short stature and delayed puberty are common.

In an effort to minimize the side effects, a variety of alternative regimens are in use. These alternative regimens include prednisone on a 10 days on and 10 days off regimen, or for the first 10 days a month. A weekend dosing regimen of 10 mg per kilogram per week (divided on weekend days) has been shown to be roughly equivalent to daily dosing in terms of efficacy, with a similar side effect regimen.[69] Despite a consensus that treatment with some corticosteroid regimen will increase ambulation by up to 1 to 3 years,[70–74] these regimens have not been well characterized head to head in clinical trials. The ongoing National Institutes of Health–sponsored multicenter FOR-DMD trial is a randomized double-blinded trial that should provide clear information on the relative efficacy and side effects of these alternate regimens.

Several other outstanding issues regarding corticosteroid therapy exist. One issue is at what age to initiate corticosteroid therapy, and at what age to stop it. Published recommendations suggest starting therapy between ages 2 and 5 years in boys whose strength has plateaued or is declining.[66] Although treatment in boys who have reached the motor plateau is clearly recommended, earlier treatment may be beneficial, and in fact, may be associated with a longer-term benefit.[75,76] The second issue is how exactly to alter dosing as boys grow. Most practitioners do not adhere strictly to a 0.75 mg per kilogram dose of prednisone at every visit, but instead modify dosing related to tolerance and side effects. A third issue regards the use of corticosteroids after the boy has lost ambulation. The use of low-dose steroids in nonambulant boys may result in diminished scoliosis and improved ventilation,[74,77] but standard dosing by weight may result in significant obesity and further respiratory impairment.

Cardiac

Cardiomyopathy is a major feature of DMD. Although the median age of onset has been described as around 14 to 15 years,[78,79] other studies estimate the incidence is as high as 25% by age 6 years and 59% by 10 years.[80,81] Clearly, the importance of cardiomyopathy has come to the forefront over the past decades, as improvements in ventilatory and orthopedic care have prolonged life. Cardiac MRI may be used to demonstrate cardiac fibrosis and the diastolic dysfunction that is present before systolic dysfunction is noted.[77,82–86] However, in most clinical settings, systolic dysfunction is first detected by standard clinical echocardiograms. For this reason, a baseline echocardiogram is recommended at diagnosis, with screening echocardiograms every 2 years up to age 8 years, and yearly after age 10 years.[66] Cardiomyopathy is typically treated with afterload reduction, using angiotensin-converting enzyme inhibitors or angiotensin receptor blockers; some data suggest that use of these drugs should be initiated before symptoms occur, although these studies are limited.[87–89] Although systolic dysfunction is often emphasized in cardiac care, cardiac conduction disturbances are frequent and may require Holter monitoring for assessment.[90–92] In BMD, cardiomyopathy is also frequent and may be severe, even necessitating cardiac transplantation. The age of onset of cardiomyopathy is likely largely related to the structure and features of the residual dystrophin protein.[28]

Nonpharmacologic Management

Pulmonary

Because pulmonary insufficiency is the major cause of mortality, aggressive manage-ment of pulmonary insufficiency has been the greatest contributor to prolonged life and quality of life in adults with DMD.[93] Routine use of mechanical insufflator/exsuffla-tor (eg, CoughAssist) devices decreases pulmonary morbidity, and their early use should be considered. Forced vital capacity typically declines after loss of ambulation, and as pulmonary function declines, the incidence of nocturnal hypoxemia and hyper-capnia increases.[94] Thorough evaluation of these variables during sleep is critical in early identification of these issues, so yearly polysomnograms after loss of ambulation are indicated. Introduction of nocturnal ventilation, typically, with bilevel continuous positive airway pressure ventilation, can improve quality of life by decreasing morning headaches and general fatigue while improving sleep efficiency.[94,95]

Spine/scoliosis

Scoliosis ultimately affects up to 77% of boys with DMD and is typically seen after loss of ambulation, but it may be delayed or minimized by use of steroids. Orthopedic consultation should be considered for curves past 20°, and yearly radiographs may be needed to assess progression. Nocturnal ventilation combined with spinal stabili-zation has been shown to prolong survival into the fourth decade.[96]

Contractures

Regular use of night splints can decrease contracture progression because they pro-vide a stretch or maintain ankle position across several hours. A dynamic splint has the potential to provide a passive muscle stretch throughout the night, whereas a solid brace will maintain the ankle in a 90° position. Often dynamic splints are recommen-ded because they can provide a continuous stretch to the muscle over an extended period of time. A combination of active, active-assisted, and passive stretching can be implemented throughout the day alongside splints or in the child unable to with-stand nightly use of splints. Other muscle groups prone to contracture and targeted for passive stretching are the iliotibial band, hip flexors, hamstrings, and elbow and finger flexors. Although an aggressive stretching program may not prevent progres-sion of contracture, it may delay the progression and maintain patient comfort.

Use of bracing during the day is not recommended in ambulatory children with DMD or BMD. Gait deviations are compensatory mechanisms used to prolong ambulation in the presence of progressive muscle weakness. Use of ankle-foot-orthoses (AFOs) are often misprescribed in this population and can lead to reduced walking speed, decreased stability, and increased falls.[97] In rare instances, AFO use can be useful in individual cases to temporarily prolong ambulation in the presence of severe ankle instability.

Exercise

Parents frequently ask whether exercise is beneficial for improving strength. Progres-sive, high-intensity, resistive exercises are not recommended in DMD and BMD because of the impaired muscle regeneration process.[66] Similarly, activities requiring repetitive eccentric contractions are also to be avoided because of the potential to damage dystrophic muscles. Some limited data support the recommendation of main-taining an active lifestyle in an attempt to maintain strength by limiting atrophy because of nonuse or muscle damage because of overwork.[98–101] Encouraging pa-tients to be active in functional activities (ie, swimming, walking, playing with friends) is likely to be helpful in maintaining strength and establishing some normalcy in childhood.

Balancing activity with components of energy conservation to limit fatigue throughout the day is also important in maximizing participation and independence in children and adults with DMD and BMD. Consultation with a physical therapist in the community or school-based program is often helpful in assisting patients and families find ways to conserve energy throughout the day. For example, using a wheelchair to transition between classes or move long distances in the community conserves energy, thus allowing the child to participate in meaningful activities rather than expending all their energy getting to the activity location. Mastering energy conservation techniques requires effective collaboration between the child, family, and therapist, especially during phases of transition.

Functional Outcomes

Currently available outcome measures are used clinically to predict loss of function and in research to measure change over time after introduction of a therapeutic agent. Children with DMD tend to improve scores on functional tests until the age of 7 years, at which point their function begins to decline. Timed functional tests, such as time to rise from the floor, 10 m walk/run test, timed stair climbing, and timed walking tests such as the 6-minute walk test (6MWT), are easy to implement in a clinical setting and can predict the loss of function, including ambulation, based on performance. For example, a child taking greater than 12 seconds to walk 10 m or unable to rise from the floor is highly likely to lose the ability to ambulate independently within 1 year.[14] The 6MWT has become the accepted standard for measuring change across clinical trials. Although the rate of decline on the 6MWT varies between cohorts, a 30-m change on the 6MWT is considered the minimal clinically significant change.[102,103] More specifically, a child walking less than 350 m is at a high risk for a significant function decline, with those walking less than less than 325 m being at risk for an imminent loss of ambulation.[104] The North Star Ambulatory Assessment (NSAA) is an evaluator-administered scale designed for children with DMD. The NSAA grades a child's ability on 17 items, and the total score has been shown to correlate to 6MWT and functional decline over time.[105]

EMERGING THERAPIES

Several novel therapies have reached clinical trial that seek to address the fundamental molecular defect in DMD by inducing expression of a functional or semifunctional version of the dystrophin protein.

Gene Transfer

The goal of gene transfer is a functional version of the gene to skeletal muscle (and, ultimately, cardiac muscle and diaphragm) under control of an appropriate promoter. The full-length *DMD* gene can be cloned into a plasmid, but delivering a naked DNA plasmid to skeletal muscle is highly inefficient and does not result in significant dystrophin protein expression.[106] Instead, current approaches make use of an adeno-associated virus (AAV) to package the transgene, selecting serotypes that show muscle tropism.[107] AAVs are limited in the size of transgene they can encapsidate, so instead of the full-length *DMD* mRNA, a microdystrophin lacking large portions of the central rod domain have been developed. An initial trial with an early microdystrophin vector version did not show significant dystrophin expression following injection into the extensor digitorum brevis muscle[108]; nevertheless, successful AAV-mediated gene expression of the α-sarcoglycan demonstrates a general proof-in-principle of the AAV approach for muscular dystrophy genes,[109] and clinical trials with second-generation vectors are near initiation.[110]

Alternate approaches to gene therapy for DMD are in development and should soon reach clinical trials. One alternate approach is surrogate gene transfer, in which overexpression of a different protein allows functional correction of muscle pathologic abnormality or dysfunction. One such example is overexpression of the α7-integrin gene, encoding a protein that directly links the extracellular matrix to the actin cytoskeleton.[111] Another surrogate gene is *GALGT2*, which encodes a GalNAc transferase normally expressed at the neuromuscular synapse; transgenic or AAV-mediated overexpression of *GALGT2* results in the presence of synaptic DGC across the entire muscle, with the inclusion of synaptic proteins such as utrophin resulting in improvements in muscle physiology and pathologic abnormality. Plans for clinical trials are underway.[112,113] A third approach is to deliver the gene encoding follistatin, which inhibits the action of the circulating myostatin protein, which itself negatively regulates muscle mass. Treatment of BMD patients with an AAV-delivered follistatin gene results in improvements in 6MWT distance in 4 of 6 subjects. Future trials in DMD are planned.[114]

Exon Skipping

The principle of exon-skipping therapies is based on the reading frame rule (**Fig. 3**). Splicing of pre-mRNA containing out-of-frame exon deletions is altered such that an exon is excluded, resulting in an in-frame mature mRNA that encodes a BMD-like protein.[115] In trials to date, this skipping has been accomplished by the use of antisense oligonucleotides (AONs) based on 1 of 2 different chemistries: 2′O-methyl phosphorothioate (2′O-Me) AONs,[116,117] or phosphorodiamidate morpholino oligomers (PMO).[118–120] These antisense molecules bind to exon splice junctions, masking them from the spliceosome. Targeting of a given exon may be a potential therapy for more than one mutation; for example, targeting of exon 51 will restore the reading frame of deletions of exon 45 to 50, exon 50 alone, or exon 52, among others. For this reason, targeting a limited number of exons (44, 45, 51, and 53) could result in therapy for around 35% of patients, and targeting 2 exons simultaneously could treat around 83%.[121]

To date, randomized placebo-controlled trials have been published for molecules targeting exon 51. Treatment of 12 patients with the PMO eteplirsen resulted, at 48 weeks, in a significant difference in the distance walked in the 6MWT between patients treated with the compound at the start of the study and those who initially received a placebo for 24 weeks before receiving active drug; the number of dystrophin-expressing fibers was also increased.[118] Similarly, treatment of 53 patients with the 2′O-Me drisapersen for 48 weeks resulted in a significant increase in 6MWT distance walked at 25 weeks in those patients treated with continuous treatment, rather than intermediate treatment or placebo.[116] Follow-up studies of each compound are ongoing, and studies targeting other exons will soon be underway.

Nonsense Suppression

The principle of nonsense suppression therapy for DMD (see **Fig. 3**) was first demonstrated in the *mdx* mouse, which carries a nonsense mutation in exon 23.[122] Treatment with gentamicin was shown to result in dystrophin expression, because binding to the ribosome results in a conformational change such that instead of translation termination an amino acid is inserted and translation proceeds. Although gentamicin treatment of DMD patients is possible and results in some increased dystrophin expression,[123] it is not practical, because of the requirement for intravenous

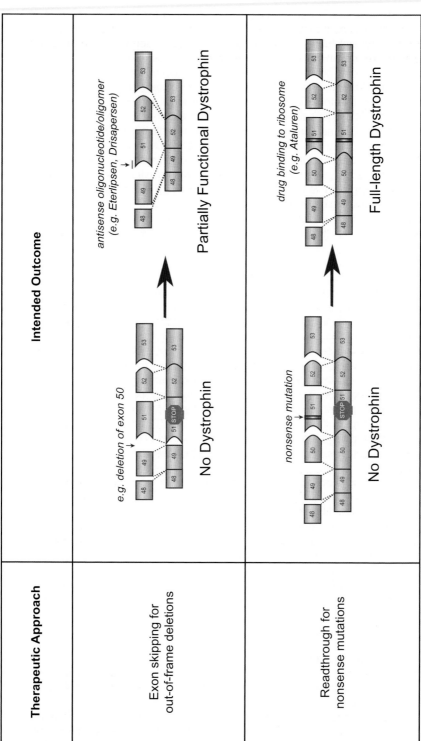

Fig. 3. Representation of the mechanism of 2 gene corrective therapeutic strategies currently in clinical trials. *Exon skipping* of exon 51 using 2'O-Me AONs or PMOs (see text) restores the *DMD* reading frame, allowing the production of an internally truncated but functional BMD-like protein. *Nonsense suppression* (or "readthrough") results in a premature translation termination codon being decoded by a near-cognate rather than a cognate tRNA. As a result, rather than disassembly of the ribosomal complex, an amino acid is inserted into the nascent peptide chain and translation continues, resulting in a functional protein.

treatment, ototoxicity, and nephrotoxicity of aminoglycosides. An orally available nonsense suppression agent, ataluren, has demonstrated promising clinical efficacy into early phase clinical trials[124] and received conditional approval in Europe. An ongoing presumably confirmatory trial is underway.

SUPPLEMENTARY DATA

Supplementary data related to this article can be found online at http://dx.doi.org/10.1016/j.pcl.2015.03.008.

REFERENCES

1. Mendell JR, Shilling C, Leslie ND, et al. Evidence-based path to newborn screening for Duchenne muscular dystrophy. Ann Neurol 2012;71(3):304–13.
2. Emery AE. Population frequencies of neuromuscular diseases–II. Amyotrophic lateral sclerosis (motor neurone disease). Neuromuscul Disord 1991;1(5):323–5.
3. Bushby KM, Thambyayah M, Gardner-Medwin D. Prevalence and incidence of Becker muscular dystrophy. Lancet 1991;337(8748):1022–4.
4. Monaco AP, Bertelson CJ, Liechti-Gallati S, et al. An explanation for the phenotypic differences between patients bearing partial deletions of the DMD locus. Genomics 1988;2(1):90–5.
5. Flanigan KM, Dunn DM, von Niederhausern A, et al. Mutational spectrum of DMD mutations in dystrophinopathy patients: application of modern diagnostic techniques to a large cohort. Hum Mutat 2009;30(12):1657–66.
6. Ciafaloni E, Fox DJ, Pandya S, et al. Delayed diagnosis in duchenne muscular dystrophy: data from the Muscular Dystrophy Surveillance, Tracking, and Research Network (MD STARnet). J Pediatr 2009;155(3):380–5.
7. Connolly AM, Florence JM, Cradock MM, et al. Motor and cognitive assessment of infants and young boys with Duchenne Muscular Dystrophy: results from the Muscular Dystrophy Association DMD Clinical Research Network. Neuromuscul Disord 2013;23(7):529–39.
8. Noritz GH, Murphy NA, Neuromotor Screening Expert Panel. Motor delays: early identification and evaluation. Pediatrics 2013;131(6):e2016–27.
9. Cotton S, Voudouris NJ, Greenwood KM. Intelligence and Duchenne muscular dystrophy: full-scale, verbal, and performance intelligence quotients. Dev Med Child Neurol 2001;43(7):497–501.
10. Cotton SM, Voudouris NJ, Greenwood KM. Association between intellectual functioning and age in children and young adults with Duchenne muscular dystrophy: further results from a meta-analysis. Dev Med Child Neurol 2005;47(4):257–65.
11. Cyrulnik SE, Fee RJ, De Vivo DC, et al. Delayed developmental language milestones in children with Duchenne's muscular dystrophy. J Pediatr 2007;150(5):474–8.
12. Brooke MH, Fenichel GM, Griggs RC, et al. Clinical investigation in Duchenne dystrophy: 2. Determination of the "power" of therapeutic trials based on the natural history. Muscle Nerve 1983;6(2):91–103.
13. Brooke MH, Griggs RC, Mendell JR, et al. The natural history of Duchenne muscular dystrophy: a caveat for therapeutic trials. Trans Am Neurol Assoc 1981;106:195–9.
14. McDonald CM, Abresch RT, Carter GT, et al. Profiles of neuromuscular diseases. Duchenne muscular dystrophy. Am J Phys Med Rehabil 1995;74(5 Suppl):S70–92.

15. Nicholson LV, Johnson MA, Bushby KM, et al. Integrated study of 100 patients with Xp21 linked muscular dystrophy using clinical, genetic, immunochemical, and histopathological data. Part 1. Trends across the clinical groups. J Med Genet 1993;30(9):728–36.
16. Tangsrud S, Petersen IL, Lodrup Carlsen KC, et al. Lung function in children with Duchenne's muscular dystrophy. Respir Med 2001;95(11):898–903.
17. Eagle M, Baudouin SV, Chandler C, et al. Survival in Duchenne muscular dystrophy: improvements in life expectancy since 1967 and the impact of home nocturnal ventilation. Neuromuscul Disord 2002;12(10):926–9.
18. Becker PE. Dystrophia Musculorum Progressiva. Eine genetische und klinische Untersuchung der Muskeldystrophien. Stuttgart (Germany): Thieme; 1953.
19. Becker PE. Two families of benign sex-linked recessive muscular dystrophy. Rev Can Biol 1962;21:551–66.
20. Bushby KM, Gardner-Medwin D. The clinical, genetic and dystrophin characteristics of Becker muscular dystrophy. I. Natural history. J Neurol 1993;240(2):98–104.
21. Heald A, Anderson LV, Bushby KM, et al. Becker muscular dystrophy with onset after 60 years. Neurology 1994;44(12):2388–90.
22. Yazaki M, Yoshida K, Nakamura A, et al. Clinical characteristics of aged Becker muscular dystrophy patients with onset after 30 years. Eur Neurol 1999;42(3):145–9.
23. Sunohara N, Arahata K, Hoffman EP, et al. Quadriceps myopathy: forme fruste of Becker muscular dystrophy. Ann Neurol 1990;28(5):634–9.
24. Minetti C, Tanji K, Chang HW, et al. Dystrophinopathy in two young boys with exercise-induced cramps and myoglobinuria. Eur J Pediatr 1993;152(10):848–51.
25. Melis MA, Cau M, Muntoni F, et al. Elevation of serum creatine kinase as the only manifestation of an intragenic deletion of the dystrophin gene in three unrelated families. Eur J Paediatr Neurol 1998;2(5):255–61.
26. North KN, Miller G, Iannaccone ST, et al. Cognitive dysfunction as the major presenting feature of Becker's muscular dystrophy. Neurology 1996;46(2):461–5.
27. Young HK, Barton BA, Waisbren S, et al. Cognitive and psychological profile of males with Becker muscular dystrophy. J Child Neurol 2008;23(2):155–62.
28. Kaspar RW, Allen HD, Ray WC, et al. Analysis of dystrophin deletion mutations predicts age of cardiomyopathy onset in becker muscular dystrophy. Circ Cardiovasc Genet 2009;2(6):544–51.
29. Zatz M, Rapaport D, Vainzof M, et al. Serum creatine-kinase (CK) and pyruvate-kinase (PK) activities in Duchenne (DMD) as compared with Becker (BMD) muscular dystrophy. J Neurol Sci 1991;102(2):190–6.
30. Plauchu H, Dorche C, Cordier MP, et al. Duchenne muscular dystrophy: neonatal screening and prenatal diagnosis. Lancet 1989;1(8639):669.
31. Skinner R, Emery AE, Scheuerbrandt G, et al. Feasibility of neonatal screening for Duchenne muscular dystrophy. J Med Genet 1982;19(1):1–3.
32. Doriguzzi C, Palmucci L, Mongini T, et al. Exercise intolerance and recurrent myoglobinuria as the only expression of Xp21 Becker type muscular dystrophy. J Neurol 1993;240(5):269–71.
33. Flanigan KM, Dunn DM, von Niederhausern A, et al. DMD Trp3X nonsense mutation associated with a founder effect in North American families with mild Becker muscular dystrophy. Neuromuscul Disord 2009;19(11):743–8.
34. Shoji T, Nishikawa Y, Saito N, et al. A case of Becker muscular dystrophy and massive myoglobinuria with minimal renal manifestations. Nephrol Dial Transplant 1998;13(3):759–60.

35. Thakker PB, Sharma A. Becker muscular dystrophy: an unusual presentation. Arch Dis Child 1993;69(1):158–9.
36. Morse RP, Rosman NP. Diagnosis of occult muscular dystrophy: importance of the "chance" finding of elevated serum aminotransferase activities. J Pediatr 1993;122(2):254–6.
37. Vajro P, Del Giudice E, Veropalumbo C. Muscular dystrophy revealed by incidentally discovered elevated aminotransferase levels. J Pediatr 2010; 156(4):689.
38. Veropalumbo C, Del Giudice E, Esposito G, et al. Aminotransferases and muscular diseases: a disregarded lesson. Case reports and review of the literature. J Paediatr Child Health 2012;48(10):886–90.
39. Rosales XQ, Chu ML, Shilling C, et al. Fidelity of gamma-glutamyl transferase (GGT) in differentiating skeletal muscle from liver damage. J Child Neurol 2008;23(7):748–51.
40. Viollet L, Gailey S, Thornton DJ, et al. Utility of cystatin C to monitor renal function in Duchenne muscular dystrophy. Muscle Nerve 2009;40(3):438–42.
41. Bushby K, Finkel R, Birnkrant DJ, et al. Diagnosis and management of Duchenne muscular dystrophy, part 1: diagnosis, and pharmacological and psychosocial management. Lancet Neurol 2010;9(1):77–93.
42. Dent KM, Dunn DM, von Niederhausern AC, et al. Improved molecular diagnosis of dystrophinopathies in an unselected clinical cohort. Am J Med Genet A 2005;134:295–8.
43. Tuffery-Giraud S, Beroud C, Leturcq F, et al. Genotype-phenotype analysis in 2,405 patients with a dystrophinopathy using the UMD-DMD database: a model of nationwide knowledgebase. Hum Mutat 2009;30(6):934–45.
44. Beggs AH, Koenig M, Boyce FM, et al. Detection of 98% of DMD/BMD gene deletions by polymerase chain reaction. Hum Genet 1990;86(1):45–8.
45. Chamberlain JS, Gibbs RA, Ranier JE, et al. Multiplex PCR for the diagnosis of Duchenne muscular dystrophy. In: Innis MA, Gelfand DH, Sninsky JJ, et al, editors. PCR protocols: a guide to methods and applications. San Francisco (CA): Academic Press; 1990. p. 272–81.
46. Janssen B, Hartmann C, Scholz V, et al. MLPA analysis for the detection of deletions, duplications and complex rearrangements in the dystrophin gene: potential and pitfalls. Neurogenetics 2005;6(1):29–35.
47. Schwartz M, Duno M. Improved molecular diagnosis of dystrophin gene mutations using the multiplex ligation-dependent probe amplification method. Genet Test 2004;8(4):361–7.
48. del Gaudio D, Yang Y, Boggs BA, et al. Molecular diagnosis of Duchenne/ Becker muscular dystrophy: enhanced detection of dystrophin gene rearrangements by oligonucleotide array-comparative genomic hybridization. Hum Mutat 2008;29(9):1100–7.
49. Hegde MR, Chin EL, Mulle JG, et al. Microarray-based mutation detection in the dystrophin gene. Hum Mutat 2008;29(9):1091–9.
50. Saillour Y, Cossee M, Leturcq F, et al. Detection of exonic copy-number changes using a highly efficient oligonucleotide-based comparative genomic hybridization-array method. Hum Mutat 2008;29(9):1083–90.
51. Yan J, Feng J, Buzin CH, et al. Three-tiered noninvasive diagnosis in 96% of patients with Duchenne muscular dystrophy (DMD). Hum Mutat 2004;23(2): 203–4.
52. Gurvich OL, Tuohy TM, Howard MT, et al. DMD pseudoexon mutations: splicing efficiency, phenotype, and potential therapy. Ann Neurol 2008;63(1):81–9.

53. Tuffery-Giraud S, Saquet C, Chambert S, et al. Pseudoexon activation in the DMD gene as a novel mechanism for Becker muscular dystrophy. Hum Mutat 2003;21(6):608–14.

54. Matsumura K, Burghes AH, Mora M, et al. Immunohistochemical analysis of dystrophin-associated proteins in Becker/Duchenne muscular dystrophy with huge in-frame deletions in the NH2-terminal and rod domains of dystrophin. J Clin Invest 1994;93(1):99–105.

55. Disset A, Bourgeois CF, Benmalek N, et al. An exon skipping-associated nonsense mutation in the dystrophin gene uncovers a complex interplay between multiple antagonistic splicing elements. Hum Mol Genet 2006;15(6):999–1013.

56. Flanigan KM, Dunn DM, von Niederhausern A, et al. Nonsense mutation-associated Becker muscular dystrophy: interplay between exon definition and splicing regulatory elements within the DMD gene. Hum Mutat 2011;32(3): 299–308.

57. Ginjaar IB, Kneppers AL, v d Meulen JD, et al. Dystrophin nonsense mutation induces different levels of exon 29 skipping and leads to variable phenotypes within one BMD family. Eur J Hum Genet 2000;8(10):793–6.

58. Barbujani G, Russo A, Danieli GA, et al. Segregation analysis of 1885 DMD families: significant departure from the expected proportion of sporadic cases. Hum Genet 1990;84(6):522–6.

59. Grimm T, Muller B, Muller CR, et al. Theoretical considerations on germline mosaicism in Duchenne muscular dystrophy. J Med Genet 1990;27(11):683–7.

60. Burrow KL, Coovert DD, Klein CJ, et al. Dystrophin expression and somatic reversion in prednisone-treated and untreated Duchenne dystrophy. CIDD Study Group. Neurology 1991;41(5):661–6.

61. Fanin M, Danieli GA, Vitiello L, et al. Prevalence of dystrophin-positive fibers in 85 Duchenne muscular dystrophy patients. Neuromuscul Disord 1992;2(1):41–5.

62. Klein CJ, Coovert DD, Bulman DE, et al. Somatic reversion/suppression in Duchenne muscular dystrophy (DMD): evidence supporting a frame-restoring mechanism in rare dystrophin-positive fibers. Am J Hum Genet 1992;50(5): 950–9.

63. Nicholson LV, Johnson MA, Gardner Medwin D, et al. Heterogeneity of dystrophin expression in patients with Duchenne and Becker muscular dystrophy. Acta Neuropathol 1990;80(3):239–50.

64. Hoffman EP, Kunkel LM, Angelini C, et al. Improved diagnosis of Becker muscular dystrophy by dystrophin testing. Neurology 1989;39(8):1011–7.

65. Anthony K, Arechavala-Gomeza V, Taylor LE, et al. Dystrophin quantification: biological and translational research implications. Neurology 2014;83(22): 2062–9.

66. Bushby K, Finkel R, Birnkrant DJ, et al. Diagnosis and management of Duchenne muscular dystrophy, part 2: implementation of multidisciplinary care. Lancet Neurol 2010;9(2):177–89.

67. Mendell JR, Moxley RT, Griggs RC, et al. Randomized, double-blind six-month trial of prednisone in Duchenne's muscular dystrophy. N Engl J Med 1989; 320(24):1592–7.

68. Bonifati MD, Ruzza G, Bonometto P, et al. A multicenter, double-blind, randomized trial of deflazacort versus prednisone in Duchenne muscular dystrophy. Muscle Nerve 2000;23(9):1344–7.

69. Escolar DM, Hache LP, Clemens PR, et al. Randomized, blinded trial of weekend vs daily prednisone in Duchenne muscular dystrophy. Neurology 2011; 77(5):444–52.

70. Fenichel GM, Florence JM, Pestronk A, et al. Long-term benefit from prednisone therapy in Duchenne muscular dystrophy. Neurology 1991;41(12): 1874–7.
71. Fenichel GM, Mendell JR, Moxley RT 3rd, et al. A comparison of daily and alternate-day prednisone therapy in the treatment of Duchenne muscular dystrophy. Arch Neurol 1991;48(6):575–9.
72. Griggs RC, Moxley RT 3rd, Mendell JR, et al. Prednisone in Duchenne dystrophy. A randomized, controlled trial defining the time course and dose response. Clinical Investigation of Duchenne Dystrophy Group. Arch Neurol 1991;48(4): 383–8.
73. Manzur AY, Kuntzer T, Pike M, et al. Glucocorticoid corticosteroids for Duchenne muscular dystrophy. Cochrane Database Syst Rev 2008;(1):CD003725.
74. Moxley RT 3rd, Pandya S, Ciafaloni E, et al. Change in natural history of Duchenne muscular dystrophy with long-term corticosteroid treatment: implications for management. J Child Neurol 2010;25(9):1116–29.
75. Merlini L, Cicognani A, Malaspina E, et al. Early prednisone treatment in Duchenne muscular dystrophy. Muscle Nerve 2003;27(2):222–7.
76. Merlini L, Gennari M, Malaspina E, et al. Early corticosteroid treatment in 4 Duchenne muscular dystrophy patients: 14-year follow-up. Muscle Nerve 2012;45(6):796–802.
77. King WM, Ruttencutter R, Nagaraja HN, et al. Orthopedic outcomes of long-term daily corticosteroid treatment in Duchenne muscular dystrophy. Neurology 2007;68(19):1607–13.
78. Connuck DM, Sleeper LA, Colan SD, et al. Characteristics and outcomes of cardiomyopathy in children with Duchenne or Becker muscular dystrophy: a comparative study from the Pediatric Cardiomyopathy Registry. Am Heart J 2008;155(6):998–1005.
79. Viollet L, Thrush PT, Flanigan KM, et al. Effects of angiotensin-converting enzyme inhibitors and/or beta blockers on the cardiomyopathy in Duchenne muscular dystrophy. Am J Cardiol 2012;110(1):98–102.
80. Cox GF, Kunkel LM. Dystrophies and heart disease. Curr Opin Cardiol 1997; 12(3):329–43.
81. Nigro G, Comi LI, Politano L, et al. The incidence and evolution of cardiomyopathy in Duchenne muscular dystrophy. Int J Cardiol 1990;26(3):271–7.
82. Giglio V, Pasceri V, Messano L, et al. Ultrasound tissue characterization detects preclinical myocardial structural changes in children affected by Duchenne muscular dystrophy. J Am Coll Cardiol 2003;42(2):309–16.
83. Takenaka A, Yokota M, Iwase M, et al. Discrepancy between systolic and diastolic dysfunction of the left ventricle in patients with Duchenne muscular dystrophy. Eur Heart J 1993;14(5):669–76.
84. Soslow JH, Damon BM, Saville BR, et al. Evaluation of post-contrast myocardial t1 in duchenne muscular dystrophy using cardiac magnetic resonance imaging. Pediatr Cardiol 2015;36(1):49–56.
85. Hor KN, Kissoon N, Mazur W, et al. Regional circumferential strain is a biomarker for disease severity in duchenne muscular dystrophy heart disease: a cross-sectional study. Pediatr Cardiol 2014;36(1):111–9.
86. Menon SC, Etheridge SP, Liesemer KN, et al. Predictive value of myocardial delayed enhancement in Duchenne muscular dystrophy. Pediatr Cardiol 2014; 35(7):1279–85.
87. Romfh A, McNally EM. Cardiac assessment in duchenne and becker muscular dystrophies. Curr Heart Fail Rep 2010;7(4):212–8.

88. Allen HD, Flanigan KM, Thrush PT, et al. A randomized, double-blind trial of lisinopril and losartan for the treatment of cardiomyopathy in duchenne muscular dystrophy. PLoS Curr 2013;5.

89. Duboc D, Meune C, Lerebours G, et al. Effect of perindopril on the onset and progression of left ventricular dysfunction in Duchenne muscular dystrophy. J Am Coll Cardiol 2005;45(6):855–7.

90. Chenard AA, Becane HM, Tertrain F, et al. Ventricular arrhythmia in Duchenne muscular dystrophy: prevalence, significance and prognosis. Neuromuscul Disord 1993;3(3):201–6.

91. Corrado G, Lissoni A, Beretta S, et al. Prognostic value of electrocardiograms, ventricular late potentials, ventricular arrhythmias, and left ventricular systolic dysfunction in patients with Duchenne muscular dystrophy. Am J Cardiol 2002;89(7):838–41.

92. Thrush PT, Allen HD, Viollet L, et al. Re-examination of the electrocardiogram in boys with Duchenne muscular dystrophy and correlation with its dilated cardiomyopathy. Am J Cardiol 2009;103(2):262–5.

93. Birnkrant DJ, Bushby KM, Amin RS, et al. The respiratory management of patients with duchenne muscular dystrophy: a DMD care considerations working group specialty article. Pediatr Pulmonol 2010;45(8):739–48.

94. Bersanini C, Khirani S, Ramirez A, et al. Nocturnal hypoxaemia and hypercapnia in children with neuromuscular disorders. Eur Respir J 2012;39(5):1206–12.

95. Raphael JC, Dazord A, Jaillard P, et al. Assessment of quality of life for home ventilated patients with Duchenne muscular dystrophy. Rev Neurol (Paris) 2002;158(4):453–60 [in French].

96. Eagle M, Bourke J, Bullock R, et al. Managing Duchenne muscular dystrophy–the additive effect of spinal surgery and home nocturnal ventilation in improving survival. Neuromuscul Disord 2007;17(6):470–5.

97. Townsend EL, Tamhane H, Gross KD. Effects of AFO use on walking in boys with Duchenne muscular dystrophy: a pilot study. Pediatr Phys Ther 2014;27(1):24–9.

98. Alemdaroglu I, Karaduman A, Yilmaz OT, et al. Different types of upper extremity exercise training in Duchenne muscular dystrophy: effects on functional performance, strength, endurance, and ambulation. Muscle Nerve 2014. [Epub ahead of print].

99. Eagle M. Report on the muscular dystrophy campaign workshop: exercise in neuromuscular diseases Newcastle, January 2002. Neuromuscul Disord 2002;12(10):975–83.

100. Jansen M, van Alfen N, Geurts AC, et al. Assisted bicycle training delays functional deterioration in boys with Duchenne muscular dystrophy: the randomized controlled trial "no use is disuse". Neurorehabil Neural Repair 2013;27(9):816–27.

101. Markert CD, Case LE, Carter GT, et al. Exercise and Duchenne muscular dystrophy: where we have been and where we need to go. Muscle Nerve 2012;45(5):746–51.

102. Henricson E, Abresch R, Han JJ, et al. The 6-minute walk test and person-reported outcomes in boys with duchenne muscular dystrophy and typically developing controls: longitudinal comparisons and clinically-meaningful changes over one year. PLoS Curr 2013;5.

103. McDonald CM, Henricson EK, Abresch RT, et al. The 6-minute walk test and other clinical endpoints in duchenne muscular dystrophy: reliability, concurrent validity, and minimal clinically important differences from a multicenter study. Muscle Nerve 2013;48(3):357–68.

104. McDonald CM, Henricson EK, Abresch RT, et al. The 6-minute walk test and other endpoints in Duchenne muscular dystrophy: longitudinal natural history observations over 48 weeks from a multicenter study. Muscle Nerve 2013; 48(3):343–56.

105. Mazzone E, Vasco G, Sormani MP, et al. Functional changes in Duchenne muscular dystrophy: a 12-month longitudinal cohort study. Neurology 2011; 77(3):250–6.

106. Romero NB, Braun S, Benveniste O, et al. Phase I study of dystrophin plasmid-based gene therapy in Duchenne/Becker muscular dystrophy. Hum Gene Ther 2004;15(11):1065–76.

107. Mendell JR, Rodino-Klapac L, Sahenk Z, et al. Gene therapy for muscular dystrophy: lessons learned and path forward. Neurosci Lett 2012;527(2):90–9.

108. Mendell JR, Campbell K, Rodino-Klapac L, et al. Dystrophin immunity in Duchenne's muscular dystrophy. N Engl J Med 2010;363(15):1429–37.

109. Mendell JR, Rodino-Klapac LR, Rosales XQ, et al. Sustained alpha-sarcoglycan gene expression after gene transfer in limb-girdle muscular dystrophy, type 2D. Ann Neurol 2010;68(5):629–38.

110. Rodino-Klapac LR, Montgomery CL, Bremer WG, et al. Persistent expression of FLAG-tagged micro dystrophin in nonhuman primates following intramuscular and vascular delivery. Mol Ther 2010;18(1):109–17.

111. Heller KN, Montgomery CL, Janssen PM, et al. AAV-mediated overexpression of human alpha7 integrin leads to histological and functional improvement in dystrophic mice. Mol Ther 2013;21(3):520–5.

112. Martin PT, Xu R, Rodino-Klapac LR, et al. Overexpression of Galgt2 in skeletal muscle prevents injury resulting from eccentric contractions in both mdx and wild-type mice. Am J Physiol Cell Physiol 2009;296(3):C476–88.

113. Chicoine LG, Rodino-Klapac LR, Shao G, et al. Vascular delivery of rAAVrh74.MCK.GALGT2 to the gastrocnemius muscle of the rhesus macaque stimulates the expression of dystrophin and laminin alpha2 surrogates. Mol Ther 2014;22(4):713–24.

114. Mendell JR, Sahenk Z, Malik V, et al. A phase 1/2a follistatin gene therapy trial for becker muscular dystrophy. Mol Ther 2015;23(1):192–201.

115. Touznik A, Lee JJ, Yokota T. New developments in exon skipping and splice modulation therapies for neuromuscular diseases. Expert Opin Biol Ther 2014;14(6):809–19.

116. Voit T, Topaloglu H, Straub V, et al. Safety and efficacy of drisapersen for the treatment of Duchenne muscular dystrophy (DEMAND II): an exploratory, randomised, placebo-controlled phase 2 study. Lancet Neurol 2014;13(10): 987–96.

117. Hammond SM, Wood MJ. PRO-051, an antisense oligonucleotide for the potential treatment of Duchenne muscular dystrophy. Curr Opin Mol Ther 2010;12(4): 478–86.

118. Mendell JR, Rodino-Klapac LR, Sahenk Z, et al. Eteplirsen for the treatment of Duchenne muscular dystrophy. Ann Neurol 2013;74(5):637–47.

119. Cirak S, Feng L, Anthony K, et al. Restoration of the dystrophin-associated glycoprotein complex after exon skipping therapy in Duchenne muscular dystrophy. Mol Ther 2012;20(2):462–7.

120. Cirak S, Arechavala-Gomeza V, Guglieri M, et al. Exon skipping and dystrophin restoration in patients with Duchenne muscular dystrophy after systemic phosphorodiamidate morpholino oligomer treatment: an open-label, phase 2, dose-escalation study. Lancet 2011;378(9791):595–605.

121. Aartsma-Rus A, Fokkema I, Verschuuren J, et al. Theoretic applicability of antisense-mediated exon skipping for Duchenne muscular dystrophy mutations. Hum Mutat 2009;30(3):293–9.
122. Barton-Davis ER, Cordier L, Shoturma DI, et al. Aminoglycoside antibiotics restore dystrophin function to skeletal muscles of mdx mice. J Clin Invest 1999;104(4):375–81.
123. Malik V, Rodino-Klapac LR, Viollet L, et al. Gentamicin-induced readthrough of stop codons in Duchenne muscular dystrophy. Ann Neurol 2010;67(6):771–80.
124. Bushby K, Finkel R, Wong B, et al. Ataluren treatment of patients with nonsense mutation dystrophinopathy. Muscle Nerve 2014;50(4):477–87.

Spinal Muscular Atrophies

Basil T. Darras, MD

KEYWORDS

- Spinal muscular atrophy • 5q SMA • Non-5q SMAs
- Survival of motor neuron protein • Werdnig-Hoffmann disease • Dubowitz disease
- Kugelberg-Welander disease

KEY POINTS

- Spinal muscular atrophies (SMAs) are hereditary degenerative disorders of lower motor neurons associated with progressive muscle weakness and atrophy.
- SMA subtypes are classified by severity of weakness: type I nonsitters, type II sitters, type III walkers, and type IV adult-onset patients with mild phenotype.
- The survival of motor neuron (SMN) gene is present in 2 copies on each chromosome 5, designated *SMN1* and *SMN2*. A majority of cases are caused by homozygous deletions of exon 7 of the telomeric *SMN1* gene on chromosome 5q.
- An approximate inverse correlation exists between *SMN2* gene copy number, which varies normally in the population, the level of SMN protein, and severity of disease; however, the role of the SMN protein is still under active investigation.
- No cure exists for SMA. Treatment consists of multidisciplinary management of symptoms. Trials are under way to identify agents for therapy.

INTRODUCTION

Spinal muscular atrophies (SMAs) are genetic disorders clinically characterized by progressive muscle weakness and atrophy associated with degeneration of spinal and, in the most severely affected patients, lower bulbar motor neurons. Classic proximal SMA, the most common form of SMA and the leading genetic cause of infant mortality, seems to be found in practically all populations, but it is diagnosed more frequently in infants and children than in adults. The severe form of SMA was first described in the early 1890s by clinician Guido Werdnig[1] of the University of Graz, Austria, and physician Johann Hoffmann[2] of Heidelberg, Germany. Their reports described the neuromuscular phenotype of the disease and the associated loss of anterior horn cells in the spinal cord.

Disclosures: Dr. Darras receives research support from PTC Therapeutics and ISIS Pharmaceuticals.
This article was funded in part by the SMA Foundation (New York, NY).
Division of Clinical Neurology, Department of Neurology, Boston Children's Hospital, 300 Longwood Avenue, Fegan 11, Boston, MA 02115, USA
E-mail address: basil.darras@childrens.harvard.edu

0031-3955/15/$ – see front matter © 2015 Elsevier Inc. All rights reserved.

SMA results from homozygous deletions or mutations involving the "survival of motor neuron" (SMN) gene at locus 5q13. The *SMN* gene is present in 2 copies on each chromosome 5, designated *SMN1* and *SMN2*, forming an inverted duplication (**Fig. 1**). *SMN2* is differentiated from *SMN1* by 5 nucleotide changes that do not change amino acids. The crucial single nucleotide change in *SMN2* creates an exonic splicing suppressor in exon 7 that leads to exclusion of exon 7 in most transcripts[3]; thus, the duplicated (*SMN2*) gene produces less functional SMN protein. Most patients with 5q proximal recessive SMA harbor homozygous deletions involving exon 7 of the *SMN1* gene but maintain at least 1 copy of *SMN2*. An approximate correlation exists between *SMN2* gene copy number, which varies normally in the population, the level of SMN protein, and severity of disease; however, the role of the SMN protein is still under active investigation. Modifying genes that serve other roles in motor neuron function seem present as well. SMA may involve dysfunction of more than lower motor neurons, with abnormalities of the neuromuscular junction noted in animal models and abnormal muscle development in the most severely affected patients. There are also many other types of SMA, known as non-5q SMAs, which are related to mutations in various genes expressed in a wide range of tissues, including the nervous system.

EPIDEMIOLOGY

The incidence of SMA has been estimated at 1 in 6000 to 11,000 live births[4–7] or approximately 7.8 to 10 per 100,000 live births[8–10] and at 4.1 per 100,000 live births for type I SMA.[8] The estimated panethnic disease frequency is approximately 1 in 11,000.[7] The carrier frequency for mutations in the *SMN1* gene has been estimated from 1:38 to 1:70. Despite the high carrier frequency, the incidence of SMA is lower than expected. It has been postulated that this may reflect that some fetuses have a 0/0 SMN1/SMN2 genotype (ie, no SMN protein is present at all), which is known in other species to be embryonic lethal.[11]

CLINICAL CHARACTERISTICS

Although most patients with SMA have deletions or mutations involving the *SMN1* gene, a range of phenotypic severity permits division into 4 broad clinical subtypes. It is recognized that the subtypes represent a phenotypic continuum extending from the very severe, with onset in utero, to the very mild, with onset during adulthood; there is also a spectrum of severity within each of these groups (**Table 1**).[12,13] For the purposes of clinical classification or of guidelines developed for standards of care, the maximal functional status achieved approach, which classifies type I patients as non-sitters, type II patients as sitters, and type III patients as walkers, has been used.[14,15] Patients with a mild phenotype and onset during middle or late age are classified as type IV. The age at onset is also considered in the classification but because of potential overlap between subtypes and the difficulty in accurately determining the onset of symptoms, it has not been considered as the sole determinant of disease subtype.

Type I Spinal Muscular Atrophy

After the initial description of infantile SMA by Werdnig and Hoffmann in the early 1890s and further descriptions made by Sylvestre in 1899[16] and Beevor in 1902,[17] infantile or type I SMA was described again in detail, both clinically and pathologically, by Randolph Byers and Betty Banker at Boston Children's Hospital in 1961.[18] Patients with type I SMA, also known as Werdnig-Hoffmann disease, present between birth and 6 months of age. Type I SMA has been further subdivided into 3 groups: type IA (or type 0 in certain reports[19]) with onset in utero and presentation at birth, type

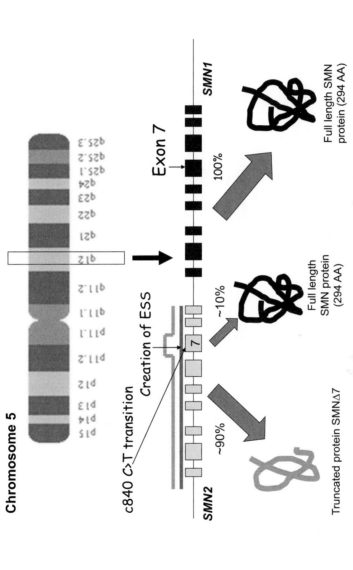

Fig. 1. Schematic diagram of human *SMN1* and *SMN2* genes on chromosome 5. Patients with SMA have deletions or mutations in both copies of *SMN1*. A C-to-T transition at position 6 of *SMN2* creates an exonic splicing suppressor (ESS) that leads to skipping of exon 7 during transcription and production of truncated, nonfunctional SMN protein. A small amount (approximately 10%) of full-length messenger RNA, however, is produced from the *SMN2* gene, resulting in functional, full-length SMN protein. (AA, amino acids.)

Table 1
Clinical classification of spinal muscular atrophy

Spinal Muscular Atrophy Type	Other Names	Age at Onset	Life Span	Highest Motor Milestone Achieved	Other Features	Proportion of Total Spinal Muscular Atrophy (%)
Type IA	Prenatal, congenital SMA, Werdnig-Hoffmann disease	Prenatal	<6 mo	Mostly unable to achieve motor milestones	• Severe weakness at birth • Profound hypotonia • Facial diplegia • Areflexia • Early respiratory failure • Joint contractures	60[a]
Type IB, type IC	Werdnig-Hoffmann disease, Severe SMA (nonsitters)	Type IB (0–3 mo) Type IC (3–6 mo)	<2 y without respiratory support	Never sits unsupported	• Weakness • Frog-leg posture, hypotonia • Tongue fasciculations • Hyporeflexia, areflexia • Suck and swallow difficulties • Respiratory failure	60

Type II	Intermediate SMA (sitters), Dubowitz disease	6–18 mo	>2 y ~70% alive at 25 y of age	Sits independently, never stands or walks	• Proximal weakness, hypotonia • Postural hand tremor • Hyporeflexia • Average or above-average intellectual skills by adolescence • Scoliosis	27
Type III	Kugelberg-Welander disease, Mild SMA (walkers)	>18 mo Type IIIA (prior to 3 y) Type IIIB (after 3 y)	Almost normal	Stands and walks	• May have hand tremor • Resembles muscular dystrophy	12
Type IV	Adult SMA	>21 y	Normal	Normal		1

[a] SMA types I, IA, IB, and IC all have a 60% proportion of total SMA.

Adapted from Markowitz JA, Singh P, Darras BT. Spinal muscular atrophy: a clinical and research update. Pediatr Neurol 2012;46:2; with permission.

IB with onset of symptoms prior to 3 months of age, and type IC with onset between 3 and 6 months of age. Infants with SMA type I have progressive proximal weakness that affects the legs more than the arms. They have poor head control, hypotonia that causes them to assume a frog-leg posture when lying and to slip through on vertical suspension, and areflexia. They are never able to sit (nonsitters) (see **Table 1**). There is also weakness of the intercostal muscles with relative sparing of the diaphragm, producing a bell-shaped chest and a pattern of paradoxic or belly breathing. Infants with type I SMA also classically exhibit tongue fasciculations and eventually have difficulty swallowing, with risk for aspiration and failure to thrive. Other cranial nerves are not as affected, although facial weakness does occur at later stages of the disease. Cognition is normal, and they are often noted at diagnosis to have a bright, alert expression that contrasts with their generalized weakness. Infants with type I SMA usually develop respiratory failure by age 2 years or much earlier, and in the past most did not survive past 2 years; however, there has been some increase in survival in recent years with the use of assisted ventilation (described in more detail later) and other interventions.[12,20–22] Prior natural history studies have reported shortened life span, with 68% mortality within 2 years and 82% by 4 years of age.[23,24] The application of nutritional and respiratory interventions has reduced the mortality to approximately 30% at 2 years, but approximately half the survivors are fully dependent on noninvasive ventilation.[25] In a recent observational study, the median age at reaching the combined endpoint of requiring at least 16 h/d of noninvasive ventilation or death was 13.5 months. Infants with 2 *SMN2* copies had greater morbidity and mortality than those with 3 copies. The need for nutritional support preceded that for ventilation support.[26]

It was previously believed that SMA is a purely motor neuron disorder. Recent studies have shown, however, that severe type I SMA can result in various organ manifestations, apart from spinal cord motor neurons, such as brain, cardiac, vascular, and even sensory nerve involvement. Recent autopsy studies have shown increasing evidence of congenital heart disorders in severe SMA, most commonly hypoplastic left heart syndrome[27]; however, a chance association has not been firmly excluded. Studies on various mouse models have also found that severe SMN protein deficiency might present as vasculopathy. This was also noted in the case reports of 2 unrelated patients with severe type I SMA . Both infants developed ulcerations and necroses of the fingers and toes.[28] Autonomic dysfunction is thought to be the primary cause of this vasculopathy.[29] In a different biopsy study done by Rudnik-Schöneborn and colleagues[30] on 19 patients with infantile SMA, significant sensory nerve pathology was found in severe type I SMA patients, whereas no sensory involvement was found in type II and type III SMA patients.

Type II Spinal Muscular Atrophy

This intermediate form of SMA was first reported in 1893[31] at the University of Edinburgh, United Kingdom, and described again by Byers and Banker in 1961[18] and in detail by Dubowitz in 1964.[32] Patients with type II SMA, also known as intermediate SMA or Dubowitz disease, are able to sit unsupported at some point (sitters) but are never able to stand alone or walk (see **Table 1**). The onset of symptoms is between 6 and 18 months of age. They have progressive proximal weakness affecting legs more than arms, hypotonia, and areflexia. They also develop progressive scoliosis, which, in combination with intercostal muscle weakness, results in significant restrictive lung disease as they grow older. They develop joint contractures and can have ankylosis of the mandible. They exhibit tremor, or polyminimyoclonus, of the hands.[12,22] Although their body mass index may be low (at the third percentile or less when compared with normal children), the high-functioning, nonambulatory patients have a higher relative fat mass index and are at risk of becoming overweight.[33] Cognition is normal and verbal intelligence may be above average.[34] In a study done on 240 type II patients, survival rates were found to be 98.5% at 5 years and 68.5% at 25 years.[35] Patients may live into the third decade, but life expectancy is shortened due to the risk of respiratory compromise.[12,22]

Type III Spinal Muscular Atrophy

In 1956, Kugelberg and Welander[36] described a much milder form of SMA characterized by prolonged ambulation. Patients with type III SMA, also known as Kugelberg-Welander disease, are able to stand alone and walk at some point (walkers). The onset of symptoms occurs after the age of 18 months; it has further been subdivided into type IIIA (onset between 18 months and 3 years) and type IIIB (onset after 3 years). They have progressive proximal weakness affecting legs more than arms and may ultimately need to use a wheelchair, but they generally develop little to no respiratory muscle weakness or severe scoliosis. Loss of ambulation increases the risk of these complications. They may have tremor or polyminimyoclonus of the hands. Sometimes, the calves of these patients can be prominent and hence type III SMA can be confused with Becker muscular atrophy. Life expectancy is not significantly different compared with the normal population (see **Table 1**).[12,22,35]

There has been much debate about the appropriate classification of patients into these 3 types of SMA because, as discussed previously, there are patients who within these categories exhibit phenotypes of differing severities. A classification system based on a continuous rather than discrete variable (eg, type 1.8 SMA in cases of less severely affected type I patients) has been proposed to better capture the clinical spectrum of these patients.[13]

Outliers

There are also patients who are outliers on either end of the phenotypic spectrum. As discussed previously, a type IA SMA (formerly known as type 0) has been used to describe neonates who present with severe weakness and profound hypotonia, probably of prenatal onset, as well as with a history of decreased fetal movements. A majority do not attain any motor milestones. Other findings include areflexia, facial diplegia, atrial septal defects, and joint contractures. In type IA SMA, respiratory failure forms an important cause of morbidity and mortality, requiring noninvasive ventilation and endotracheal intubation at birth. Life expectancy is reduced and most of them are unable to survive beyond 6 months of age (see **Table 1**).[19,37] Furthermore, arthrogryposis multiplex congenita (congenital joint contractures involving at least 2 regions of body) has been noted in SMA patients with *SMN1* gene deletions,[38] and congenital axonal neuropathy involving motor and sensory nerves in conjunction with facial weakness, joint contractures, ophthalmoplegia, and respiratory failure at birth has been reported in 3 newborn siblings with deletions in the SMA chromosomal region.[39]

A milder adult-onset SMA, or type IV SMA, has also been described with onset of symptoms after age 21 years and essentially normal life span. Most patients with the SMA types IA and IV phenotypes have homozygous deletions of exon 7 in *SMN1*, but, as discussed later, the *SMN2* copy number is usually only 1 in type IA SMA and 4 to 5 in type IV SMA.[12,40]

Other Spinal Muscular Atrophies

The non-5q13–associated SMAs are a heterogeneous group of motor neuron diseases associated with mutations in a variety of different genes (eg, X-linked and autosomal dominant or recessive SMAs), distal SMAs (DSMAs) or segmental SMAs, or distal hereditary motor neuropathies or neuronopathies (dHMNs).[12,40,41] Patients with these disorders generally have some clinical characteristics that can help differentiate them from those with 5q13-associated or classic SMA.[42]

Non-5q SMAs are genetically heterogeneous, clinically diverse, and rare compared with 5q SMA.[42,43] Classification by distribution of weakness (distal, proximal, or bulbar) and mode of inheritance is currently used by most experts in this field.[44,45] The classification scheme outlined in **Table 2**, although based on these premises, has its own limitations.[42] It does not include all non-5q motor axonopathies or neuro-nopathies or SMA plus syndromes, and especially excludes conditions with uncertain nosology or those with no gene/locus information.

DSMAs present with predominantly distal weakness and exhibit significant phenotypic overlap with dHMNs. There is a condition known as SMA with respiratory distress type 1 (SMARD1) that needs to be differentiated from type I SMA. In SMARD1, most patients have low birth weight and present within the first 3 to 6 months of life with diaphragmatic paralysis, hypotonia, and distal more than proximal weakness as well as with sensory and autonomic nerve involvement; these infants become ventilator dependent. In a series of 141 *SMN1* mutation-negative patients presenting with respiratory distress and diaphragmatic and intercostal weakness, 3 distinct phenotypes were noted[46]: (1) congenital contractures with associated respiratory failure at birth; (2) respiratory distress with onset between 3 and 6 months, hip flexion with minimal or no movements of the distal muscle groups; and (3) respiratory distress after age 6 months with congenital contractures. In a series of 10 patients with SMARD1 from the Netherlands, significant phenotypic variability was noted with no clear phenotype-genotype correlations.[47] CPK is usually normal and there is no cardiac involvement. In children with SMARD1, life expectancy is limited but rarely patients can have only mild sleep hyperventilation.[48] SMARD1 is caused by mutations in the gene *IGHMBP2* encoding the immunoglobulin μ-binding protein.[48]

HMN5A and Charcot-Marie-Tooth (CMT) type 2D are allelic conditions due to *GARS* gene mutations and are characterized initially by upper limb predominance of the weakness, with selective atrophy of the thenar eminence and first dorsal interosseous muscles; by contrast, the hypothenar eminence is spared until later in the course of the disease. Mutations in *BSCL2* gene result in allelic phenotypes, including spastic paraplegia with amyotrophy of hands and feet (Silver syndrome/SPG17), congenital generalized lipodystrophy type 2, and DSMA with early hand involvement (HMN5B).

Non-5q SMAs with proximal or diffuse weakness include SMA with lower extremity predominance caused by dominant mutations in the dynein gene (*DYNC1H1*), which encodes a microtubule motor protein and one of its cargo adaptors, BICD2.[45,49] In a cohort of 32 patients with *BICD2* mutations, the main features were lower extremity predominant weakness and wasting of both proximal and distal muscle groups, resulting in delayed motor milestones and ankle contractures.[50] At presentation, other features include congenital dislocation of the hips and arthrogryposis. In this cohort, a subset of patients had upper motor neuron signs, but all members had static or only slowly progressive lower motor neuron disease, and most remained ambulant throughout their lives.[50]

TRPV4-related disorders are another example of diverse phenotypes, ranging from congenital SMA with contractures to CMT2C associated with vocal cord and phrenic nerve paralysis and to SMA with scapuloperoneal and laryngeal distribution of weakness. There are also non-5q spinal and bulbar muscular atrophies and SMA plus types (see **Table 2**). Some of the arthrogryposis multiplex congenita syndromes need to be considered in the differential diagnosis of type IA SMA due to *SMN1* mutations but

Table 2
Simplified classification of non-5q spinal muscular atrophies

Gene/Locus	Disease/Phenotype, Selected Distinguishing Features	Selected OMIM Designations
DSMA/dHMN		
Autosomal recessive		
IGHMBP2	SMA with respiratory distress or diaphragmatic SMA	SMARD1/HMN6 or DSMA1
9p21.1-pL2	dHMN	DSMA2/HMNJ
11q13	DSMA	DSMA3/HMN3,4
PLEKHG5	Lower motor neuron syndrome with childhood onset	DSMA4
Autosomal dominant		
7q34-q36	dHMN/DSMA, juvenile	HMN1
HSPB8	Distal adult HMN, type IIA	HMN2A
HSPB1	dHMN, type IIB	HMN2B
HSPB3	dHMN, type IIC	HMN2C
GARS	DSMA with upper limb predominance, type VA CMT disease 2D	HMN5A[a] CMT2D
BSCL2	DSMA with upper limb predominance, type VB Silver syndrome/SPG17	HMN5B[a]
SLCA7	dHMN with vocal cord paralysis	HMN7A
Dynactin1	dHMN with vocal cord paralysis	HMN7B
Proximal SMA (± distal involvement)		
Autosomal dominant		
VAPB	SMA with late-onset, Finkel type/ALS8	
TRPV4	Congenital SMA with contractures/SMA, congenital, nonprogressive, with lower limb predominance Scapuloperoneal SMA CMT, type 2C	SPSMA HMSN2C
DYNC1H1, BICD2	SMA with lower extremity predominance (early onset)	SMALED
TFG	HMSN, proximal (Okinawa type)	HMSNP
Other non-5q spinal and bulbar muscular atrophies, SMA plus types		
Autosomal recessive		
GLE1	Lethal arthrogryposis with anterior horn cell disease or lethal congenital contracture syndrome	LAAHD
VRK1, EXOCS3	PCH with SMA	SMA-PCH1
RFT2 (C20ORF54)	BVVLS Fazio-Londe disease, bulbar palsy	BVVLS
X-linked recessive		
Androgen receptor	Bulbo-SMA, Kennedy disease	SBMA/SMAX1
UBA1	Infantile SMA with arthrogryposis	SMAX2
ATP7A	DSMA, X-linked	SMAX3

[a] Listed in the Online Mendelian Inheritance in Man (OMIM) catalog as HMN5.

also other non-5q SMAs presenting at birth with arthrogryposis, like the lethal congenital contracture syndrome related to *GLE1* gene mutations. Brown-Vialetto-van Laere syndrome (BVVLS) and Fazio-Londe disease are clinically overlapping motor neuron diseases involving primarily the lower cranial nerves and presenting with pontobulbar palsy, sensorineural deafness (BVVLS), and respiratory failure. BVVLS and Fazio-Londe disease have been linked to mutations in the *RFT2* (C20ORF54) gene and defective riboflavin transport.[51]

The autosomal recessive pontocerebellar hypoplasias (PCH) feature postnatal progressive microcephaly combined with brainstem and cerebellar hemispheres that are hypoplastic at birth, with the cerebellar vermis relatively spared. To date, 7 PCH clinical syndromes have been described (PCH1–7).[52]

When PCH is combined with anterior horn cell degeneration, the designation PCH1 is applied; PCH1 has been linked to mutations in the *VRK1* gene.[53] This is an unusual phenotype, in that a characteristic brain malformation is combined with abnormalities of motor neurons in the spinal cord. Recently, Rudnik-Schöneborn and colleagues[54] sequenced *EXOCS3* in a cohort of 27 families with PCH1, and found mutations in 37%. A common c.395A > C, p.D132A mutation was present in approximately half of these families. Although there was some variation in clinical features, enough phenotype-genotype correlation was present to underscore the continued usefulness of PCH1 as a clinical category.

Other non-5q spinal and bulbar SMAs include X-linked SMA type 1 (SMAX1) and spinal-bulbar muscular atrophy (SBMA), also known as Kennedy disease. SBMA has an onset between 20 and 50 years; adult men with SBMA often present with proximal muscle weakness and atrophy, bulbar symptoms, fasciculations, gynecomastia, testicular atrophy, and reduced fertility. It is related to an expansion of a CAG trinucleotide repeat in the androgen receptor gene.[55] Furthermore, infantile SMA with arthrogryposis with or without bone fractures, dysmorphic features, myopathic facies, hypotonia, areflexia, and digital contractures may represent a lethal X-linked form of SMA (SMAX2) and be confused with type IA SMA; mutations in the *UBA1* gene have been detected in this group of patients.[56] A clinical and pathologic study of a *UBA1* gene mutation–positive SMAX2 case showed white matter abnormalities on MRI brain imaging and prominent motor and sensory systems as well as cerebellar involvement and widespread inflammatory changes on muscle biopsy.[57]

GENETICS
The Survival of Motor Neuron Gene

In 1995, Lefebvre and colleagues[58] identified the *SMN* gene within the SMA chromosomal region, which was absent or interrupted in 98.6% of the patients in their group. The structure of this region is complex, with a large inverted duplication of a 500-kb element. This contains the *SMN1* gene, which is deleted or interrupted in patients with SMA and is evolutionarily older, in the telomeric portion of the region; and the *SMN2* gene, a duplication of *SMN1* that differs from it by only 5 nucleotides, in the centromeric portion (see **Fig. 1**). The critical difference between *SMN1* and *SMN2* is a C to T transition that creates an exon splicing suppressor in exon 7 of *SMN2*. Although this splice modulator change is translationally silent (ie, it does not change the amino acid sequence), it affects the alternative splicing of the gene, so that exon 7 is spliced out of or excluded from most *SMN2* mRNA transcripts. This altered mRNA results in production of a truncated version of the SMN protein, which does not oligomerize efficiently and is degraded. Because exon 7 is not always spliced out of all

SMN2 mRNA, a small amount of full-length transcript and hence functional protein is produced by SMN2, but it yields only on average approximately 10% as much as that produced by SMN1.[59] In patients with SMA, both copies of the SMN1 gene are deleted or disrupted, so the individual is left with only the small amount of SMN protein produced by the remaining copies of SMN2. The amount of SMN protein is inversely correlated with the severity of disease.[60]

Approximately 95% to 98% of patients with SMA harbor homozygous deletions of exon 7 of the telomeric SMN1 gene (**Table 3**). The remainder have small intragenic mutations or have undergone gene conversions from SMN1 to SMN2. De novo mutations occur at a rate of approximately 2%, which is relatively high, and explained by the fact that this region of chromosome 5 is unstable, containing not only the inverted repeat of SMN1 and SMN2, but other surrounding low copy number repeats.

The number of copies of SMN2 per chromosome 5 varies among normal individuals, and 10% to 15% of the population possess no copies of SMN2.[6,61] Among patients with SMA, a clear correlation has been established between SMN2 copy number and phenotypic severity. Feldkotter and colleagues[61] in 2002 found that, in their series, 80% of patients with type I SMA had 1 or 2 copies of SMN2, 82% of patients with type II had 3 copies of SMN2, and 96% of patients with type III had 3 or 4 SMN2 copies (**Fig. 2**). Studies by Mailman and colleagues[10] in 2002 and Arkblad and colleagues[62] in 2009 found similar results (95%–100% of type I patients had 1 or 2 copies of SMN2, and all type III patients had at least 3 copies of SMN2). This correlation is not so perfect, however, as to permit the absolute prediction of clinical severity based on SMN2 copy number, especially in the intermediate forms of the disease where there is some overlap (patients with 3 copies of SMN2 have been described with all 3 phenotypes).[63,64] One reason for the overlap is that not all copies of SMN2 gene are equal; in terms of full-length SMN protein production, some copies probably produce less and some more than 10% functional protein. In general, however, a patient with 1 or 2 copies of SMN2 is highly likely to present with type IA, IB, or IC SMA.[10,61] Unaffected

Table 3
Genetic diagnostic testing in spinal muscular atrophy

Type of Mutation	Test Applied	Mutation Detection Rate
Homozygous deletion of exon 7[a]	SMN1 Targeted mutation analysis PCR/restriction enzyme analysis or MLPA methodologies	~95%–98%
Compound heterozygosity (deletion of SMN1 exon 7 [allele 1] and an intragenic mutation of SMN1[b] [allele 2])	Targeted mutation analysis combined with SMN1 gene sequence analysis[c]	2%–5%
SMN2 copy number[d]	Quantitative PCR analysis and other methodologies[e]	N/A

[a] Testing for exon 8 deletion is not necessary.
[b] Small intragenic deletions/insertions and nonsense, missense, and splice site mutations.
[c] Whole-gene deletions/duplications are not detected.
[d] SMN2 copy number ranges from 0 to 5.
[e] MLPA, long-range PCR, CMA that includes the SMN1, SMN2 chromosomal segment.
  Adapted from Markowitz JA, Singh P, Darras BT. Spinal muscular atrophy: a clinical and research update. Pediatr Neurol 2012;46:5; with permission.

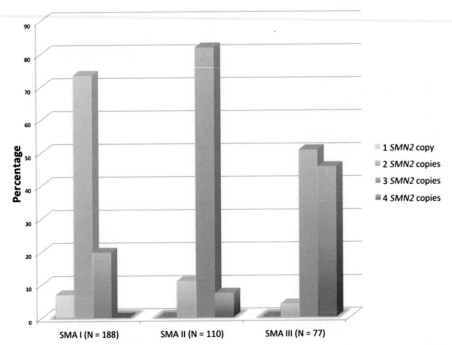

Fig. 2. Frequency of patients with SMA types I, II, and III and *SMN2* copy numbers. In SMA type I, 80% of patients had 1 or 2 copies of SMN2, 82% of patients with type II had 3 copies of *SMN2*, and 96% of patients with type III carried 3 or 4 *SMN2* copies. (*From* Feldkotter M, Schwarzer V, Wirth R, et al. Quantitative analyses of *SMN1* and *SMN2* based on based on real-time lightCycler PCR: fast and highly reliable carrier testing and prediction of severity of spinal muscular atrophy. Am J Hum Genet 2002;70:363, Philadelphia: Elsevier; with permission.)

family members with homozygous *SMN1* deletions and 5 copies of *SMN2* have been described, which suggests that *SMN2* copy number alone cannot be the sole modifying factor in disease severity because there are patients with type III SMA who also have 5 copies of *SMN2*.[10,65]

Regarding the level of SMN protein itself, although there is in general an inverse correlation between the level of SMN protein and severity of disease, this correlation does not seem to be as close as that between *SMN2* copy number and phenotype.[66]

Genetic Diagnosis

Genetic testing for SMA can be performed with polymerase chain reaction (PCR)–based targeted mutation analysis using a restriction enzyme that digests exon 7 of the *SMN1* gene (see **Table 3**). Multiplex ligation probe amplification (MLPA) methodology, however, is currently applied in most DNA diagnostic laboratories for deletion analysis of exon 7 of the *SMN1* gene in potential probands and carriers. This type of targeted mutation testing in conjunction with sequence analysis can also detect individuals who are compound heterozygotes[61] with a deletion of exon 7 in 1 *SMN1* allele and an intragenic point mutation in the other allele. In such a case (approximately 2%–5% of individuals with clinical diagnosis of SMA), sequence analysis of the *SMN* gene detects the mutation; this sequence testing, however, does not detect exonic deletions or duplications[67] and does not determine whether the point mutation is in the SMN1 gene or SMN2 gene (if 1 of these genes is not deleted). Fortunately, certain point mutations have been described in more than 1 SMA patient already and thus the detection of a previously reported mutation supports its pathogenicity and its location in the SMN1 gene. The use of long-range PCR or subcloning can also allow specific analysis of SMN1 and confirm that the mutation is present in SMN1.[67]

Carrier testing is feasible and accurate in the parents of patients with homozygous deletions of exon 7 or compound heterozygosity using a PCR-based dosage assay, known as SMN gene dosage analysis. It can also be performed using other techniques like long-range PCR, MLPA, and chromosomal microarray (CMA) that includes this gene segment. Sequencing of the SMN gene detects point mutations in nondeletion carriers. Rarely, carriers may have 2 copies of SMN1 on 1 chromosome (a so-called 2 + 0 carrier); the incidence of this genotype is approximately 4% of the general population. In the 2 + 0 carriers, the SMA dosage carrier test is falsely normal and thus other methods may need to be pursued, such as family linkage analysis, to identify the disease-associated genotype in families in which a deletion mutation has been transmitted more than once from a parent with 2 copies of the SMN1 gene on gene dosage testing.[68–71] Due to the occurrence of de novo mutations in 2% of patients with SMA, 1 of the parents may not be a carrier.[67] So, in approximately 6% of parents of a child with SMA secondary to a homozygous SMN1 deletion, SMN1 gene dosage testing is normal.

As discussed previously, a general correlation has been found between SMN2 copy number and disease severity, and it is relatively straightforward to determine SMN2 copy number in individual patients using various methodologies. This correlation is not so strict, however, that the severity or type of disease can be reliably predicted based on copy number, and it is hence not advisable to offer families prognostic information based on SMN2 copy number assays.

OTHER DIAGNOSTIC TESTS

In patients with SMA, the serum creatine kinase may be 2- to 4-fold elevated but not more than 10 times normal.[22] Nerve conduction studies demonstrate normal sensory potentials but may show diminished compound motor action potential amplitudes.[72] Needle electromyography (EMG) in patients with type II/III SMA demonstrates a neurogenic pattern with high-amplitude, long-duration motor unit potentials with reduced recruitment pattern. Needle EMG in patients with type I SMA shows denervation changes but may not show evidence of reinnervation, because there may not have been enough SMN protein and/or time for this to occur yet. As discussed later, muscle biopsy in all types of SMA demonstrates a neurogenic pattern, with grouped atrophy; the small atrophic fibers are of both types (type 1 and type 2) whereas the large ones are always type 1 fibers. Although a neurogenic pattern with large group atrophy is common, a fetal appearance has been noted in muscle biopsy specimens from patients with type I SMA, leading some to question whether type I SMA may actually result from arrested development of the motor unit rather than degeneration of the motor neuron. A morphometric analysis of fetuses with type I SMA at 12 to 15 weeks showed delayed maturation of myotubes when compared with controls.[73] Although EMG continues to be used in the diagnosis of SMA in selected atypical cases, the use of muscle biopsy has become essentially obsolete.

DIFFERENTIAL DIAGNOSIS

The differential diagnosis of 5q SMA is listed in **Box 1**.

Box 1
Differential diagnosis of 5q spinal muscular atrophy

Spinal cord disorders

　Neoplasms (SMA types I, II, III)

　Other myelopathies (SMA types I, II, III)

Other motor neuron disorders

　SMARD1 (SMA type I)

　Juvenile muscular atrophy of distal upper extremity (Hirayama disease)

　Fazio-Londe disease, BVVLS

　Other non-5q SMAs (SMA types I, II, III)

　Juvenile ALS (SMA types I, II, III)

Neuropathies

　Congenital hypomyelinating or axonal neuropathies (SMA types I, II)

　Hereditary motor and sensory neuropathies (SMA types I, II, III)

　CIDP (SMA types II, III)

Neuromuscular junction disorders

　Botulism (SMA type I)

　Congenital myasthenic syndromes (SMA types I, II, III)

　Lambert-Eaton myasthenic syndrome (SMA type III)

　Autoimmune myasthenia gravis (SMA types II, III)

Myopathies

　Congenital myopathies (SMA types I, II, III)

　Congenital myotonic dystrophy (SMA type I)

　Congenital muscular dystrophies (SMA types I, II)

　Muscular dystrophies (DMD/BMD, LGMD) (SMA type III)

　Mitochondrial myopathies (SMA types I, II, III)

　Acid maltase/Pompe disease (SMA types I, II, III)

　Other metabolic myopathies (SMA types I, II, III)

　Inflammatory myopathies (SMA type III)

　Channelopathies (SMA type III)

Other disorders

　Chromosomal abnormalities (SMA types I, II, III)

　Prader-Willi syndrome (SMA type III)

　Central nervous system abnormalities (SMA types I, II, III)

　Hexosaminidase A deficiency (SMA types III, IV)

ALS, amyotrophic lateral sclerosis; BMD, Becker muscular dystrophy; CIDP, chronic inflammatory demyelinating polyneuropathy; DMD, Duchenne muscular dystrophy; LGMD, limb-girdle muscular dystrophy.

Modified from Markowitz JA, Singh P, Darras BT. Spinal muscular atrophy: a clinical and research update. Pediatr Neurol 2012;46:4; with permission.

TREATMENT

Currently, there is no cure for SMA. Despite the presence of homozygous deletions of *SMN1* in a majority of patients with SMA,[74] however, the unique structure of the 5q11.1-13.3 inverted duplication provides potential therapeutic targets. There has been great interest in identifying agents that can increase the amount of full-length SMN protein by up-regulating the expression of the *SMN2* gene or promoting inclusion of exon 7. Researchers are also actively exploring several other approaches to treatment.

Clinical Trials in Spinal Muscular Atrophy—Therapeutics

SMA is a unique translational disease because of the presence of the *SMN2* gene, which is a well-validated target for therapeutic interventions. The status of therapeutics development is shown in **Table 4**. The effort on therapeutics is aimed at finding pharmaceutical compounds that can up-regulate *SMN2* expression or affect other modifying genes to produce more functional SMN protein.

Agents that Up-regulate Survival of Motor Neuron 2 Gene Expression and Promote Exon 7 Inclusion

Small molecules

A class of drugs known as histone deacetylase inhibitors (HDACIs) has been investigated extensively as potential therapeutic agents in SMA.[75,76] Histones, which are core proteins in chromatin, play a role in epigenetic regulation of gene expression via their acetylation status. Several compounds that are HDACIs have been shown to increase full-length *SMN2* transcript levels in cell lines from patients,[66,77,78] usually by activating the human *SMN2* promoter, enhancing transcription, and correcting the splicing pattern. Clinical trials of HDACIs, phenybutyrate,[79] and valproic acid have shown no difference in motor function scores compared with placebo group in a non-ambulatory cohort of type II SMA.

Table 4		
Status of therapeutics development in spinal muscular atrophy		
Therapeutic Targets	**Approaches**	**Clinical Trials**
Increase SMN transcript	HDACIs Non-HDACIs Quinazoline Prolactin	Valproic acid, sodium 4-phenylbutyrate Hydroxyurea Repligen RG3039
SMN2 exon 7 inclusion	ASOs	ISIS Rx
Stabilization of SMN protein	Aminoglycoside Proteasome inhibitors Indoprofen	
Neuroprotection	Neurotrophic factors	Riluzole Gabapentin Olesoxime (TRO19622)
Cell therapy	Stem cells	
Replacement of *SMN1*	Gene therapy	

Reprinted from Singh P, Liew WK, Darras BT. Current advances in drug development in spinal muscular atrophy. Curr Opin Pediatr 2013;25:685, Lippincott Williams and Wilkins/Wolters Kluwer Health; with permission.

A proprietary small molecule developed by PTC Therapeutics (South Plainfield, NJ) extends the life expectancy of the SMNΔ7 severe mouse model from 14 days to more than 6 months. Along with the quinazoline derivatives, this compound is further developed by Hoffmann-La Roche (Basel, Switzerland) for clinical trials in humans. The distinct advantage of these small molecules is that they can cross the blood-brain barrier (BBB).

The Food and Drug Administration–approved drug, hydroxyurea, a non-HDACI, was identified in the course of drug screens using cell lines from SMA patients to increase the amount of full-length SMN transcript and protein in vitro.[80–82] A small pilot study of hydroxyurea at 3 different doses for 8 weeks in 33 types II and III patients, however, showed no statistically significant benefit.[81] A randomized, double-blind, placebo-controlled trial failed to show any improvement over an 18-month period.[83]

Albuterol, a β-adrenergic agonist, was evaluated in a pilot study of 13 patients with type II and III SMA due to its reported positive effect on muscle strength in healthy individuals. At 6 months, a significant improvement was noted in myometry, forced vital capacity, and dual-energy x-ray absorptiometry scores, but there was no significant change in Medical Research Council strength score.[84] Another pilot study of 23 patients with SMA type II treated with salbutamol (a form of albuterol) for 12 months showed improved functional scores on the Hammersmith Functional Motor Scale after 6 and 12 months, but this was not a placebo-controlled study and must be interpreted with caution.[85] On an in vitro level, salbutamol has been shown to increase full-length SMN mRNA, SMN protein, and gem numbers by promoting inclusion of exon 7.[86] The response was directly proportional to SMN2 gene copy number.[87] This finding prompts further interest in exploring the effects of β-agonists on SMA with randomized controlled trials.

Quinazoline compounds like RG3039 increase expression of SMN2 transcripts and are currently under investigation.[88,89]

Neuroprotective, Survival of Motor Neuron Protein Stabilization Agents

Other small molecules

Riluzole and gabapentin, the neuroprotective agents, were studied to assess the effect on motor performance in SMA. Unfortunately, the results were not found encouraging or the studies were not adequate to show efficacy.[90–93] A phase II multicenter, randomized, double-blind study is currently being conducted to assess the efficacy and safety of riluzole in young adults with types II and III SMA.

Olesoxime (TRO19622), a novel neuroprotective compound, is currently being tested in a randomized, multicenter, parallel group, double-blind, placebo-controlled trial conducted in Europe. More than 150 nonambulant patients with type II and III SMA ages 3 to 25 years have been enrolled in this efficacy and safety trial with the primary endpoint being a change in the Motor Function Measure scale.[94]

Other Approaches

Antisense oligonucleotides

Antisense oligonucleotides (ASOs) have been developed that block an intronic splicing suppressor element, which in turn prevents skipping of exon 7.[95] Hua and colleagues[96] in their work on transgenic mice found these intronic splicing suppressors to be located in intron 7 as tandem motifs, namely hnRNP A1/A2. Blocking of these motifs by ASOs enhanced exon 7 inclusion in the SMA mouse model. Similar work by Singh and colleagues[97] demonstrated enhanced production of full-length SMN mRNA in fibroblasts from patients treated by ASOs. Periodic intracerebroventricular deliveries of ASOs in SMA mice models have been found to improve the motor phenotype.[98,99] Based on the promise of preclinical studies, a multicenter phase I trial developed by ISIS Pharmaceuticals is currently being conducted to assess the safety, tolerability, and dose-range finding of multiple doses of ASO (ISIS-SMNRx), which is delivered intrathecally into the subarachnoid space of SMA patients.

Stem cells

Interest in the use of stem cells also continues, both as potential treatment of SMA and for use in constructing model systems for therapeutics development. During the past few years, pluripotent stem cells with the capacity to differentiate into motor neurons that lacked *SMN1* expression were induced from a patient with type 1 SMA and his mother; this could serve as an important model system for testing of new compounds and eventually for stem cell approaches to the treatment of SMA.[100,101]

Gene therapy

Among other therapeutic targets, gene therapy has shown potential in animal models.[102,103] Foust and colleagues[102] demonstrated that self-complementary adeno-associated virus 9 (scAAV9) could cross the BBB and infect approximately 60% of motor neurons when injected intravenously into neonatal mice. It was more beneficial when administered on postnatal day 1 when compared with postnatal day 5 and 10. Similar results were obtained in nonhuman primates. With the discovery of novel serotypes of adeno-associated virus (AAV), such as AAV9, which not only infects numerous cell types but also appears to traverse the BBB, there has been renewed interest in applying gene replacement protocols to treat SMA. Neonatal SMA model mice injected systemically with scAAV9 engineered to carry the wild-type *SMN* gene expressed high levels of protein in multiple tissues and derived remarkable therapeutic benefit, surviving in some instances to 12 months or more with no evidence of muscle weakness.[104–106] Considering proof-of-concept studies demonstrating the ability of scAAV9 to penetrate the mature BBB and infect adult motor neurons,[107] an SMN replacement strategy to treat SMA is a promising alternative to pharmacologic approaches.

CARE OF PATIENTS WITH SPINAL MUSCULAR ATROPHY

Patients with SMA and their families benefit greatly from a multidisciplinary approach to care. This approach involves members from neurology/neuromuscular medicine, orthopedics, physical and occupational therapy, pulmonology, nutrition and gastroenterology. For severely affected patients with type I SMA, early involvement of the pediatric advanced care or palliative care team can provide parents with support and assistance in making decisions that are consonant with their values and help to maximize their child's quality of life. In 2007 a Consensus Statement for Standard of Care in Spinal Muscular Atrophy was released by a multidisciplinary team regarding the current best recommendations for management of patients with SMA.[15]

Pulmonary

Respiratory failure is the major cause of mortality in patients at the more severe end of the disease spectrum, namely types I and II SMA. Infants with type I SMA have weak intercostal muscles with relatively preserved diaphragm strength, resulting in a bell-shaped chest, pectus excavatum, and in some cases underdevelopment of the lungs. Patients with type II SMA have weak intercostal muscles with scoliosis contributing to progressive restrictive lung disease.[108,109] The restrictive lung disease results in insidious onset of sleep hypoventilation. Proper use of bilevel positive airway pressure, with correct pressure adjustments and mask placement, has no significant side effects on patient hemodynamics.[110] There should also be a low threshold for the use of antibiotics during acute illnesses in these patients, due to the risk of pneumonia.[15,108,109] Patients should be followed regularly by a pulmonologist experienced in caring for patients with neuromuscular diseases, with home visits by a home ventilation team if available.

Gastrointestinal

Patients with type I SMA are extremely weak and hence tire during feedings, which can lead to failure to thrive and aspiration with recurrent respiratory infections.[108] In a small retrospective study, Durkin and colleagues.[111] found that early laparoscopic Nissen fundoplication and gastrostomy in patients with type I SMA was associated with improved nutritional status in these patients and also perhaps with a trend toward fewer long-term aspiration events. Patients with SMA are also at risk of constipation, which, if severe (especially in young patients with type I), can worsen reflux or even respiratory symptoms.[108]

Nutrition

Failure to thrive and growth failure are common in infants with type I SMA and in some severely affected patients with type II. Although many patients with type II plot as having a normal BMI (often as low as third percentile for a healthy child of their age), they may actually have excessive fat mass relative to their muscle mass. Clinically high-functioning nonambulatory SMA patients (Hammersmith Functional Motor Scale score ≥12) are at risk of becoming overweight.[33,112] Hence, close attention must be paid to nutritional status in patients with all types of SMA, and consultation with a dietician who is aware of these special concerns is vital.

Orthopedic

Patients with SMA at the severe end of the disease spectrum require close orthopedic follow-up for the development of scoliosis and contractures. Surgical intervention for scoliosis is often required, and careful coordination of perioperative respiratory and nutritional support can help minimize complications.[15] Fractures and hip subluxation are commonly seen in patients with milder type II and type III SMA. Distal femur is the most common fracture site followed by lower leg, ankle, and upper arm. Most of the fractures can be treated conservatively.[113]

Fatigue

Physiologic fatigue is a common complaint in patients with milder SMA and can be measured by the decrement in distance walked from the first to sixth minute of the six-minute walk test.[114–116] The mechanism(s) underlying fatigue in SMA remains to be elucidated but may be related at least in part to the neuromuscular junction defects (described previously). Anecdotal evidence suggests that oral albuterol in usual pediatric doses is an effective agent in the treatment of fatigue in SMA patients, thus is frequently used; however, fatigue has not been studied directly in the conducted albuterol pilot studies that showed improvement in motor function.[84,85]

SUMMARY

SMA is a chronic, inherited motor neuron disease for which there is no established treatment. Yet there is cause for optimism, because it is an area of active research, and knowledge about the molecular genetics and pathogenesis of SMA is ever increasing. Several groups are actively exploring pharmacologic treatments, whether through the use of approved drugs, identification of new agents via high-throughput screens, or development of novel pharmaceutical compounds. Consortia of clinicians and researchers are working together to organize multicenter trials and identify the best outcome measures. The SMA Patient Registry has helped facilitate inclusion of patients in these studies. Standards of care have also been developed to optimize the long-term multidisciplinary management of patients with SMA. Patient support and advocacy groups (SMA Foundation, Families of SMA, FightSMA, Project Cure, and others) have played a vital role in supporting research efforts and providing a community for children and families affected by SMA. Although it may seem at times that a treatment of SMA is far in the future, the advances made since the gene was identified in 1995 permit a modicum of hope to patients, their families, and those with the privilege to care for SMA patients.

REFERENCES

1. Werdnig G. Two early infantile hereditary cases of progressive muscular atrophy simulating dystrophy, but on a neural basis [article in German]. Arch Psychiat Neurol 1891;22:437–81.
2. Hoffmann J. Ueber chronische spinale Muskelatrophie im Kindesalter, auf familiärer Basis. Dtsch Z Nervenheilkd 1893;3:427–70.
3. Monani UR, Lorson CL, Parsons DW, et al. A single nucleotide difference that alters splicing patterns distinguishes the SMA gene SMN1 from the copy gene SMN2. Hum Mol Genet 1999;8:1177–83.
4. Pearn J. Incidence, prevalence, and gene frequency studies of chronic childhood spinal muscular atrophy. J Med Genet 1978;15:409–13.
5. Ogino S, Leonard DG, Rennert H, et al. Genetic risk assessment in carrier testing for spinal muscular atrophy. Am J Med Genet 2002;110:301–7.
6. Ogino S, Wilson RB, Gold B. New insights on the evolution of the SMN1 and SMN2 region: simulation and meta-analysis for allele and haplotype frequency calculations. Eur J Hum Genet 2004;12:1015–23.
7. Sugarman EA, Nagan N, Zhu H, et al. Pan-ethnic carrier screening and prenatal diagnosis for spinal muscular atrophy: clinical laboratory analysis of >72,400 specimens. Eur J Hum Genet 2012;20:27–32.
8. Mostacciuolo ML, Danieli GA, Trevisan C, et al. Epidemiology of spinal muscular atrophies in a sample of the Italian population. Neuroepidemiology 1992;11:34–8.
9. Thieme A, Mitulla B, Schulze F, et al. Epidemiological data on Werdnig-Hoffmann disease in Germany (West-Thuringen). Hum Genet 1993;91:295–7.
10. Mailman MD, Heinz JW, Papp AC, et al. Molecular analysis of spinal muscular atrophy and modification of the phenotype by SMN2. Genet Med 2002;4:20–6.
11. Prior TW, Snyder PJ, Rink BD, et al. Newborn and carrier screening for spinal muscular atrophy. Am J Med Genet A 2010;152A:1608–16.
12. Zerres K, Davies KE. 59th ENMC International Workshop: spinal muscular atrophies: recent progress and revised diagnostic criteria 17-19 April 1998, Soestduinen, The Netherlands. Neuromuscul Disord 1999;9:272–8.
13. Dubowitz V. Chaos in the classification of SMA: a possible resolution. Neuromuscul Disord 1995;5:3–5.
14. Iannaccone ST, Russman BS, Browne RH, et al. Prospective analysis of strength in spinal muscular atrophy. DCN/Spinal Muscular Atrophy Group. J Child Neurol 2000;15:97–101.
15. Wang CH, Finkel RS, Bertini ES, et al. Consensus statement for standard of care in spinal muscular atrophy. J Child Neurol 2007;22:1027–49.

16. Sylvestre M. Paralysie flasque de quatre membres et des muscles du tronc (sauf le diaphragme) chez un nouveau-ne. Bull Soc Pediatr Paris 1899;1:3–10.

17. Beevor CE. A case of congenital spinal muscular atrophy (family type) and a case of hemorrhage into the spinal cord at birth, giving similar symptoms. Brain 1902;25:85–108.

18. Byers RK, Banker BQ. Infantile muscular atrophy. Arch Neurol 1961;5:140–64.

19. Dubowitz V. Very severe spinal muscular atrophy (SMA type 0): an expanding clinical phenotype. Eur J Paediatr Neurol 1999;3:49–51.

20. O'Hagen JM, Glanzman AM, McDermott MP, et al. An expanded version of the Hammersmith Functional Motor Scale for SMA II and III patients. Neuromuscul Disord 2007;17:693–7.

21. Thomas NH, Dubowitz V. The natural history of type I (severe) spinal muscular atrophy. Neuromuscul Disord 1994;4:497–502.

22. Darras BT, Markowitz JA, Monani UR, et al. Spinal muscular atrophies. In: Darras BT, Jones HR Jr, Ryan MM, et al, editors. Neuromuscular Disorders of Infancy, Childhood, and Adolescence: A Clinician's Approach. 2nd edition. San Diego: Academic Press; 2014. p. 117–45.

23. Zerres K, Rudnik-Schoneborn S. Natural history in proximal spinal muscular atrophy. Clinical analysis of 445 patients and suggestions for a modification of existing classifications. Arch Neurol 1995;52:518–23.

24. Munsat T, Davies K. Spinal muscular atrophy. 32nd ENMC International Workshop. Naarden, The Netherlands, 10-12 March 1995. Neuromuscul Disord 1996;6:125–7.

25. Oskoui M, Levy G, Garland CJ, et al. The changing natural history of spinal muscular atrophy type 1. Neurology 2007;69:1931–6.

26. Finkel RS, McDermott MP, Kaufmann P, et al. Observational study of spinal muscular atrophy type I and implications for clinical trials. Neurology 2014;83:810–7.

27. Menke LA, Poll-The BT, Clur SA, et al. Congenital heart defects in spinal muscular atrophy type I: a clinical report of two siblings and a review of the literature. Am J Med Genet A 2008;146A:740–4.

28. Rudnik-Schöneborn S, Vogelgesang S, Armbrust S, et al. Digital necroses and vascular thrombosis in severe spinal muscular atrophy. Muscle Nerve 2010;42:144–7.

29. Araujo Ade Q, Araujo M, Swoboda KJ. Vascular perfusion abnormalities in infants with spinal muscular atrophy. J Pediatr 2009;155:292–4.

30. Rudnik-Schöneborn S, Goebel HH, Schlote W, et al. Classical infantile spinal muscular atrophy with SMN deficiency causes sensory neuronopathy. Neurology 2003;60:983–7.

31. Thompson J, Bruce A. A case of progressive muscular atrophy in a child with a spinal lesion. Edinb Hosp Rep 1893;1:372.

32. Dubowitz V. Infantile muscular atrophy. a prospective study with particular reference to a slowly progressive variety. Brain 1964;87:707–18.

33. Sproule DM, Montes J, Montgomery M, et al. Increased fat mass and high incidence of overweight despite low body mass index in patients with spinal muscular atrophy. Neuromuscul Disord 2009;19:391–6.

34. von Gontard A, Zerres K, Backes M, et al. Intelligence and cognitive function in children and adolescents with spinal muscular atrophy. Neuromuscul Disord 2002;12:130–6.

35. Zerres K, Rudnik-Schöneborn S, Forrest E, et al. A collaborative study on the natural history of childhood and juvenile onset proximal spinal muscular atrophy (type II and III SMA): 569 patients. J Neurol Sci 1997;146:67–72.

36. Kugelberg E, Welander L. Heredofamilial juvenile muscular atrophy simulating muscular dystrophy. AMA Arch Neurol Psychiatry 1956;75:500–9.
37. MacLeod MJ, Taylor JE, Lunt PW, et al. Prenatal onset spinal muscular atrophy. Eur J Paediatr Neurol 1999;3:65–72.
38. Bingham PM, Shen N, Rennert H, et al. Arthrogryposis due to infantile neuronal degeneration associated with deletion of the SMNT gene. Neurology 1997;49: 848–51.
39. Korinthenberg R, Sauer M, Ketelsen UP, et al. Congenital axonal neuropathy caused by deletions in the spinal muscular atrophy region. Ann Neurol 1997; 42:364–8.
40. Russman BS. Spinal muscular atrophy: clinical classification and disease heterogeneity. J Child Neurol 2007;22:946–51.
41. Guillot N, Cuisset JM, Cuvellier JC, et al. Unusual clinical features in infantile Spinal Muscular Atrophies. Brain Dev 2008;30:169–78.
42. Darras BT. Non-5q spinal muscular atrophies: the alphanumeric soup thickens. Neurology 2011;77:312–4.
43. Zerres K, Rudnik-Schoneborn S. 93rd ENMC international workshop: non-5q-spinal muscular atrophies (SMA) - clinical picture (6-8 April 2001, Naarden, The Netherlands). Neuromuscul Disord 2003;13:179–83.
44. Pestronk A. Hereditary motor syndromes. St Louis (MO): Washington University; 2013 [cited December 27, 2013]. Available at: http://neuromuscular.wustl.edu/synmot.html.
45. Harms MB, Allred P, Gardner R Jr, et al. Dominant spinal muscular atrophy with lower extremity predominance: linkage to 14q32. Neurology 2010;75: 539–46.
46. Guenther UP, Varon R, Schlicke M, et al. Clinical and mutational profile in spinal muscular atrophy with respiratory distress (SMARD): defining novel phenotypes through hierarchical cluster analysis. Hum Mutat 2007;28:808–15.
47. Stalpers XL, Verrips A, Poll-The BT, et al. Clinical and mutational characteristics of spinal muscular atrophy with respiratory distress type 1 in The Netherlands. Neuromuscul Disord 2013;23:461–8.
48. Joseph S, Robb SA, Mohammed S, et al. Interfamilial phenotypic heterogeneity in SMARD1. Neuromuscul Disord 2009;19:193–5.
49. Harms MB, Ori-McKenney KM, Scoto M, et al. Mutations in the tail domain of DYNC1H1 cause dominant spinal muscular atrophy. Neurology 2012;78:1714–20.
50. Rossor AM, Oates EC, Salter HK, et al. Phenotypic and molecular insights into spinal muscular atrophy due to mutations in BICD2. Brain 2014;138(Pt 2): 293–310.
51. Ciccolella M, Catteruccia M, Benedetti S, et al. Brown-Vialetto-van Laere and Fazio-Londe overlap syndromes: a clinical, biochemical and genetic study. Neuromuscul Disord 2012;22:1075–82.
52. Namavar Y, Barth PG, Poll-The BT, et al. Classification, diagnosis and potential mechanisms in pontocerebellar hypoplasia. Orphanet J Rare Dis 2011;6:50.
53. Renbaum P, Kellerman E, Jaron R, et al. Spinal muscular atrophy with pontocerebellar hypoplasia is caused by a mutation in the VRK1 gene. Am J Hum Genet 2009;85:281–9.
54. Rudnik-Schoneborn S, Senderek J, Jen JC, et al. Pontocerebellar hypoplasia type 1: clinical spectrum and relevance of EXOSC3 mutations. Neurology 2013;80:438–46.
55. La Spada AR, Wilson EM, Lubahn DB, et al. Androgen receptor gene mutations in X-linked spinal and bulbar muscular atrophy. Nature 1991;352:77–9.

56. Ramser J, Ahearn ME, Lenski C, et al. Rare missense and synonymous variants in UBE1 are associated with X-linked infantile spinal muscular atrophy. Am J Hum Genet 2008;82:188–93.

57. Dlamini N, Josifova DJ, Paine SM, et al. Clinical and neuropathological features of X-linked spinal muscular atrophy (SMAX2) associated with a novel mutation in the UBA1 gene. Neuromuscul Disord 2013;23:391–8.

58. Lefebvre S, Burglen L, Reboullet S, et al. Identification and characterization of a spinal muscular atrophy-determining gene. Cell 1995;80:155–65.

59. Lorson CL, Androphy EJ. An exonic enhancer is required for inclusion of an essential exon in the SMA-determining gene SMN. Hum Mol Genet 2000;9:259–65.

60. Lefebvre S, Burlet P, Liu Q, et al. Correlation between severity and SMN protein level in spinal muscular atrophy. Nat Genet 1997;16:265–9.

61. Feldkotter M, Schwarzer V, Wirth R, et al. Quantitative analyses of SMN1 and SMN2 based on real-time lightCycler PCR: fast and highly reliable carrier testing and prediction of severity of spinal muscular atrophy. Am J Hum Genet 2002;70:358–68.

62. Arkblad E, Tulinius M, Kroksmark AK, et al. A population-based study of genotypic and phenotypic variability in children with spinal muscular atrophy. Acta Paediatr 2009;98:865–72.

63. Saito M, Chen Y, Mizuguchi M, et al. Quantitative analysis of SMN2 based on real-time PCR: correlation of clinical severity and SMN2 gene dosage. No To Hattatsu 2005;37:407–12 [in Japanese].

64. Rudnik-Schöneborn S, Berg C, Zerres K, et al. Genotype-phenotype studies in infantile spinal muscular atrophy (SMA) type I in Germany: implications for clinical trials and genetic counselling. Clin Genet 2009;76:168–78.

65. Prior TW, Swoboda KJ, Scott HD, et al. Homozygous SMN1 deletions in unaffected family members and modification of the phenotype by SMN2. Am J Med Genet A 2004;130A:307–10.

66. Sumner CJ, Kolb SJ, Harmison GG, et al. SMN mRNA and protein levels in peripheral blood: biomarkers for SMA clinical trials. Neurology 2006;66:1067–73.

67. Prior TW, Russman BS. Spinal muscular atrophy. In: Pagon RA, Bird TC, Dolan CR, et al, editors. GeneReviews. Seattle (WA): University of Washington; 2013 [Internet].

68. McAndrew PE, Parsons DW, Simard LR, et al. Identification of proximal spinal muscular atrophy carriers and patients by analysis of SMNT and SMNC gene copy number. Am J Hum Genet 1997;60:1411–22.

69. Eggermann T, Zerres K, Anhuf D, et al. Somatic mosaicism for a heterozygous deletion of the survival motor neuron (SMN1) gene. Eur J Hum Genet 2005;13:309–13.

70. Prior TW. Spinal muscular atrophy diagnostics. J Child Neurol 2007;22:952–6.

71. Smith M, Calabro V, Chong B, et al. Population screening and cascade testing for carriers of SMA. Eur J Hum Genet 2007;15:759–66.

72. Swoboda KJ, Prior TW, Scott CB, et al. Natural history of denervation in SMA: relation to age, SMN2 copy number, and function. Ann Neurol 2005;57:704–12.

73. Martinez-Hernandez R, Soler-Botija C, Also E, et al. The developmental pattern of myotubes in spinal muscular atrophy indicates prenatal delay of muscle maturation. J Neuropathol Exp Neurol 2009;68:474–81.

74. Markowitz JA, Singh P, Darras BT. Spinal muscular atrophy: a clinical and research update. Pediatr Neurol 2012;46:1–12.

75. Darras BT, Kang PB. Clinical trials in spinal muscular atrophy. Curr Opin Pediatr 2007;19:675–9.

76. Singh P, Liew WK, Darras BT. Current advances in drug development in spinal muscular atrophy. Curr Opin Pediatr 2013;25:682–8.

77. Lunke S, El-Osta A. The emerging role of epigenetic modifications and chromatin remodeling in spinal muscular atrophy. J Neurochem 2009;109:1557–69.

78. Chang JG, Hsieh-Li HM, Jong YJ, et al. Treatment of spinal muscular atrophy by sodium butyrate. Proc Natl Acad Sci U S A 2001;98:9808–13.

79. Mercuri E, Bertini E, Messina S, et al. Randomized, double-blind, placebo-controlled trial of phenylbutyrate in spinal muscular atrophy. Neurology 2007; 68:51–5.

80. Grzeschik SM, Ganta M, Prior TW, et al. Hydroxyurea enhances SMN2 gene expression in spinal muscular atrophy cells. Ann Neurol 2005;58:194–202.

81. Liang WC, Yuo CY, Chang JG, et al. The effect of hydroxyurea in spinal muscular atrophy cells and patients. J Neurol Sci 2008;268:87–94.

82. Xu C, Chen X, Grzeschik SM, et al. Hydroxyurea enhances SMN2 gene expression through nitric oxide release. Neurogenetics 2011;12:19–24.

83. Chen TH, Chang JG, Yang YH, et al. Randomized, double-blind, placebo-controlled trial of hydroxyurea in spinal muscular atrophy. Neurology 2010;75: 2190–7.

84. Kinali M, Mercuri E, Main M, et al. Pilot trial of albuterol in spinal muscular atrophy. Neurology 2002;59:609–10.

85. Pane M, Staccioli S, Messina S, et al. Daily salbutamol in young patients with SMA type II. Neuromuscul Disord 2008;18:536–40.

86. Angelozzi C, Borgo F, Tiziano FD, et al. Salbutamol increases SMN mRNA and protein levels in spinal muscular atrophy cells. J Med Genet 2008;45:29–31.

87. Tiziano FD, Lomastro R, Pinto AM, et al. Salbutamol increases survival motor neuron (SMN) transcript levels in leucocytes of spinal muscular atrophy (SMA) patients: relevance for clinical trial design. J Med Genet 2010;47:856–8.

88. Butchbach ME, Singh J, Thorsteinsdottir M, et al. Effects of 2,4-diaminoquinazoline derivatives on SMN expression and phenotype in a mouse model for spinal muscular atrophy. Hum Mol Genet 2010;19:454–67.

89. Van Meerbeke J, Gibbs R, Plasterer H, et al. The therapeutic effects of RG3039 in severe spinal muscular atrophy mice and normal human volunteers [abstract]. Neurology 2012;78(S25):003.

90. Haddad H, Cifuentes-Diaz C, Miroglio A, et al. Riluzole attenuates spinal muscular atrophy disease progression in a mouse model. Muscle Nerve 2003; 28:432–7.

91. Russman BS, Iannaccone ST, Samaha FJ. A phase 1 trial of riluzole in spinal muscular atrophy. Arch Neurol 2003;60:1601–3.

92. Miller RG, Moore DH, Dronsky V, et al. A placebo-controlled trial of gabapentin in spinal muscular atrophy. J Neurol Sci 2001;191:127–31.

93. Merlini L, Solari A, Vita G, et al. Role of gabapentin in spinal muscular atrophy: results of a multicenter, randomized Italian study. J Child Neurol 2003;18: 537–41.

94. Lloyd A, Hunter N, editors. Trophos completes patient enrolment in pivotal efficacy study of olesoxime in spinal muscular atrophy. Marseille, France: Trophos; 2011. Available at: http://www.trophos.com/news/pr20110908.htm.

95. Burghes AH, McGovern VL. Antisense oligonucleotides and spinal muscular atrophy: skipping along. Genes Dev 2010;24:1574–9.

96. Hua Y, Vickers TA, Okunola HL, et al. Antisense masking of an hnRNP A1/A2 intronic splicing silencer corrects SMN2 splicing in transgenic mice. Am J Hum Genet 2008;82:834–48.

97. Singh NN, Shishimorova M, Cao LC, et al. A short antisense oligonucleotide masking a unique intronic motif prevents skipping of a critical exon in spinal muscular atrophy. RNA Biol 2009;6:341–50.

98. Hua Y, Sahashi K, Hung G, et al. Antisense correction of SMN2 splicing in the CNS rescues necrosis in a type III SMA mouse model. Genes Dev 2010;24:1634–44.

99. Williams JH, Schray RC, Patterson CA, et al. Oligonucleotide-mediated survival of motor neuron protein expression in CNS improves phenotype in a mouse model of spinal muscular atrophy. J Neurosci 2009;29:7633–8.

100. Corti S, Nizzardo M, Nardini M, et al. Embryonic stem cell-derived neural stem cells improve spinal muscular atrophy phenotype in mice. Brain 2010;133:465–81.

101. Ebert AD, Yu J, Rose FF Jr, et al. Induced pluripotent stem cells from a spinal muscular atrophy patient. Nature 2009;457:277–80.

102. Foust KD, Wang X, McGovern VL, et al. Rescue of the spinal muscular atrophy phenotype in a mouse model by early postnatal delivery of SMN. Nat Biotechnol 2010;28:271–4.

103. Passini MA, Bu J, Roskelley EM, et al. CNS-targeted gene therapy improves survival and motor function in a mouse model of spinal muscular atrophy. J Clin Invest 2010;120:1253–64.

104. Valori CF, Ning K, Wyles M, et al. Systemic delivery of scAAV9 expressing SMN prolongs survival in a model of spinal muscular atrophy. Sci Transl Med 2010;2:35ra42.

105. Dominguez E, Marais T, Chatauret N, et al. Pereira de Moura A, Voit T, Barkats M. Intravenous scAAV9 delivery of a codon-optimized SMN1 sequence rescues SMA mice. Hum Mol Genet 2011;20:681–93.

106. Duque S, Joussemet B, Riviere C, et al. Intravenous administration of self-complementary AAV9 enables transgene delivery to adult motor neurons. Mol Ther 2009;17:1187–96.

107. Gowing G, Svendsen CN. Stem cell transplantation for motor neuron disease: current approaches and future perspectives. Neurotherapeutics 2011;8:591–606.

108. Iannaccone ST. Modern management of spinal muscular atrophy. J Child Neurol 2007;22:974–8.

109. Schroth MK. Special considerations in the respiratory management of spinal muscular atrophy. Pediatrics 2009;123(Suppl 4):S245–9.

110. Markstrom A, Cohen G, Katz-Salamon M. The effect of long term ventilatory support on hemodynamics in children with spinal muscle atrophy (SMA) type II. Sleep Med 2010;11:201–4.

111. Durkin ET, Schroth MK, Helin M, et al. Early laparoscopic fundoplication and gastrostomy in infants with spinal muscular atrophy type I. J Pediatr Surg 2008;43:2031–7.

112. Sproule DM, Montes J, Dunaway S, et al. Adiposity is increased among high-functioning, non-ambulatory patients with spinal muscular atrophy. Neuromuscul Disord 2010;20:448–52.

113. Fujak A, Kopschina C, Forst R, et al. Fractures in proximal spinal muscular atrophy. Arch Orthop Trauma Surg 2010;130:775–80.

114. Montes J, McDermott MP, Martens WB, et al. Six-Minute Walk Test demonstrates motor fatigue in spinal muscular atrophy. Neurology 2010;74:833–8.

115. Montes J, Dunaway S, Montgomery MJ, et al. Fatigue leads to gait changes in spinal muscular atrophy. Muscle Nerve 2011;43:485–8.

116. Montes J, Blumenschine M, Dunaway S, et al. Weakness and fatigue in diverse neuromuscular diseases. J Child Neurol 2013;28:1277–83.

Pediatric Charcot-Marie-Tooth Disease

Agnes Jani-Acsadi, MD[a], Sylvia Ounpuu, MSc[b], Kristan Pierz, MD[c],
Gyula Acsadi, MD, PhD[d],*

KEYWORDS

- Charcot-Marie-Tooth disease • Pediatric • Electrophysiology • Gait

KEY POINTS

- Charcot-Marie-Tooth disease (CMT) is the most prevalent genetic neuromuscular disease in children.
- Dejerine-Sottas syndrome is the infantile form of inherited neuropathy.
- CMT is divided into 2 major groups: demyelinating and axonal neuropathy.
- More than 80 CMT-causing genes have been identified with the aid of new-generation DNA sequencing.
- PMP22 duplication in CMT1A is the most frequent cause of CMT.
- Standardized evaluation tools have been developed, including a pediatric neuropathy scoring system and gait analysis (computerized motion analysis).
- Therapeutic management consists of physical and orthopedic therapies that should be tailored individually in order to maintain the quality of life of children with CMT.

INTRODUCTION

Charcot-Marie-Tooth disease (CMT), or hereditary motor and sensory neuropathy, has long been recognized as a heterogeneous group of inherited neuropathies.[1,2] These two terms have been used interchangeably, but the scientific literature tends to use the eponym CMT more often.

Perhaps the first description of this neuropathy in medical literature originated from Friedreich[3] or Eichhorst[4] in 1873. Familial length-dependent peripheral neuropathy

Disclosures: None.
[a] Department of Neurology, University of Connecticut School of Medicine, Farmington, CT, USA; [b] Department of Orthopedic Surgery, Connecticut Children's Medical Center, Farmington, CT, USA; [c] Department of Orthopedic Surgery, Center of Motion Analysis, Connecticut Children's Medical Center, Farmington, CT, USA; [d] Division of Neurology, Department of Neurology, Connecticut Children's Medical Center, University of Connecticut School of Medicine, 505 Farmington Avenue, Farmington, CT 06032, USA
* Corresponding author. Department of Pediatrics, Connecticut Children's Medical Center, University of Connecticut School of Medicine, 505 Farmington Avenue, Farmington, CT 06032.
E-mail address: gacsadi@connecticutchildrens.org

Pediatr Clin N Am 62 (2015) 767–786
http://dx.doi.org/10.1016/j.pcl.2015.03.012
0031-3955/15/$ – see front matter © 2015 Elsevier Inc. All rights reserved.

was later described by the French neurologists, Charcot[5] and Marie, and independently by a British neurologist, Tooth,[6] in 1886 referring to the prominent distal muscle wasting of the weak muscles as peroneal muscular atrophy. The infantile form was first reported by Dejerine and Sottas[7] in 1893. Dyck and Lambert[8] in 1968 published their work on the major electrophysiologic characteristics of inherited neuropathies and later initiated the first classification based on the electrophysiologic features of their patients. They identified 2 major groups: 1 as CMT1, with slow nerve conduction velocities (NCVs) along with pathologic finding of hypertrophic demyelination; and CMT2, with normal or mildly reduced NCVs along with pathologic evidence of axonopathy. Most patients with CMT (~70%) belong to the first group and have autosomal dominant inheritance pattern.[9]

According to Ouvrier and Nicholson's[10] estimation, about 30% of pediatric neuromuscular patients have some form of neuropathy, but only about 10% of these are acquired, whereas the rest are likely to have genetic causes. CMT represents the largest group of inherited neuromuscular diseases with an estimated prevalence of 0.5 to 1 in 2500.[11,12] During a 33-year retrospective analysis of data from 260 patients, Wilmshurst and colleagues[13] documented that about 1 in 5 cases had an infantile (less than 1 year of age) presentation. The medical literature has been sparse in pediatric CMT until recently, which can be attributed to an absence of national or international data collection programs, uniform evaluation tools, and long-term natural history studies.[14,15] Another contributing factor is the significant delay in diagnosis for the pediatric CMT population. Based on our own observation of 117 pediatric patients with CMT at the former Wayne State University CMT Clinic (Detroit, MI), the average delay of clinical diagnosis was more than 10 years even in families known to have CMT (Acsadi and Shy, unpublished observation, 2005). In another cohort of 39 patients, we documented that the mean age at CMT diagnosis was 8 ± 5 years (range, 18 months to 16 years).[16] Most adults with CMT experienced some clinical signs during their childhood; however, these signs, such as motor delay, hip dysplasia, foot abnormalities, scoliosis, pain, or decreased athletic abilities, can be subtle.[17]

FORMS AND GENETICS OF CHARCOT-MARIE-TOOTH DISEASE

The initial term hereditary sensorimotor neuropathy was based on the pathology and inheritance pattern.[18] Based on the pathology and electrophysiology, there are 2 major types of CMTs: the most frequent is the dysmyelinating form caused by defects in myelin-forming Schwann cells, and the less common is the axonal form caused by primary abnormalities in the nerve axon and/or its interactions with Schwann cells (reviewed by Saporta and Shy[19] in 2013). Motor and sensory or autonomic nerves are variably affected in CMT; however, autonomic symptoms are uncommon.[20] After detailed electrophysiologic characterization of various neuropathies[8] and in the era of molecular genetic association, the CMT eponym has gained popularity in the scientific literature.

CMT is monogenic and the rate of gene discovery has been exponential since the availability of new-generation whole-exome DNA sequencing (WES) techniques. More than 80 genes have been identified as disease-causing genes.[21] Because of space limitation, this article cannot describe all of the CMT-related gene defects. For a comprehensive list of CMT genes, see the recent review by Timmerman and colleagues[21] (2014) and Gene Reviews (http://www.ncbi.nlm.nih.gov/books/NBK1205/). Depending on the molecular techniques used to identify the genetic cause in individual patients, about 20% to 30% of patients with inherited neuropathy have unknown genetic causes; however, this rate is rapidly declining because of new-generation sequencing tools.[22]

Charcot-Marie-Tooth type 1 (CMT1) is the autosomal dominant demyelinating type and it is the most common because about 70% of all inherited neuropathies are in this category (**Table 1**). The first chromosomal localization, and eventually the disease-causing gene defect, was reported in 1991.[1,23] The peripheral myelin protein 22 gene (PMP22) duplication on chromosome 17p11.2 causes the classic demyelinating CMT1A phenotype with characteristic slow NCV of less than 35 m/s.[8,24] Point mutations in the same gene are rare (~1%) and it cause early onset (sometimes infantile) and typically severe demyelinating neuropathy. In contrast, deletion or some point mutations (CMT1E) of the same gene cause hereditary neuropathy with pressure palsy (HNPP).[25,26] HNPP is the third most common CMT and causes multiple compression neuropathies in adults (median, ulnar, and peroneal) but it rarely manifests in children. CMT1B is the third most common demyelinating neuropathy (after Charcot-Marie-Tooth Type X [CMTX]) and is associated with abnormalities in the major peripheral myelin protein, MPZ gene on chromosome 1q22.[27] The clinical variations of this group are very large, starting from the infantile form to a late-onset and milder phenotype with dysmyelinating, axonal, and intermediate NCVs.[27,28] CMT1C has similar clinical features as CMT1A and is related to mutations in the lipopolysaccharide-induced tumor necrosis factor-alpha factor gene (LITAF/SIMPLE).[29]

Charcot-Marie-Tooth type 2 (CMT2) groups together the various dominant forms of axonal neuropathies, which are often clinically indistinguishable from CMT1 except that the myotatic reflexes and NCVs are typically preserved. CMT2A is the most prevalent axonal (~20%) form and caused by mutations in the mitofusin 2 (MFN2) gene.[30,31] This type is one of the most progressive among CMTs.[32–34] CMT2B is associated with severe distal sensory loss leading to foot ulcerations, and it is caused by RAB7 (a small GTP-ase) gene mutations.[35,36] Vocal cord and diaphragm paralysis have been described in CMT2C and this form is caused by mutations in the TRP4 (a phosphoribosyltransferase) gene.[37] The GARS (glycyl-tRNA synthetase) gene is responsible for the CMT2D phenotype, which is different from the classic CMTs because of the more severe upper extremity involvement compared with lower extremity, and because some mutations can cause severe disease in children.[38,39] It is notable that a few distinct mutations in many CMT2 genes may cause recessive inheritance and these forms belong to the Charcot-Marie-Tooth type 4 (CMT4) category.

Charcot-Marie-Tooth type 3 (CMT3) is reserved for patients with infantile onset neuropathy or Dejerine-Sottas syndrome (DSS) and hypomyelinating neuropathy. The classic pathologic description recognized the hypertrophy of nerve fibers with

Table 1
Features of the most common Charcot-Marie-Tooth neuropathies

CMT Type	Disorder	NCV (m/s)	Inheritance	Common Genes
CMT1	Dysmyelinating	UE<30; LE<25	Dominant	PMP22; MPZ; SIMPLE
CMT2	Axonal	>35; low CMAP denervation	Dominant	MFN2; RAB7; TRP4; GARS
CMT3 (DSS)	Dysmyelinating	<20	Dominant or Recessive	PMP22; MPZ; EGR2
CMT4	Dysmyelinating or axonal	Low NCV or CMAP denervation	Recessive	GDAP1; FIG4; MTMR2; NEFL
CMTX	Dysmyelinating	30–40	X-linked dominant	Connexin32 (GJB1)

Abbreviations: LE, lower extremity; NCV, nerve conduction velocity; UE, upper extremity.

onion-bulb formation.[40] The NCVs are uniformly slow (<15 m/s). The genetic causes of CMT3 include de novo dominant point mutations in PMP22, MPZ, and recessive mutations in the EGR2 (early growth response 2) gene.[22]

CMT4 incorporates various recessive demyelinating or axonal neuropathy phenotypes that are rare and distinct from each other. Some entities have motor neuron–like features, also referred to as distal SMA (eg, FIG4, a phosphoinositide phosphatase). CMT4A is caused by mutations in ganglioside-induced differentiation-associated protein 1 (GDAP1), CMT4B by the myotubularin-related protein (MTMR2), and CMT4C by SH3TC2 (src homology 3 domains and tetratricopeptide repeat domain protein) genes.[41–43] Both forms have a severe phenotype with early childhood onset.

CMTX is an X-linked recessive demyelinating neuropathy with variably severe phenotype. CMTX is clinically more severe in male compared with female patients. Females carriers may not have symptoms or have the HNPP phenotype. The NCVs are slowed to between 25 and 40 m/s in the intermediate NCV range. It is the second most common CMT (10%) caused by mutations in the GJB1 gene.[44,45]

PATHOMECHANISMS OF NEUROPATHY

The peripheral nervous system is a complex anatomic structure that has to maintain its integrity in order to provide the propagation of electrical impulses between the cell body of motor neurons and muscle cells or the sensory receptors and the sensory neurons. The functional integrity of Schwann cells, myelin sheet, Ranvier node, and the axon depends on complex biological processes and a dynamic orchestrated interplay between the various components (reviewed by Berger and colleagues,[46] 2006; Saporta and Shy,[19] 2013; Brennan and colleagues,[47] 2015). PMP22, MPZ, and GJB1 are essential for forming normal compact myelin and gene dosage/gene expression is important to provide the integrity of myelin structure. Overexpressed PMP22 results in a toxic protein aggregation and overloads the protein degradation process, thus leading to demyelination. Many gene products in CMT2 (eg, MFN2) participate in crucial axonal processes, including transport, trophic support, and energy production, and a dysfunction in these processes leads to axonal damage and wallerian degeneration of axons (reviewed by Juárez and Palau,[48] 2012). It is notable that demyelination in a nerve eventually results in axonal damage; therefore, the two pathologic processes cannot be separated from each other.[49,50] Despite this heterogeneity in CMT, there is a good prospect that identifying converging molecular pathways in the disease process will eventually lead to specific therapies for CMTs.

CLINICAL FEATURES

The neuropathy in CMT is length dependent, which means that the longest nerves in the body are affected first and most severely. Therefore, the first dominating clinical signs are distal limb weakness and muscle atrophy. The lower extremities are usually affected earlier than the upper extremities in the course of disease progression. In toddlers the earliest clinical signs are delayed motor development and toe walking along with tripping or falling. These signs are not specific because many other childhood neurologic diseases (eg, cerebral palsy, myopathies) can present similarly. In older children, slow running, ankle injuries, and clumsiness in sport activities are the concerns. However, it is common to see good athletic abilities in later onset cases even if typical foot deformity is present. It is commonly seen that a foot deformity such as flat foot or high arch takes the patient initially to a podiatrist or an orthopedic specialist. Between 50% and 80% of such foot problems, particularly if bilateral, are eventually proved to be caused by CMT.[51] Although some asymmetry in foot alignment exists in some children, it is not a typical finding[52,53]; therefore it is important to consider diagnoses other than CMT in asymmetric cases (eg, spinal cord disease and mononeuropathies). Significant discrepancy between the degree of symptoms and weakness or sensory deficit can often be seen on physical examination.[54] For example, children usually do not complain much about numbness, tingling, or pain even if sensory loss is evident. Muscle cramps can be present more often in the axonal forms of CMT. The first signs of hand weakness may not be obvious until the child has some trouble dressing, tying shoes, or writing at school.

DSS, the rare severe infantile CMT, presents with floppy-infant features; nonspecific clinical signs such as generalized hypotonia; hip dysplasia; decreased sucking effort; and, in more severe cases, breathing problems (reviewed by Gabreëls-Festen,[55] 2002). After the neonatal period, most infants survive and eventually improve to achieve motor skills with variable delay.

PHYSICAL EXAMINATION FINDINGS
Weakness and Muscle Atrophy

A variable degree of distal weakness can be seen affecting hallux and ankle plantar flexion, dorsiflexion, eversion, and inversion. The weakness makes voluntary toe walking difficult unless heel cord contracture is present.[56] The most typical foot abnormalities are high arch (pes cavus) and hammer toes (claw feet), but less frequently flat foot is present (**Fig. 1**).[57] Thinning of the ankle and atrophy of the anterior and/or posterior compartments of the lower legs can be observed mainly in the more advanced cases. The abnormal foot structure and weakness results in abnormal weight distribution and pressure on the bottom of the foot (**Fig. 2**).

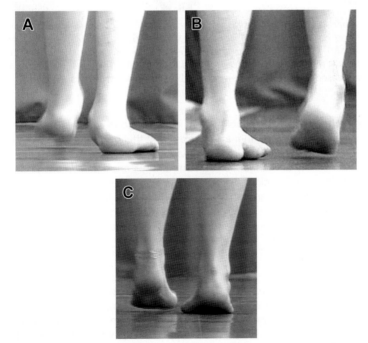

Fig. 1. Typical presentations of CMT foot and ankle during gait. (*A*) Flail foot and ankle, (*B*) cavovarus deformity, and (*C*) toe walking with plantar flexor and/or cavus deformity.

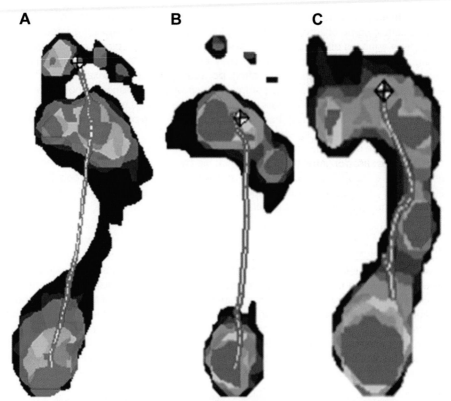

Fig. 2. Comparison of right foot pressure patterns. The foot pressure patterns show the variations among patients with CMT depending on foot deformity. (*A*) Normally developing foot, (*B*) a child with CMT who has a cavus deformity with a reduction in weight bearing over the lateral midfoot and reduced ground contact with the toes, (*C*) a child with CMT who has increased lateral weight bearing and no toe contact with the ground.

The signs for initial hand involvement include subtle wasting (flattening) in the hypothenar and base of the thenar muscles, and this can be seen even before any obvious weakness or dexterity problems. As the disease progresses, further interosseous muscle atrophy and finger flexion contractures are noticeable. Hand weakness can be examined in the clinic by testing the finger flexors and extensors, thumb adduction and abduction, and opposition; however, these require good cooperation and effort by the patient. Grip strength measurement by hand-held myometry and dexterity testing using a 9-hole peg test are reliable tools to monitor changes in hand functions over time.[58]

Sensation

Signs of sensory nerve dysfunction are usually less severe compared with motor nerve dysfunction and they are typically associated with decreased vibration and joint position sense rather than change in pin-prick or temperature sensation.[56] Sensory nerve dysfunction can be the cause of decreased balance, which can be evaluated by Romberg test and tandem gait.[59] The sensory deficit may also cause fine essential tremor and dry skin in hands and feet.

Stretch Reflex

The muscle stretch (myotatic) reflexes are diminished more in ankles and knees compared with biceps and triceps, but they can be preserved or even brisk in axonal forms of CMT.[56]

Additional neurologic signs may include sensorineural hearing loss as well as vocal cord or phrenic nerve paralysis in some forms of CMT.

The neurologic examination in DSS (or infantile CMT) is consistent with floppy-infant syndrome. Generalized hypotonia, distal weakness (eg, wrist drop), absent myotatic reflexes, and lack of muscle fasciculation are the most pertinent findings.[40]

Gait Findings: Motion Analysis

Weakness and deformity in the lower extremities are the prime sources of gait deviations in persons with CMT. These gait deviations may result in instability (caused by weakness of ankle musculature), clearance issues (caused by foot drop or internal foot progression), and compensations (steppage gait to clear the lower extremity). Gait patterns in children and youth with CMT vary substantially from person to person and are best documented and understood using comprehensive computerized motion analysis techniques. Using motion analysis, 3 distinct patterns with respect to foot and ankle function: flail foot, cavovarus foot, and toe walking (see **Fig. 1**) have been identified.[19] These gait issues are caused by weakness, contractures, and bone deformities of the ankles and feet and can also be categorized in terms of the ankle sagittal plane kinematic and kinetic patterns; specifically peak dorsiflexion in terminal stance greater than, within, and less than the normal control range (**Fig. 3**).

Ankle plantar flexor weakness results in the most common kinematic finding of delayed peak dorsiflexion in terminal stance (90% of patients), and may be the only gait abnormality present.[16] It is likely that delayed peak dorsiflexion or delayed heel rise is the first gait sign of CMT. Plantar flexor weakness may also lead reduced peak ankle plantar flexor moments and powers in terminal stance compared with normal age-matched controls. Plantar flexor weakness is the cause of complaints reported by many patients, such as the inability to toe walk and difficulties in running. Foot drop (or increased equinus) in swing is also a common finding (about 60% of patients) in CMT[16,60] and can lead to tripping; however, it may be caused by either ankle dorsiflexor weakness or plantar flexor tightness, which require different interventions.

Functional compensations are also common components of gait in patients with CMT.[16,61] However, the gait abnormalities vary individually, so the needed compensations also vary from patient to patient. Patients with excessive plantar flexion in swing phase caused by ankle dorsiflexor weakness compensate with hip flexion and pelvic hiking to clear the swinging limb. Patients with internally rotated foot caused by forefoot adductus compensate with increased external hip rotation to minimize the effect of the adductus. The most common compensation is increased hip abduction, which has been found by multiple investigators.[16,62] Increased hip abduction makes a widened base possible and as a result improves stability.

ELECTROPHYSIOLOGIC FINDINGS

Before the introduction of electromyography (EMG) and NCV testing, peripheral neuropathies were grouped based on clinical presentation, inheritance pattern, and microscopic pathology of nerves. With the help of electrodiagnostic evaluation, it was possible to establish a diagnostic correlation between the clinical and pathologic features.[8] The first disease classification was based on electrophysiologic findings

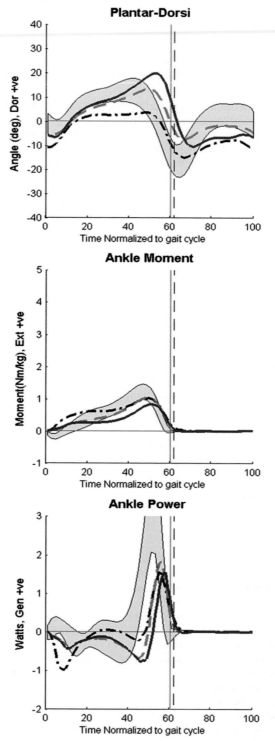

Fig. 3. Comparison of 3 ankle sagittal plane kinematic, moment, and power patterns found in CMT gait. Flail foot (*solid line*), cavovarus foot (*long dashed line*), and toe walking (*dashed/dotted line*). Normal reference data are provided in the gray band.

seen in the upper extremities (median nerve) because many patients with more advanced disease had unobtainable responses on the lower extremity.

NCV and EMG are minimally invasive and can be performed in patients of any age. They give immediate results and are helpful in the differential diagnosis between acquired or inherited processes.[63,64] Electrodiagnostic studies using surface electrodes allow an assessment of motor and sensory nerves. The needle examination may provide evidence of acute and chronic denervation patterns by analyzing the motor unit action potentials, which helps to determine whether a neuropathy is axonal or demyelinating.[24]

In order to differentiate between the two CMT forms, the most important parameter is the conduction velocity of the motor nerve fiber. This measurement depends on the axon diameter and the degree of myelination. The longer the nerve fiber (in the legs), the slower is the NCV compared with the shorter upper limb nerves as the nerve diameter tapers off, which explains the normal difference in NCV of about 10 m/s between the median motor nerve ($\sim$ 50 m/s) and peroneal nerve ($\sim$ 40 m/s). Slowing of motor nerve conduction to less than 30 m/s in the upper limb and 25 m/s in the lower is considered an absolute indicator of demyelination.[65,66] The other variability is the age of the child; adult values are reached when peripheral nerve myelination is finished, at around age 4 years.[67] Because of this age factor, pediatric normative values should be used when evaluating NCVs. Uniform nerve conduction slowing is a classic feature of CMT1A, which is the most common form of CMT. Focal segmental nerve conduction slowing is more typical for acquired demyelinating neuropathies (eg, acute inflammatory demyelinating polyneuropathy or chronic demyelinating polyneuropathy) but is also seen in HNPP.[68] Less uniform conduction velocities may be seen in CMTX. NCV always reflects the pathophysiology of the fastest conducting fibers. The presence of temporal dispersion (the presence of fibers that conduct at lower speed) is notable in both hereditary and acquired neuropathies but the findings are more uniform in CMT1A. Conduction block, a significant reduction in compound muscle action potential amplitude between distal and proximal stimulation sites, is a feature of acquired neuropathies and is not usually seen in CMT.

The CMT2 group includes the axonal neuropathies. Electrodiagnostic findings usually show slowly progressive axonal degeneration.[24,69] NCVs are preserved in early stages with mild slowing noted later as the axonopathy leads to loss of larger diameter, fast-conducting nerve fibers. There is reduction in sensory and compound motor action potential (CMAP) amplitudes because they represent a summated action potential and as such are a measure of total axon loss.

DIAGNOSIS AND TESTING STRATEGY

The clinical signs of length-dependent neuropathy, including the family history, foot abnormalities, gait disturbance, and balance problems, should raise an appropriate suspicion for CMT. The diagnosis can be established by abnormal neurologic findings, such as sensorimotor findings and diminished myotatic reflexes, in most cases. Electrodiagnostic testing (EMG/NCV) is the first test of choice for confirming a form of neuropathy and differentiating between demyelinating and axonal types.[19] Furthermore, EMG/NCV helps to exclude other types of neuromuscular diseases, such as motor neuron diseases, neuromuscular junction defects, as well as muscle disorders. The role of nerve and muscle biopsy has diminished in the diagnosis of CMT but pathologic studies can be useful in the diagnosis of various other neuropathies (eg, vasculitic neuropathies).[64] If the EMG/NCV test confirms a demyelinating CMT, the most informative and cost-effective next test is a genetic test for PMP22 duplication, which is positive in

70% of patients.[19,70–72] If there is evidence for maternal transmission in a case of demyelinating CMT based on the family history, a single genetic test can focus on sequencing of the connexin 32 gene (GJB1). For a dominant axonal CMT it is reasonable to do a selective mutation analysis including the MFN2.[54] If these initial gene tests are negative, it is a reasonable approach to do exome sequencing of a panel of CMT genes.[21] At present, selected commercial laboratories offer WES sequencing of at least 70 of the CMT genes. Caution is needed because WES sequencing may miss PMP22 duplications and intronic mutations. Insurance coverage presents barriers for this approach, but this limitation is expected to improve with the declining costs of the new genetic technologies.

MANAGEMENT

At present, there is no curative treatment available for CMT. Regular multidisciplinary surveillance of the disease status and anticipation of potential progression should take place in order to implement interventions that are directed to the preservation of quality of life of the pediatric patients. Natural history of pediatric CMT has until recently been largely unknown because of the lack of standardized assessment tools and data collection.[14,73,74] A pediatric multidimensional neuropathy scoring system has been developed and validated in pediatric patients with CMT.[75,76] This tool is available online at http://cmtpeds.org. The ability to walk without falling is a crucial factor for the quality of life of children with CMT. Computerized gait analysis is an accurate tool for quantitative assessment and monitoring of the disease-related changes over time; however, it is not available in all neuromuscular centers.[16] Analysis of disease progression from diagnosis using standardized techniques (eg, CMTPeds: a validated pediatric neuropathy scoring system, some timed tests, motion analysis techniques) in collaborative studies would help improve understanding of the specific factors affecting disability and prognosis for future ambulation status, and would allow clinicians to optimize interventions to preserve ambulation and improve the quality of life of children with CMT.

Physical Therapy

Regular physical therapy should focus on strengthening, range of motion, and balance training in order to maintain the mobility of patients.[77] Swimming and other pool-based therapies may be useful for maintaining axial strength and preventing scoliosis. The role of occupational therapy is to provide tools for accomplishing daily routine activities, particularly those hand functions that help children in school activities.[78]

For patients with significant weakness of the foot and ankle musculature, support can be provided with an appropriately molded ankle foot orthosis (AFO) that limits ankle motion, specifically excessive dorsiflexion in terminal stance and/or plantar flexion in swing.[79] The impact of the AFO is shown by a comparison of the barefoot versus AFO sagittal plane ankle kinematic, moment, and power for a variety of AFO designs (**Fig. 4**). An example of a hinged AFO and a solid AFO shows the pros and cons of different brace designs and how the variation in patient presentation requires different options for brace design.[80]

Orthopedic Treatment

Because the term CMT represents a spectrum of clinical phenotypes, there is no single treatment recommendation for the condition. In addition, the progressive nature of the condition makes it difficult to compare treatments because results may vary based on when in the course of the disease process such treatments are initiated. Despite

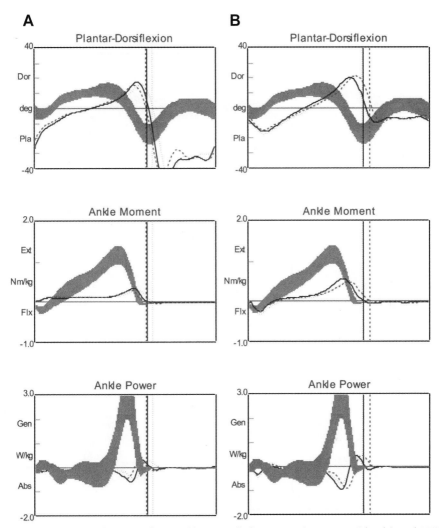

Fig. 4. Comparison of the barefoot and brace walk for two patients one with a hinged AFO (*A* and *B*) and one with a solid AFO (*C* and *D*). The sagittal plane right ankle kinematic, moment, and power during walking are plotted for 3 gait cycles in each condition. The hinged AFO (*B*) in comparison to barefoot (*A*) eliminates the excessive plantar flexion and allows for free dorsiflexion and therefore the ankle continues to show excessive dorsiflexion in terminal stance because of weak plantar flexors. Ankle dorsiflexion is beneficial for stair descent. The solid AFO (*D*) in comparison to barefoot (*C*) limits the excessive peak ankle dorsiflexion in terminal stance, which is a result of ankle plantar flexor weakness. This limitation also provides more support for the knee. However, there is a reduction in ankle plantar flexion and ankle power generation that may limit the ability to walk fast and run. Normal reference data are provided in the gray band; (*A*) barefoot patient #1; (*B*) hinged AFO patient #1; (*C*) barefoot patient #2; (*D*) solid AFO patient #2.

the variability, it is common for individuals with CMT to present with foot and ankle problems, including pain, weakness, deformity, and problems with shoe wear. Clinicians must carefully consider the progression of the neurologic dysfunction, the distribution of the muscular weakness, the flexibility of the foot deformity, and the current

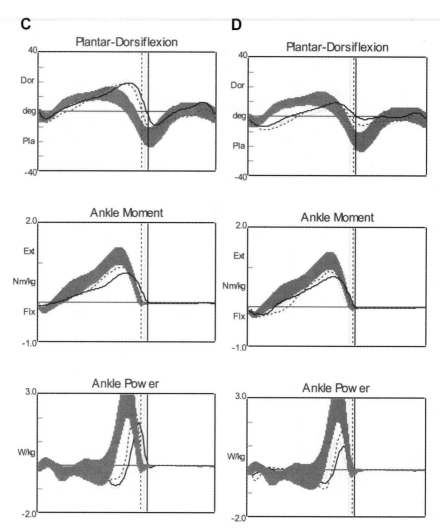

Fig. 4. (*continued*).

and future foot demands before making treatment recommendations. Understanding the gait characteristics on presentation can help clinicians to tailor treatment. Computerized comprehensive gait analysis is a useful tool for documenting and analyzing gait disorders. Objective assessment of patients with CMT using gait analysis techniques has identified 3 characteristic presentations (flail foot, cavovarus foot, and toe walking), as described earlier.[16] Decision making can be improved by understanding these patterns and applying appropriate treatment to achieve specific functional goals.

Patients who present with a flail foot typically have weak ankle dorsiflexors, plantar flexors, invertors, and evertors. This weakness may result in instability in stance as well as tripping caused by clearance problems in swing. Bracing, such as an AFO, should be considered for these individuals. Such braces are typically made of lightweight material and are designed to fit into a shoe while holding the ankle in a neutral (right angle) position. By supporting the foot and ankle externally, an AFO can provide stability in stance.[80] In addition, it can limit excessive ankle dorsiflexion in stance, thus allowing the center of mass to move forward over the forefoot without collapsing. This support can increase push-off power in some patients. In addition, by decreasing foot drop (excessive equinus) in swing, an AFO can limit tripping and falling by improving swing limb clearance.

Cavovarus deformity is characterized by a high arch (cavus) and a C-shaped appearance (varus) of the foot. Increased deformity results in altered pressure distribution on the plantar aspect of the foot, manifested by abnormal calluses, pain, and difficulties with shoe wear (see **Figs. 1** and **2**). Although multiple muscles are typically affected, the imbalance between the peroneus longus (which plantar flexes the first ray) and the anterior tibialis (which dorsiflexes the first ray) likely contributes to the cavus, whereas the imbalance between the posterior tibialis (which inverts the hindfoot) and the peroneus brevis (which everts the hindfoot) likely contributes to the varus.[81,82]

Treatment of the cavovarus foot must be tailored to the patient's complaints as well as the flexibility of the foot because an initially flexible deformity can become fixed over time. Stretching of the plantar fascia as well as exercises designed to strengthen the ankle evertors can be tried, and bracing may help delay deformity progression. Surgical options include soft tissue and plantar fascia releases for flexible deformity, osteotomy for a fixed deformity, and tendon transfers to improve muscle balance.[82–84] In particular, a dorsiflexing osteotomy of the first metatarsal combined with plantar fascia release can correct cavus and relieve metatarsal head pain, transfer of the peroneus longus to peroneus brevis may decrease recurrence of cavus, transfer of the extensor hallucis longus to the neck of the first metatarsal improves clawing of the toe, and a calcaneal osteotomy may be necessary to correct persistent varus (**Fig. 5**).[85] Transfer of the tibialis posterior tendon has been shown to improve the drop-foot component of the cavovarus foot deformity; however, it is associated with reduced active plantar flexion at push-off.[86] Care must be taken to avoid overlengthening the already weak plantar flexors because this can result in increased peak ankle dorsiflexion in stance and ultimately lead to increased knee flexion. Triple arthrodesis (fusion of the talus-calcaneal, calcaneocuboid, and talonavicular joints) is reserved for severe progressive or recurrent cases. Although most patients with CMT and pes cavus have normal or increased dorsiflexion at the tibiotalar joint, a subset can present with true plantar flexor tightness or contracture and toe walking.[16] The abnormal foot contact in toe walking may result in instability in stance as well as increased metatarsal pressure and pain. Treatment should be designed to address the functional limitations. If aggressive stretching, casting, and/or bracing are unsuccessful, surgery can be considered. Because CMT is associated with progressive plantar flexor weakness, care must be taken to avoid overlengthening the plantar flexors, which has the potential to cause the opposite deformity of excessive dorsiflexion in stance and diminished push-off power. Surgically addressing the cavus deformity with plantar fascia release (and possible dorsiflexing metatarsal osteotomy) may be adequate to treat the symptoms and increase ankle dorisflexion range of motion through reposition of the calcaneous so that additional plantar flexor lengthening can usually be avoided.

Pain Management

Pain is typically not a neuropathic pain in CMT. It is instead related to the structural and functional problems in the lower extremity or muscle cramps.[87,88] Therefore, pain management is complex and should be aligned with physical therapy and orthopedic management. Painful callus formation on the bottom of the foot is related to abnormal pressure distribution (see **Fig. 2**). Certain shoe inserts or special shoes may help to redistribute the abnormal pressure points but surgical interventions are often needed.

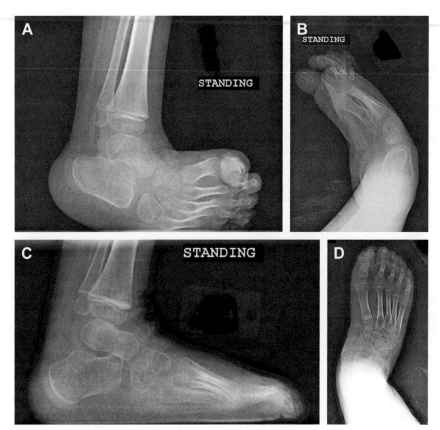

Fig. 5. Preoperative and postoperative foot radiographs of a 3-year-old patient with CMT. (A) Anteroposterior (AP) and (B) lateral preoperative views of flail foot and cavovarus deformity. Bracing resulted in skin blisters and pressure sores. Despite stretching and casting, the foot could not be held in a position that could be braced so surgery was performed, which included lengthening of the Achilles tendon, plantar fascia, flexor digitorum longus and flexor hallucis longus tendons, and abductor hallucis muscle, as well as capsulotomies of the posterior subtalar and ankle joints and medial talonavicular joint, plus a closing cuboid osteotomy. Following surgery, postoperative (C) AP and (D) lateral weight-bearing radiographs reveal a plantigrade foot that is able to be braced.

Muscle cramps are most typical in the gastrocnemius group and are often related to decreased ankle range and toe walking. Therefore, stretching, bracing, and orthopedic interventions need to be implemented for pain management. Knee and hip pain are often related to the compensatory gait mechanisms. Appropriate bracing or other orthopedic interventions (detailed earlier) are likely to be helpful to reduce this problem.[89] The medical management of pain and/or muscle cramps is often disappointing. Gabapentin, pregabalin, muscle-relaxing agents, and nonsteroidal antiinflammatory medication can be helpful for a short period of time; however, their chronic use is problematic.

Charcot-Marie-Tooth Disease and Neurotoxic Drugs

Certain medications can deleteriously affect patients with CMT, causing increased weakness and paresthesia by inducing nerve damage. The most typical drug that may worsen the neuropathy is vincristine, which is used as a chemotherapeutic drug in cancer treatment.[90,91] It is not impossible to discover underlying CMT after severe weakness develops during this treatment. Some centers advocate screening of patients for CMT using NCV/EMG before vincristine administration. There are other chemotherapeutic agents (eg, cisplatin), antibiotics (eg, nitrofurantoin, metronidazole, isoniazid), antiretrovirals (eg, d4T), and vitamins (eg, pyridoxine) that have the potential to affect adversely patient with CMT.[92] A comprehensive list of these drugs is available online at http://www.hnf-cure.org/neurotoxic-drugs/; http://www.cmtausa.org/; http://www.mda.org.nz/media/32478/CMT_medic_alert_list.pdf.

SUMMARY AND FUTURE DIRECTIONS

CMT is the most prevalent inherited neurologic disease in children. Understanding of CMT has greatly improved because of advances in genetics and biology. New in vitro and in vivo models for many genetic forms have been developed[19,49,92] that provide efficient biological platforms for searching for disease-modifying therapies.[93] The genetic heterogeneity and biological complexity of CMTs lead to significant challenges. A high dose of ascorbic acid (vitamin C), curcumin, or onapristone (a progesterone antagonist) were able to decrease the expression of PMP22 in animal models but they have either failed to lead to good therapeutic effect in humans or have proved to be toxic.[94–97] There is a promising ongoing search for small molecules that can influence the deleterious effects of the misfolded proteins that are responsible for some dominant CMT forms.[98]

Gene therapy can be considered for replacing the defective genes responsible for recessive CMT types or to express protective neurotrophic molecules.[99,100] The optimal selective gene delivery system has not yet been discovered. Other genetics-based therapies, such as molecules that can correct nonsense mutations or facilitate gene expression regulations, hold promise in specific therapies for CMT.[101,102]

REFERENCES

1. Lupski JR, de Oca-Luna RM, Slaugenhaupt S, et al. DNA duplication associated with Charcot-Marie-Tooth disease type 1A. Cell 1991;66(2):219–32.
2. Baets J, De Jonghe P, Timmerman V. Recent advances in Charcot-Marie-Tooth disease. Curr Opin Neurol 2014;27(5):532–40.
3. Friedreich N. Uber progressive Muskelatrophie, uber wahre und falsche Muskelhypertrophie. Berlin: A Hirschwald; 1873.
4. Eichhorst K. Uber hereditare Formen der progressiven Muskelatrophie. Berlin Klin Wochenschrift 1873;42.
5. Charcot JM. Sur une forme particuliere d'atrophie musculaire progressive souvent familial debutant par les pieds et les jambes et atteignant plus tard les mains. Rev Méd Paris 1886;6:97–138.
6. Tooth HH. The peroneal type of progressive muscular atrophy, (thesis for the degree of M.D.), University of Cambridge. London: HK Lewis; 1886.
7. Dejerine J, Sottas J. Sur la névrite interstitielle hypertrophique et progressive de l'enfance. Comp Rend Soc Biol 1893;45:63–96.
8. Dyck PJ, Lambert EH. Lower motor and primary sensory neuron diseases with peroneal muscular atrophy. I. Neurologic, genetic, and electrophysiologic findings in hereditary polyneuropathies. Arch Neurol 1968;18:603–18.
9. Jani-Acsadi A, Krajewski K, Shy ME. Charcot-Marie-Tooth neuropathies: diagnosis and management [review]. Semin Neurol 2008;28(2):185–94.

10. Ouvrier RA, Nicholson GA. Advances in the genetics of hereditary hypertrophic neuropathy in childhood. Brain Dev 1995;17(Suppl):31–8.

11. Skre H. Genetic and clinical aspects of Charcot-Marie-Tooth's disease. Clin Genet 1974;6(2):98–118.

12. Martyn CN, Hughes RA. Epidemiology of peripheral neuropathy. J Neurol Neurosurg Psychiatry 1997;62:310–8.

13. Wilmshurst JM, Pollard JD, Nicholson G, et al. Peripheral neuropathies of infancy. Dev Med Child Neurol 2003;45(6):408–14.

14. Fridman V, Bundy B, Reilly MM, et al. CMT subtypes and disease burden in patients enrolled in the Inherited Neuropathies Consortium natural history study: a cross-sectional analysis. J Neurol Neurosurg Psychiatry 2014. [Epub ahead of print].

15. Pagliano E, Moroni I, Baranello G, et al. Outcome measures for Charcot-Marie-Tooth disease: clinical and neurofunctional assessment in children. J Peripher Nerv Syst 2011;16(3):237–42.

16. Õunpuu S, Garibay E, Solomito M, et al. A comprehensive evaluation of the variation in ankle function during gait in children and youth with Charcot-Marie-Tooth disease. Gait Posture 2013;38(213):900–6.

17. Yagerman SE, Cross MB, Green DW, et al. Pediatric orthopedic conditions in Charcot-Marie-Tooth disease: a literature [review]. Curr Opin Pediatr 2012; 24(1):50–6.

18. Thomas PK, Calne DB, Stewart G. Hereditary motor and sensory polyneuropathy (peroneal muscular atrophy). Ann Hum Genet 1974;38:111–53.

19. Saporta MA, Shy ME. Inherited peripheral neuropathies [review]. Neurol Clin 2013;31(2):597–619.

20. Wilmshurst JM, Ouvrier R. Hereditary peripheral neuropathies of childhood: an overview for clinicians. Neuromuscul Disord 2011;21(11):763–75.

21. Timmerman V, Strickland AV, Züchner S. Genetics of Charcot-Marie-Tooth (CMT) disease within the frame of the Human Genome Project success. Genes (Basel) 2014;5(1):13–32.

22. Baets J, Deconinck T, De Vriendt E, et al. Genetic spectrum of hereditary neuropathies with onset in the first year of life. Brain 2011;134(Pt 9):2664–76.

23. Raeymaekers P, Timmerman V, Nelis E, et al. Duplication in chromosome 17p11.2 in Charcot-Marie-Tooth neuropathy type 1a (CMT 1a). The HMSN Collaborative Research Group. Neuromuscul Disord 1991;1(2):93–7.

24. Pareyson D, Scaioli V, Laurà M. Clinical and electrophysiological aspects of Charcot-Marie-Tooth disease [review]. Neuromolecular Med 2006;8(1–2):3–22.

25. Shy ME, Scavina MT, Clark A, et al. T118M PMP22 mutation causes partial loss of function and HNPP-like neuropathy. Ann Neurol 2006;59(2):358–64.

26. Li J, Parker B, Martyn C, Natarajan C, et al. The PMP22 gene and its related diseases [review]. Mol Neurobiol 2013;47(2):673–98.

27. Su Y, Brooks DG, Li L, et al. Myelin protein zero gene mutated in Charcot-Marie-tooth type 1B patients. Proc Natl Acad Sci U S A 1993;90(22):10856–60.

28. Shy ME, Jáni A, Krajewski K, et al. Phenotypic clustering in MPZ mutations [review]. Brain 2004;127(Pt 2):371–84.

29. Street VA, Bennett CL, Goldy JD, et al. Mutation of a putative protein degradation gene LITAF/SIMPLE in Charcot-Marie-Tooth disease 1C. Neurology 2003; 60(1):22–6.

30. Zuchner S, Mersiyanova IV, Muglia M, et al. Mutations in the mitochondrial GTPase mitofusin 2 cause Charcot-Marie-Tooth neuropathy type 2A. Nat Genet 2004;36(5):449–51.

31. Züchner S, De Jonghe P, Jordanova A, et al. Axonal neuropathy with optic atrophy is caused by mutations in mitofusin 2. Ann Neurol 2006;59(2):276–81.
32. Verhoeven K, Claeys KG, Züchner S, et al. MFN2 mutation distribution and genotype/phenotype correlation in Charcot-Marie-Tooth type 2. Brain 2006; 129(Pt 8):2093–102.
33. Calvo J, Funalot B, Ouvrier RA, et al. Genotype-phenotype correlations in Charcot-Marie-Tooth disease type 2 caused by mitofusin 2 mutations. Arch Neurol 2009;66(12):1511–6.
34. Ouvrier R, Grew S. Mechanisms of disease and clinical features of mutations of the gene for mitofusin 2: an important cause of hereditary peripheral neuropathy with striking clinical variability in children and adults. Dev Med Child Neurol 2010;52(4):328–30.
35. Verhoeven K, De Jonghe P, Coen K, et al. Mutations in the small GTP-ase late endosomal protein RAB7 cause Charcot-Marie-Tooth type 2B neuropathy. Am J Hum Genet 2003;72(3):722–7.
36. Züchner S, Vance JM. Molecular genetics of autosomal-dominant axonal Charcot-Marie-Tooth disease [review]. Neuromolecular Med 2006;8(1–2):63–74.
37. Landoure G, Zdebik AA, Martinez TL, et al. Mutations in TRPV4 cause Charcot-Marie-Tooth disease type 2C. Nat Genet 2010;42(2):170–4.
38. Antonellis A, Ellsworth RE, Sambuughin N, et al. Glycyl tRNA synthetase mutations in Charcot-Marie-Tooth disease type 2D and distal spinal muscular atrophy type V. Am J Hum Genet 2003;72(5):1293–9.
39. James PA, Cader MZ, Muntoni F, et al. Severe childhood SMA and axonal CMT due to anticodon binding domain mutations in the GARS gene. Neurology 2006; 67(9):1710–2.
40. Ouvrier RA, McLeod JG, Conchin TE. The hypertrophic forms of hereditary motor and sensory neuropathy. A study of hypertrophic Charcot-Marie-Tooth disease (HMSN type I) and Dejerine-Sottas disease (HMSN type III) in childhood. Brain 1987;110(Pt 1):121–48.
41. Baxter RV, Ben Othmane K, Rochelle JM, et al. Ganglioside-induced differentiation-associated protein-1 is mutant in Charcot-Marie-Tooth disease type 4A/8q21. Nat Genet 2002;30(1):21–2.
42. Senderek J, Bergmann C, Weber S, et al. Mutation of the SBF2 gene, encoding a novel member of the myotubularin family, in Charcot-Marie-Tooth neuropathy type 4B2/11p15. Hum Mol Genet 2003;12(3):349–56.
43. Senderek J, Bergmann C, Stendel C, et al. Mutations in a gene encoding a novel SH3/TPR domain protein cause autosomal recessive Charcot-Marie-Tooth type 4C neuropathy. Am J Hum Genet 2003;73(5):1106–19.
44. Bergoffen J, Scherer SS, Wang S, et al. Connexin mutations in X-linked Charcot-Marie-Tooth disease. Science 1993;262(5142):2039–42.
45. Andersson PB, Yuen E, Parko K, et al. Electrodiagnostic features of hereditary neuropathy with liability to pressure palsies. Neurology 2000;54:40–4.
46. Berger P, Niemann A, Suter U. Schwann cells and the pathogenesis of inherited motor and sensory neuropathies (Charcot-Marie-Tooth disease) [review]. Glia 2006;54(4):243–57.
47. Brennan KM, Bai Y, Shy ME. Demyelinating CMT-what's known, what's new and what's in store? Neurosci Lett 2015. [Epub ahead of print].
48. Juárez P, Palau F. Neural and molecular features on Charcot-Marie-Tooth disease plasticity and therapy. Neural Plast 2012;2012:171636.
49. Scherer SS, Wrabetz L. Molecular mechanisms of inherited demyelinating neuropathies. Glia 2008;56(14):1578–89.

50. Nave KA, Sereda MW, Ehrenreich H. Mechanisms of disease: inherited demyelinating neuropathies–from basic to clinical research. Nat Clin Pract Neurol 2007;3(8):453–64.

51. Karakis I, Gregas M, Darras BT, et al. Clinical correlates of Charcot-Marie-Tooth disease in patients with pes cavus deformities. Muscle Nerve 2013;47(4):488–92.

52. Nagai MK, Chan G, Guille JT, et al. Prevalence of Charcot-Marie-Tooth disease in patients who have bilateral cavovarus feet. J Pediatr Orthop 2006;26(4):438–43.

53. Burns J, Ouvrier R, Estilow T. Symmetry of foot alignment and ankle flexibility in paediatric Charcot-Marie-Tooth disease. Clin Biomech (Bristol, Avon) 2012; 27(7):744–7.

54. Lawson V, Garibshahi S. Alphabet soup: making sense of genetic testing in CMT. Semin Neurol 2010;3(4):373–86.

55. Gabreëls-Festen A. Dejerine-Sottas syndrome grown to maturity: overview of genetic and morphological heterogeneity and follow-up of 25 patients. J Anat 2002;200(4):341–56.

56. Thomas PK. Overview of Charcot-Marie-Tooth disease type 1A [review]. Ann N Y Acad Sci 1999;4(883):1–5.

57. Hoellwarth JS, Mahan ST, Spencer SA. Painful pes planovalgus: an uncommon pediatric orthopedic presentation of Charcot-Marie-Tooth disease. J Pediatr Orthop B 2012;21(5):428–33.

58. Burns J, Bray P, Cross LA, et al. Hand involvement in children with Charcot-Marie-Tooth disease type 1A. Neuromuscul Disord 2008;18(12):970–3.

59. Silva TR, Testa A, Baptista CR, et al. Balance and muscle power of children with Charcot-Marie-Tooth. Braz J Phys Ther 2014;18(4):334–42.

60. Don R, Serrao M, Vinci P, et al. Foot drop and plantar flexion failure determine different gait strategies in Charcot-Marie-Tooth patients. Clin Biomech (Bristol, Avon) 2007;22(8):905–16.

61. Ramdharry GM, Day BL, Reilly MM, et al. Hip flexor fatigue limits walking in Charcot-Marie-Tooth disease. Muscle Nerve 2009;40(1):103–11.

62. Newman CJ, Walsh M, O'Sullivan R, et al. The characteristics of gait in Charcot-Marie-Tooth disease types I and II. Gait Posture 2007;26(1):120–7.

63. Szigeti K, Lupski JR. Charcot-Marie-Tooth disease. Eur J Hum Genet 2009; 17(6):703–10.

64. Jani-Acsadi A, Lewis RA. Evaluation of a patient with suspected chronic demyelinating polyneuropathy [review]. Handb Clin Neurol 2013;115:253–64.

65. Bird TD, Kraft GH, Lipe HP, et al. Clinical and pathological phenotype of original family with Charcot-Marie-Tooth type 1B: a 20-year study. Ann Neurol 1997;41: 463–9.

66. Birouk N, Gouider R, Le Guern E, et al. Charcot-Marie-Tooth disease type 1A with 17p11.2 duplication. Clinical and electrophysiological phenotype study and factors influencing disease severity in 119 cases. Brain 1997;120:813–23.

67. Vecchierini-Blineau MF, Guiheneuc P. Electrophysiological study of the peripheral nervous system in children. Changes in proximal and distal conduction velocities from birth to age 5 years. J Neurol Neurosurg Psychiatry 1979;42(8): 753–9.

68. Li J, Krajewski K, Shy ME, et al. Hereditary neuropathy with liability to pressure palsy: the electrophysiology fits the name. Neurology 2002;58(12):1769–73.

69. Lawson VH, Gordon Smith A, Bromberg MB. Assessment of axonal loss in Charcot-Marie-Tooth neuropathies. Exp Neurol 2003;184(2):753–7.

70. Tousignant R, Trepanier A, Shy ME, et al. Genetic testing practices for Charcot-Marie-Tooth type 1A disease. Muscle Nerve 2014;49(4):478–82.

71. Murphy SM, Laurá M, Reilly MM. DNA testing in hereditary neuropathies [review]. Handb Clin Neurol 2013;115:213–32.
72. Miller LJ, Saporta AS, Sottile SL, et al. Strategy for genetic testing in Charcot-Marie-disease. Acta Myol 2011;30(2):109–16.
73. Pareyson D, Marchesi C. Natural history and treatment of peripheral inherited neuropathies. Adv Exp Med Biol 2009;652:207–24.
74. Padua L, Pareyson D, Aprile I, et al. Natural history of Charcot-Marie-Tooth 2: 2-year follow-up of muscle strength, walking ability and quality of life. Neurol Sci 2010;31(2):175–8.
75. Burns J, Ouvrier R, Estilow T, et al. Validation of the Charcot-Marie-Tooth disease pediatric scale as an outcome measure of disability. Ann Neurol 2012;71(5): 642–52.
76. Burns J, Ramchandren S, Ryan MM. Determinants of reduced health-related quality of life in pediatric inherited neuropathies. Neurology 2010;75(8): 726–31.
77. Burns J, Raymond J, Ouvrier R. Feasibility of foot and ankle strength training in childhood Charcot-Marie-Tooth disease. Neuromuscul Disord 2009;19(12): 818–21.
78. Matyjasik-Liggett M, Wittman P. The utilization of occupational therapy services for persons with Charcot-Marie-Tooth disease. Occup Ther Health Care 2013; 27(3):228–37.
79. Ramdharry GM, Day BL, Reilly MM, et al. Foot drop splints improve proximal as well as distal leg control during gait in Charcot-Marie-Tooth disease. Muscle Nerve 2012;46(4):512–9.
80. Phillips MF, Robertson Z, Killen B, et al. A pilot study of a crossover trial with randomized use of ankle-foot orthoses for people with Charcot-Marie-tooth disease. Clin Rehabil 2012;26(6):534–44.
81. Olney B. Treatment of the cavus foot. Deformity in the pediatric patient with Charcot-Marie-Tooth. Foot Ankle Clin 2000;5(2):305–15.
82. Schwend RM, Drennan JC. Cavus foot deformity in children. J Am Acad Orthop Surg 2003;11(3):201–11.
83. Boffeli TJ, Tabatt JA. Minimally invasive early operative treatment of progressive foot and ankle deformity associated with Charcot-Marie-Tooth. J Foot Ankle Surg 2014. [Epub ahead of print].
84. McCluskey WP, Lovell WW, Cummings RJ. The cavovarus foot deformity. Etiology and management. Clin Orthop Relat Res 1989;(247):27–37.
85. Leeuwesteijn AE, de Visser E, Louwerens JW. Flexible cavovarus feet in Charcot-Marie-Tooth disease treated with first ray proximal dorsiflexion osteotomy combined with soft tissue surgery: a short-term to mid-term outcome study. Foot Ankle Surg 2010;16(3):142–7.
86. Dreher T, Wolf SI, Heitzmann D, et al. Tibialis posterior tendon transfer corrects the foot drop component of cavovarus foot deformity in Charcot-Marie-Tooth disease. J Bone Joint Surg Am 2014;96(6):456–62.
87. Crosbie J, Burns J, Ouvrier RA. Pressure characteristics in painful pes cavus feet resulting from Charcot-Marie-Tooth disease. Gait Posture 2008;28(4): 545–51.
88. Johnson NE, Sowden J, Dilek N, et al. Prospective study of muscle cramps in Charcot-Marie-Tooth disease. Muscle Nerve 2014. [Epub ahead of print].
89. Carter GT, England JD, Chance PF. Charcot-Marie-Tooth disease: electrophysiology, molecular genetics and clinical management. IDrugs 2004;7(2): 151–9.

90. Wang MS, Wu Y, Culver DG, et al. Pathogenesis of axonal degeneration: parallels between Wallerian degeneration and vincristine neuropathy. J Neuropathol Exp Neurol 2000;59(7):599–606.

91. Weimer LH, Podwall D. Medication-induced exacerbation of neuropathy in Charcot Marie Tooth disease. J Neurol Sci 2006;242(1–2):47–54.

92. Harel T, Lupski JR. Charcot-Marie-Tooth disease and pathways to molecular based therapies. Clin Genet 2014;86(5):422–31.

93. Saporta MA, Dang V, Volfson D, et al. Axonal Charcot-Marie-Tooth disease patient-derived motor neurons demonstrate disease-specific phenotypes including abnormal electrophysiological properties. Exp Neurol 2015;263:190–9.

94. Jerath NU, Shy ME. Hereditary motor and sensory neuropathies: understanding molecular pathogenesis could lead to future treatment strategies. Biochim Biophys Acta 2015;1852(4):667–78.

95. Pareyson D, Reilly MM, Schenone A, et al. Ascorbic acid in Charcot-Marie-Tooth disease type 1A (CMT-TRIAAL and CMT-TRAUK): a double-blind randomised trial. Lancet Neurol 2011;10(4):320–8.

96. Meyer zu Horste G, Prukop T, Liebetanz D, et al. Antiprogesterone therapy uncouples axonal loss from demyelination in a transgenic rat model of CMT1A neuropathy. Ann Neurol 2007;61(1):61–72.

97. Khajavi M, Shiga K, Wiszniewski W, et al. Oral Curcumin mitigates the clinical and neuropathologic phenotype of the trembler-J mouse: a potential therapy for inherited neuropathy. Am J Hum Genet 2007;81(3):438–53.

98. Chumakov I, Milet A, Cholet N, et al. Polytherapy with a combination of three re-purposed drugs (PXT3003) down-regulates Pmp22 over-expression and improves myelination, axonal and functional parameters in models of CMT1A neuropathy. Orphanet J Rare Dis 2014;9(1):201.

99. Jani A, Menichella D, Jiang H, et al. Modulation of cell-mediated immunity prolongs adenovirus-mediated transgene expression in sciatic nerve. Hum Gene Ther 1999;10(5):787–800.

100. Sahenk Z, Galloway G, Clark KR, et al. AAV1.NT-3 gene therapy for Charcot-Marie-Tooth neuropathy. Mol Ther 2014;22(3):511–21.

101. Ryan NJ. Ataluren: first global approval. Drugs 2014;74(14):1709–14.

102. Miller JN, Pearce DA. Nonsense-mediated decay in genetic disease: friend or foe? Mutat Res Rev Mutat Res 2014;762:52–64.

Ethical and Policy Issues in Newborn Screening of Children for Neurologic and Developmental Disorders

Lainie Friedman Ross, MD, PhD[a,b,c],*

KEYWORDS

- Newborn screening • Genetic screening • Ethics • Public policy
- Duchenne muscular dystrophy • Krabbe disease • Fragile X syndrome

KEY POINTS

- The primary justification for genetic testing and screening of children is the child's best interest.
- To justify mandatory newborn screening for a specific condition, there must be an early intervention that is needed to prevent or reduce morbidity or mortality.
- Genetic testing methodologies are far more advanced than treatments for many neurologic and development disorders.

INTRODUCTION: A BRIEF HISTORY OF NEWBORN SCREENING

Virtually every infant in the United States has a few drops of blood collected within the first few days of life that is used to screen for more than 40 metabolic, endocrine, and hematologic, the vast majority of which are genetic in origin. Most infants also undergo hearing screening and pulse oximetry screening for critical congenital heart disease which may also be genetic in origin. The goal is to identify and treat conditions that present in infancy to reduce mortality and prevent morbidity.

Newborn screening (NBS) began in the 1960s when Dr Robert Guthrie developed the bacterial inhibition assay to diagnose phenylketonuria (PKU) and the filter paper on which to collect the blood samples for large-scale screening.[1] If untreated, children

Disclosures: None.
[a] Department of Pediatrics, University of Chicago, 5841 South Maryland Avenue, Chicago, IL 60637, USA; [b] Department of Medicine, University of Chicago, 5841 South Maryland Avenue, Chicago, IL 60637, USA; [c] Department of Surgery, University of Chicago, 5841 South Maryland Avenue, Chicago, IL 60637, USA
* Department of Pediatrics, University of Chicago, 5841 South Maryland Avenue, MC 6082, Chicago, IL 60637.
E-mail address: Lross@uchicago.edu

with PKU experience both intellectual disability and autistic behaviors. If treatment with a low-protein diet is begun within a few weeks of birth, these individuals can have a normal life span with normal mental development.

Although PKU screening was voluntary initially, Guthrie advocated for mandatory universal screening.[1] However, mandatory screening had its opponents. Pediatricians expressed concern that there were not enough data and that the government should not tell physicians how to practice medicine.[2(p209)] Despite these concerns, mandatory universal PKU screening was adopted in 43 states by 1975. [3(p48)] Screening for hypothyroidism followed shortly thereafter.

The next major breakthrough in NBS was in 1990 with the application of tandem mass spectrometry, a platform technology that allows for multiplex testing for many metabolic conditions using 1 sample.[4] The adoption of tandem mass spectrometry in some states led to wide variability in the number of conditions included in each state's NBS panels. In 2000, the Maternal and Child Health Bureau Health Resources Services Administration (HRSA) commissioned the American College of Medical Genetics (now the American College of Medical Genetics and Genomics [ACMG]) to outline a process of standardization of outcomes and guidelines for state NBS programs. In 2005, the ACMG/HRSA Committee proposed a "uniform panel" including 25 primary and 29 secondary conditions.[5] In 2006, the Secretary's Advisory Committee of Heritable Disorders of Newborns and Children endorsed the uniform panel, which was quickly adopted by all states.

The expansion had a number of critics. A major concern was that screening had expanded to include conditions that did not meet the Wilson and Jungner criteria. In 1969, Wilson and Jungner published a World Health Organization report that established 10 criteria that had to be met to justify a public health screening program.[6] Although not designed specifically for screening newborns for rare metabolic conditions, the Wilson and Jungner criteria have become the gold standard for judging proposed NBS additions. The 10 criteria are enumerated in **Box 1**. Although a number of

---

Box 1
Wilson and Jungner classic screening criteria

1. The condition sought should be an important health problem.

2. There should be an accepted treatment for patients with recognized disease.

3. Facilities for diagnosis and treatment should be available.

4. There should be a recognizable latent or early symptomatic stage.

5. There should be a suitable test or examination.

6. The test should be acceptable to the population.

7. The natural history of the condition, including development from latent to declared disease, should be understood adequately.

8. There should be an agreed policy on whom to treat as patients.

9. The cost of case finding (including diagnosis and treatment of patients diagnosed) should be economically balanced in relation to possible expenditure on medical care as a whole.

10. Case finding should be a continuing process and not a "once and for all" project.

From Wilson JM, Jungner JF. Principles and practice of screening for disease. Geneva (Switzerland): World Health Organization Public Health Papers, no 34; 1968. p. 26–7.

modifications have been proposed, the basic principles remain: the condition should be treatable, the natural history should be understood, a screening test should exist that is acceptable to the population, and diagnostic testing should be accurate and accessible. If a condition does not meet all of the criteria of Wilson and Jungner, it is unclear on what grounds universal screening can be justified.

Although Wilson and Jungner did not address consent, most national guidelines and consensus reports that examine the ethics of screening, both before and after the expansion, have supported seeking parental permission for all NBS on the grounds that parents must decide what is in their child's best interest.[7–10] This was most recently articulated in a joint policy statement and technical report by the American Academy of Pediatrics (AAP) and the ACMG.[11,12]

In this article, we examine 3 neurologic and developmental disorders that have been considered for inclusion in the uniform panel: Duchenne muscular dystrophy (DMD), Krabbe disease, and fragile X syndrome. We consider the pros and cons of expanding NBS to include each disorder and the ethical and policy issues it raises. We will then evaluate ethical issues raised by the proposal to use genomic sequencing in NBS.

DUCHENNE MUSCULAR DYSTROPHY
Empirical Data

DMD is an X-linked degenerative disease of skeletal muscle that affects approximately 1 in 3500 to 5000 males.[13] The condition is characterized by progressive loss of muscle strength in boys leading to loss of ambulation and wheelchair dependency by adolescence. The 2 leading causes of death are respiratory and cardiac failure. The use of steroids in childhood prolongs ambulation.

The earliest DMD pilot screening program was in New Zealand in 1979 in which 10,000 boys were screened and 2 cases were identified.[14] The largest number of boys have been screened in West Germany, Belgium, and Wales where the frequency is approximately 1 in 5000 boys.[15] Most of the screening programs did not enroll girls. Although boys are much more severely affected than girls, and are affected at an earlier age, some girls do develop some musculoskeletal problems (between 2.5 and 7.8% of girls are manifesting carriers).[16] In addition, more than one-half of female carriers have some cardiac involvement as adults, although fewer than 10% develop severe cardiomyopathy.[17]

Early NBS programs measured creatinine kinase (CK) from the newborn blood spot in newborn males. CK can be falsely increased owing to birth trauma and so a repeat test is recommended several weeks later. Traditionally, those who still have an elevated CK would undergo biopsy. In the past decade, some NBS programs adopted genetic testing (either as first tier to reduce the number of false positives) or as an alternative to biopsy. The only active NBS program for DMD is in Belgium, which uses first tier CK testing alone.[15]

Ethical and Policy Considerations

One way to evaluate the ethics of NBS for DMD is to evaluate whether it meets the Wilson and Jungner criteria. There is a suitable screen (CK) and accurate diagnostic testing by either genetic testing or biopsy is widely available. However, there is no treatment that is needed in infancy. Although steroids are the treatment of choice to prolong ambulation and reduce scoliosis, the initiation of glucocorticoid treatment is not recommended for a child who is still gaining motor skills, which occurs until approximately age 4 to 6 years.[18] Because the mean age of diagnosis is approximately 5 years of age, opponents of NBS for DMD point out that these children are diagnosed early enough even without screening. Proponents argue, in contrast, that there are some preliminary data suggesting that earlier initiation of steroids may be helpful in retaining ambulation.[19] They also argue that the earlier diagnosis avoids the diagnostic odyssey and allows for parental reproductive planning.

Avoiding the diagnostic odyssey is a true benefit for the child and family. A study published in 1982 found that the gap between first parental concern and diagnosis was about 2.5 years.[20] More recent studies find that the gap has not changed.[21] Symptoms also begin earlier than was originally thought.[22] Many boys with DMD have delayed speech and delayed walking by 12 to 18 months of age. However, early intervention recommendations for developmental delays should apply regardless of the cause, and so again, it is not clear that there is a clinical need for early identification.

Does NBS produce a reproductive benefit? In Wales, the incidence of DMD dropped from a prescreening rate of 1 in 4046 boys to 1 in 5136 boys,[23] whereas none of the families in Manitoba chose to have prenatal diagnosis.[13] But even if NBS can reduce the number of children born with DMD, it is controversial whether this is a valid goal of NBS, because it reduces the child to his disorder and does not value the unborn child as a whole person.[24] Although reproductive benefit may be included in a NBS risk–benefit calculation,[25] the utility of this benefit would be greater if screening were offered in the prenatal or preconception screening period.

Even if one finds that the benefits of NBS for DMD outweigh the risks and harms, one must ask whether screening can be done outside of the newborn period. Screening later in infancy would avoid conflating those conditions that require immediate intervention to prevent early morbidity and mortality (public health emergencies) from those conditions that provide "less dramatic or immediate benefit, as well as benefits beyond those to the newborn."[26(p923)] Uptake will be lower because it will require a separate blood test, although this may be appropriate.

A second problem with the current design of NBS for DMD is that it only screens boys. Targeting NBS to a subpopulation ignores the equity value of universal screening programs.[27] The main ethical reason to screen girls is to identify manifesting carriers. Identifying manifesting carriers is in the girl's best interest because, to the extent that one is less likely to suspect DMD in girls, a screening program reduces disparities by identifying them. However, the benefits are confounded by identifying many carriers, many of whom will be asymptomatic for life. The concern here is in creating a "vulnerable child" and of creating the potential for stigma and discrimination.[28]

Screening girls can provide (1) adult-onset cardiac risk information, (2) reproductive information to the girl's parents (possibly before a first affected male is born), and (3) future reproductive information for the girl herself. But screening infants for adult-onset conditions is contrary to the national ethics guidelines that recommend deferring predictive genetic testing for adult-onset conditions and reproductive information until adulthood.[7,9–12] If those are the goals of screening, screening women as young adults may be more appropriate.

Where Are We Now?

In the United States, there was a NBS pilot for DMD in the late 1980s in Western Pennsylvania.[22] In the 2005 ACMG/HRSA report, DMD was considered and rejected for the uniform panel in part because CK was considered too nonspecific.[5] The ability to perform CK/genetic testing as first tier resolves that concern, although it does not resolve the question of the need for early diagnosis.

Despite a number of programs over 35 years, there is currently only 1 active program.[22] Until there is a specific treatment for boys with DMD that needs to begin before the development of symptoms, the benefit–risk ratio does not justify universal NBS; at least, it does not justify its inclusion in a mandatory universal NBS program.

KRABBE DISORDER
Empirical Data

Krabbe disease is a lysosomal storage disorder that is caused by diminished or absent activity of the lysosomal enzyme β-galactocerebrosidase (GALC), which is responsible for the degradation of galactolipids in the myelin sheath. There are known to be 4 distinct phenotypes: early infantile (<6 months), later infantile (7 months–1 year); later onset (1–10 years), and adolescent–adult onset (>10 years).[29] The most common early symptoms of the infantile form include excessive crying and irritability, stiffness, seizures, poor head control, poor feeding, and fisting.[30]

Hunter Kelly (February 14, 1997–August 5, 2005), the son of Jim Kelly, a famous Buffalo Bills quarterback, was diagnosed with Krabbe disease in 1997. His parents established the Hunter's Hope Foundation shortly after his diagnosis. The foundation began collecting clinical data on patients who had been diagnosed with Krabbe disease. As of June 2006, 334 families had returned questionnaires. Seventy-one percent of patients developed symptoms at 0 to 6 months of age, 19% between 7 and 12 months, and 10% at 13 months and beyond (13 months–5.5 years).[31]

In addition to supporting the development of a Krabbe registry, the foundation funded research, and lobbied for the inclusion of Krabbe disease into the NBS program. Despite a unanimous recommendation against screening by a New York State Task Force composed of metabolic specialists, genetic specialists, neurologists, and pediatricians,[32] Governor Pataki of New York announced in January 2005 the decision to add Krabbe disease screening to the New York NBS panel. Once the legislation was passed, this multidisciplinary team worked together to develop a uniform approach to the evaluation and follow-up of all infants who have positive Krabbe disease results on NBS.[32]

The data in the Hunter's Hope Registry suggested that 90% of affected individuals would have early onset condition, but the early data from New York showed otherwise. In the first 5 years of NBS in New York, more than 1 million infants were screened and 228 had an initial positive test. On repeat testing, 114 were found to be normal, 84 were of "low risk," and the remaining 30 had enzyme levels that placed them at either moderate (n = 19) or high (n = 11) risk for the disease.[30] The high rate of false positives is problematic for the parents, the public health department, and the confirmatory diagnostic programs.[32,33]

Of the 11 classified as high risk, all have 2 GALC mutations, but based on additional laboratory measurements and neurodiagnostic studies, 7 were deemed not to be in need of a bone marrow transplant. The outcomes of the other 4 were described by Dees and Kwon: "Of these four, the parents of one refused treatment and the child has developed Krabbe disease; the treatment of one was done after neurologic symptoms had developed, and the child has severe neurologic problems; one had the treatment and is doing relatively well with motor delays; and one died of complications from the treatment."[32(p116)]

Ethical and Policy Considerations

The first ethical question is whether Krabbe disease meets the Wilson and Jungner criteria for NBS because the natural history is not well-defined. As noted, registry data suggested that 90% of affected individuals would have early onset of the condition, but the New York data found it closer to 10% and the timing of onset in the other individuals is unknown. In addition, although 11 infants were identified as high risk, and 4 had a mutation known to be highly associated with early-onset disease, none of the other 7 have developed any symptoms to date. No symptoms have developed in any of those classified as moderate risk, and it is unclear how often they should be followed.[32]

A second problem with NBS for Krabbe disease is that the only treatment available is stem cell transplantation, which is performed ideally before symptoms develop. However, it is not clear which infants will develop an early-onset condition requiring stem cell transplant and which children will not. In addition, even with presymptomatic transplantation, significant neurologic morbidity may still develop.[34] Infantile Krabbe disease may begin in utero such that transplanting in infancy cannot prevent all of the symptoms.[35]

A third ethical concern is the timing of testing. Given that more than 90% of children diagnosed in New York to date are later onset, it is not clear that the newborn period is the appropriate time to identify cases. There is a successful prenatal screening program in 2 Moslem Arab villages in the Jerusalem area and in a Druze community in northern Israel. This was possible only because in the 2 Arab villages there is 1 founder mutation [D528N], and 1 founder mutation in the Druze community [I583 S].[36,37] Over 4 decades, the rate of Krabbe disease has fallen from 1.6 per 1000 live births to 0.82 per 1000 in this region.[38] This is probably not replicable in other areas because of the large number of mutations that have been found, although once a microarray for neuromuscular disease carrier status is developed, the analysis may change.

Where Are We Now?

Krabbe disease was not included in the 2005 uniform panel, but it was nominated for reconsideration in 2007. Based on the evidence, the Secretary's Advisory Committee on Heritable Disorders in Newborns and Children did not recommend its adoption.[39] Nevertheless, several states are preparing or have introduced NBS for Krabbe disease. Like New York, these states plan to incorporate Krabbe disease screening into their mandatory NBS programs.

Ethicists have been unanimous against the inclusion of Krabbe disease into mandatory universal screening. Some argue that the natural history is so poorly understood that it should only be performed under a research protocol with institutional review board approval and parental permission.[32,33] Others agree that it is not ready for prime time, but are not convinced that a research paradigm requiring informed consent is the solution.[40,41] Krabbe disease will not be ready for universal NBS until there is a better algorithm to predict phenotype and a treatment that is safer and has better long-term outcomes.

If a microarray chip were developed, prenatal testing may be more appropriate than NBS given that the treatment for Krabbe disease leaves much to be desired. Which mutations to include would be controversial. One could focus only on those mutations associated directly with early onset Krabbe disease because we do not know how likely it is that other mutations lead to disease nor its predicted severity, although some might argue to identify all pathologic variants to increase informed reproductive decision making.

FRAGILE X SYNDROME
Empirical Data

Fragile X syndrome is the most well-known and most common single-gene cause of inherited intellectual disabilities and autism. Fragile X syndrome is caused by a mutation in which a DNA segment, known as the CGG triplet repeat, is expanded within the *FMR1* gene. Individuals with fewer than 44 repeats are described as within the normal range, 45 to 54 repeats are in the gray zone, 55 to 199 repeats are within the premutation range (and are known as carriers), and those with 200 or more repeats have a full mutation and are said to have fragile X syndrome. The phenotype varies depending on number and gender. The frequency of males with fragile X syndrome is approximately 1 in 4000 and the frequency of affected females is somewhere between 1 in 5000 and 1 in 8000.[42] Males with fragile X syndrome have moderate to significant intellectual disability and autistic-like behaviors. Females with the full mutation show greater clinical variability. One-half of affected girls manifest some degree of intellectual impairment, although it is often milder than what is seen with boys. Emotional and psychiatric problems are common, even among those with normal intelligence.[43] Premutation carriers are at risk for 2 late-onset health conditions, fragile X–associated tremor/ataxia syndrome and fragile X premature ovarian insufficiency. Fragile X–associated tremor/ataxia syndrome is characterized by intention tremor, cerebellar ataxia, atypical parkinsonism, and dementia. A study from Spain found that it affects about 16.5% of female premutation carriers and 45.5% of male premutation carriers older than 50 years of age.[44] Fragile X premature ovarian insufficiency causes premature menopause (before the age of 40 years) in approximately 20% of female premutation carriers.[44] Some data suggest other health issues in women with premutation alleles, including mental health issues, hypertension, thyroid disorders, fibromyalgia, and tremors.[45] Whether intermediate alleles have any associated symptoms is controversial.[45]

Because the triple repeat mutation that causes fragile X syndrome is located on the X chromosome 50% of the offspring of women with a fragile X premutation will inherit the normal X chromosome and 50% will inherit the one with the mutation. The number of repeats in the premutation range is unstable and may expand in maternal transmission. In contrast, men with a premutation will have unaffected sons and their daughters will inherit the premutation (which does not expand in paternal transmission). Asymptomatic women with a full mutation have a 50% of having children with a full mutation, who may be severely affected.

The symptoms of fragile X syndrome can be managed to help the child maximize his or her potential. Current approaches include speech therapy, occupational therapy, special educational services, and behavioral interventions, including some adjunctive psychopharmacologic intervention to modify behavioral problems.

Ethical and Policy Considerations

The first ethical and policy issue is whether to test only male newborns or newborns of both genders. Testing of only boys is technically easier because of the issue of distinguishing between the 2 X chromosomes in female samples. To the extent that NBS for fragile X is justified to provide earlier services to affected children; girls with intellectual disabilities can benefit from earlier services just like boys. However, at least one-half of girls may be asymptomatic. Although there are no data to suggest that early intervention can harm those of normal intelligence, the concern would be in stigma and discrimination from the labeling. It would also make it difficult to measure the efficacy of these programs.

The second ethical and policy question is whether to develop and use a test that identifies all the different repeat ranges, or whether to only use a test that identifies the full mutation. Testing only for the full mutation focuses on those who are in most of need of services, but given that some individuals with premutations have learning difficulties, these children would also benefit from early diagnosis and implementation of services. However, testing only for the full mutation does remove the risk of identifying children who are at risk, as adults, for adult-onset conditions like fragile X–associated tremor/ataxia syndrome and fragile X premature ovarian insufficiency. It also removes the harm of identifying those in the gray zone, about which little is understood.

The third question involves timing of screening. Traditionally, the focus of NBS was to identify children for whom early intervention improved clinical outcome. To the extent that children with fragile X syndrome will be identified by behavioral and developmental screening, the specific diagnosis of fragile X syndrome by NBS is less urgent until specific pharmacologic therapies are developed that target fragile X.

NBS for the various fragile X repeat ranges can reduce the diagnostic odyssey. However, to the extent that NBS may overdiagnose females, this will be a financial cost to the system (and an emotional cost to the family). It may also lead to cascade testing and the ethical issues raised by identifying family members who may not want to know.[46]

Preconception counseling and screening, in contrast, allows women to be informed of their genotype, the possibility of expansion in progeny, and the range of phenotypes in both full and premutation offspring even before an affected child is born.

Where Are We Now?

In 2006, fragile X was not recommended for inclusion in the uniform NBS panel, both because there was no simple and inexpensive test and because it was not clear what clinical benefit early diagnosis offered families. Since then, new testing methodologies have been developed, and today a variety of different testing methodologies are available. Some are only accurate in boys (because they only have 1 X chromosome), and some can identify full, premutation, and gray zone sized repeats whereas others can only identify full mutations.[47] Depending on the methodology, sex chromosome abnormalities may also be identified. Proving clinical benefit from early diagnosis remains elusive.

Surveys of parents and physicians all agree that the ideal testing time is preconception.[48,49] Uptake of fragile X screening in nonpregnant women and pregnant women, however, has been variable, depending in part on timing of the screening and ease of enrollment.[50] Currently, the American College of Obstetricians and Gynecologists (ACOG) only recommends screening for "women with a family history of fragile X syndrome or undiagnosed mental retardation, developmental delay, or autism or for those with ovarian insufficiency," even though they concede that these guidelines will not detect most premutation carriers.[51] The ACOG does recommend providing testing along with genetic counseling to women who request it regardless of family history.[51] The ACMG also does not believe that fragile X is ready for population screening (preconception, prenatal or NBS) at this time.[52]

Two pilot NBS programs have been conducted. An Australian NBS pilot was performed in 2009 and 2010.[53] Of the 2094 women approached, 1971 (94%) consented to testing of 2000 infants. Virtually all (99%) elected to be informed of premutation and full mutation both to prepare for a child with additional needs (93%) and for reproductive planning (64%).[53] In 2009 and 2010, women at the University of California at Davis Medical Center, Rush University Medical Center (Chicago), and the University of North Carolina Hospital were invited to participate in an NBS pilot. Study recruiters approached 2137 mothers, and 2045 (95.7%) were willing to hear about the study.[54] About two-thirds (67.5%) of the 2045 consented to have their newborn screened. Because the study was determined to involve more than minimal risk without the prospect of direct benefit, the researchers were required to get consent from both parents. Because some fathers actively declined screening or failed to return a signed consent form after the mother consented, the rate of consent for couples dropped to 63%.[54]

There was high uptake in both NBS pilots despite requiring consent. The not insignificant refusal rate may be due in part to the complexity of fragile X spectrum and its meaning to women and families. However, its complexity demands a robust consent process. The consent process must include a discussion about the impact of a diagnosis on a family, because there may be many asymptomatic relatives or relatives with misdiagnoses (eg, Parkinsonism or autism spectrum disorder).[43] There are some who support broad cascade screening because it is efficient, but there are also concerns of the amount of resources that would be needed and the ethical issues raised by identifying unsuspecting and uninterested if not downright hostile family members who do not want to know.[46]

MOVING FORWARD

In 2012, the National Institutes of Health committed $25 million over 5 years to 4 research teams under a new Genomic Sequencing and Newborn Screening Disorders program. The projects will "examine whether sequencing newborns' genomes or exomes can provide useful medical information beyond what is already delivered by current newborn screening."[55] These pilots were conceived in part owing to the decreasing cost of whole genome sequencing and whole exome sequencing,[56] although even at $1000 it is too expensive for a public health program, and ignores the additional costs of data storage, data management, and laboratory and counseling staff.[57] Whole genome sequencing and whole exome sequencing can provide information about most of the conditions currently included in the uniform panel (except for hypothyroidism, which is often nongenetic), as well as a lot of other information including carrier status and risks of adult-onset conditions. Thus, like fragile X screening, it challenges a mandatory system because there are individuals who do not want information that is not imminently needed.[58,59] If parental permission is required, as it ought to be, pediatricians will need to explain the risks and benefits of screening using genomic sequencing and the alternatives. They will need to explain that genotype does not always correlate with phenotype, that sequencing will identify variants of unknown significance, and that additional health information unrelated to newborn conditions may be uncovered. A survey of members of the National Society of Genetic Counselors found that the majority (82%) did not feel prepared to counsel for whole genome sequencing results from NBS and advocated for additional education before implementation.[60] Pediatricians will also need to increase their knowledge, because even if whole genome sequencing and whole exome sequencing do not become part of NBS in the near future, they are already included in clinical guidelines for the identification of intellectual and global developmental disabilities.[61]

REFERENCES

1. Koch JH. Robert Guthrie: the PKU story: a crusade against mental retardation. Pasadena (CA): Hope Publishing House; 1997.
2. Paul D. Contesting consent: the challenge to compulsory neonatal screening for PKU. Perspect Biol Med 1999;42:207–19.
3. National Research Council. Committee for the study of inborn errors of metabolism. Genetic screening: programs, principles and research. Washington, DC: National Academy of Sciences; 1975.
4. Millington DS, Kodo N, Norwood DL, et al. Tandem mass spectrometry: a new method for acylcarnitine profiling with potential for neonatal screening for inborn errors of metabolism. J Inherit Metab Dis 1990;13:321–4.

5. American College of Medical Genetics Newborn Screening Expert Group. Newborn screening: toward a uniform screening panel and system. Genet Med 2006;8(Suppl 1):1S–252S.

6. Wilson JM, Jungner G. Principles and practice of screening for disease. Public health papers 34. Geneva (Switzerland): World Health Organization; 1968.

7. The Committee on Assessing Genetic Risks, Institute of Medicine (IOM), Andrews LB, et al, editors. Assessing genetic risks: implications for health and social policy. Washington, DC: National Academy Press; 1994.

8. American Society of Human Genetics Board of Directors. American College of Medical Genetics Board of Directors. Points to consider: ethical, legal, and psychosocial implications of genetic testing in children and adolescents. Am J Hum Genet 1995;57:1233–41.

9. Newborn Screening Task Force. Serving the family from birth to the medical home: newborn screening: a blueprint for the future. A call for a national agenda on state newborn screening programs. Pediatrics 2000;106:389–422.

10. American Academy of Pediatrics, Committee on Bioethics. Ethical issues with genetic testing in pediatrics. Pediatrics 2001;107:1451–5.

11. American Academy of Pediatrics Committee on Bioethics, Committee on Genetics and the American College of Medical Genetics and Genomics Social, Ethical and Legal Issues Committee. Policy statement ethical and policy issues in genetic testing and screening of children. Pediatrics 2013;131:620–2.

12. Ross LF, Saal HM, David KL, The American Academy of Pediatrics, American College of Medical Genetics and Genomics, et al. Ethical and policy issues in genetic testing and screening of children. Genet Med 2013;15:234–45.

13. Ellis JA, Vroom E, Muntoni F. 195th ENMC international workshop: newborn screening for Duchenne muscular dystrophy 14–16th December, 2012, Naarden, The Netherlands. Neuromuscul Disord 2013;23:682–9.

14. Drummond LM. Creatine phosphokinase levels in the newborn and their use in screening for Duchenne muscular dystrophy. Arch Dis Child 1979;54:362–6.

15. Mendell JR, Shilling C, Leslie ND, et al. Evidence-based path to newborn screening for Duchenne muscular dystrophy. Ann Neurol 2012;71:304–13.

16. Norman A, Harper P. A survey of manifesting carriers of Duchenne and Becker muscular dystrophy in Wales. Clin Genet 1989;36:31–7.

17. Hoogerwaard EM, van der Wouw PA, Wilde AA, et al. Cardiac involvement in carriers of Duchenne and Becker muscular dystrophy. Neuromuscul Disord 1999;9: 347–51.

18. Bushby K, Finkel R, Birnkrant DJ, for the DMD care considerations working group. Diagnosis and management of Duchenne muscular dystrophy, part 2: implementation of multidisciplinary care. Lancet Neurol 2010;9:177–89.

19. Sato Y, Yamauchi A, Urano M, et al. Corticosteroid therapy for Duchene muscular dystrophy: improvement of psychomotor function. Pediatr Neurol 2014;50:31–7.

20. Crisp DE, Ziter FA, Bray PF. Diagnostic delay in Duchenne's muscular dystrophy. JAMA 1982;247:478–80.

21. Bushby K, Hill A, Steel J. Failure of early diagnosis in symptomatic Duchenne muscular dystrophy. Lancet 1999;353:557–8.

22. Mendell JR, Lloyd-Puryear M. Report of MDA muscle disease symposium on newborn screening for Duchenne muscular dystrophy. Muscle Nerve 2013;48: 21–6.

23. Moat SJ, Bradley DM, Salmon R, et al. Newborn bloodspot screening for Duchenne muscular dystrophy: 21 years experience in Wales (UK). Eur J Hum Genet 2013;21:1049–53.

24. Parens E, Asch A. Special supplement: the disability rights critique of prenatal genetic testing reflections and recommendations. Hastings Cent Rep 1999; 29(5):S1–22.
25. Bombard Y, Miller FA, Hayeems RZ, et al. Reconsidering reproductive benefit through newborn screening: a systematic review of guidelines on preconception, prenatal and newborn screening. Eur J Hum Genet 2010;18:751–60.
26. Grosse SD, Boyle CA, Kenneson A, et al. From public health emergency to public health service: the implications of evolving criteria for newborn screening panels. Pediatrics 2006;117:923–9.
27. Brosco JP, Grosse SD, Ross LF. Universal state newborn screening programs can reduce health disparities. JAMA Pediatr 2015;169:7–8.
28. Ross LF. Screening for conditions that do not meet the Wilson and Jungner criteria: the case of Duchenne muscular dystrophy. Am J Med Genet 2006; 140A:914–22.
29. Duffner PK, Barczykowski A, Kay DM, et al. Later onset phenotypes of Krabbe disease: results of the world-wide registry. Pediatr Neurol 2012;46:298–306.
30. Duffner PK, Barczykowski A, Jalal K, et al. Early infantile Krabbe disease: results of the World-Wide Krabbe Registry. Pediatr Neurol 2011;45:141–8.
31. Duffner PK, Jalal K, Carter RL. The hunter's hope Krabbe family database. Pediatr Neurol 2009;40:13–8.
32. Dees RH, Kwon JM. The ethics of Krabbe newborn screening. Publ Health Ethics 2013;6:114–28.
33. Ross LF. Newborn screening for lysosomal storage diseases: an ethical and policy analysis. J Inherit Metab Dis 2012;35:627–34.
34. Duffner PK, Caviness VS, Erbe RW, et al. The long term outcomes of presymptomatic infants transplanted for Krabbe disease: report of the workshop held July 11 and 12, 2008, Holiday Valley, New York. Genet Med 2009;11:450–4.
35. Ida H, Rennert OM, Watabe K, et al. Pathological and biochemical studies of fetal Krabbe disease. Brain Dev 1994;16:480–4.
36. Zlotogora J, Regev R, Zeigler M, et al. Krabbe disease: increased incidence in a highly inbred community. Am J Med Genet 1985;21:765–70.
37. Zlotogora J, Levy-Lahad E, Legum C, et al. Krabbe disease in Israel. Isr J Med Sci 1991;27(4):196–8.
38. Macarov M, Zlotogora J, Meiner V, et al. Genetic screening for Krabbe disease: learning from the past and looking to the future. Am J Med Genet 2011;155A:574–6.
39. Kemper AR, Knapp AA, Green NS, et al. Weighing the evidence for newborn screening for early-infantile Krabbe disease. Genet Med 2010;12:539–43.
40. Miller FA. The sad story of newborn screening for Krabbe: the need for good governance. Publ Health Ethics 2013;6:123–6.
41. Nijsingh N. Krabbe newborn screening: the issue of informed consent. Publ Health Ethics 2013;6:126–8.
42. Biancalana V, Glaeser D, McQuaid S, et al. EMQN best practice guidelines for the molecular genetic testing and reporting of fragile X syndrome and other fragile X-associated disorders. Eur J Hum Genet 2014. http://dx.doi.org/10.1038/ejhg.2014.185.
43. Finucane B, Abrams L, Cronister A, et al. Genetic counseling and testing for FMR1 gene mutations: practice guidelines of the national society of genetic counselors. J Genet Couns 2012;21:752–60.
44. Rodriguez-Revenga L, Madrigal I, Pagonabarraga J, et al. Penetrance of FMR1 premutation associated pathologies in fragile X syndrome families. Eur J Hum Genet 2009;17:1359–62.

45. Tassone F. Newborn screening for fragile X syndrome. JAMA Neurol 2014;71(3):355.
46. McConkie-Rosell A, Abrams L, Finucane B, et al. Recommendations from multi-disciplinary focus groups on cascade testing and genetic counseling for fragile X-associated disorders. J Genet Couns 2007;16:593–606.
47. Monaghan KG, Lyon E, Spector EB, for the American College of Medical Genetics and Genomics. ACMG Standards and Guidelines for fragile X testing: a revision to the disease-specific supplements to the standards and guidelines for clinical genetics laboratories of the American College of Medical Genetics and Genomics. Genet Med 2013;15:575–86.
48. Archibald AD, Jacques AM, Wake S, et al. "It's something I need to consider": decisions about carrier screening for fragile X syndrome in a population of non-pregnant women. Am J Med Genet 2009;149A:2731–8.
49. Acharya K, Ross LF. Fragile X screening: attitudes of genetic health professionals. Am J Med Genet 2009;149A:626–32.
50. Hill MK, Archibald AD, Cohen J, et al. A systematic review of population screening for fragile X syndrome. Genet Med 2010;12:396–410.
51. American College of Obstetricians and Gynecologists Committee on Genetics. ACOG Committee Opinion No. 469: carrier screening for fragile X syndrome. Obstet Gynecol 2010;116:1008–10.
52. Sherman S, Pletcher BA, Driscoll DA. ACMG practice guidelines: fragile X syndrome; diagnostic and carrier testing. Genet Med 2005;7:584–7.
53. Christie L, Wotton T, Bennetts B, et al. Maternal attitudes to newborn screening for fragile X syndrome. Am J Med Genet 2013;161A:301–11.
54. Skinner D, Choudhury S, Sideris J, et al. Parents' decisions to screen newborns for FMR1 gene expansions in a pilot research project. Pediatrics 2011;127: e1455–63.
55. NIH Awards up to $25M over Five Years to Teams Testing Genome Sequencing in Newborn Screening. Available at: http://www.genomeweb.com/sequencing/nih-awards-25m-over-five-years-teams-testing-genome-sequencing-newborn-screening. Accessed September 4, 2013.
56. Hayden EC. Is the $1,000 genome for real? Nature News http://dx.doi.org/10.1038/nature.2014.14530. Accessed January 15, 2014.
57. Mardis ER. The $1,000 genome, the $100,000 analysis? Genome Med 2010; 2(11):84. Available at: http://genomemedicine.com/content/2/11/84.
58. Goldenberg AJ, Dodson DS, Davis MM, et al. Parents' interest in whole-genome sequencing of newborns. Genet Med 2014;16:78–84.
59. Bombard Y, Miller FA, Hayeems RZ, et al. Public views on participating in newborn screening using genome sequencing. Eur J Hum Genet 2014;22: 1248–54.
60. Nardini MD, Matthews AL, McCandless SE, et al. Genomic counseling in the newborn period: experiences and views of genetic counselors. J Genet Couns 2014;23:506–15.
61. Moeschler JB, Shevell M, the American Academy of Pediatrics Committee on Genetics. Comprehensive evaluation of the child with intellectual disability or global developmental delays. Pediatrics 2014;134:e903–18.

Index

Note: Page numbers of article titles are in **bold face** type.

A

Pediatr Clin N Am 62 (2015) 799–819
http://dx.doi.org/10.1016/S0031-3955(15)00061-9
0031-3955/15/$ – see front matter © 2015 Elsevier Inc. All rights reserved.

Moving?

Make sure your subscription moves with you!

To notify us of your new address, find your **Clinics Account Number** (located on your mailing label above your name), and contact customer service at:

Email: journalscustomerservice-usa@elsevier.com

800-654-2452 (subscribers in the U.S. & Canada)
314-447-8871 (subscribers outside of the U.S. & Canada)

Fax number: 314-447-8029

Elsevier Health Sciences Division
Subscription Customer Service
3251 Riverport Lane
Maryland Heights, MO 63043

*To ensure uninterrupted delivery of your subscription, please notify us at least 4 weeks in advance of move.